Why Are There So Many Banking Crises?

Why Are There So Many Banking Crises?

The Politics and Policy of Bank Regulation

Jean-Charles Rochet

PRINCETON UNIVERSITY PRESS

PRINCETON AND OXFORD

Published by Princeton University Press,
41 William Street, Princeton, New Jersey 08540

In the United Kingdom: Princeton University Press,
3 Market Place, Woodstock, Oxfordshire OX20 1SY

ISBN-13: 978-0-691-13146-7 (alk. paper)

Library of Congress Control Number: 2007938554

British Library Cataloging-in-Publication Data is available

This book has been composed in Lucida

Typeset by T&T Productions Ltd, London

Printed on acid-free paper ∞

press.princeton.edu

Printed in the United States of America

10 9 8 7 6 5 4 3 2 1

Contents

Preface and Acknowledgments

In November 2000, I was invited by the University of Leuven to give the Gaston Eyskens Lectures. The main topic of my research at the time provided the title: "Why are there so many banking crises?" These lectures were based on the content of ten articles: four had already been published in academic journals and the other six were still work in progress.

Since then, I have been invited to teach these lectures in many other places: the Oslo BI School of Management (March 2002), the Bank of Finland (April 2002), the Bank of England (May 2002), Wuhan University (November 2002 and December 2004), and the Bank of Uruguay (August 2004). Now that all these articles have been published in academic journals, I have collected them into a single volume that will, I hope, be useful to all economists—either from academic institutions, central banks, financial services authorities or from private banks—who are interested in this difficult topic. I thank my coauthors—Jean-Paul Décamps, Xavier Freixas, Bruno Parigi, Benoît Roger, Jean Tirole, and Xavier Vives—for allowing me to publish our joint work.

I also thank the academic journals—CESIfo, the Journal of Money, Credit and Banking, Review of Financial Stability, European Economic Review, the Journal of the European Economic Association, the Journal of Financial Intermediation, and the Economic Review of the Federal Reserve of New York—for giving me the right to use my articles for this monograph. Chapter 1 was originally published in *CESIfo Economic Studies* (2003) 49(2):141–56; chapter 2 in *Journal of the European Economic Association* (2004) 6:1116–47; chapter 3 in *Journal of the European Economic Association* (2004) 6:1085–115; chapter 4 in *Journal of Financial Stability* (2004) 1:93–110; chapter 5 in *Journal of Money, Credit and Banking* (1996) 28(Part 2):733–62; chapter 6 in *Journal of Money, Credit and Banking* (1996) 28:832–62; chapter 7 in *Journal of Money, Credit and Banking* (2000) 32(Part 2):611–38; chapter 8 in *European Economic Review* (1992) 36:1137–78; chapter 9 in *Economic Policy Review*, Federal Reserve Bank of New York, September 7–25, 2004; and chapter 10 in *Journal of Financial Intermediation* (2004) 13:132–55.

I have benefited a great deal from the comments of the audiences to the lectures, as well as from many colleagues. I am particularly grateful to Sudipto Bhattacharya, who organized my one-year visit to the London School of Economics, and David Webb, who kindly offered me hospitality in the Financial Markets Group. I thank my editor, Richard Baggaley, for actively supporting the project from the very beginning. Without him, this book would never have come out. Thanks also to Jon Wainwright of T&T Productions Ltd, who provided wonderful assistance in proofreading. Finally, I thank my colleagues at the University of Leuven (particularly Frans Spinnewyn) for starting the whole process by inviting me to give the prestigious Gaston Eyskens Lectures.

Why Are There So Many Banking Crises?

General Introduction and
Outline of the Book

The recent episode of the Northern Rock bank panic in the United Kingdom, with depositors queuing from 4 a.m. in order to get their money out, reminds us that banking crises are a recurrent phenomenon. An interesting IMF study back in 1997 identified 112 systemic banking crises in 93 countries and 51 borderline crises in 46 countries between 1975 and 1995, including the Savings and Loan crisis in the United States in the late 1980s, which cost more than $150 billion to the American taxpayers. Since then, Argentina, Russia, Indonesia, Turkey, South Korea, and many other countries have also experienced systemic banking crises.

The object of this book is to try and explain why these crises have occurred and whether they could be avoided in the future. It is fair to say that, in almost every country in the world, public authorities already intervene a great deal in the functioning of the banking sector. The two main components of this public intervention are on the one hand the financial safety nets (composed essentially of deposit insurance systems and emergency liquidity assistance provided to commercial banks by the central bank) and on the other hand the prudential regulation systems, consisting mainly of capital adequacy (and liquidity) requirements, and exit rules, establishing what supervisory authorities should do when they close down a commercial bank.

This book suggests several ways for reforming the different components of the regulatory-supervisory system: the lender of last resort (part 2), prudential supervision and the management of systemic risk (part 3), and solvency regulations (part 4) so that future banking crises can be avoided, or at least their frequency and cost can be reduced significantly.

Why Are There So Many Banking Crises?

Part 1 contains a nontechnical presentation of these banking crises and a first, easily accessible, discussion of how the regulatory–supervisory system could be reformed to limit the frequency and the cost of these crises. The main conclusions of this part are the following:

- Although many banking crises have been initiated by financial deregulation and globalization, these crises were amplified largely by political interference.

- Public intervention in the banking sector faces a fundamental commitment problem, analogous to the time consistency problem confronted by monetary policy.

- The key to successful reform is independence and accountability of banking supervisors.

The Lender of Last Resort

Part 2 explores the concept of lender of last resort (LLR), which was elaborated in the nineteenth century by Thornton (1802) and Bagehot (1873). The essential point of the "classical" doctrine associated with Bagehot asserts that the LLR role is to lend to "solvent but illiquid" banks under certain conditions. More precisely, the LLR should lend freely against good collateral, valued at precrisis levels, and at a penalty rate. These conditions can be found in Bagehot (1873) and are also presented, for instance, in Humphrey (1975) and Freixas et al. (1999).

This policy was clearly effective: traditional banking panics were eliminated with the LLR facility and deposit insurance by the end of the nineteenth century in Europe, after the crisis of the 1930s in the United States and, by and large, in emerging economies, even though they have suffered numerous crises until today.[1] Modern liquidity crises associated with securitized money or capital markets have also required the intervention of the LLR. Indeed, the Federal Reserve intervened in the crises provoked by the failure of Penn Central in the U.S. commercial paper market in 1970, by the stock market crash of October 1987, and by Russia's default in 1997 and subsequent collapse of LTCM (in the latter case a "lifeboat" was arranged by the New York Fed). For example, in October 1987 the Federal Reserve supplied liquidity to banks through the discount window.[2]

---

[1] See Gorton (1988) for U.S. evidence and Lindgren et al. (1996) for evidence on other IMF member countries.

[2] See Folkerts-Landau and Garber (1992). See also chapter 7 of this book for a modeling of the interactions between the discount window and the interbank market.

The LLR's function of providing emergency liquidity assistance has been criticized for provoking moral hazard on the banks' side.[3] Perhaps more importantly, Goodfriend and King (1988) (see also Bordo 1990; Kaufman 1991; Schwartz 1992) remark that Bagehot's doctrine was elaborated at a time when financial markets were underdeveloped. They argue that, whereas central bank intervention on aggregate liquidity (monetary policy) is still warranted, individual interventions (banking policy) are not anymore: with sophisticated interbank markets, banking policy has become redundant. Goodfriend and Lacker (1999) suggest that commercial banks could instead provide each other with multilateral credit lines, remunerated *ex ante* by commitment fees.

Part 2 contains two articles. Chapter 2, written with Xavier Vives, provides a theoretical foundation for Bagehot's doctrine in a model that fits the modern context of sophisticated and presumably efficient financial markets. Our approach bridges a gap between the "panic" and "fundamental" views of crises by linking the probability of occurrence of a crisis to the fundamentals. We show that in the absence of intervention by the central bank, some solvent banks may be forced to liquidate if too large a proportion of wholesale deposits are not renewed.

The second article, chapter 3, written with Xavier Freixas and Bruno Parigi, formalizes two common criticisms of the Bagehot doctrine of the LLR: that it may be difficult to distinguish between illiquid and insolvent banks (Goodhart 1995) and that LLR policies may generate moral hazard. They find that when interbank markets are efficient, there is still a potential role for an LLR but only during crisis periods, when market spreads are too high. In "normal" times, liquidity provision by interbank markets is sufficient.

Prudential Regulation and the Management of Systemic Risk

Part 3 is dedicated to prudential regulation and the management of systemic risk. Although the topic is still debated in the academic literature (see Bhattacharya and Thakor (1993), Freixas and Rochet (1995), and Santos (2000) for extended surveys), a large consensus seems to have emerged on the rationale behind bank prudential regulation. It is now widely accepted that it has essentially two purposes:

- To protect small depositors, by limiting the frequency and cost of individual bank failures. This is often referred to as *microprudential* policy.[4]

---

[3] However, Cordella and Levy-Yeyati (2003) show that, in some cases, moral hazard can be *reduced* by the presence of LLR.

[4] See, for example, Borio (2003) or Crockett (2001) for a justification for this terminology.

- To protect the banking system as a whole, by limiting the frequency and cost of systemic banking crises. This is often referred to as *macroprudential* policy.

Notice that, from the point of view of economic analysis, these two types of policies have very different justifications:

- Microprudential policy is justified by the (presumed)[5] inability of small depositors to control the use of their money by bankers. This is why most countries have organized deposit insurance funds (DIFs) that guarantee small deposits against the risk of failure of their bank.[6] The role of bank supervisors is then to represent the interests of depositors (or rather of the DIF) vis-à-vis banks' managers and shareholders.[7]

- Macroprudential policy is justified by the (partial) failure of the market to deal with aggregate risks, and by the public good component of financial stability. As for other public goods, the total (declared) willingness to pay of individual banks (or more generally of investors) for financial stability is less that the social value of this financial stability. This is because each individual (bank or investor) free-rides on the willingness of others to pay for financial stability.

These differences imply in particular that, while microprudential policy (and supervision) can in principle be dealt with at a purely private level (it amounts to a collective representation problem for depositors), macroprudential policy has intrinsically a public good component. This being said, governments have traditionally controlled both dimensions of prudential policy, which may be the source of serious time consistency problems[8] (this is because democratic governments cannot commit on long-run decisions that will be made by their successors) leading to political pressure on supervisors, regulatory forbearance, and misman-agement of banking crises.

The first article in part 3, chapter 4, builds a simple model of the banking industry where both micro and macro aspects of prudential policies can be integrated. This model shows that the main cause behind the poor management of banking crises may not be the "safety net" per

---

[5]The supporters of the "free banking school" challenge this view.

[6]Contrary to what is often asserted, the need for a microprudential regulation is not a consequence of any "*mispricing*" of deposit insurance (or other form of government subsidies) but simply of the *existence* of deposit insurance.

[7]This is the "representation theory" of Dewatripont and Tirole (1994).

[8]A similar time consistency problem used to exist for monetary policy, until indepen-dence was granted to the central banks of many countries.

se as argued by many economists, but instead the lack of commitment power of banking authorities, who are typically subject to political pressure. However, the model also shows that the use of private monitors (market discipline) is a very imperfect means of solving this commitment problem. Instead, I argue in favor of establishing independent and accountable banking supervisors, as has been done for monetary authorities. I also suggest a differential regulatory treatment of banks according to the costs and benefits of a potential bailout. In particular, I argue that independent banking authorities should make it clear from the start (in a credible fashion) that certain banks with an excessive exposure to macroshocks should be denied the access to emergency liquidity assistance by the central bank. By contrast, banks that have access to the LLR either because they have a reasonable exposure to macroshocks or because they are too big to fail should face a special regulatory treatment, with increased capital ratio and deposit insurance premium (or liquidity requirements).

The three other articles in part 3 study the mechanisms of propagation of failure from one bank to other banks, or even to the banking system as a whole.

Chapter 5, written with Jean Tirole, shows that "peer-monitoring," i.e., the notion that banks should monitor each other, as a complement to centralized monitoring by a public supervisor, is central to the risk of propagation of bank failures through interbank markets.

Chapter 6, also written with Jean Tirole, studies the risk of propagation of bank failures through large-value interbank payment systems.

Finally, chapter 7, written with Xavier Freixas and Bruno Parigi, shows that the architecture of the financial system, and in particular the matrix of interbank relations has a large impact on the resilience of the banking system and its ability to absorb systemic shocks. This paper is related to several important papers on the sources of fragility of the banking system, notably Allen and Gale (1998), Diamond and Rajan (2001), and Goodhart et al. (2006).

Solvency Regulations

Part 4 contains three articles, which are all concerned with the regulation of banks' solvency, and more precisely with the first and second Basel Accords. The first Basel Accord, elaborated in July 1988 by the Basel Committee on Banking Supervision (BCBS), required internationally active banks from the G10 countries to hold a minimum total capital equal to 8% of risk-adjusted assets. It was later amended to cover market risks. It has been revised by the BCBS, which has released for comment several proposals of amendment, commonly referred to as Basel II (Basel Committee 1999, 2001, 2003).

The first article, chapter 8, is mainly concerned with the possibilities of regulatory arbitrage implied by this first accord. It shows that improperly chosen risk weights induce banks to select inefficient portfolios and to undertake regulatory arbitrage activities which might paradoxically result in increased risk taking.[9]

This article belongs to a strand of the theoretical literature (e.g., Furlong and Keeley 1990; Kim and Santomero 1988; Koehn and Santomero 1980; Thakor 1996) focusing on the distortion of the allocation of the banks' assets that could be generated by the wedge between market assessment of asset risks and its regulatory counterpart in Basel I.

Hellman et al. (2000) argue in favor of reintroducing interest rate ceilings on deposits as a complementary instrument to capital requirements for mitigating moral hazard. By introducing these ceilings, the regulator increases the franchise value of the banks (even if they are not currently binding) which relaxes the moral hazard constraint. Similar ideas are put forward in Caminal and Matutes (2002).

The empirical literature (e.g., Bernanke and Lown (1991); see also Thakor (1996), Jackson et al. (1999), and the references therein) has tried to relate these theoretical arguments to the spectacular (yet apparently transitory) substitution of commercial and industrial loans by investment in government securities in U.S. banks in the early 1990s, shortly after the implementation of the Basel Accord and the Federal Deposit Insurance Corporation Improvement Act (FDICIA).[10]

Hancock et al. (1995) study the dynamic response to shocks in the capital of U.S. banks using a vector autoregressive framework. They show that U.S. banks seem to adjust their capital ratios much faster than they adjust their loan portfolios. Furfine (2001) extends this line of research by building a structural dynamic model of banks' behavior, which is calibrated on data from a panel of large U.S. banks for the period 1990–97. He suggests that the credit crunch cannot be explained by demand effects but rather by the rise in capital requirements and/or the increase in regulatory monitoring. He also uses his calibrated model to simulate the effects of Basel II and suggests that its implementation would not provoke a second credit crunch, given that average risk weights on good quality commercial loans will decrease if Basel II is implemented.

---

[9]These activities are analyzed in detail in Jones (2000).

[10]Peek and Rosengren (1995) find that the increase in supervisory monitoring also had a significant impact on bank lending decisions, even after controlling for bank capital ratios. Blum and Hellwig (1995) analyze the macroeconomic implications of bank capital regulation.

The other two articles in part 4 focus on the reform of the Basel Accord (nicknamed Basel II), which relies on three "pillars": capital adequacy requirements, supervisory review, and market discipline. Yet, as shown in chapter 9, the interaction between these three instruments is far from being clear. The recourse to market discipline is rightly justified by common sense arguments about the increasing complexity of banking activities and the impossibility for banking supervisors to monitor in detail these activities. It is therefore legitimate to encourage monitoring of banks by professional investors and financial analysts as a complement to banking supervision. Similarly, a notion of gradualism in regulatory intervention is introduced (in the spirit of the reform of U.S. banking regulation, following the FDIC Improvement Act of 1991). It is suggested that commercial banks should, under "normal circumstances," maintain economic capital way above the regulatory minimum and that supervisors could intervene if this is not the case. Yet, and somewhat contradictorily, while the proposed reform states very precisely the complex refinements of the risk weights to be used in the computation of this regulatory minimum, it remains silent on the other intervention thresholds.

The third article, chapter 10, written with Jean-Paul Décamps and Benoît Roger, analyzes formally the interaction between the three pillars of Basel II in a dynamic model. It also suggests that regulators should put more emphasis on implementation issues and institutional reforms.

Market Discipline versus Regulatory Intervention

Let me conclude this introductory chapter by discussing an important topic that is absent from the papers collected here, namely the respective roles of market discipline and regulatory intervention. Conceptually, market discipline can be used by banking authorities in two different ways:

- *Direct* market discipline, which aims at inducing market investors to *influence*[11] the behavior of bank managers, and works as a *substitute* for prudential supervision.

- *Indirect* market discipline, which aims at inducing market investors to *monitor* the behavior of bank managers, and works as a *complement* to prudential supervision. The idea is that indirect market discipline provides new, objective information that can be used by supervisors not only to improve their control on problem banks but

---

[11]This distinction between influencing and monitoring is due to Bliss and Flannery (2001).

also to implement prompt corrective action (PCA) measures that limit forbearance.

The instruments for implementing market discipline are essentially of three types:

- *Imposing more transparency*, i.e., forcing bank managers to disclose publicly various types of information that can be used by market participants for a better assessment of banks' management.

- *Changing the liability structure of banks*, e.g., forcing bank managers to issue periodically subordinated debt.

- *Using market information* to improve the efficiency of supervision.

We now examine these three types of instruments.

Imposing More Transparency

In a recent empirical study of disclosure in banking, Baumann and Nier (2003) find that more disclosure tends to be beneficial to banks: it decreases stock volatility, increases market values, and increases the usefulness of accounting data. However, as argued by D'Avolio et al. (2001): "market mechanisms...are unlikely themselves to solve the problems raised by misleading information.... For the future of financial markets in the United States, disclosure [of accurate information] is likely to be critical for continued progress." In other words, financial markets will not by themselves generate enough information for investors to allocate their funds appropriately and efficiently, and in some occasions will even tend to propagate misleading information. This means that disclosure of accurate information has to be imposed by regulators. A good example of such regulations are the disclosure requirements imposed in the United States by the Securities and Exchange Commission (and in other countries by the agencies regulating security exchanges) for publicly traded companies. However, the banking sector is peculiar in two respects: banks' assets are traditionally viewed as "opaque,"[12] and banks are subject to regulation and supervision, which implies that bank supervisors are already in possession of detailed information on the banks' balance sheets. Thus it may seem strange to require public disclosure of information already possessed by regulatory authorities:

---

[12] Morgan (2002) provides indirect empirical evidence on this opacity by comparing the frequency of disagreements among bond-rating agencies about the values of firms across sectors of activity. He shows that these disagreements are much more frequent, all else being equal, for banks and insurance companies than for other sectors of the economy.

why can't these authorities disclose the information themselves,[13] or even publish their regulatory ratings (BOPEC, CAMELS, and the like)? There are basically two reasons for this:

- First, as argued in chapter 2, too much disclosure may trigger bank runs and/or systemic banking crises. This happens in any situation where coordination failures may occur between many dispersed investors.

- Second, as we explain below, the crucial benefit of market discipline is to limit the possibilities of regulatory forbearance by generating "objective" information that can be used to force supervisors to intervene before it is too late when a bank is in trouble. This would not be possible if the information was disclosed by the supervisors themselves.

In any case, there are intrinsic limits to transparency in banking: we have to recall that the main economic role of banks is precisely to allocate funds to projects of small and medium enterprises that are "opaque" to outside investors. If these projects were transparent, commercial banks would not be needed in the first place.

Changing the Liability Structure of Banks

The economic idea behind *direct market discipline* is that, by changing the liability structure of banks (e.g., forcing banks to issue uninsured debt of a certain maturity),[14] one can change the incentives of bank managers and shareholders. In particular, some proponents of the mandatory subdebt proposal claim that informed investors have the possibility to "influence" bank managers. This idea has been discussed extensively in the academic literature on corporate finance: short-term debt can in theory be used to mitigate the debt overhang problem (Myers 1984) and the free cash flow problem (Jensen 1986). In the banking literature, Calomiris and Kahn (1991) and Carletti (1999) have shown how demandable debt could be used in theory to discipline bank managers. The subdebt proposal has been analyzed formally in only very few articles: Levonian (2001) uses a Black–Scholes–Merton type of model

---

[13]One could also argue that the information of supervisors is "proprietary" information that could be used inappropriately by the bank's competitors if publicly disclosed. This is not an argument against regulatory disclosure since regulators can select which pieces of information they disclose.

[14]The "subordinated debt proposal" is discussed, for example, in Calomiris (1998, 1999), Evanoff (1993), Evanoff and Wall (2000), Gorton and Santomero (1990), and Wall (1989).

(where the bank's return on assets and closure date are exogenous) to show that mandatory subdebt is typically not a good way to prevent bankers from taking too much risk.[15] Décamps et al. (chapter 10) and Rochet (chapter 9) modify this model by endogenizing the bank's return on assets and closure date. They find that under certain conditions (sufficiently long maturity of the debt, sufficient liquidity of the subdebt market, limited scope for asset substitution by the bank managers) mandating a periodic issuance of subordinated debt could allow regulators to reduce equity requirements (tier 1). However, it would always increase total capital requirements (tier 1 + tier 2).

In any case, empirical evidence for direct market discipline is weak: Bliss and Flannery (2001) find very little support for equity or bond holders influencing U.S. bank holding companies.[16] It is true that studies of crisis periods—either in the recent crises in emerging countries (Martinez Peria and Schmukler 2001; Calomiris and Powell 2000), during the Great Depression (Calomiris and Mason 1997), or the U.S. Savings and Loan crisis (Park and Peristiani 1998)—have found that in extreme circumstances depositors and other investors were able to distinguish between "good" banks and "bad" banks and "vote with their feet." There is no doubt indeed that depositors and private investors have the possibility to provoke bank closures, and thus ultimately discipline bankers. But it is hard to see this as "influencing" banks managers, and it is not necessarily the best way to manage banking failures or systemic crises. This leads me to an important dichotomy within the tasks of regulatory-supervisory systems: one is to limit the *frequency* of bank failures, the other is to *manage* them in the most efficient way once they become unavoidable. I am not aware of any piece of empirical evidence showing that depositors and private investors can directly influence bank managers before their bank becomes distressed (i.e., help supervisors in their first task). As for the second task (i.e., managing closures in the most efficient way), it seems reasonable to argue that supervisors should in fact aim at an orderly resolution of failures, i.e., exactly *preventing* depositors and private investors from interfering with the closure mechanism.

---

[15] The reason is that subdebt behaves like equity in the region close to liquidation (which is precisely the region where influencing managers becomes crucial) so subdebt holders have the some incentives as shareholders to take too much risk.

[16] A recent article by Covitz et al. (2003) partially challenges this view. However, Covitz et al. (2003) focus exclusively on funding decisions. More specifically they find that in the United States riskier banks are less likely to issue subdebt. This does not necessarily imply that mandating subdebt issuance would prevent banks from taking too such risk.

Using Market Information

The most convincing mechanism through which market discipline can help bank supervision is indirect: by *monitoring* banks, private investors can generate new, "objective" information on the financial situation of these banks. This information can then be used to complement the information already possessed by supervisors. There is a large academic literature on this question.[17] Most empirical studies of market discipline indeed focus on market monitoring, i.e., indirect market discipline. The main question examined by this literature is: what is the informational content of prices and returns of the securities issued by banks? More precisely, is this information new with respect to what supervisors already know? Some authors also examine if bond yields and spreads are good predictors of bank risk.

Flannery (1998) reviews most of the empirical literature on these questions. More recent contributions are Jagtiani et al. (2000) and De Young et al. (2001). The main stylized facts are:

- Bond yields and spreads contain information not contained in regulatory ratings and vice versa. More precisely, bank closures can be predicted more accurately by using both market data and regulatory information than by using each of them separately.[18]

- Subdebt yields typically contain bank risk premiums. However, in the United States this is only true since explicit too-big-to-fail policies were abandoned (that is, after 1985–86). This shows that market discipline can work only if regulatory forbearance is not anticipated by private investors.

- However, as shown by Covitz et al. (2003), bond and subdebt yields can also reflect things other than bank risk. In particular, liquidity premiums are likely to play an important role.

In any case, even if there seems to be a consensus that complementing the information set of banking supervisors by market information is useful, it seems difficult to justify, on the basis of existing evidence, mandating all banks to issue subordinated debt for the sole purpose of generating additional information. Large banks and U.S. bank holding

---

[17]See, for example, De Young et al. (2001), Evanoff and Wall (2001, 2002, 2003), Flannery (1998), Flannery and Sorescu (1996), Gropp et al. (2002), Hancock and Kwast (2001), Jagtiani et al. (2000), and Pettway and Sinkey (1980).

[18]A similar point was made earlier by Pettway and Sinkey (1980). They showed that both accounting information and equity returns were useful to predict bank failures. Berger et al. (2000) obtain similar conclusions by testing causality relations between changes in supervisory ratings and in stock prices.

companies already issue publicly traded securities, and therefore this information is already available, while small banks would probably find it difficult to issue such securities on a regular basis and the market for them would probably not be very liquid.[19]

There is also a basic weakness in most empirical studies of indirect market discipline: for data availability reasons they have essentially used cross-sectional data sets containing a vast majority of well-capitalized banks. Remember that the problem at stake is the dynamic behavior of undercapitalized banks. Thus what we should be interested in is instead the informational content of subdebt yields for predicting banks' problems. That is, empirical studies should essentially focus on panel data and restrict analysis to problem banks.

Finally, most of the academic literature (both theoretical and empirical) has focused on the asset substitution effect, exemplified by some spectacular cases, like those of "zombie" Savings and Loan in the U.S. crisis of the 1980s. However, as convincingly argued by Bliss (2001), "poor investments are as problematic as excessively risky projects.... Evidence suggests that poor investments are likely to be the major explanation for banks getting into trouble." Thus there is a need for a more thorough investigation of the performance of weakly capitalized banks: is asset substitution the only problem or is poor investment choice also at stake?

In fact, the crucial aspect about using market regulation to improve banking supervision is probably the possibility of limiting regulatory forbearance by triggering PCA, based on "objective" information. As soon as stakeholders of any sort (private investors, depositors, managers, shareholders or employees of a bank in trouble) can check that supervisors have done their job, i.e., have reacted soon enough to "objective" information (provided by the market) on the bank's financial situation, the scope for regulatory forbearance will be extremely limited. Of course, the challenge is to design (*ex ante*) sufficiently clear rules (i.e., set up a clear agenda for the regulatory agency) specifying how regulatory action has to be triggered by well-specified market events.

How to Integrate Market Discipline and Banking Supervision

A few conclusions emerge from our short review:

---

[19]The argument that subordinated debt has the same profile as (uninsured) deposits and can thus be used to replace forgone market discipline (due to deposit insurance) is not convincing. Indeed, as pointed out by Levonian (2001), the profile of subdebt changes according to the region of scrutiny: it indeed behaves like deposits (or debt) in the region where the bank starts have problems, but like equity when the bank comes closer to the failure region.

- First, it seems that supervision and market discipline are more *complements* than *substitutes*: one cannot work efficiently without the other. Without credible closure policies implemented by supervisors, market discipline is ineffective. Conversely, without the objective data generated by prices and yields of banks' bonds and equity, closure policy is likely to be plagued by "ambiguity" and forbearance.

- Second, *indirect* market discipline (private investors *monitoring* bank managers) seems to be more empirically relevant than *direct* market discipline (private investors *influencing* bank managers). Also, mandating all banks to regularly issue a certain type of subordinated debt would not generate a lot of new information on large bank holding companies (because most of them already issue publicly traded securities), but would be very costly for smaller banks.[20]

- Third, more attention should be directed to the precise ways in which supervisory action can be gradually triggered by market signals. Instead of spending so much time and energy refining the first pillar of the new Basel Accord, the Basel Committee should concentrate on this difficult issue, crucial to creating a level playing field for international banking.

There is also clearly a lot more to be done, both by academics and regulators, if one really wants to understand the interactions between banking supervision and market discipline. In particular, very little attention has been drawn[21] so far to macroprudential regulation: how to prevent and manage systemic banking crises. It seems clear that market discipline is probably not a good instrument for improving macroprudential regulation. Indeed, market signals often become erratic during crises, and the very justification for macroprudential regulation is that markets do not deal efficiently with aggregate shocks of sufficient magnitude. Macroprudential control therefore lies almost exclusively on the shoulders of bank supervisors, in coordination with the central bank and the Treasury. A difficult question is then how to organize the two dimensions (macro and micro) of prudential regulation in such a way that systemic crises are efficiently managed by governments and central banks, while individual bank closure decisions remain protected from political interference.

---

[20]The only convincing argument for mandating regular issuance of a standardized form of subdebt is that it may improve liquidity of such a market, and therefore increase informational content of prices and yields.

[21]Borio (2003) is one exception.

References

Allen, F., and D. Gale. 1998. Optimal financial crises. *Journal of Finance* 53:1245–84.

Bagehot, W. 1873. *Lombard Street: A Description of the Money Market.* London: H. S. King.

Basel Committee. 1999. A new capital adequacy framework. Consultative Paper, Basel Committee on Banking Supervision. Basel, Switzerland: Bank for International Settlements.

———. 2001. Overview of the new Basel Capital Accord. Second consultative document, Basel Committee on Banking Supervision, Basel, Switzerland: Bank for International Settlements.

———. 2003. The new Basel Capital Accord. Third consultative document, Basel Committee on Banking Supervision, Basel, Switzerland: Bank for International Settlements.

Baumann, U., and E. Nier. 2003. Disclosure in banking: what matters most? Paper presented at the NYFed–Chazen Institute Conference, October 2003, New York.

Berger, A., S. M. Davies, and M. J. Flannery. 2000. Comparing market and supervisory assessments of bank performance: who knows what when? *Journal of Money, Credit and Banking* 32:641–67.

Bernanke, B., and C. Lown. 1991. The credit crunch. *Brookings Papers on Economic Activity* 2:205–47.

Bhattacharya, S., and A. V. Thakor. 1993. Contemporary banking theory. *Journal of Financial Intermediation* 3:2–50.

Bliss, R. 2001. Market discipline and subordinated debt: a review of salient issues. *Economic Perspectives, FRB of Chicago* 1:24–45.

Bliss, R., and M. Flannery. 2001. Market discipline in the governance of U.S. bank holding companies: monitoring vs influencing. *European Finance Review* 6:363–95.

Blum, J., and M. Hellwig. 1995. The macroeconomic implications of capital adequacy requirements for banks. *European Economic Review* 39:739–49.

Bordo, M. D. 1990. The lender of last resort: alternative views and historical experience. Federal Reserve Bank of Richmond *Economic Review* (January/February), pp. 18–29.

Borio, C. E. V. 2003. Towards a macroprudential framework for financial supervision and regulation? Working Paper 128. Basel, Switzerland: Bank for International Settlements.

Calomiris, C. W. 1998. Blueprints for a new global financial architecture. (Available at www.house.gov/jec/imf/blueprnt.htm.)

———. 1999. Building an incentive-compatible safety net. *Journal of Banking and Finance* 23:1499–519.

Calomiris, C. W., and C. Kahn. 1991. The role of demandable debt in structuring optimal banking arrangements. *American Economic Review* 81:497–513.

Calomiris, C. W., and J. Mason. 1997. Contagion and bank failures during the Great Depression. *American Economic Review* 87:863–83.

Calomiris, C. W., and P. Powell. 2000. Can emerging markets bank regulators establish credible discipline? The case of Argentina. Mimeo, Banco Central de la Republica Argentina.

Caminal, R., and C. Matutes. 2002. Market power and banking failures. *International Journal of Industrial Organization* 20:1341-61.

Carletti, E. 1999. Bank moral hazard and market discipline. Mimeo, FMG, London School of Economics.

Cordella, T., and E. Levy-Yeyati. 2003. Bank bailouts: moral hazard vs value effect. *Journal of Financial Intermediation* 12:300-30.

Covitz, D. M., D. Hancock, and M. L. Kwast. 2003. Market discipline in banking reconsidered: the role of deposit insurance reform and funding manager decisions and bond market liquidity. Paper presented at the NYFed–Chazen Institute Conference, October 2003, New York.

Crockett, A. 2001. Market discipline and financial stability. Speech delivered at the "Banks and Systemic Risk" conference, Bank of England, London.

D'Avolio, G., E. Gildor, and A. Shleifer. 2001. Technology, information production, and market efficiency. Proceedings of the Jackson Hole Conference, Federal Reserve Bank of Kansas City.

De Young, R., M. J. Flannery, W. W. Lang, and S. M. Sorescu. 2001. The informational content of bank exam ratings and subordinated debt prices. *Journal of Money, Credit and Banking* 33:900-25.

Dewatripont, M., and J. Tirole. 1994. *The Prudential Regulation of Banks.* Cambridge, MA: MIT Press.

Diamond, D., and R. Rajan. 2001. Liquidity risk, liquidity creation and financial fragility: a theory of banking. *Journal of Political Economy* 109:287-327.

Evanoff, D. D. 1993. Preferred sources of market discipline. *Yale Journal of Regulation* 10:347-67.

Evanoff, D. D., and L. D. Wall. 2000. Subordinated debt and bank capital reform. Federal Reserve Bank of Chicago, Working Paper 2000-07.

——. 2001. SND yield spreads as bank risk measures. *Journal of Financial Services Research* 20:121-46.

——. 2002. Measures of the riskiness of banking organizations: subordinated debt yields, risk-based capital. Federal Reserve Bank of Chicago and Atlanta.

——. 2003. Subordinated debt and prompt corrective regulatory action. Federal Reserve Bank of Chicago, Working Paper 2003-03.

Flannery, M. J. 1998. Using market information in prudential bank supervision: a review of the U.S. empirical evidence. *Journal of Money, Credit and Banking* 30:273-305.

Flannery, M. J., and S. Sorescu. 1996. Evidence of bank market discipline in subordinated debenture yields. *Journal of Finance* 51:1347-77.

Folkerts-Landau, D., and P. Garber. 1992. The ECB: a bank or a monetary policy rule? In *Establishing a Central Bank: Issues in Europe and Lessons from the U.S.* (ed. M. B. Canzoneri, V. Grilland, and P. R. Masson), chapter 4, pp. 86–110. CEPR, Cambridge University Press.

Freixas, X., and J.-C. Rochet. 1995. *Microeconomics of Banking*. Cambridge, MA: MIT Press.

Freixas, X., C. Giannini, G. Hoggarth, and F. Soussa. 1999. Lender of last resort: a review of the literature. Financial Stability Review, Bank of England, Issue 7, pp. 151–67.

Furfine, C. 2001. Bank portfolio allocation: the impact of capital requirements, regulatory monitoring, and economic conditions. *Journal of Financial Services Research* 20:33–56.

Furlong, F., and N. Keeley. 1990. A reexamination of mean–variance analysis of bank capital regulation. *Journal of Banking and Finance* 14:69–84.

Goodfriend, M., and R. G. King. 1988. Financial deregulation, monetary policy, and central banking. In *Restructuring Banking and Financial Services in America* (ed. W. Haraf and R. M. Kushmeider). AEI Studies 481, Lanham, MD.

Goodfriend, M., and J. Lacker. 1999. Loan commitment and central bank lending. Federal Reserve Bank of Richmond, Working Paper 99-2.

Goodhart, C. 1995. *The Central Bank and the Financial System*. Cambridge, MA: MIT Press.

Goodhart, C., P. Sunir, and D. Tsomocos. 2006. A model to analyze financial fragility. *Economic Theory* 27:107–42.

Gorton, G. 1988. Banking panics and business cycles. *Oxford Economic Papers* 40:751–81.

Gorton, G., and A. Santomero. 1990. Market discipline and bank subordinated debt. *Journal of Money, Credit and Banking* 22:119–28.

Gropp, R., J. Vesala, and G. Vulpes. 2002. Equity and bond market signals as leading indicators of bank fragility. ECB Working Paper 150, ECB, Frankfurt, Germany.

Hancock, D., and M. L. Kwast. 2001. Using subordinated debt to monitor bank holding companies: is it feasible? *Journal of Financial Services Research* 20:147–87.

Hancock, D., A. J. Laing, and J. A. Wilcox. 1995. Bank capital shocks: dynamic effects on securities, loans, and capital. *Journal of Banking and Finance* 19:661–77.

Hellman, T. F., K. C. Murdock, and J. E. Stiglitz. 2000. Liberalization, moral hazard in banking, and prudential regulation: are capital requirements enough? *American Economic Review* 90:147–65.

Humphrey, T. M. 1975. The classical concept of the lender of last resort. Federal Reserve Bank of Richmond *Economic Review* (January/February), pp. 2–9.

Jackson, P., C. Furfine, H. Groeneveld, D. Hancock, D. Jones, W. Perraudin, L. Redecki, and N. Yoneyama. 1999. Capital requirements and bank behaviour: the impact of the Basel Accord. Basel Committee on Bank Supervision, Working Paper 1.

Jagtiani, J., G. Kaufman, and C. Lemieux. 2000. Do markets discipline banks and bank holding companies? Federal Reserve Bank of Chicago, Working Paper.

Jensen, M. 1986. Agency cost of free cash-flow, corporate finance and takeovers. *American Economic Review* 76:323–39.

Jones, D. J. 2000. Emerging problems with the Basel Accord: regulatory capital arbitrage and related issues. *Journal of Banking and Finance* 14:35–58.

Kaufman, G. 1991. Lender of last resort: a contemporary perspective. *Journal of Financial Services Research* 5:95–110.

Kim, D., and A. M. Santomero. 1988. Risk in banking and capital regulation. *Journal of Finance* 43:1219–33.

Koehn, M., and A. M. Santomero. 1980. Regulation of bank capital and portfolio risk. *Journal of Finance* 35:1235–44.

Levonian, M. 2001. Subordinated debt and the quality of market discipline in banking. Mimeo, Federal Reserve Bank of San Francisco, CA.

Lindgren, C.-J., G. Garcia, and M. Saal. 1996. *Bank Soundness and Macroeconomic Policy*. Washington, DC: IMF.

Martinez Peria, S., and S. Schmukler. 2001. Do depositors punish banks for "bad" behavior? Market discipline, deposit insurance and banking crises. *Journal of Finance* 56:1029–51.

Morgan, D. 2002. Rating banks: risk and uncertainty in an opaque industry. *American Economic Review* 92:874–88.

Myers, S. 1984. The capital structure puzzle. *Journal of Finance* 39:575–92.

Park, S., and S. Peristiani. 1998. Market discipline by thrift depositors. *Journal of Money, Credit and Banking* 26:439–59.

Peek, J., and E. Rosengren. 1995. Bank capital regulation and the credit crunch. *Journal of Banking and Finance* 19:679–92.

Pettway, R. H., and J. F. Sinkey. 1980. Establishing on site bank examination priorities: an early-warning system using accounting and market information. *Journal of Finance* 35:137–50.

Santos, J. A. C. 2000. Bank capital regulation in contemporary banking theory: a review of the literature. Working Paper 90. Basel, Switzerland: Bank for International Settlements.

Schwartz, A. J. 1992. The misuse of the Fed's discount window. Federal Reserve Bank of St. Louis *Review* 74(5):58–69.

Thakor, A. V. 1996. Capital requirements, monetary policy, and aggregate bank lending. *Journal of Finance* 51:279–324.

Thornton, H. 1802. *An Enquiry into the Nature and Effects of Paper Credit of Great Britain*. London: Hatchard.

Wall, L. D. 1989. A plan for reducing future deposit insurance losses: puttable subordinated debt. *Economic Review* 74(4):2–17.

PART 1

Why Are There So Many
Banking Crises?

Chapter One

Why Are There So Many Banking Crises?

Jean-Charles Rochet

1.1 Introduction

The last thirty years have seen an impressive number of banking and financial crises all over the world. In an interesting study, Caprio and Klingebiel (1997) identify 112 systemic banking crises in 93 countries and 51 borderline crises in 46 countries since the late 1970s (see also Lindgren et al. 1996). More than 130 out of 180 of the IMF countries have thus experienced crises or serious banking problems. Similarly, the cost of the Savings and Loan crisis in the United States in the late 1980s has been estimated as over USD 150 billion, which is more than the cumulative loss of all U.S. banks during the Great Depression, even after adjusting for inflation. On average the fiscal cost of each of these recent banking crises was of the order of 12% of the country's GDP but exceeded 40% in some of the most recent episodes in Argentina, Indonesia, South Korea, and Malaysia. Figure 1.1 shows the universality of the problem.

These crises have renewed interest of economic research about two questions: the causes of fragility of banks and the possible ways to remedy this fragility, and the justifications and organization of public intervention. This public intervention can take several forms:

- emergency liquidity assistance by the central bank acting as a lender of last resort;

- organization of deposit insurance funds for protecting the depositors of failed banks;

- minimum solvency requirements and other regulations imposed by banking authorities;

- and finally supervisory systems, supposed to monitor the activities of banks and to close the banks that do not satisfy these regulations.

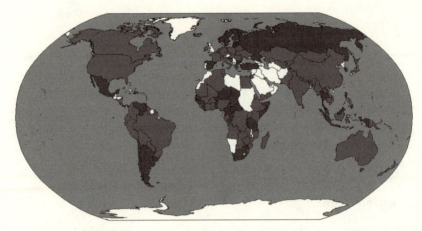

Figure 1.1. Banking problems worldwide, 1980–96. Light gray, banking crisis; dark gray, significant banking problems; white, no significant banking problems or insufficient information. This map was constructed by the author from table 2 in Lindgren et al. (1996).

Important reforms have recently been introduced in banking supervisory systems. For example, the American Congress enacted the Federal Deposit Insurance Corporation Improvement Act in 1991 after the Savings and Loan crisis. Several countries, notably the United Kingdom, have created integrated supervisory authorities for all financial services including banking, insurance, and securities dealing. Finally, in 1989, the G10 countries harmonized their solvency regulations for international active banks. This harmonization, known as the Basel Accord, since it was designed by the Basel Committee of Banking Supervision, was later adopted at national levels by a large number of countries. The Basel Committee is currently working on a revision of this Accord, aiming in particular at giving more importance to market discipline.

The object of this article is to build on recent findings of economic research in order to better understand the causes of banking crises and to possibly offer policy guidelines for reform of regulatory supervisory systems. In a nutshell, my main conclusions will be:

- Banking crises are largely amplified, if not provoked, by political interference.

- Supervision systems face a fundamental commitment problem, analogous to the time consistency confronted by monetary policy.[1]

---

[1] After finishing this paper, I became aware of an article of Quintyn and Taylor (2002), also presented at the Venice Summer Institute of CESIfo (July 2002), that basically arrives to the same conclusions.

- And, finally, the key to successful reform is independence and accountability of banking supervisors.

The plan of this article is as follows. I will start by studying the historical sources of banking fragility. Then I will examine possible remedies: creation of a lender of last resort, and/or deposit insurance combined with solvency regulations. Then I will try to draw a few lessons from recent crises. And finally I will conclude by examining the future of banking supervision.

1.2   The Sources of Banking Fragility

Historically, banks started as money changers. This is testified by etymology. "Trapeza," the Greek word for a bank, refers to the trapezoidal balance that was used by money changers to weigh the precious coins. Similarly, "banco" or "banca," the Italian word for a bank, refers to the bench used by money changers to display their currencies. Interestingly, this money changing activity naturally led early bankers to also provide deposit facilities to merchants using the vaults and safes already in place for storing their precious coins. In England the same movement was initiated by goldsmiths. Similarly, some merchants exploited their networks of trading posts to offer payment services to other merchants, by transferring bills of exchange from one person to another instead of carrying species and gold along the road. In both cases, early bankers very soon realized that the species and gold deposited in their vaults could be profitably reinvested in other commercial and industrial activities. This was the beginning of the fractional reserve system in which a fraction of demandable deposits are used to finance long-term illiquid loans. This is represented by this simplified balance sheet of a representative bank:

Reserves	Deposits
Loans	Capital

As long as the bank keeps enough reserves to cover the withdrawals of the depositors who actually need their money, which is much less than the total amount of the deposits, the system can function smoothly and efficiently. But this system is intrinsically fragile. If all depositors demand their money simultaneously, as they are entitled to (the situation is referred to as a bank run), the bank is forced to liquidate its assets at short notice, which may provoke its failure.[2] Whereas bank runs are often inefficient, bank closures are also necessary in order to eliminate inefficient institutions. Such closures correspond to what are known as fundamental runs, where depositors withdraw their money because the banks' assets are revealed to be bad investments. This Darwinian mechanism is useful to eliminate unsuccessful banks and incentivize bankers to select carefully their investments. But, unfortunately, bank runs can also happen for purely speculative reasons. A recent example of a speculative run occurred in 1991 in Rhode Island in the United States, where a perfectly solvent bank was forced to close after the television channel CNN used a picture of this bank to illustrate a story on bank closures, which led the bank's customers to believe the bank was insolvent (it was not).

As we will see, small depositors are now insured in many countries, which means that the modern form of a bank run is more what is called a silent run, where professional investors stop renewing their large deposits, or Certificates of Deposits as they are called, which is the case, for example, in the Continental Illinois failure in 1984 in the United States.

The mechanism of a speculative run is simple. If each depositor anticipates that other depositors are going to withdraw en masse, then it is in their interest to join the movement, even if they know for sure that the bank's assets are fundamentally safe. Given that these speculative runs are seriously damaging to the banking sector, several mechanisms have been elaborated to eliminate those speculative runs. The first example was the institution of a lender of last resort.

1.3   The Lender of Last Resort

The lender of last resort, which consists of emergency liquidity assistance provided by the central bank to the bank in trouble, was invented, so to speak, in the United Kingdom and the doctrine was articulated in 1873 by the English economist Walter Bagehot, elaborating on previous ideas of Henry Thornton. Bagehot's doctrine was influenced by the systemic crises that followed the failure of Overend & Guerney and Company in May 1866. Overend & Guerney was at the time the greatest discounting house, i.e., a broker of bills of exchange, in the world. During the previous financial crisis of 1825 it was able to make short loans, i.e., to provide liquidity assistance to most of the banks on the London

---

[2]A spectacular example of a bank run occurred in October 1995 in Japan, where the Hyogo Bank experienced more than the equivalent of USD 1 billion withdrawals in just one day.

place and it became known as the bankers' banker. After the death of its founder, Samuel Guerney in 1856, the company was placed under less competent control. Experiencing big losses on some of its loans, it was forced to declare bankruptcy in May 1866 with more than UKP 11 million in liabilities. As a result of this failure, many small banks lost their only provider of liquidity and were forced to close as well, even though they were intrinsically solvent. In order to avoid such crises, Bagehot recommended that the Bank of England be ready to provide liquidity assistance to individual banks in distress. The main points of Bagehot's doctrine were that the central bank should (a) lend only against good collateral, so that only solvent banks might borrow, and that the central bank would be protected against losses; (b) lend at a "very high" interest rate so that only "illiquid" banks are tempted to borrow and that ordinary liquidity provision would be performed by the market, not by the central bank; and (c) announce in advance its readiness to lend without limits in order to establish its credibility to nip the contagion process in the bud. The doctrine was first put into application by the Bank of England in the Barings' crisis of 1890. It was then adopted in continental Europe, resulting in the absence of a major banking crisis for more than thirty years. In the United States, prior to the creation of the Federal Reserve System in 1913, commercial banks organized a clearing house system which served as a private lender of last resort for several decades.

Among more recent examples where Bagehot's doctrine was followed to the letter are the Bank of New York case of 1985 and the second Barings crisis in 1995. On November 21, 1985, the Bank of New York experienced a computer bug. It was a leading participant in the U.S. Treasury bond market and the computer had paid out good funds for the bonds bought by the bank, but would not accept cash in payments for the bonds sold. This quickly led to a USD 22.6 billion deficit. Even if there was no doubt about the solvency of the Bank of New York, no single bank was in a position to cover such a huge deficit by an emergency loan. Similarly there was not enough time to organize a consortium of lenders. So the New York Fed solved the problem by providing an emergency loan against good collateral.[3] Similarly, on February 24, 1995, Barings (once again!) made it known to the Bank of England that its securities subsidiary in Singapore had lost USD 1.4 billion, three times the capital of the bank, due to the fraudulent operation of one of its traders.[4] The Bank of England decided that, since bilateral exposures were relatively limited and the source of Barings failure was a specific case of fraud, the threat of contagion in the U.K. financial system was not large enough

---

[3] This account is drawn from Goodhart (1999).
[4] This account is drawn from Hoggarth and Soussa (2001).

to justify the commitment of public funds. As a result the bank failed on February 26. However, the Bank of England clearly made public its willingness to provide adequate liquidity to the U.K. banking system in case of a market disturbance and, as matter of fact, the announcement itself was enough to avoid any such disturbance.

It is interesting to notice that in these two episodes the intervention of the central banks was triggered by different types of situations. It was a failure of the market to provide liquidity assistance to a solvent bank in the case of the Bank of New York, and in the Barings case, it was a desire to provide liquidity support to the market, and more specifically to the bank, that might have been affected by the closure of a major participant. However, in both cases Bagehot's doctrine was followed and taxpayers' money was not involved. This is unfortunately not always the case. There are indeed several reasons why the central bank might consider supporting insolvent institutions. The first is systemic risk, i.e., the fear that the failure of a large institution might propagate to the rest of the financial system. Given that the central bank is typically responsible for the overall stability of the financial system, it is conceivable that it considers assisting large insolvent institutions whose failure might propagate to other banks. This reason was invoked on several occasions, for example, in the bailout of Johnson Matthey Bankers by the Bank of England in 1984, even if the Bank waited for more than a year before organizing a consortium. A similar case is that of Continental Illinois in the United States, also in 1984. Incidentally, the bailout of Continental Illinois (which effectively amounted to subsidizing the bank's shareholders and uninsured depositors with taxpayers' money) led to the unfortunate notion of a bank that would be "too big to fail."

A second reason why insolvent banks might be bailed out is political interference. Let me take as an illustration the case of my own country, France, where it is interesting to contrast two episodes. The first episode corresponds to the failure in 1988 and 1989 of two Franco-Arab banks, Al Saudi Bank and Kuwaiti-French bank, which were essentially recycling petrodollars in loans to developing countries. They experienced important losses on their lending portfolios. The Bank of France decided not to intervene and the two banks were forced to close. By contrast the largest French bank at the time, the Credit Lyonnais, whose slogan was ironically "The Power to Say 'Yes'," started in 1988 a disastrous policy of bad investments which initially resulted in a spectacular increase of the size of its total balance sheet (30% in two years) and a 200% increase of its industrial holdings. However, very soon, heavy losses materialized: the equivalent of USD 0.3 billion in 1992, USD 1.2 billion in 1993 and USD 2 billion in 1994. After some time the French government felt compelled to intervene. The total cost of the three successive rescue plans that were implemented was estimated to be USD 25 billion, which, in per capita terms, is of the same order of magnitude as the total cost of the Savings and Loan crisis in the United States. A similar situation occurred in Japan during the Jusen crisis in 1995–99. Jusens were non-deposit-taking subsidiaries of banks, created to provide affordable home financing for individual borrowers. The frenetic lending activity of these institutions contributed to the building up of the Japanese real estate bubble. When this bubble burst in 1995 the Japanese authorities had to inject the equivalent of USD 24 billion in order to avoid a collapse of the Japanese financial system. Japanese banks are also famous for several spectacular episodes of fraud. For example, in 1990 it was disclosed by Daiwa Bank that a security trader in its New York branch had been able to conceal a cumulative loss of USD 1.1 billion on the U.S. securities over eleven years. Similarly, in 1996 Sumitomo acknowledged that one of its copper traders was responsible for fraudulent transactions that amounted to a cumulative loss of USD 1.8 billion over ten years.

Let me now turn to two other fundamental mechanisms of public intervention in the banking sector, namely deposit insurance and solvency regulations.

1.4 Deposit Insurance and Solvency Regulations

In the United States the first federal deposit insurance fund was created in 1934,[5] when the Federal Deposit Insurance Corporation (FDIC) was set up in order to prevent bank runs and to protect small and unsophisticated depositors. The initial coverage was USD 2,500 but it was gradually increased to the present figure of USD 100,000. In the United Kingdom the system is less generous: its coverage is limited to only 75% of the first USD 20,000. In continental Europe deposit insurance has long been implicit in the sense that losses were often covered *ex post* by taxpayers' money or by a compulsory contribution of surviving banks, what the Bank of France used to call "solidarité de place." A European Union directive of 1994 requires a minimum harmonization among member countries, with the implementation of explicit deposit insurance systems having a minimum coverage of 20,000 euros, funded by risk-based insurance premiums. It has been argued that these deposit insurance systems were partly responsible, paradoxically, for the fragility of the banking system, whereas in fact they were imagined, or designed, exactly for the opposite purpose. Several studies of the IMF tend indeed to show that countries that have implemented such systems are more likely to

---

[5] State deposit insurance funds were created much earlier, starting in 1829 (New York State). For a good history of deposit insurance in the United States, see FDIC (1998).

experience banking crises, surprisingly. The proposed explanation is that in such countries bankers feel free to take excessive risks, given that their insured depositors are not concerned by the possibility of a failure of their bank, since they are insured in all cases. In the absence of a deposit insurance system, as in New Zealand, for example, bankers are disciplined by the threat of massive withdrawals when depositors become aware of any excessive risk taking by their bank. The doctrine in New Zealand since December 1994 is thus "freedom with publicity." Banks are not really supervised but are only required to disclose detailed information on their accounts to their customers, and bank directors are personally liable in case of false disclosure statements.

In most other countries the reaction to banking crises has been to reinforce banking regulations and in particular solvency regulations. This started at the international level, where the Basel Committee of Banking Supervision enacted in 1988 a regulation requiring a minimum capital level of 8% of risk-weighted assets for internationally active banks of the G10 countries. The different weights were supposed to reflect the credit risk of the corresponding assets. This regulation was later amended to incorporate interest rate risk and market risk. It was also implemented with small variations at the domestic level by the banking authorities of several countries. In particular in the United States, the reform of the FDIC system introduced an important notion, that of prompt corrective action which is some form of gradualism in the intervention of supervisors in order to force them to intervene before it is too late. This is based on a full set of indicators known as CAMELS Ratings.

Let me now discuss the justifications for these solvency regulations, which are essentially twofold. First, they provide a minimum buffer against losses on a bank's assets and therefore decrease its probability of failure. The second justification is to provide incentives to the bank's stockholders to monitor the bank's managers more closely, because these stockholders have more to lose in case of failure. This was the spirit of the Basel Accord of 1988, which was, however, severely criticized for being too crude and for encouraging regulatory arbitrage by commercial banks. It was argued in particular that it was responsible for a credit crunch in the 1990s because banks found it profitable to substitute government securities to commercial and industrial loans in their portfolios of assets.

1.5 Lessons from Recent Crises

Let me try to draw some lessons from the crises of the last twenty-five years, which have provided very useful evidence for research. Economists have examined several questions. For example, evaluation of the social cost of these crises is not easy. Hoggarth et al. (2001) criticize the use of fiscal costs, i.e., the amount transferred from taxpayer to creditors of failed banks, as a true measure of the economic cost of banking crises. Indeed those fiscal costs are more a transfer than an aggregate cost to society. So they propose instead to evaluate the output loss, i.e., the amount of wealth that would have been provided or produced in the country in the absence of a crisis. They find that this estimated output loss is large, around 15-20% of the annual GDP and even larger in the case of a twin crisis, that is to say, a currency crisis occurring simultaneously with a banking crisis. This confirms previous studies of Kaminsky and Reinhart (1996, 1999), who also show that a different pattern seems to emerge in developed countries and developing countries, respectively. In developed countries, banking crises alone are already very costly, whereas in developing countries it seems that the cost is significant only in the case of a twin crisis.[6] Other economists (e.g., Bell and Pain 2000; Davis 1999) have tried to establish common patterns of banking crises and derive indicators for predicting those crises. Davis argues in particular that the East Asian crisis that started in 1997 exhibited features very similar to earlier crises in Scandinavia or Japan, namely vulnerability to real shocks, such as export price variations and foreign currency exposure. However, the East Asian crisis had very little impact on the securities market of the OECD countries by contrast with the Russian crisis of August 1998. The reason seems to be that the moratorium on Russian public debt generated an unwinding of leverage positions on U.S. Treasury markets—USD 80 billion for LTCM alone, more than USD 3,000 billion for commercial banks altogether. By contrast, the Asian crisis only resulted in bank runs instead of affecting markets and so the consequence was only the failure of several domestic banks.

Also, economists have tried to assess the characteristics of banking systems that were more likely to be associated with a large probability of crisis or a large cost of resolution. Honohan and Klingebiel (2000) show in particular that precrisis provision of liquidity support, which is often used by governments to delay the recognition of a crisis, is the most significant predictor of a high fiscal cost, once the crisis erupts.

Finally, the Scandinavian banking crisis (1988-93) was much more dramatic in Finland and to a lesser extent in Norway than in Sweden. The common causes were the deregulation of financial markets, an economic boom, and an asset market bubble (accompanied with a spectacular increase in USD denominated foreign debt) followed by a real shock. In

---

[6]For a thorough analysis of currency crises and international financial architecture, see Tirole (2002).

the case of Finland it was the collapse of the Soviet Union. After the rise in European interest rates in 1989, Finland, and to some extent other Nordic economies, faced a serious competitiveness problem partly due to their indebtedness. An attempt to defend fixed exchange rates led to very high interest rates and deflation. The final result in Finland was a massive devaluation, followed by an asset bubble burst. Some large commercial banks and the entire savings bank sector had to be taken over by the government. Nonperforming assets were separated and transferred to a defeasance structure, usually referred to as a bad bank. Public support was provided to all of the banks, but the stockholders of the banks were not expropriated and some managers remained in charge. As a result the cost was huge, of the order of 8% of GDP.

For Norway (and even more so for Sweden), the real shock was more the decrease in the price of oil rather than the collapse of the Soviet Union. But the symptoms were similar: three large commercial banks and two regional savings banks had to bailed out by public funds because they incurred large losses on their loan portfolios, and as a result became undercapitalized. But the Norwegian government was tougher: it injected money only in exchange for drastic reduction in loan portfolios, import and cost cuts, and shareholders were fully expropriated, which was not the case in Finland. Of course, the shareholders of failed Norwegian banks later required compensation arguing that the banks were not actually closed, but they lost the case. Bank managers and directors were almost systematically replaced and as a result the cost of the crisis was much smaller, less than 3% of GDP.[7]

1.6 The Future of Banking Supervision

Let me now conclude by trying to assess the possible future of banking supervision, starting with the remark that the traditional approach to banking supervision was very paternalistic. In the 1960s and 1970s, banks were in many countries protected from competition through entry restrictions and price controls, in exchange for accepting that they follow the detailed prescription of supervisors. This quid pro quo between banks and governments is no longer viable, for several reasons.

First of all, globalization and deregulation have made competition very fierce, in particular by nonbanks, i.e., firms that are not regulated. Also, the increased complexity of financial markets and banking activities implies that supervisors are no longer in a position to monitor closely the activities of all banks. This feature is illustrated by the failure of the

---

[7]The rebound of oil price due to the first Gulf War may also have helped the crisis resolution. I thank Jon Danielson for this remark.

Basel Committee to impose the standardized approach to market risks. Instead, the Committee was obliged to accept that large banks use their own internal models. It is expected that in the future few banks will follow the standardized approach, since they will probably prefer to use one of the models developed by the large banks.

The proposed reform of the Basel Accord is supposed to rely on three "pillars." The first pillar is a refined capital requirement with very complex weights, designed to be more in line with market assessments of risks. The second pillar is a more proactive role of banking supervisors, and the third pillar is an increased recourse to market discipline. The problem is that supervisors have a general tendency to interfere too much when the banks are well run and to intervene too little when the banks have problems. Too much attention in my opinion has been devoted to the first pillar, namely the design of a very complicated system of risk weights. In my opinion it is not the job of the regulators to tell the banks what they have to do when they are not in trouble. On the contrary, their job is to take care of ailing banks. Thus, I believe more attention should be devoted to the other two pillars of Basel II, namely supervision and market discipline. In particular, it should be stated precisely when and how supervisors will intervene and which instruments should be used to generate market discipline. Several U.S. economists (e.g., Calomiris 1999; Evanoff and Wall 2000) have proposed such an instrument, namely compulsory subordinated debt. Without going into the details, let me just mention why subordinated debt can sometimes be a good instrument for generating market discipline. It can indeed provide direct market discipline since the cost of issuing new debt increases when the risk profile of the bank increases. Thus, if the bank is forced to issue subordinated debt on a regular basis, it will have incentives not to take too much risk. But there is also indirect market discipline because the price of subordinated debt in secondary markets decreases when the risk of failure of the bank increases. So the secondary market price of subordinated debt provides additional information to the regulator on the perceived risk of failure of the bank. But the real concern is supervision, not regulation. One needs to be sure that supervisors impose corrective measures or even close the bank before it is too late. The core of the problem is that any bank is always worth more alive than dead. This is so in particular because the informational capital of the bank is lost if it closes. So, even a competent and benevolent planner would always find preferable *ex post* to provide liquidity assistance to a bank in distress. But, of course, if this is anticipated by bankers *ex ante*, this can be the source of moral hazard. Proper incentives can only be provided if stockholders and top managers are truly expropriated in case of problems (the Norwegian case is a good illustration). Empirical evidence on the resolution of bank defaults suggests that failed banks are more often rescued than liquidated. For example, Goodhart and Schoenmaker (1995) show that the effective methods of resolving banking problems vary a lot from country to country, but in most cases they result in bailouts. Out of a sample of 104 failing banks, Goodhart and Schoenmaker find that 73 resulted in rescue and only 31 in actual liquidation.[8] This is confirmed by other studies. For example, Santomero and Hoffman (1998) show that in the United States the discount window, i.e., the lender of last resort facility, was often used improperly to rescue banks that subsequently failed. So market discipline can be useful in two respects: by directly penalizing the banks that take too much risk without the need for an intervention by supervisors; by indirectly providing new objective information, such as private ratings, interest rate spreads, or secondary prices of debt that can be used by supervisors. But market discipline can also be dangerous. In particular, market prices become erratic during crises and diverge from fundamentals. Coordination failures may occur between investors whereby each of them has a good and justified opinion of the solvency of a given bank but refuses to buy its subordinated debt because it anticipates that other investors will not lend to the bank. This is what game theoreticians call self-fulfilling prophecies. The theoretical analysis of this was done by Morris and Shin (1998) for currency crises and, later, Rochet and Vives (chapter 2) developed an extension for banking crises.

But there are other dangers of market discipline. For example, it is proposed by the reform of the Basel Accord to condition capital requirements on private ratings. But can we really trust ratings agencies? They often have less information than the supervisors and sometimes even less than other banks. Secondly, the market for ratings is not really competitive and conflicts of interest between auditing and consulting activities may occur, as was exemplified by the recent Enron–Andersen case. Finally, market discipline can be the vehicle for contagion. It could be a good disciplining device during good times, in particular subordinated debt, but it can also be the source of systemic risk during crises.[9]

However, the main difficulty is to obtain credibility of regulation and to get rid of political pressure on banking supervisors. The source of this difficulty is not only corruption and regulatory capture, but more fundamentally the absence of commitment power of governments. It is a classical time consistency problem, which is even more severe in the case

---

[8] The "purchase and assumption" method, whereby the failing bank is merged with a safe bank, is often used in the United States. This allows to some extent a preservation of the failed bank's "informational capital."

[9] A theoretical analysis of this is provided in chapter 5.

of democracies than in the case of corrupt regimes. I therefore argue in favor of independence and accountability of banking supervisors as has been done for monetary policy. So, instead of discretionary power given to bank supervisors, sometimes referred to as the constructive ambiguity proposal, I advocate an explicit mandate given to banking supervisory agencies. This is of course difficult to design and is a challenge for further research. For example, it would be useful to define objective criteria for deciding when a bank has to be bailed out for systemic reasons, and also how to organize *ex post* accountability with sanctions on supervisors if they do not perform well.

To summarize, I believe the main reason behind the frequency and magnitude of recent banking crises is neither deposit insurance, nor bad regulation, nor the incompetence of supervisors. It is essentially the commitment problem of political authorities who are likely to exert pressure for bailing out insolvent banks. The remedy to political pressures on bank supervisors is not to substitute supervision by market discipline, because market discipline can only be effective if absence of government intervention is anticipated. So, the crucial problem is the credibility of political authorities, and the way to restore this credibility is to ensure the independence and accountability of bank supervisors. More work needs to be done in specifying the precise institutional reforms that are necessary to achieve this goal.

References

Bell, J., and D. L. Pain. 2000. Leading indicator models of banking crises: a critical review. Financial Stability Review, December, Bank of England.

Calomiris, C. W. 1999. Building an incentive-compatible safety net. *Journal of Banking and Finance* 23:1499–519.

Caprio, G., and D. Klingebiel. 1997. Bank insolvency: bad luck, bad policy or bad banking? In *Annual World Bank Report* (ed. M. Bruno and B. Pleskovic). Washington, DC: The International Bank for Reconstruction and Development.

Davis, E. P. 1999. Financial data needs for macroprudential surveillance. Lecture Series 2, Bank of England.

Evanoff, D. D., and L. A. Wall. 2000. Subordinated debt as bank capital: a proposal for regulatory reform. *FRB of Chicago Review* 24:40–53.

FDIC. 1998. *A Brief History of Deposit Insurance in the USA.* (Available at www.fdic.gov/bank/historical/brief/brhist.pdf.)

Goodhart, C. 1999. Myths about the lender of last resort. FMG Special Paper 120, London School of Economics.

Goodhart, C., and D. Schoenmaker. 1995. Institutional separation between supervisory and monetary agencies. FMG Special Paper, London School of Economics.

Hoggarth, G., and F. Soussa. 2001. Crisis management, lender of last resort and the changing nature of the banking industry. In *Financial Stability and Central Bank: A Global Perspective* (ed. R. A. Brealey et al.), chapter 6. London and New York: Routledge.

Hoggarth, G., R. Ries, and V. Saporta. 2001. Costs of banking system instability: some empirical evidence. Financial Stability Review, Summer, Bank of England.

Honohan, P., and D. Klingebiel. 2000. Controlling fiscal costs of banking crises. Mimeo, World Bank.

Kaminsky, G. L., and C. M. Reinhart. 1996. The twin crises: the causes of banking and balance-of-payments problems. International Finance Discussion Paper 544, Board of Governors of the Federal Reserve System, March.

——. 1999. The twin crises: the causes of banking and balance-of-payments problems. *American Economic Review* 89:473–500.

Lindgren, C. J., G. Garcia, and M. Seal. 1996. *Bank Soundness and Macroeconomic Policy*. Washington, DC: IMF.

Morris, S., and H. Shin. 1998. Unique equilibrium a model of self-fulfilling currency attacks. *American Economic Review* 88:587–97.

Quintyn, M., and M. Taylor. 2002. Regulatory and supervisory independence and financial stability. IMF Discussion Paper.

Santomero, A. M., and P. Hoffman. 1998. Problem bank resolution: evaluating the options, financial institutions. Working Paper, the Wharton School, University of Pennsylvania.

Tirole, J. 2002. *Financial Crises, Liquidity and the International Monetary System*. Princeton University Press.

PART 2
The Lender of Last Resort

Chapter Two

Coordination Failures and the Lender of Last Resort: Was Bagehot Right After All?

Jean-Charles Rochet and Xavier Vives

2.1 Introduction

There have been several recent controversies about the need for a lender of last resort (LLR) both within national banking systems (the central banks) and at an international level (the IMF).[1] The concept of an LLR was elaborated in the nineteenth century by Thornton (1802) and Bagehot (1873). An essential point of the "classical" doctrine associated with Bagehot asserts that the LLR role is to lend to "solvent but illiquid" banks under certain conditions.[2]

Banking crises have been recurrent in most financial systems. The LLR facility and deposit insurance were instituted precisely to provide stability to the banking system and to avoid unfavorable consequences for the real sector. Indeed, financial distress may cause important damage to the economy, as the example of the Great Depression makes clear.[3] Traditional banking panics had been eliminated with the LLR facility and deposit insurance by the end of the nineteenth century in Europe and after the crisis of the 1930s in the United States; and they have almost disappeared from emerging economies, which have until now suffered numerous crises.[4] Modern liquidity crises associated with securitized money or capital markets have also required the intervention of the LLR. Indeed, the Federal Reserve intervened in the crises provoked by the failure of Penn Central in the U.S. commercial paper market in 1970, by the stock market crash of October 1987, and by Russia's default in

---

[1] See, for instance, Calomiris (1998a,b), Kaufman (1991), Fischer (1999), Mishkin (2000), and Goodhart and Huang (1999, 2000).

[2] The LLR should lend freely against good collateral, valued at precrisis levels, and at a penalty rate. These conditions are due to Bagehot (1873) and are also presented, for instance, in Humphrey (1975) and Freixas et al. (1999).

[3] See Bernanke (1983) and Bernanke and Gertler (1989).

[4] See Gorton (1988) for U.S. evidence and Lindgren et al. (1996) for evidence on other IMF member countries.

1997 and subsequent collapse of LTCM (in the latter case a "lifeboat" was arranged by the New York Fed). For example, in October 1987 the Federal Reserve supplied liquidity to banks through the discount window.[5]

The LLR's function of providing emergency liquidity assistance has been criticized for provoking moral hazard on the banks' side. Perhaps more importantly, Goodfriend and King (1988) (see also Bordo 1990; Kaufman 1991; Schwartz 1992) remark that Bagehot's doctrine was elaborated at a time when financial markets were underdeveloped. They argue that, whereas central bank intervention on aggregate liquidity (monetary policy) is still warranted, individual interventions (banking policy) are not anymore: with sophisticated interbank markets, banking policy has become redundant. Open-market operations can provide sufficient liquidity, which is then allocated by the interbank market. The discount window is not needed. In other words, Goodfriend and King argue that, when financial markets function well, a solvent institution cannot be illiquid. Banks can finance their assets with interbank funds, negotiable certificates of deposit (CDs), and repurchase agreements (repos). Well-informed participants in this interbank market will distinguish liquidity from solvency problems. This view also has consequences for the debate about the need for an international LLR. Indeed, Chari and Kehoe (1998) claim, for example, that such an international LLR is not needed because joint action by the Federal Reserve, the European Central Bank, and the Bank of Japan can take care of any international liquidity problem.[6]

Those developments have led qualified observers to dismiss bank panics as a phenomenon of the past and to express confidence in the efficiency of financial markets—especially the interbank market—for resolving liquidity problems of financial intermediaries. This is based on the view that participants in the interbank market are the best-informed agents to ascertain the solvency of an institution with liquidity problems.[7]

---

[5]See Folkerts-Landau and Garber (1992). See also Freixas et al. (chapter 3) for a modeling of the interactions between the discount window and the interbank market.

[6]Jeanne and Wyplosz (2003) compare the required size of an international LLR under the "open market monetary policy" and the "discount window banking policy" views.

[7]For example, Tommaso Padoa-Schioppa, a member of the European Central Bank's executive committee in charge of banking supervision, has gone as far as saying that classical bank runs may occur only in textbooks, precisely because measures like deposit insurance and capital adequacy requirements have been put in place. Furthermore, despite recognizing that "rapid outflows of uninsured interbank liabilities" are more likely, Padoa-Schioppa (1999) states: "However, since interbank counterparties are much better informed than depositors, this event would typically require the market to have a strong suspicion that the bank is actually insolvent. If such a suspicion were to be unfounded and not generalized, the width and depth of today's interbank market is

The main objective of this article is to provide a theoretical foundation for Bagehot's doctrine in a model that fits the modern context of sophisticated and presumably efficient financial markets. We are thinking of a short time horizon that corresponds to liquidity crises. We shift emphasis from maturity transformation and liquidity insurance of small depositors to the "modern" form of bank runs, where large well-informed investors refuse to renew their credit (CDs for example) on the interbank market. The decision not to renew credit may arise as the result of an event (e.g., failure of Penn Central, October 1987 crash, LTCM failure) that renders doubtful the repayment capacity of an intermediary or a number of intermediaries. The central bank may then decide to provide liquidity to those troubled institutions. The question arises of whether such intervention is warranted.

Since Diamond and Dybvig (1983) (and Bryant 1980), banking theory has insisted on the fragility of banks due to possible coordination failures between depositors (bank runs). However, it is hard to base any policy recommendation on their model since it systematically possesses multiple equilibria. The selection among these multiple equilibria is usually explained by the presence of sunspots that coordinate the behavior of investors. This view of banking instability has been disputed by Gorton (1985) and others who argue that crises are related to fundamentals and not to self-fulfilling panics. On this view, crises are triggered by bad news about the returns to be obtained by the bank. Gorton (1988) studies panics in the U.S. national banking era and concludes that crises were predictable by indicators of the business cycle. The phenomenon has been theorized in the literature on information-based bank runs (see Chari and Jagannathan 1988; Jacklin and Bhattacharya 1988; Allen and Gale 1998). There is an ongoing empirical debate about whether crises are predictable and their relation to fundamentals.[8]

Our approach is inspired by Postlewaite and Vives (1987), who present an incomplete information model featuring a unique Bayesian equilibrium with a positive probability of bank runs. However, the model of Postlewaite and Vives (1987) differs from our model here in several respects. In particular, in Postlewaite and Vives there is no uncertainty about the fundamental value of the bank's assets (no solvency problems) but incomplete information about the liquidity shocks suffered by depositors. The uniqueness of equilibrium in their case comes from a more complex specification of technology and liquidity shocks for depositors than in Diamond and Dybvig (1983). The present model is

---

such that other institutions would probably replace (possibly with the encouragement of the public authorities as described above) those which withdraw their funds."

[8] See also Kaminsky and Reinhart (1999) and Radelet and Sachs (1998) for perspectives on international crises.

instead adapted from the "global game" analysis of Carlsson and Van Damme (1993) and Morris and Shin (1998).[9] This approach builds a bridge between the "panic" and "fundamentals" views of crises by linking the probability of occurrence of a crisis to the fundamentals. A crucial property of the model is that, when the private information of investors is precise enough, the game among them has a unique equilibrium. Moreover, at this unique equilibrium there is an intermediate interval of values of the bank's assets for which, in the absence of intervention by the central bank, the bank is solvent but can still fail if too large a proportion of investors withdraw their money. In other words, in this intermediate range for the fundamentals there exists a potential for coordination failure. Furthermore, the range in which such a coordination failure occurs diminishes with the *ex ante* strength of fundamentals.

Given that this equilibrium is unique and is based on the fundamentals of the bank, we are able to provide some policy recommendations on how to avoid such failures. More specifically, we discuss the interaction between *ex ante* regulation of solvency and liquidity ratios and *ex post* provision of emergency liquidity assistance. It is found that liquidity and solvency regulation can solve the coordination problem, but typically the cost is too high in terms of forgone returns. This means that prudential measures must be complemented with emergency discount-window loans.

In order to complete the policy discussion we introduce moral hazard and endogenize banks' short-term debt structure as a way to discipline bank managers. This framework allows us to discuss early closure policies of banks as well as the interaction of the LLR, prompt corrective action, and orderly resolution of failures. We can then study the adequacy of Bagehot's doctrine in a richer environment and derive the complementarity between public (LLR and other facilities) and private (market) involvement in crisis resolution.

Finally, we provide a reinterpretation of the model in terms of the banking sector of a small open economy and derive lessons for an international LLR facility.

The rest of the paper is organized as follows. Section 2.2 presents the model. Section 2.3 discusses runs and solvency. Section 2.4 characterizes the equilibrium of the game between investors. Section 2.5 studies the properties of this equilibrium and the effect of prudential regulation on coordination failure. Section 2.6 makes a first pass at the LLR policy implications of our model and its relation to Bagehot's doctrine. Section 2.7 shows how to endogenize the liability structure and proposes a

---

[9]See also Goldstein and Pauzner (2003), Heinemann and Illing (2002), and Corsetti et al. (2004).

welfare-based LLR facility with attention to crisis resolution. Section 2.8 provides the international reinterpretation of the model and discusses the role of an international LLR and associated facilities. Concluding remarks end the paper in section 2.9.

2.2 The Model

Consider a market with three dates: $\tau = 0, 1, 2$. At date $\tau = 0$ the bank possesses own funds E and collects uninsured wholesale deposits (CDs for example) for some amount D_0 that is normalized to unity. These funds are used in part to finance some investment I in risky assets (loans), the rest being held in cash reserves M. Under normal circumstances, the returns RI on these assets are collected at date $\tau = 2$, the CDs are repaid, and the stockholders of the bank receive the difference (when it is positive). However, early withdrawals may occur at an interim date $\tau = 1$, following the observation of private signals on the future realization of R. If the proportion x of these withdrawals exceeds the cash reserves M of the bank, then the bank is forced to sell some of its assets. To summarize our notation, the bank's balance sheet at $\tau = 0$ is represented as:

I	$D_0 = 1$
M	E

The terms in this representation are defined as follows.

1. D_0 $(= 1)$ is the volume of uninsured wholesale deposits that are normally repaid at $\tau = 2$ but can also be withdrawn at $\tau = 1$. The nominal value of deposits upon withdrawal is $D \geqslant 1$ independently of the withdrawal date. Thus, early withdrawal entails no cost for the depositors themselves (when the bank is not liquidated prematurely).

2. E represents the value of equity (or, more generally, long-term debt; it may also include insured deposits[10]).

3. I denotes the volume of investment in risky assets, which have a random return R at $\tau = 2$.

4. M is the amount of cash reserves (money) held by the bank.

---

[10]If they are fully insured, these deposits have no reason to be withdrawn early and can therefore be assimilated into stable resources.

We assume that the withdrawal decision is delegated to fund managers who typically prefer to renew the deposits (i.e., not to withdraw early) but are penalized by the investors if the bank fails. This is consistent with the fact that the vast majority of wholesale deposits are held by collective investment funds and the empirical evidence on the remuneration of fund managers (see, for example, Chevalier and Ellison 1997, 1999). Indeed, the salaries of fund managers depend on the size of their funds and are not directly indexed on the returns on these funds. Instead, managers are promoted (i.e., get more funds to manage) if they build a good reputation, and demoted otherwise. Accordingly, we suppose that fund managers' payoffs depend on whether they take the "right decision." When the bank does not fail, the differential payoff of withdrawing with respect to rolling over the CD is negative and equal to $-C < 0$. When the bank does fail, the differential payoff of withdrawing with respect to rolling over the CD is positive and equal to $B > 0$. Therefore, fund managers adopt the following behavioral rule: withdraw if and only if they anticipate $PB - (1 - P)C > 0$ or $P > y = C/(B + C)$, where P is the probability that the bank fails.

This payoff structure is obtained, for example, if fund managers obtain a benefit $B > 0$ if they get the money back or if they withdraw and the bank fails. They get nothing otherwise. However, to withdraw involves a cost $C > 0$ for the managers (for example, because their reputation suffers if they have to recognize that they have made a bad investment) as well as not withdrawing and the bank failing.

At $\tau = 1$, fund manager i privately observes a signal $s_i = R + \varepsilon_i$, where the ε_i are i.i.d. and also independent of R. As a result, a proportion x of them decides to "withdraw" (i.e., not to renew their CDs). By assumption there is no other source of financing for the bank (except perhaps the central bank, see below), so if $x > M/D$ then the bank is forced to sell a volume y of assets.[11] If the needed volume of sales y is greater than the total of available assets I, the bank fails at $\tau = 1$; if not, the bank continues until date 2. Failure occurs at $\tau = 2$ whenever

$$R(I - y) < (1 - x)D. \tag{2.1}$$

Our modeling tries to capture, in the simplest possible way, the main institutional features of modern interbank markets. In our model, banks essentially finance themselves by two complementary sources: stable resources (equity and long-term debt) and uninsured short-term deposits (or CDs), which are uncollateralized and involve fixed repayments. However, in the case of a liquidity shortage at date 1, banks may

---

[11]These sales are typically accompanied with a repurchase agreement (or repo). They are thus equivalent to a collateralized loan.

also sell some of their assets (or equivalently borrow against collateral) on the repo market. This secondary market for bank assets is assumed to be informationally efficient in the sense that the secondary price aggregates the decentralized information of investors about the quality of the bank's assets.[12] Therefore, we assume that the resale value of the bank's assets depends on R. However, banks cannot obtain the full value of these assets but only a fraction $1/(1 + \lambda)$ of this value, with $\lambda > 0$. Accordingly, the volume of sales needed to face withdrawals x is given by

$$y = (1 + \lambda)\frac{[xD - M]_+}{R},$$

where $[xD - M]_+ = \max(0, xD - M)$.

The parameter λ measures the cost of "fire sales" in the secondary market for bank assets. It is crucial for our analysis and can be explained via considerations of asymmetric information or liquidity problems.[13]

Indeed, asymmetric information problems may translate into either limited commitment of future cash flows (as in Hart and Moore (1994) or Diamond and Rajan (2001)), moral hazard (as in Holmström and Tirole (1997)), or adverse selection (as in Flannery (1996)). We have chosen to stress the last explanation because it gives a simple justification for the superiority of the central bank over financial markets in the provision of liquidity to banks in trouble. This adverse selection premium comes from the fact that a bank may want to sell its assets for two reasons: because it needs liquidity or because it wants to get rid of its bad loans (with a value normalized to zero). Investors only accept to pay $R/(1 + \lambda)$ because they assess a probability $1/(1 + \lambda)$ to the former case. The superiority of the central bank comes from its supervisory knowledge of banks.[14] The presence of an adverse selection discount in credit markets is well established (see, for example, Broecker 1990; Riordan 1993). Flannery (1996) presents a specific mechanism that explains why the secondary market for bank assets may be plagued by a winner's curse, inducing a fire-sale premium. He argues, furthermore, that this fire-sale premium is likely to be higher during crises, given that investors are

---

[12]We can imagine, for instance, that the bank organizes an auction for the sale of its assets. If there is a large number of bidders and their signals are (conditionally) independent, then the equilibrium price p of this auction will be a deterministic function of R.

[13]For a similar assumption in a model of an international lender of last resort, see Goodhart and Huang (2000).

[14]The empirical evidence points at the superiority of the central bank information because of its access to supervisory data (see, for example, Peek et al. 1999). Similarly, Romer and Romer (2000) find evidence of a superiority of the Federal Reserve over commercial forecasters in forecasting inflation.

then probably more uncertain about the precision of their signals. This makes the winner's curse more severe because it is then more difficult to distinguish good from bad risks.

The parameter λ can also be interpreted as a liquidity premium, i.e., the interest margin that the market requires for lending at short notice. (See Allen and Gale (1998) for a model in which costly asset sales arise owing to the presence of liquidity-constrained speculators in the resale market.) In a generalized banking crisis we would have a liquidity shortage, implying a large λ. Interpreting it as a market rate, λ can also spike temporarily in response to exogenous events, such as September 11.

In our model we will be thinking mostly of the financial distress of an individual bank (a bank is close to insolvency when R is small), although—for sufficiently correlated portfolio returns of the banks— the interpretation could be broadened (see also the interpretation in an international context in section 2.8).

Operations on interbank markets do not involve any physical liquidation of bank assets. However, we will show that, when a bank is close to insolvency (R small) or when there is a liquidity shortage (λ large), the interbank markets do not suffice to prevent early closure of the bank. Early closure involves the physical liquidation of assets, and this is costly. We model this liquidation cost (not to be confused with the fire-sale premium λ) as being proportional to the future returns on the bank's portfolio. If the bank is closed at $\tau = 1$, then the (per-unit) liquidation value of its assets is νR, with $\nu \ll 1/(1 + \lambda)$.

2.3 Runs and Solvency

We focus in this section on some features of banks' liquidity crises that cannot be properly taken into account within the classical Bryant–Diamond–Dybvig (BDD) framework. In doing so we take the banks' liability structure (and, in particular, the fact that an important fraction of these liabilities can be withdrawn on demand) as exogenous. A possible way to endogenize the bank's liability structure is to introduce a disciplining role for liquid deposits. In section 2.7 we explore such an extension.

We adopt explicitly the short time horizon (say, two days) that corresponds to liquidity crises. This means that we shift the emphasis from maturity transformation and liquidity insurance of small depositors to the "modern" form of bank runs, i.e., large investors refusing to renew their CDs on the interbank market.

A second element that differentiates our model from BDD is that our bank is not a mutual bank but rather a corporation that acts in the best interest of its stockholders. This allows us to discuss the role of equity as well as the articulation between solvency requirements and provision of emergency liquidity assistance. In section 2.7 we endogenize the choice of assets by the bank through the monitoring effort of its managers (first-order stochastic dominance), but we take as given the amount of equity E. It would be interesting to extend our model by endogenizing the level of equity in order to capture the impact of leverage on the riskiness of assets chosen by banks (second-order stochastic dominance). In this model, however, both the amount of equity and the riskiness of assets are taken as given.

As a consequence of our assumptions, the relation between the proportion x of early withdrawals and the failure of the bank is different from that in BDD. To see this, let us recapitulate the different cases.

1. $xD \leqslant M$: there is no sale of assets at $\tau = 1$. In this case, there is failure at $\tau = 2$ if and only if

$$RI + M < D \quad \Longleftrightarrow \quad R < R_s = \frac{D - M}{I} = 1 - \frac{1 + E - D}{I}.$$

   Here R_s can be interpreted as the solvency threshold of the bank. Indeed, if there are no withdrawals at $\tau = 1$ ($x = 0$), then the bank fails at $\tau = 2$ if and only if $R < R_s$. The threshold R_s is a decreasing function of the solvency ratio E/I.

2. $M < xD \leqslant M + RI/(1 + \lambda)$: there is a partial sale of assets at $\tau = 1$. Failure occurs at $\tau = 2$ if and only if

$$RI - (1 + \lambda)(xD - M) < (1 - x)D$$
$$\Longleftrightarrow \quad R < R_s + \lambda \frac{xD - M}{I} = R_s \left[1 + \lambda \frac{xD - M}{D - M} \right].$$

   This formula illustrates how, because of the premium λ, solvent banks can fail when the proportion x of early withdrawals is too large.[15] Note, however, an important difference with BDD: when the bank is "supersolvent" ($R > (1 + \lambda)R_s$) it can never fail, even if everybody withdraws ($x = 1$).

3. $xD > M + RI/(1 + \lambda)$, the bank is closed at $\tau = 1$ (early closure).

The failure thresholds are summarized in figure 2.1.

---

[15]We may infer that to obtain resources $xD - M > 0$ we must liquidate a fraction $\mu = [(xD - M)/(RI)](1 + \lambda)$ of the portfolio; hence, $\tau = 2$ we have $R(1 - \mu)I = RI - (1 + \lambda)(xD - M)$ remaining.

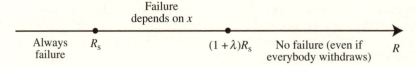

Figure 2.1. The failure thresholds.

A few comments are in order. In our model, early closure is never *ex post* efficient because physically liquidating assets is costly. However, as discussed in section 2.7, early closure may be *ex ante* efficient for disciplining bank managers and inducing them to exert effort. The perfect information benchmark of our model (where R is common knowledge at $\tau = 1$) has different properties than in BDD: here, the multiplicity of equilibria arises only in the median range $R_s \leqslant R \leqslant (1 + \lambda)R_s$. When $R < R_s$ everybody runs ($x = 1$), when $R > (1 + \lambda)R_s$ nobody runs ($x = 0$), and only in the intermediate region do both equilibria coexist.[16] This pattern is crucial for being able to select a unique equilibrium via the introduction of private noisy signals (when noise is not too important, as in Morris and Shin (1998)).[17]

The different regimes of the bank are represented in figure 2.2 as functions of R and x.

The critical value of R below which the bank is closed early (early closure threshold R_{EC}) is given by

$$R_{EC}(x) = (1 + \lambda)\frac{[xD - M]_+}{I},$$

and the critical value of R below which the bank fails (failure threshold R_F) is given by

$$R_F(x) = R_s + \lambda\frac{[xD - M]_+}{I}. \tag{2.2}$$

The parameters R_s, M, and I are not independent. Since we want to study the impact of prudential regulation on the need for central bank intervention, we will focus on R_s (a decreasing function of the solvency

---

[16]When $R < R_s$ the differential payoff of withdrawing for fund managers is B. When $R > (1 + \lambda)R_s$ the differential payoff of withdrawing is $-C$.

[17]Goldstein and Pauzner (2003) adapt the same methodology to the BDD model, in which the perfect information game always has two equilibria, even for very large R. Accordingly, they have to make an extra assumption, namely that short-term returns are high when the value of the bank's assets is large, or that there exists a potential lender who can cover the liquidity needs of the bank, in order to get an upper dominance region. Goldstein and Pauzner (2003) provides a very useful extension of the methodology of global games to cases where strategic complementarity is not satisfied. See also Morris and Shin (2000).

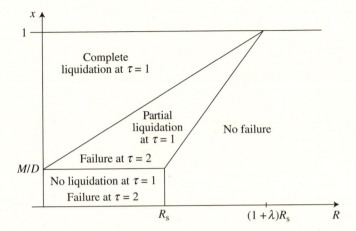

Figure 2.2. The different regimes in the (R, x) plane.

ratio E/I) and $m = M/D$ (the liquidity ratio). Replacing I by its value $(D - M)/R_s$, we obtain

$$R_{EC}(x) = R_s(1 + \lambda)\frac{[x - m]_+}{1 - m}$$

and

$$R_F(x) = R_s\left(1 + \lambda\frac{[x - m]_+}{1 - m}\right).$$

It should be obvious that $R_{EC}(x) < R_F(x)$, since early closure implies failure whereas the converse is not true (see figure 2.2).

2.4 Equilibrium of the Investors' Game

In order to simplify the presentation we concentrate on "threshold" strategies, in which each fund manager decides to withdraw if and only if his signal is below some threshold t.[18] As we shall see, this is without loss of generality. For a given R, a fund manager withdraws with probability

$$\Pr[R + \varepsilon < t] = G(t - R),$$

where G is the c.d.f. of the random variable ε. Given our assumptions, this probability also equals the proportion of withdrawals $x(R, t)$.

---

[18]It is assumed that the decision on whether to withdraw is taken before the secondary market is organized and thus before fund managers have the opportunity to learn about R from the secondary price. (On this issue see Atkeson's comments on Morris and Shin (2000).)

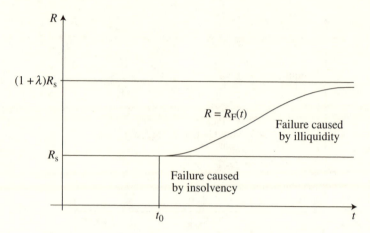

Figure 2.3. The different regimes in the (R, t) plane.

A fund manager withdraws if and only if the probability of failure of the bank (conditional on the signal s received by the manager and the threshold t used by other managers) is large enough. That is, $P(s, t) > y$, where

$$P(s, t) = \Pr[\text{failure} \mid s, t]$$
$$= \Pr[R < R_F(x(R, t)) \mid s].$$

Before we analyze the equilibrium of the investor's game, let us look at the region of the plane (t, R) where failure occurs. For this, transform figure 2.2 by replacing x by $x(R, t) = G(t - R)$; this yields figure 2.3. Notice that the critical R that triggers failure $R_F(t)$ is equal to the solvency threshold R_s when t is low and fund managers are confident about the strength of fundamentals:

$$R_F(t) = R_s \quad \text{if } t \leqslant t_0 = R_s + G^{-1}(m).$$

For $t > t_0$, however, $R_F(t)$ is an increasing function of t and is defined implicitly by

$$R = R_s\left(1 + \lambda\left[\frac{G(t - R) - m}{1 - m}\right]\right).$$

Let us denote by $G(\cdot \mid s)$ the c.d.f. of R conditional on signal s:

$$G(r \mid s) = \Pr[R < r \mid s].$$

Then, given the definition of $R_F(t)$,

$$P(s, t) = \Pr[R < R_F(t) \mid s] = G(R_F(t) \mid s). \tag{2.3}$$

It is natural to assume that $G(r \mid s)$ is decreasing in s: the higher s, the lower the probability that R lies below any given threshold r. Then it is immediate that P is decreasing in s and nondecreasing in t: $\partial P / \partial s < 0$ and $\partial P / \partial t \geqslant 0$. This means that the depositors' game is one of strategic complementarities. Indeed, given that other fund managers use the strategy with threshold t, the best response of a manager is to use a strategy with threshold $\bar{s}$: withdraw if and only if $P(s,t) > \gamma$ or (equivalently) if and only if $s < \bar{s}$, where $P(\bar{s}, t) = \gamma$. Let $\bar{s} = S(t)$. Now we have that $S' = -(\partial P / \partial t)/(\partial P / \partial s) \geqslant 0$: a higher threshold t by others induces a manager to use a higher threshold also.

The strategic complementarity property holds for general strategies. For a fund manager, all that matters is the conditional probability of failure for a given signal, and this depends only on aggregate withdrawals. Recall that the differential payoff to a fund manager for withdrawing versus not withdrawing is given by $PB - (1 - P)C$. A strategy for a fund manager is a function $a(s) \in \{\text{not withdraw, withdraw}\}$. If more managers withdraw, then the probability of failure conditional on receiving signal s increases. This just means that the payoff to a fund manager displays increasing differences with respect to the actions of others. The depositor's game is a supermodular game that has a largest and a smallest equilibrium. In fact, the game is symmetric (i.e., exchangeable against permutations of the players) and hence the largest and smallest equilibria are symmetric.[19] At the largest equilibrium, every fund manager withdraws on the largest number of occasions; at the smallest equilibrium, every fund manager withdraws on the smallest number of occasions. The largest (smallest) equilibrium can then be identified with the highest (lowest) threshold strategy $\bar{t}$ $(\underline{t})$.[20] These extremal equilibria bound the set of rationalizable outcomes. That is, strategies outside this set can be eliminated by iterated deletion of dominated strategies.[21] We will make assumptions so that $\bar{t} = \underline{t}$ and equilibrium will be unique.

---

[19]See remark 15 in Vives (1999, p. 34). See also chapter 2 in the same reference for an exposition of the theory of supermodular games.

[20]The extremal equilibria can be found with the usual algorithm in a supermodular game (Vives 1990), starting at the extremal points of the strategy sets of players and iterating using the best responses. For example, to obtain $\bar{t}$, let all investors withdraw for any signal received (i.e., start from $\bar{t}_0 = +\infty$ and $x = 1$) and apply iteratively the best response $S(\cdot)$ of a player to obtain a decreasing sequence $\bar{t}_k$ that converges to $\bar{t}$. Note that $S(+\infty) = \bar{t}_1 < +\infty$, where $\bar{t}_1$ is the unique solution to $P(t, +\infty) = G(R_s(1 + \lambda) \mid t) = \gamma$ given that G is (strictly) decreasing in t. The extremal equilibria are in strategies that are monotone in type, which with two actions means that the strategies are of the threshold type. The game among mutual fund managers is an example of a "monotone supermodular game" for which, according to Van Zandt and Vives (2003), extremal equilibria are monotone in type.

[21]See Morris and Shin (2000) for an explicit demonstration of the outcome of iterative elimination of dominated strategies in a similar model.

The threshold $t = t^*$ corresponds to a (symmetric) Bayesian Nash equilibrium if and only if $P(t^*, t^*) = y$. Indeed, suppose that fund managers use the threshold strategy t^*. Then for $s = t^*$ we have $P = y$ and, since P is decreasing in s for $s < t^*$, it follows that $P(s, t^*) > y$ and the manager withdraws. Conversely, if t^* is a (symmetric) equilibrium, then, for $s = t^*$, there is no withdrawal and hence $P(t^*, t^*) \leqslant y$. If $P(t^*, t^*) < y$, then, by continuity, for s close to but less than t^* we would have $P(s, t^*) < y$ a contradiction. It is clear then that the largest and smallest solutions to $P(t^*, t^*) = y$ correspond respectively to the largest and smallest equilibria.

An equilibrium can also be characterized by a couple of equations in two unknowns (a withdrawal threshold t^* and a failure threshold R^*):

$$G(R^* \mid t^*) = y, \tag{2.4}$$

$$R^* = R_s \left(1 + \lambda \left[\frac{G(t^* - R^*) - m}{1 - m} \right]_+ \right). \tag{2.5}$$

Equation (2.4) states that, conditional on observing a signal $s = t^*$, the probability that $R < R^*$ is y. Equation (2.5) states that, given a withdrawal threshold t^*, R^* is the critical return (i.e., the one below which failure occurs). Equation (2.5) implies that R^* belongs to $[R_s, (1 + \lambda)R_s]$. Notice that early closure occurs whenever $x(R, t^*)D > M + IR/(1 + \lambda)$, where $x(R, t^*) = G(t^* - R)$. This happens if and only if R is smaller than some threshold $R_{EC}(t^*)$. We will have that $R_{EC}(t^*) < R^*$, because early closure implies failure whereas the converse is not true, as remarked upon earlier.

In order to simplify the analysis of this system, we shall make distributional assumptions on returns and signals. More specifically, we will assume that the distributions of R and ϵ are normal, with respective means $\bar{R}$ and 0 and respective precisions (i.e., inverse variances) α and β. Denoting by Φ the c.d.f. of a standard normal distribution allows us to characterize the equilibrium by a pair (t^*, R^*) such that

$$\Phi \left(\sqrt{\alpha + \beta} R^* - \frac{\alpha \bar{R} + \beta t^*}{\sqrt{\alpha + \beta}} \right) = y \tag{2.6}$$

and

$$R^* = R_s \left(1 + \lambda \left[\frac{\Phi(\sqrt{\beta}(t^* - R^*)) - m}{1 - m} \right]_+ \right). \tag{2.7}$$

We now can now state our first result.

Proposition 2.1. *When β (the precision of the private signal of investors) is large enough relative to α (prior precision), there is a unique t^* such that $P(t^*, t^*) = y$. The investor's game then has a unique (Bayesian) equilibrium. In this equilibrium, fund managers use a strategy with threshold t^*.*

Proof. We show that $\varphi(s) \overset{\text{def}}{=} P(s,s)$ is decreasing for

$$\beta \geqslant \beta_0 \overset{\text{def}}{=} \frac{1}{2\pi} \left(\frac{\lambda \alpha D}{I} \right)^2$$

with $I = D - M/R_s$. Under our assumptions, R conditional on signal realization s follows a normal distribution

$$N\left(\frac{\alpha \bar{R} + \beta s}{\alpha + \beta}, \frac{1}{\alpha + \beta} \right).$$

Denoting by Φ the c.d.f. of a standard normal distribution, it follows that

$$\varphi(s) = P(s,s) = \Pr[R < R_F(s) \mid s]$$
$$= \Phi\left[\sqrt{\alpha + \beta}\, R_F(s) - \frac{\alpha \bar{R} + \beta s}{\sqrt{\alpha + \beta}} \right]. \tag{2.8}$$

This function is clearly decreasing for $s < t_0$ since, in this region, we have $R_F(s) \equiv R_s$. Now, if $s > t_0$ then $R_F(s)$ is increasing and its inverse is given by

$$t_F(R) = R + \frac{1}{\sqrt{\beta}} \Phi^{-1}\left(\frac{I}{\lambda D}(R - R_s) + m \right).$$

The derivative of t_F is

$$t_F'(R) = 1 + \frac{1}{\sqrt{\beta}} \frac{I}{\lambda D} \left[\Phi'\left(\Phi^{-1}\left(\frac{I}{\lambda D}(R - R_s) + m \right) \right) \right]^{-1}.$$

Since Φ' is bounded above by $1/\sqrt{2\pi}$, it follows that t_F' is bounded below:

$$t_F'(R) \geqslant 1 + \sqrt{\frac{2\pi}{\beta}} \frac{I}{\lambda D}.$$

Thus

$$R_F'(s) \leqslant \left[1 + \sqrt{\frac{2\pi}{\beta}} \frac{I}{\lambda D} \right]^{-1}.$$

Given formula (2.8), $\varphi(s)$ will be decreasing provided that

$$\sqrt{\alpha + \beta}\left(1 + \sqrt{\frac{2\pi}{\beta}} \frac{I}{\lambda D} \right)^{-1} \leqslant \frac{\beta}{\sqrt{\alpha + \beta}},$$

which (after simplification) yields

$$\beta \geqslant \frac{1}{2\pi} \left(\frac{\lambda \alpha D}{I} \right)^2.$$

If this condition is satisfied, then there is at most one equilibrium. Existence is easily shown. When s is small, $R_F(s) = R_s$ and formula (2.8) implies that $\lim_{s \to -\infty} \varphi(s) = 1$. On the other hand, if $s \to +\infty$ then $R_F(s) \to (1 + \lambda)R_s$ and $\varphi(s) \to 0$. $\square$

The limit equilibrium when β tends to infinity can be characterized as follows. From equation (2.6) we have that $\lim_{\beta \to +\infty} \sqrt{\beta}(R^* - t^*) = \Phi^{-1}(y)$. Given that $\Phi\{-z\} = 1 - \Phi\{z\}$ we obtain from formula (2.7) that, in the limit,

$$t^* = R^* = R_s\left(1 + \frac{\lambda}{1-m}[\max\{1 - y - m, 0\}]\right).$$

The critical cutoff R^* is decreasing with y and ranges from R_s for $y \geqslant 1 - m$ to $(1+\lambda)R_s$ for $y = 0$. It is also nonincreasing in m. As we establish in the next section, these features of the limit equilibrium are also valid for $\beta \geqslant \beta_0$.

It is worth noting also that, with a diffuse prior ($\alpha = 0$), the equilibrium is unique for any private precision of investors (indeed, we have that $\beta_0 = 0$). From (2.6) and (2.7) we obtain immediately that

$$R^* = R_s\left(1 + \frac{\lambda}{1-m}[\max\{1 - y - m, 0\}]\right)$$

and $t^* = R^* - \Phi^{-1}(y)/\sqrt{\beta}$. Both the cases $\beta \to +\infty$ and $\alpha = 0$ have in common that each investor faces maximal uncertainty about the behavior of other investors at the switching point $s_i = t^*$. Indeed, it can be easily checked that in either case the distribution of the proportion $x(R, t^*) = \Phi(\sqrt{\beta}(t^* - R))$ of investors withdrawing is uniformly distributed over $[0, 1]$ conditional on $s_i = t^*$. This contrasts with the certainty case with multiple equilibria when $R \in (R_s, (1 + \lambda)R_s)$, where (for example) in a run equilibrium an investor thinks that with probability 1 all other investors will withdraw. It is precisely the need to entertain a wider range of behavior of other investors in the incomplete information game that pins down a unique equilibrium, as in Carlsson and Van Damme (1993) or Postlewaite and Vives (1987).

The analysis could be easily extended to allow for fund managers to have access to a public signal $v = R + \eta$, where $\eta \sim N(0, 1/\beta_p)$ is independent of R and from the error terms ε_i of the private signals. The only impact of the public signal is to replace the unconditional moments $\bar{R}$ and $1/\alpha$ of R by its conditional moments, taking into account the public signal v. A disclosure of a signal of high enough precision will imply the existence of multiple equilibria—much in the same manner as a sufficiently precise prior.

The public signal could be provided by the central bank. Indeed, the central bank typically has information about banks that the market does not have (and, conversely, market participants also have information that is unknown to the central bank).[22] The model allows for the information

---

[22] See Peek et al. (1999), De Young et al. (1998), and Berger et al. (2000).

structures of the central bank and investors to be nonnested. Our discussion then has a bearing on the slippery issue of the optimal degree of transparency of central bank announcements. Indeed, Alan Greenspan has become famous for his oblique way of saying things, fostering an industry of "Greenspanology" or interpretation of his statements. Our model may rationalize oblique statements by central bankers that seem to add noise to a basic message. Precisely because the central bank may be in a unique position to provide information that becomes common knowledge, it has the capacity to destabilize expectations in the market (which in our context means to move the interbank market to a regime of multiple equilibria). By fudging the disclosure of information, the central bank makes sure that somewhat different interpretations of the release will be made, preventing destabilization.[23] Indeed, in the initial game (without a public signal) we may well be in the uniqueness region, but adding a precise enough public signal will mean we have three equilibria. At the interior equilibrium we have a result similar to that with no public information, but run and no-run equilibria also exist. We may therefore end up in an "always run" situation when disclosing (or increasing the precision of) the public signal while the economy is in the interior equilibrium without public disclosure. In other words, public disclosure of a precise enough signal may be destabilizing. This means that a central bank that wants to avoid entering the "unstable" region may have to add noise to its signal if that signal is otherwise too precise.[24]

2.5   Coordination Failure and Prudential Regulation

For β large enough, we have just seen that there exists a unique equilibrium whereby investors adopt a threshold t^* characterized by

$$\Phi\left(\sqrt{\alpha + \beta}\, R_F(t^*) - \frac{\alpha \bar{R} + \beta t^*}{\sqrt{\alpha + \beta}}\right) = \gamma$$

or

$$R_F(t^*) = \frac{1}{\sqrt{\alpha + \beta}}\left(\Phi^{-1}(\gamma) + \frac{\alpha \bar{R} + \beta t^*}{\sqrt{\alpha + \beta}}\right). \tag{2.9}$$

For this equilibrium threshold, the failure of the bank will occur if and only if

$$R < R_F(t^*) = R^*.$$

---

[23] The potentially damaging effects of public information is a theme also developed in Morris and Shin (2001).

[24] See Hellwig (2002) for a treatment of the multiplicity issue.

This means that the bank fails if and only if fundamentals are weak, $R < R^*$. When $R^* > R_s$ we have an intermediate interval of fundamentals $R \in [R_s, R^*)$ where there is a coordination failure: the bank is solvent but illiquid. The occurrence of a coordination failure can be controlled by the level of the liquidity ratio m, as the following proposition shows.

Proposition 2.2. *There is a critical liquidity ratio $\bar{m}$ of the bank such that, for $m \geqslant \bar{m}$, we have $R^* = R_s$; this means that only insolvent banks fail (there is no coordination failure). Conversely, for $m < \bar{m}$ we have $R^* > R_s$; this means that, for $R \in [R_s, R^*)$, the bank is solvent but illiquid (there is a coordination failure).*

Proof. For $t^* \leqslant t_0 = R_s + 1/(\sqrt{\beta})\Phi^{-1}(m)$, the equilibrium occurs for $R^* = R_s$. By inserting this condition in formula (2.6) we obtain

$$(\alpha + \beta)R_s \leqslant \sqrt{\alpha + \beta}\, \Phi^{-1}(y) + \alpha\bar{R} + \beta R_s + \sqrt{\beta}\, \Phi^{-1}(m),$$

which is equivalent to

$$\Phi^{-1}(m) \geqslant \frac{\alpha}{\sqrt{\beta}}(R_s - \bar{R}) - \sqrt{1 + \frac{\alpha}{\beta}}\, \Phi^{-1}(y). \tag{2.10}$$

Therefore, the coordination failure disappears when $m \geqslant \bar{m}$, where

$$\bar{m} = \Phi\left(\frac{\alpha}{\sqrt{\beta}}(R_s - \bar{R}) - \sqrt{1 + \frac{\alpha}{\beta}}\, \Phi^{-1}(y)\right).$$

$\square$

Observe that, since R_s is a decreasing function of E/I, the critical liquidity ratio $\bar{m}$ decreases when the solvency ratio E/I increases.[25]

The equilibrium threshold return R^* is determined (when (2.10) is not satisfied) by the solution to

$$\phi(R) \equiv \alpha(R - \bar{R}) - \sqrt{\beta}\Phi^{-1}\left(\frac{1 - m}{\lambda R_s}(R - R_s) + m\right) - \sqrt{\alpha + \beta}\, \Phi^{-1}(y)$$

$$= 0. \tag{2.11}$$

When $\beta \geqslant \beta_0$ we have $\phi'(R) < 0$ and the comparative statics properties of the equilibrium threshold R^* are straightforward. Indeed, it follows that $\partial\phi/\partial m < 0$, $\partial\phi/\partial R_s > 0$, $\partial\phi/\partial\lambda > 0$, $\partial\phi/\partial y < 0$, and $\partial\phi/\partial\bar{R} < 0$. The following proposition states the results.

---

[25]More generally, it is easy to see that the regulator in our model can control the probabilities of illiquidity ($\Pr(R < R^*)$) and insolvency ($\Pr(R < R_s)$) of the bank by imposing appropriately high ratios of minimum liquidity and solvency.

Proposition 2.3. *The comparative statics of R^* (and of the probability of failure) can be summarized as follows:*

(i) *R^* is a decreasing function of the liquidity ratio m and the solvency (E/I) of the bank, of the critical withdrawal probability y, and of the expected return on the bank's assets $\bar{R}$.*

(ii) *R^* is an increasing function of the fire-sale premium λ and of the face value of debt D.*

We have thus that stronger fundamentals, as indicated by a higher prior mean $\bar{R}$, also imply a lower likelihood of failure. In contrast, a higher fire-sale premium λ increases the incidence of failure. Indeed, for a higher λ, a larger portion of the portfolio must be liquidated in order to meet the requirements of withdrawals. We also have that R^* is decreasing with the critical withdrawal probability y and that $R^* \to (1 + \lambda)R_s$ as $y \to 0$.

A similar analysis applies to changes in the precision of the prior α and the private information of investors β. Assume that $y = C/B < \frac{1}{2}$. Indeed, we should expect that the cost C of withdrawal is small in relation to the continuation benefit B for the fund managers. If $y < \frac{1}{2}$ then it is easy to see that:

- for large β and bad prior fundamentals ($\bar{R}$ low), increasing α increases R^* (more precise prior information about a bad outcome worsens the coordination problem); and

- increasing β decreases R^*.

2.6 Coordination Failure and LLR Policy

The main contribution of our paper so far has been to show the theoretical possibility of a solvent bank being illiquid as a result of coordination failure on the interbank market. We shall now explore the LLR policy of the central bank and present a scenario where it is possible to give a theoretical justification for Bagehot's doctrine.

We start by considering a simple central bank objective: eliminate the coordination failure with minimal involvement. The instruments at the disposal of the central bank are the liquidity ratio m and intervention in the form of open-market or discount-window operations.[26]

---

[26]Open-market operations typically involve performing a repo operation with primary security dealers. The Federal Reserve auctions a fixed amount of liquidity (reserves) and, in general, does not accept bids by dealers below the Federal Funds rate target.

We have shown in section 2.5 that a high enough liquidity ratio m eliminates the coordination failure altogether by inducing $R^* = R_s$. This is so for $m \geqslant \bar{m}$. However, it is likely that imposing $m \geqslant \bar{m}$ might be too costly in terms of forgone returns (recall that $I + M = 1 + E$, where I is the investment in the risky asset). In section 2.7 we analyze a more elaborate welfare-oriented objective and endogenize the choice of m. We look now at forms of central bank intervention that can eliminate the coordination failure when $m < \bar{m}$.

Let us see how central bank liquidity support can eliminate the coordination failure. Suppose the central bank announces it will lend at rate $r \in (0, \lambda)$, and without limits, but only to solvent banks. The central bank is not allowed to subsidize banks and is assumed to observe R. The knowledge of R may come from the supervisory knowledge of the central bank or perhaps by observing the amount of withdrawals of the bank. Then the optimal strategy of a (solvent) commercial bank will be to borrow exactly the liquidity it needs, i.e., $D[x - m]_+$. Whenever $x - m > 0$, failure will occur at date 2 if and only if

$$\frac{RI}{D} < (1 - x) + (1 + r)(x - m).$$

Given that $D/I = R_s/(1 - m)$, we obtain that failure at $t = 2$ will occur if and only if

$$R < R_s\left(1 + r\frac{[x - m]_+}{1 - m}\right).$$

This is exactly analogous to our previous formula giving the critical return of the bank, except here the interest rate r replaces the liquidation premium λ. As a result, this type of intervention will be fully effective (yielding $R^* = R_s$) only when r is arbitrarily close to zero. It is worth remarking that central bank help in the amount $D[x - m]_+$ whenever the bank is solvent ($R > R_s$), and at a very low rate, avoids early closure, and the central bank loses no money because the loan can be repaid at $\tau = 2$. Note also that, whenever the central bank lends at a very low rate, the collateral of the bank is evaluated under "normal circumstances," i.e., as if there were no coordination failure. Consider as an example the limit case of β tending to infinity. The equilibrium with no central bank help is then

$$t^* = R^* = R_s\left(1 + \frac{\lambda}{1 - m}[\max\{1 - y - m, 0\}]\right).$$

Suppose that $1 - y > m$ so that $R^* > R_s$. Then withdrawals are $x = 0$ for $R > R^*$, $x = 1 - y$ for $R = R^*$, and $x = 1$ for $R < R^*$. Whenever $R > R_s$, the central bank will help to avoid failure and will evaluate the collateral as if $x = 0$. This effectively changes the failure point to $R^* = R_s$.

Central bank intervention can take the form of open-market operations that reduce the fire-sale premium or of discount-window lending at a very low rate. The intervention with open-market operations makes sense if a high λ is due to a temporary spike of the market rate (i.e., a liquidity crunch). In this situation, a liquidity injection by the central bank will reduce the fire-sale premium. After September 11, for example, open-market operations by the Federal Reserve accepted dealers' bids at levels well below the Federal Funds Rate target and pushed the effective lending rate to lows of zero in several days.[27]

Intervention via the discount window—perhaps more in the spirit of Bagehot—makes sense when λ is interpreted as an adverse selection premium. The situation when a large number of banks is in trouble displays both liquidity and adverse selection components. In any case, the central bank intervention should be a very low rate, in contrast with Bagehot's doctrine of lending at a penalty rate.[28] This type of intervention may provide a rationale for the Fed's apparently strange behavior of lending below the market rate (but with a "stigma" associated with it, so that banks borrow there only when they cannot find liquidity in the market).[29] In section 2.7 we provide a welfare objective for this discount-window policy.

In some circumstances the central bank may not be able to infer R exactly because of noise (in the supervisory process or in the observation of withdrawals). Then the central bank will obtain only an imperfect signal of R. In this case, the central bank will not be able to distinguish perfectly between illiquid and insolvent banks (as in Goodhart and Huang 1999) and so, whatever the lending policy chosen, taxpayers' money may be involved with some probability. This situation is realistic given the difficulty in distinguishing between solvency and liquidity problems.[30]

---

[27]See Markets Group of the Federal Reserve Bank of New York (2002). Martin (2002) contrasts the classical prescription of lending at a penalty rate with the Fed's response to September 11, namely to lend at a very low interest rate. He argues that penalty rates were needed in Bagehot's view because the gold standard implied limited reserves for the central bank.

[28]Typically, the lending rate is kept at a penalty level to discourage arbitrage and perverse incentives. Those considerations lie outside the present model. For example, in a repo operation the penalty for not returning the cash on loan is to keep paying the lending rate. If this lending rate is very low, then the incentive to return the loan is small. See Fischer (1999) for a discussion of why lending should be at a penalty rate.

[29]The discount-window policy of the Federal Reserve is to lend at 50 basis points below the target Federal Funds Rate.

[30]We may even think that the central bank cannot help *ex post* once withdrawals have materialized but that it receives a noisy signal s_{CB} about R at the same time as investors.

It may also be argued that our LLR function could be performed by private banks through credit lines. Banks that provide a line of credit to another bank would then have an incentive to monitor the borrowing institution and reduce the fire-sale premium. The need for an LLR remains, but it may be privately provided. Goodfriend and Lacker (1999) draw a parallel between central bank lending and private lines of credit, putting emphasis on the commitment problem of the central bank to limit lending.[31] However, the central bank typically acts as LLR in most economies, presumably because it has a natural superiority in terms of financial capacity and supervisory knowledge.[32] For example, in the LTCM case it may be argued that the New York Fed had access to information that the private sector—even the members of the lifeboat operation—did not. This unique capacity to inspect a financial institution might have made possible the lifeboat operation orchestrated by the New York Fed. An open issue is whether this superior knowledge continues to hold in countries where the supervision of banks is basically in the hands of independent regulators like the Financial Services Authority of the United Kingdom.[33]

2.7 Endogenizing the Liability Structure and Crisis Resolution

In this section we endogenize the short-term debt contract assumed in our model, according to which depositors can withdraw at $\tau = 1$ or otherwise wait until $\tau = 2$. We have seen that the ability of investors to withdraw at $\tau = 1$ creates a coordination problem. We argue here that this potentially inefficient debt structure may be the only way that investors can discipline a bank manager subject to a moral hazard problem.

Suppose, as seems reasonable, that investment in risky assets requires the supervision of a bank manager and that the distribution of returns of the risky assets depends on the effort undertaken by the manager. For example, the manager can either exert or not exert effort, $e \in \{0, 1\}$;

The central bank can then act preventively and inject liquidity into the bank contingent on the received signal $L(s_{CB})$. In this case, the risk also exists that an insolvent bank ends up being helped. The game played by the fund managers changes, obviously, after liquidity injection by a large actor like the central bank.

[31] If this commitment problem is acute, then the private solution may be superior. However, Goodfriend and Lacker (1999) do not take a position on this issue. They state: "We are agnostic about the ultimate role of CB lending in a welfare-maximizing steady state."

[32] One of the few exceptions is the Liquidity Consortium in Germany, in which private banks and the central bank both participate.

[33] See Vives (2001) for the workings of the Financial Services Authority and its relationship with the Bank of England.

then $R \sim N(\bar{R}_0, \alpha^{-1})$ when $e = 0$, and $R \sim N(\bar{R}, \alpha^{-1})$ when $e = 1$, where $\bar{R} > \bar{R}_0$. That is, exerting effort yields a return distribution that first-order stochastically dominates the one obtained by not exerting effort. The bank manager incurs a cost if he chooses $e = 1$; if he chooses $e = 0$, the cost is 0. The manager also receives a benefit from continuing the project until date 2. Assume for simplicity that the manager does not care about monetary incentives. The manager's effort cannot be observed, so his willingness to undertake effort will depend on the relationship between his effort and the probability that the bank continues at date 1. Thus, withdrawals may enforce the early closure of the bank and so provide incentives to the bank manager.[34]

In the banking contract, short-term debt or demandable deposits can improve upon long-term debt or nondemandable deposits. With long-term debt, incentives cannot be provided to the manager because liquidation never occurs; therefore, the manager does not exert effort. Furthermore, neither can incentives be provided with renegotiable short-term debt, because early liquidation is *ex post* inefficient. Dispersed short-term debt (i.e., uninsured deposits) is what is needed.

Let us assume that it is worthwhile inducing the manager to exert effort. This will be true if $\bar{R} - \bar{R}_0$ is large enough and the (physical) cost of asset liquidation is not too large. Recall that the (per-unit) liquidation value of its assets is vR, with $v \ll 1/(1+\lambda)$, whenever the bank is closed at $\tau = 1$. We assume, as in previous sections, that the face value of the debt contract is the same in periods $\tau = 1, 2$ (equal to D), and we suppose also that investors—in order to trust their money to fund managers— must be guaranteed a minimum expected return, which we set equal to zero without loss of generality.

The banking contract will have short-term debt and will maximize the expected profits of the bank by choosing to invest in risky and safe assets and deposit returns subject to: the resource constraint $1 + E = I + Dm$ (where $Dm = M$ is the amount of liquid reserves held by the bank); the incentive-compatibility constraint of the bank manager; and the (early) closure rule associated with the (unique) equilibrium in the investors' game. This early closure rule is defined by the property $x(R, t^*)D > M + IR/(1 + \lambda)$, which is satisfied if and only if $R < R_{EC}(t^*)$. As stated before, $R_{EC}(t^*) < R^*$, because early closure implies failure whereas the converse is not true. Let R^0 be the smallest R that fulfills the incentive-compatibility constraint of the bank manager. We thus have $R_{EC}(t^*) \geqslant R^0$. The banking program will maximize the expected value of the bank's assets which consists of two terms: (i) the product of the size $I = 1 +$

---

[34]This approach is based on Grossman and Hart (1982) and is followed in Gale and Vives (2002). See also Calomiris and Kahn (1991) and Carletti (1999).

$E - Dm$ of the bank's investments by the net expected return on these investments, taking into account expected liquidation costs; and (ii) the value of liquid reserves Dm. Hence the optimal banking contract will solve

$$\max_{m}\{(1 + E - Dm)(\bar{R} - (1 - v)E(R \mid R < R_{EC}(t^*(m)))$$
$$\times \Pr(R < R_{EC}(t^*(m))) + Dm\}$$

subject to:

(i) $t^*(m)$ is the unique equilibrium of the fund managers' game; and

(ii) $R_{EC}(t^*(m)) \geqslant R^o$.

Given that $t^*(m)$, and thus $R_{EC}(t^*(m))$, decrease with m, the optimal banking contract is easy to characterize. If the net return on the bank's assets is always larger than the opportunity cost of liquidity (even when the banks have no liquidity at all), i.e., when

$$\bar{R} - (1 - v)E(R \mid R < R_{EC}(t^*(0)) \Pr(R < R_{EC}(t^*(m))) > 1,$$

then it is clear that $m = 0$ at the optimal point. If, on the contrary,

$$\bar{R} - (1 - v)E(R \mid R < R_{EC}(t^*(0)) \Pr(R < R_{EC}(t^*(0))) < 1,$$

then there is an interior optimum. An interesting question is how the banking contract compares with the incentive efficient solution, which we now describe.

Given that the pooled signals of investors reveal R, we can define the incentive-efficient solution as the choice of investment in liquid and risky assets and probability of continuation at $\tau = 1$ (as a function of R) that maximizes expected surplus subject to the resource constraint and the incentive-compatibility constraint of the bank manager.[35] Furthermore, given the monotonicity of the likelihood ratio $\phi(R \mid e = 0)/\phi(R \mid e = 1)$, the optimal region of continuation is of the cutoff form. More specifically, the optimal cutoff will be R^o, the smallest R that fulfills the incentive-compatibility constraint of the bank manager. The cutoff R^o will be (weakly) increasing with the extent of the moral hazard problem that bank managers face.

The incentive-efficient solution solves

$$\max_{m}\{(1 + E - Dm)(\bar{R} - (1 - v)E(R \mid R < R^o))\Pr(R < R^o) + Dm\},$$

[35]We disregard here the welfare of the bank manager and that of the fund managers.

where R^o is the minimal return cutoff that motivates the bank manager. If $\bar{R} - (1 - v)E(R \mid R < R^o)\Pr(R < R^o) > 1$, then $m^o = 0$. Thus, at the incentive-efficient solution it is optimal not to hold any reserves. This should come as no surprise, since we assume there is no cost of liquidity provision by the central bank. A more complete analysis would include such a cost and lead to an optimal combination of LLR policy with *ex ante* regulation of a minimum liquidity ratio.

Since $R_{EC}(t^*)$ must also fulfill the incentive-compatibility constraint of the bank manager, it follows that, at the optimal banking contract with no LLR, $R_{EC}(t^*) \geqslant R^o$. In fact, we will typically have a strict inequality, because there is no reason for the equilibrium threshold t^* to satisfy $R_{EC}(t^*) = R^o$. This means that the market solution will entail too many early closures of banks, since the banking contract with no LLR intervention uses an inefficient instrument (the liquidity ratio) to provide indirect incentives for bankers through the threat of early liquidation.

The role of a modified LLR can be viewed, in this context, as correcting these market inefficiencies while maintaining the incentives of bank managers. By announcing its commitment to provide liquidity assistance (at a zero rate) in order to avoid inefficient liquidation at $\tau = 1$ (i.e., for $R > R^o$), the LLR can implement the incentive-efficient solution. When offered help, the bank will borrow the liquidity it needs, $D[x - m]_+$.[36]

To implement the incentive-efficient solution, the modified LLR must be more concerned with avoiding inefficient liquidation at $\tau = 1$ in the range (R^o, R_{EC}) than about avoiding failure of the bank. Now the solvency threshold R_s has no special meaning. Indeed, R^o will typically be different from R_s. The reason is that R_s is determined by the promised payments to investors, cash reserves, and investment in the risky asset, whereas R^o is just the minimum threshold that motivates the banker to behave. We will have that $R^o > R_s$ when the moral hazard problem for bank managers is severe and $R^o < R_s$ when it is moderate.

This modified LLR facility leads to a view on the LLR that differs from Bagehot's doctrine and introduces interesting policy questions. Whenever $R^o > R_s$ there is a region (specifically, for R in (R_s, R^o)) where

---

[36]We could also envision help by the central bank in an ongoing crisis to implement the incentive-efficient closure rule. The central bank would then lend at a very low interest rate to illiquid banks for the amount that they could not borrow in the interbank market in order to meet their payment obligations at $\tau = 1$. It is easy to see that in this case the equilibrium between fund managers is not modified. This is so because central bank intervention does not change the instances of failure of the bank (indeed, when a bank is helped at $\tau = 1$ because $x(R, t^*)D > M + IR/(1 + \lambda)$, it will fail at $\tau = 2$). In this case the coordination failure is not eliminated, but its effects (on early closure) are neutralized by the intervention of the central bank. The modified LLR helps the bank in the range $(R^o, R_{EC}(t^*))$ in the amount $Dx(t^*, R) - (M + IR/(1 + \lambda)) > 0$. Thus LLR help (bailout) complements the money raised in the interbank market $IR/(1 + \lambda)$ (bailin).

there should be early intervention (or "prompt corrective action," to use the terminology of banking regulators). Indeed, in this region the bank is solvent but intervention is needed to control moral hazard of the banker. On the other hand, in the range (R^o, R_{EC}) an LLR policy is efficient if the central bank can commit. If it cannot and instead optimizes *ex post* (whether because building a reputation is not possible or because of weakness in the presence of lobbying), it will intervene too often. Some additional institutional arrangement is needed in the range (R_s, R^o) in order to implement prompt corrective action (i.e., early closure of banks that are still solvent).

When $R^o < R_s$, there is a range (R^o, R_{EC}) in which the bank should be helped even though it might be insolvent (and in this case money is lost). More precisely, for R in the range $(R^o, \min\{R_s, R_{EC}\})$, the bank is insolvent and should be helped. If the central bank's charter specifies that it cannot lend to insolvent banks, then another institution (deposit insurance fund, regulatory agency, treasury) financed by other means (insurance premiums or taxation) is needed to provide an "orderly resolution of failure" when R is in the range $(R^o, \min\{R_s, R_{EC}\})$. This could be interpreted, as in corporate bankruptcy practice, as a way to preserve the going-concern value of the institution and to allow its owners and managers a fresh start after the crisis.

An important implication of our analysis is the complementarity between bailins (interbank market) and bailouts (LLR) as well as other regulatory facilities (prompt corrective action, orderly resolution of failure) in crisis management. We can summarize by comparing different organizations as follows:

1. With neither an LLR nor an interbank market, liquidation takes place whenever $x > mD$, which inefficiently limits investment I.

2. With an interbank market but no LLR (as advocated by Goodfriend and King), the closure threshold is R_{EC} and there is excessive failure whenever $R_{EC} > R^o$.

3. With both an LLR facility and an interbank market:

   (a) If $R^o > R_s$ (severe moral hazard problem for the banker), then the incentive-efficient solution can be implemented, complementing the LLR with a policy of prompt corrective action in the range (R_s, R^o).

   (b) If $R^o < R_s$ (moderate moral hazard problem for the banker), then a different institution (financed by taxation or by insurance premiums) is needed to complement the central bank and implement the incentive-efficient solution. The central bank helps whenever the bank is solvent, and the other institution provides an "orderly resolution of failure" in the range $(R^o, \min\{R_s, R_{EC}\})$.

2.8 An International LLR

In this section we reinterpret the model in an international setting and provide a potential rationale for an international LLR (ILLR) à la Bagehot. Financial and banking crises, usually coupled with currency crises, have been common in emerging economies in Asia (Thailand, Indonesia, South Korea), Latin America (Mexico, Brazil, Ecuador, Argentina), and in the periphery of Europe (Turkey). These crisis have proved costly in terms of output. The question is whether an ILLR can help alleviate, or even avoid, such crises. An ILLR could follow a policy of injecting liquidity in international financial markets—by actions that range from establishing the proposed global central bank that issues an international currency to merely coordinating the intervention of the three major central banks[37]—or could act to help countries in trouble, much like a central bank acts to help individual banking institutions. The latter approach is developed in several proposals that adapt Bagehot's doctrine to international lending; see, for example, the Meltzer Report (Meltzer 2000) and Fischer (1999). As pointed out by Jeanne and Wyplosz (2003), a major difference between the approaches concerns the required size of the ILLR. The former (global CB) approach requires an issuer of international currency; in the latter, the intervention is bounded by the difference between the short-term foreign exchange liabilities of the banking sector and the foreign reserves of the country in question. We will look here at the second approach. The main tension identified in the debate is between those who emphasize the effect of liquidity support on crisis prevention (Fischer 1999) and those who are worried about generating moral hazard in the country being helped (Meltzer 2000).

2.8.1 A Reinterpretation of the Model

Suppose now that the balance sheet of section 2.2 corresponds to a small open economy for which D_0 is the foreign-denominated short-term debt, M is the amount of foreign reserves, I is the investment in risky local entrepreneurial projects, E is the equity and long-term debt (or local resources available for investment), and D is the face value of the foreign-denominated short-term debt.[38] Our fund managers are now

---

[37]See Eichengreen (1999) for a survey of the different proposals.

[38]The balance sheet corresponds to the consolidated private sector of the country. In some countries, local firms borrow from local banks and then the latter borrow in international currency.

international fund managers operating in the international interbank market. The liquidity ratio $m = M/D$ is now the ratio of foreign reserves to foreign short-term debt—a crucial ratio, according to empirical work, in determining the probability of a crisis in the country.[39] The parameter λ now represents the fire-sale premium associated with early sales of domestic bank assets in the secondary market. Furthermore, for a given amount of withdrawals by fund managers $x > m$ at $\tau = 1$, there are critical thresholds for the return R of investment below which the country is bankrupt ($R_F(x)$) or will default at $\tau = 1$ ($R_{EC}(x) < R_F(x)$). The effort e necessary to improve returns could be understood to be exerted by bank managers, entrepreneurs, or even the government. According to section 2.7, effort has a cost and the actors exerting effort are interested in continuing in their job. Default by the country at $\tau = 1$ deprives those actors from their continuation benefits (for example, because of restructuring of the banking and/or private sectors or because the government is removed from office), and consequently "default" at $\tau = 1$ for some region of realized returns is the only disciplining device.

2.8.2 Results

(i) There is a range or realizations of the return R, (R_s, R^*), for which a coordination failure occurs. This happens when the amount of withdrawals by foreign fund managers is so large that the country is bankrupt even though it is (in principle) solvent.

(ii) For a high enough foreign reserve ratio m, the range (R_s, R^*) collapses and there is no coordination failure of international investors.

(iii) The probability of bankruptcy of the banking sector is:

- decreasing in the foreign reserve ratio, the solvency ratio, the critical withdrawal probability y, and the expected mean return of the country investment;

- increasing in the fire-sale premium and the face value of foreign short-term debt; and

- increasing in the precision of public information about R when public news is bad and decreasing in the precision of private information (both provided $y < \frac{1}{2}$).

---

[39]Indeed, Radelet and Sachs (1998) as well as Rodrik and Velasco (1999) find that the ratio of short-term debt to reserves is a robust predictor of financial crisis (in the sense of a sharp reversal of capital flows). The latter also find that a greater short-term exposure aggravates the crisis once capital flows reverse.

(iv) An ILLR that follows Bagehot's prescription can minimize the incidence of coordination failure among international fund managers, provided it is well-informed about R. One possibility is that the ILLR performs in-depth country research and has supervisory knowledge of the banking system of the country where the crisis occurs.[40]

(v) The disclosure of a public signal about country return prospects may introduce multiple equilibria. A well-informed international agency may want to be cautious and not publicly disclose too precise information in order to avoid a rally of expectations in a run equilibrium.

(vi) In the presence of the moral hazard problem associated with eliciting high returns, foreign short-term debt serves the purpose of disciplining whoever must exert effort to improve returns. Note that domestic-currency-denominated short-term debt will not have a disciplining effect because it can be inflated away. There will be an optimal cutoff point R^o below which restructuring (of either the private sector or government) must occur in order to provide incentives to exert effort.

The following scenarios can be considered.

No bailin and no bailout. With no ILLR and no access to the international interbank market, country projects are liquidated whenever withdrawals by foreign fund managers are larger than foreign reserves. This inefficiently limits investment.

Bailin but no bailout. With no ILLR but with access to the international interbank market, some costly project liquidation is avoided by having fire sales of assets, but still there will be excessive liquidation of entrepreneurial projects.

Bailin and bailout. With ILLR and access to the international interbank market, we have two cases as follows:

- The moral hazard problem in the country is severe ($R^o > R_s$). In this case a policy of prompt corrective action in the range (R_s, R^o) is needed to complement the ILLR facility. A solvent country may need to "restructure" when returns are close to the solvency threshold.

- The moral hazard problem in the country is moderate ($R^o < R_s$). Then, in addition to the ILLR help for a solvent country, an orderly "resolution of failure" process is needed in the range

---

[40]Although this seems more far-fetched than in the case of a domestic LLR, the IMF (for example) is trying to enhance its monitoring capabilities by way of "financial sector assessment" programs.

($R^{\mathrm{o}}, \min\{R_s, R_{\mathrm{EC}}\}$). An insolvent country should be helped when it is not too far away from the solvency threshold. This may be interpreted as a mechanism similar to the sovereign debt restructuring mechanism (SDRM) of the sort currently studied by the IMF with the objective of restructuring unsustainable debt.[41] In our case, this would be the foreign short-term debt. In the range ($R^{\mathrm{o}}, \min\{R_s, R_{\mathrm{EC}}\}$), an institution like an international bankruptcy court could help.

As before, an important insight from the analysis is the complementarity between the market (bailins) and an ILLR facility (bailout)—together with other regulatory facilities—can provide for prompt corrective action and orderly failure resolution. Our conclusion is that an ILLR facility à la Bagehot can help to implement the incentive-efficient solution, provided that it is complemented with provisions of prompt corrective action and orderly resolution of failure.

2.9 Concluding Remarks

In this paper we have provided a rationale—in the context of modern interbank markets—for Bagehot's doctrine of helping illiquid but solvent banks. Indeed, investors in the interbank market may face a coordination failure and so intervention may be desirable. We have examined the impact of public intervention along the following three dimensions:

(i) solvency and liquidity requirements (at $\tau = 0$);

(ii) LLR policy (at the interim date $\tau = 1$); and

(iii) closure rules, which can consist of two types of policy: prompt corrective action or the orderly resolution of bank failures.

The coordination failure can be avoided by appropriate solvency and liquidity requirements. However, the cost of doing so will typically be too large in terms of forgone returns, and *ex ante* measures will only help partially. This means that prudential regulation needs to be complemented by an LLR policy. This chapter shows how discount-window loans can eliminate the coordination failure (or alleviate it, if for incentive reasons some degree of coordination failure is optimal). It also sheds light on when open-market operations will be appropriate.

A main insight of the analysis is that public and private involvement are both necessary in implementing the incentive-efficient solution. Furthermore, implementation of this solution may also require

---

[41] See Bolton (2003) for a discussion of SDRM-type facilities from the perspective of corporate bankruptcy theory and practice.

complementing Bagehot's LLR facility with prompt corrective action (intervention on a solvent bank) or orderly failure resolution (help to an insolvent bank).

The model, when given an interpretation in an international context, provides a rationale for an international LLR à la Bagehot, complemented with prompt corrective action and provisions for orderly resolution of failures, and it points to the complementarity between bailins and bailouts in crisis resolution.

References

Allen, F., and D. Gale. 1998. Optimal financial crises. *Journal of Finance* 53:1245–84.

Bagehot, W. 1873. *Lombard Street: A Description of the Money Market*. London: H. S. King.

Berger, A., S. M. Davies, and M. J. Flannery. 2000. Comparing market and supervisory assessments of bank performance: who knows what when? *Journal of Money, Credit and Banking* 32:641–67.

Bernanke, B. 1983. Nonmonetary effects of the financial crisis in the propagation of the Great Depression. *American Economic Review* 73:257–63.

Bernanke, B., and M. Gertler. 1989. Agency costs, net worth, and business fluctuations. *American Economic Review* 79:14–31.

Bolton, P. 2003. Towards a statutory approach to sovereign debt restructuring: lessons from corporate bankruptcy practice around the world. IMF Staff Papers, volume 50 (Special Issue).

Bordo, M. D. 1990. The lender of last resort: alternative views and historical experience. Federal Reserve Bank of Richmond *Economic Review* (January/February), pp. 18–29.

Broecker, T. 1990. Credit-worthiness tests and interbank competition. *Econometrica* 58:429–52.

Bryant, J. 1980. A model of reserves, bank runs and deposit insurance. *Journal of Banking and Finance* 4:335–44.

Calomiris, C. W. 1998a. The IMF's imprudent role as a lender of last resort. *Cato Journal* 17(3):275–94.

———. 1998b. Blueprints for a new global financial architecture. Joint Economics Committee, United States Congress, Washington, DC (October 7).

Calomiris, C. W., and C. Kahn. 1991. The role of demandable debt in structuring optimal banking arrangements. *American Economic Review* 81:497–513.

Carletti, E. 1999. Bank moral hazard and market discipline. Mimeo, FMG, London School of Economics.

Carlsson, H., and E. Van Damme. 1993. Global games and equilibrium selection. *Econometrica* 61:989–1018.

Chari, V. V., and R. Jagannathan. 1988. Banking panics, information, and rational expectations equilibrium. *Journal of Finance* 43:749–61.

Chari, V. V., and P. Kehoe. 1998. Asking the right questions about the IMF. *Public Affairs* 13:3–26.

Chevalier, J., and G. Ellison. 1997. Risk taking by mutual funds as a response to incentives. *Journal of Political Economy* 105:1167–200.

———. 1999. Are some mutual funds managers better than others? *Journal of Finance* 54:875–99.

Corsetti, G., A. Dasgupta, S. Morris, and H. S. Shin. 2004. Does one Soros make a difference? The role of a large trader in currency crises. *Review of Economic Studies* 71:87–114.

De Young, R., M. J. Flannery, W. W. Lang, and S. M. Sorescu. 1998. The informational advantage of specialized monitors: the case of bank examiners. Presentation at the June 1998 Annual Meeting of the Western Finance Association, Lake Tahoe, NV.

Diamond, D., and P. H. Dybvig. 1983. Bank runs, deposit insurance, and liquidity. *Journal of Political Economy* 91:401–19.

Diamond, D., and R. Rajan. 2001. Liquidity risk, liquidity creation and financial fragility: a theory of banking. *Journal of Political Economy* 109:287–327.

Eichengreen, B. 1999. *Toward a New International Financial Architecture: A Practical Post-Asia Agenda*. Washington, DC: Institute for International Economics.

Fischer, S. 1999. On the need for an international lender of last resort. *Journal of Economic Perspectives* 13:85–104.

Flannery, M. J. 1996. Financial crises, payment systems problems, and discount window lending. *Journal of Money, Credit and Banking* 28(Part 2):804–24.

Folkerts-Landau, D., and P. Garber. 1992. The ECB: a bank or a monetary policy rule? In *Establishing a Central Bank: Issues in Europe and Lessons from the U.S.* (ed. M. B. Canzoneri, V. Grilland, and P. R. Masson), chapter 4, pp. 86–110. CEPR, Cambridge University Press.

Freixas, X., C. Giannini, G. Hoggarth, and F. Soussa. 1999. Lender of last resort: a review of the literature. Financial Stability Review, Bank of England, Issue 7, pp. 151–67.

Gale, D., and X. Vives. 2002. Dollarization, bailouts, and the stability of the banking system. *Quarterly Journal of Economics* 117:467–502.

Goldstein, I., and A. Pauzner. 2003. Demand deposit contracts and the probability of bank runs. Discussion Paper, Tel-Aviv University.

Goodfriend, M., and R. G. King. 1988. Financial deregulation, monetary policy, and central banking. In *Restructuring Banking and Financial Services in America* (ed. W. Haraf and R. M. Kushmeider). AEI Studies 481, Lanham, MD.

Goodfriend, M., and J. Lacker. 1999. Loan commitment and central bank lending. Federal Reserve Bank of Richmond, Working Paper 99-2.

Goodhart, C., and H. Huang. 1999. A model of the lender of last resort. FMG, London School of Economics Discussion Paper 313.

———. A simple model of an international lender of last resort. *Economic Notes* 29(1):1–11.

Gorton, G. 1985. Bank suspension of convertibility. *Journal of Monetary Economics* 15:177–93.

Gorton, G. 1988. Banking panics and business cycles. *Oxford Economic Papers* 40:751–81.

Grossman, S., and O. Hart. 1982. Corporate financial structure and managerial incentives. In *The Economics of Information and Uncertainty* (ed. J. McCall), pp. 107–37. University of Chicago Press.

Hart, O. D., and J. Moore. 1994. A theory of debt based on the inalienability of human capital. *Quarterly Journal of Economics* 109:841–79.

Heinemann, F., and G. Illing. 2002. Speculative attacks: unique sunspot equilibrium and transparency. *Journal of International Economics* 58:429–50.

Hellwig, C. 2002. Public information, private information and the multiplicity of equilibria in coordination games. *Journal of Economic Theory* 107:191–222.

Holmström, B., and J. Tirole. 1997. Financial intermediation, loanable funds, and the real sector. *Quarterly Journal of Economics* 112:663–92.

Humphrey, T. M. 1975. The classical concept of the lender of last resort. Federal Reserve Bank of Richmond *Economic Review* (January/February), pp. 2–9.

Meltzer, A. H. (ed.). 2000. *Report of the International Financial Institution Advisory Commission.* Washington, DC: IFIAC.

Jacklin, C., and S. Bhattacharya. 1988. Distinguishing panics and information-based bank runs: welfare and policy implications. *Journal of Political Economy* 96:568–92.

Jeanne, O., and C. Wyplosz. 2003. The international lender of last resort: how large is large enough? In *Managing Currency Crises in Emerging Markets* (ed. M. P. Dooley and J. A. Frankel). University of Chicago Press.

Kaminsky, G., and C. Reinhart. 1999. The twin crises: the causes of banking and balance-of-payments problems. *American Economic Review* 89:473–500.

Kaufman, G. G. 1991. Lender of last resort: a contemporary perspective. *Journal of Financial Services Research* 5:95–110.

Lindgren, C.-J., G. Garcia, and M. Saal. 1996. *Bank Soundness and Macroeconomic Policy.* Washington, DC: IMF.

Markets Group of the Federal Reserve Bank of New York. 2002. Domestic open market operations during 2001. Federal Reserve Bank of New York.

Martin, A. 2002. Reconciling Bagehot with the Fed's response to Sept. 11. Federal Reserve Bank of Kansas City, October.

Mishkin, F. 2000. Systemic risk, moral hazard and the international lender of last resort. In *Private Capital Flows in the Age of Globalization: The Aftermath of the Asian Financial Crisis* (ed. U. Dadush, D. Dasgupta, and M. Uzan). New York: Edward Elgar.

Morris, S., and H. Shin. 1998. Unique equilibrium a model of self-fulfilling currency attacks. *American Economic Review* 88:587–97.

———. 2000. Rethinking multiple equilibria in macroeconomic modelling. National Bureau of Economic Research Macroeconomics Annual.

———. 2001. The CNBC effect: welfare effects of public information. Yale Cowles Foundation Discussion Paper 1312.

Padoa-Schioppa, T. 1999. EMU and banking supervision. *International Finance* 2:295–308.

Peek, J., E. Rosengren, and G. Tootell. 1999. Is bank supervision central to central banking. *Quarterly Journal of Economics* 114:629–53.

Postlewaite, A., and X. Vives. 1987. Bank runs as an equilibrium phenomenon. *Journal of Political Economy* 95:485–91.

Radelet, S., and J. Sachs. 1998. The onset of the Asian financial crisis. Mimeo, Harvard Institute for International Development.

Riordan, M. 1993. Competition and bank performance: a theoretical perspective. In *Capital Markets and Financial Intermediation* (ed. C. Mayer and X. Vives), pp. 328–48. Cambridge University Press.

Rodrik, D., and A. Velasco. 1999. Short-term capital flows. World Bank 1999 ABCDE Conference.

Romer, C., and D. Romer. 2000. Federal Reserve information and the behavior of interest rates. *American Economic Review* 90:429–53.

Schwartz, A. J. 1992. The misuse of the Fed's discount window. Federal Reserve Bank of St. Louis *Review* 74(5):58–69.

Thornton, H. 1802. *An Enquiry into the Nature and Effects of Paper Credit of Great Britain.* London: Hatchard.

Van Zandt, T., and X. Vives. 2003. Monotone equilibria in Bayesian games of strategic complementarities. INSEAD Working Paper.

Vives, X. 1990. Nash equilibrium with strategic complementarities. *Journal of Mathematical Economics* 19:305–21.

——. 1999. *Oligopoly Pricing: Old Ideas and New Tools.* Cambridge, MA: MIT Press.

——. 2001. Restructuring financial regulation in the European Monetary Union. *Journal of Financial Services Research* 19:57–82.

Chapter Three

The Lender of Last Resort:
A Twenty-First-Century Approach

Xavier Freixas, Bruno M. Parigi, and Jean-Charles Rochet

3.1 Introduction

This paper offers a new perspective on the role of emergency liquidity assistance (ELA) by the central bank (CB), often referred to as the lender of last resort (LLR). We take into account two well-acknowledged facts of the banking industry: first, that it is difficult to disentangle liquidity shocks from solvency shocks; second, that moral hazard and gambling for resurrection are typical behaviors for banks experiencing financial distress.

The LLR policy has a long history. Bagehot's (1873) "classical" view maintained that the LLR policy should satisfy at least three conditions: (i) lending should be open only to solvent institutions and against good collateral; (ii) these loans must be at a penalty rate, so that banks cannot use them to fund their current operations; and (iii) the CB should make clear in advance its readiness to lend without limits to a bank that fulfills the conditions on solvency and collateral.

In today's world, the "classical" Bagehotian conception of a lender of last resort has been under attack from two different fronts. First, the distinction between solvency and illiquidity is less than clear-cut. As Goodhart (1987) points out, the banks that require the assistance of the LLR are already under suspicion of being insolvent.[1] Second, it has been argued (see, for example, Goodfriend and King 1988) that the existence of a fully collateralized repo market allows central banks to provide the adequate aggregate amount of liquidity and leave the responsibility of lending uncollateralized to the banks, thus giving them a role as peer monitors and introducing market discipline.

These arguments have been so influential that the Bagehot view of the LLR is often seen as obsolete for any well-developed financial system.

---

[1] Furfine (2001a) provides empirical evidence of banks' reluctance to borrow from the Fed's discount window for fear of the stigma associated with it.

Yet, there does not seem to exist any explicit set of rules to replace it. From an institutional perspective, the discount window provides liquidity support to banks in a way that leaves some discretion to central banks (e.g., the Marginal Lending Facility in the Eurosystem). On the theory side, things may look better but only at first glance. Goodfriend and King's argument sounds attractive only if we assume perfect interbank markets (both repo and unsecured). But this contradicts the asymmetric information assumption that is regarded as the main justification for the existence of banks.[2] Goodfriend and King's argument sounds even less attractive if we take into account Goodhart's criticism: when liquidity and solvency shocks cannot be distinguished, the interbank market is far from perfect. So, to summarize, if we agree with both Goodfriend and King's and Goodhart's criticisms, then we are simply left with no theory of the LLR interventions. The main objective of this paper is to build such a new theory, taking into account bankers' incentive problems and imperfections of the interbank market.

An important motivation for ELA is the prevention of systemic risk. Systemic risk refers to two distinct issues: contagion on the one hand, and macroeconomic risk on the other. There is a large literature on LLR policies when contagion is at stake—when problems at individual financial institutions may trigger widespread financial crises with potential impact on the money supply. See, for example, the recent studies by Flannery (1996) for contagion via the payments system; Gorton and Huang (2002b) on the origin of central banking in relation to bank panics; Kaufman (1991) on the historical evolution of LLR policies; Allen and Gale (2000) and Freixas et al. (chapter 7) on coordination failures; and the surveys by Freixas et al. (1999) and de Bandt and Hartmann (2002). A common theme is that public support to individual banks may be justified to prevent contagion despite the encouragement of excessive bank risk taking that potential bailouts may encourage.

In this paper we abstract from contagion, but we direct our attention to the incentive aspects of ELA and ask under which macroeconomic conditions the CB should provide ELA and how it should operate. By focusing on the ELA incentive issues and building a model that takes into account both of the criticisms discussed previously, we find a new role for the LLR. This new role stems from the unique potential of the CB to

---

[2]The imperfection of the interbank market could be illustrated for the United Kingdom, where the effect of the announcement of BCCI's closure on July 5, 1991, rapidly accelerated the withdrawal of wholesale funds from small and medium-sized U.K. banks. In a perfect interbank market, this would have led to loans from large to small banks, since the withdrawals of funds from small banks were deposited in large banks. But the interbank market did not recycle back the funds and, within three years, a quarter of the banks in this sector were technically insolvent.

change the priority of claims on banks' assets. In periods of crisis, when banks' assets are very risky, borrowing in the interbank market may impose a high penalty on banks because of the high spread demanded on loans. As noticed by Goodfriend and Lacker (1999), if the CB has the power to change the priority of claims, then it can lend at lower rates than the market.

We construct a model in which banks are confronted with interim shocks that may come from uncertain withdrawals by impatient consumers (liquidity shocks) or from losses on the long-term projects they have financed (solvency shocks). Banks are of three types: illiquid (if they have a large fraction of impatient consumers, i.e., they suffer a liquidity shock), insolvent (if their investment is worth little, i.e., they suffer a solvency shock), or normal if they do not suffer from any shock. We take for granted that the opacity of banks' balance sheets makes it difficult for the market and for regulators to distinguish among insolvent, illiquid, and normal banks. Thus, in acting as the LLR, the CB faces the possibility that an insolvent bank may pose as an illiquid bank. In particular, we envision a situation where the insolvent bank is able to borrow either from the interbank market or from the CB and "gambles for resurrection," i.e., it invests the loan in the continuation of a project with a negative expected net present value.

We distinguish two types of moral hazard, which correspond to two important activities of banks: screening loan applicants (*ex ante* or screening moral hazard) and monitoring borrowers after loans are granted (interim or monitoring moral hazard). Because these two types of moral hazard play a key role in our analysis, it is important to clarify their economic justification as well as to understand when one of the two will be prevailing. In the first case (screening moral hazard) the problem is to provide bankers with incentives to put effort into screening loan applicants and so lower the probability of insolvency. The cost of effort depends on how difficult it is to identify the sound firms to lend to, i.e., it depends on the heterogeneity of the population that is applying for a loan. For the banks, it is easier to screen firms in a stable than in a changing environment (Rajan and Zingales 2003); it is also easier at the beginning of an upturn—because the worst firms have already gone bankrupt—than at the end of an upturn, when we may anticipate a larger proportion of lame ducks. We thus expect screening moral hazard to be less stringent on these occasions. On the other hand, we also expect this constraint to be more stringent in some countries than in others. This will indeed be the case owing to different roles of the banking industry, different costs of setting up a business, different disclosure requirements, and the presence (or not) of credit bureaus and ratings agencies (see Pagano and Jappelli 1993).

The interpretation of the monitoring moral hazard is different. The issue here is to provide banks with incentives to put effort into monitoring the firms they have already financed. This is particularly crucial in countries without developed financial markets and in developed countries for small firms that cannot directly borrow from financial markets. On the other hand, for the large firms of developed countries who have easy access to direct finance, these incentives are typically provided by market discipline (ratings agencies, financial analysts, etc.) and the monitoring activity of banks is less important. In this article we provide a full discussion of both cases.

Our main findings are that the role of LLR depends on macroeconomic conditions as well as on the nature of the incentive problems faced by the banks. When moral hazard mainly concerns the monitoring activity of banks (i.e., when market discipline is insufficient), there is no reason to lend at a penalty rate to banks seeking liquidity; hence, a fully secured interbank market allows the implementation of efficient allocation. When, instead, the main source of moral hazard is screening loan applicants, then ELA should be made at a penalty rate in order to discourage insolvent banks from borrowing as if they were merely illiquid; thus, the interbank market should be unsecured and there may be a role for central bank lending. When this occurs, the LLR overrides the priority of the deposit insurance fund (DIF) and lends against the assets of the bank. It can thus offer a better rate than the interbank market, but at a cost to the DIF. This should take place in times of crisis when market spreads on interbank loans are excessively high, and it should happen regardless of whether the DIF bails out insolvent banks or liquidates them, although the latter case will be more frequent. As a consequence, the efficient organization of the interbank market (secured or unsecured) is related to the nature of the main type of moral hazard the banks are facing (monitoring or screening, respectively). In the first case the Goodfriend–King argument applies, while in the second case there is a specific role for the LLR policy. Thus we provide a theory of the LLR in crisis periods even in the absence of contagion threats.

Our results may thus help clarify the debate on the role of the LLR: when the monitoring role of banks is less important, because of the discipline provided by financial markets, we recommend that the interbank market be unsecured. In this case an LLR is needed in order to limit excessive liquidation of assets by illiquid banks. On the other hand, in countries where the monitoring role of banks is crucial and where market discipline is insufficient, the basic role of the interbank market is to provide liquidity insurance. We recommend in this case that the interbank market claims be senior, and we do not find any role for an LLR.

Of course, information problems would be immaterial if banks had a sufficient amount of capital. This is why any model that deals with these issues must consider that capital is scarce. As a consequence, there is a trade-off between the banks' safety and their funding costs. Our approach avoids an arbitrary resolution of this trade-off by considering the overall efficiency in terms of the total value added of the banking industry. Thus, it is not surprising that our framework provides, as a by-product, a recommendation for optimal capital regulation. The amount of capital depends on how the interbank market works, which in turn depends on the moral hazard constraints that the banks are facing.

The rest of the paper is organized as follows. In section 3.2 we set up the basic model of adverse selection of banks' types and moral hazard of bankers. In section 3.3 we consider a perfect information setting and show how the interbank market can implement efficient allocation. In section 3.4 we introduce gambling for resurrection, consider the possibility of bailing out insolvent banks, and establish how the interbank market must be structured. In section 3.5 we show how and when central bank lending through the discount window will improve upon the market allocation. In section 3.6 we extend our results to an economy where it is impossible to prevent gambling for resurrection. Section 3.7 draws policy implications and concludes; a mathematical appendix appears as section 3.8.

3.2 The Model

We consider an economy with three dates ($t = 0, 1, 2$), where profit-maximizing banks offer contracts to depositors while investing in a risky long-term project. At date $t = 0$, equity is raised, deposits are collected, and investment is made. At $t = 1$, a bank can be in one of three possible states, denoted $k = S, L, N$; a bank may face a solvency shock ($k = S$), a liquidity shock ($k = L$), or no shock at all ($k = N$). The precise definitions of these states will be provided later. At date $t = 2$, returns of the investments are divided between depositors and a bank's shareholders.

3.2.1 Banks and Depositors

As in Diamond and Dybvig (1983), banks serve a large number of risk-averse depositors that need intertemporal insurance because they face idiosyncratic shocks about the timing of their consumption needs. We normalize the riskless interest rate to zero. Implicit behind this assumption is the idea that the CB conducts "regular" liquidity management operations (for purposes of monetary policy implementation) irrespective of financial stability. We also assume the existence of a deposit insurance fund that guarantees all deposits. Deposit insurance is financed by actuarially fair premiums. Since depositors are fully insured by the DIF, the optimal contract offered to depositors allows them to withdraw the amount D initially deposited in each period. Fully insured depositors are totally passive in the model. In modern banks, a sizeable portion of deposits is held by large uninsured depositors. However, in many crisis resolutions, large depositors often have been de facto fully insured as well; hence we may assume that there is only one category of depositors and that they are fully insured.

We neglect internal agency problems within banks and assume that banks are run by risk-neutral owner-managers, henceforth bankers. We will use the terms "bank" and "banker" interchangeably whenever this does not create ambiguity. We assume that there exists a supervisory agency, which we call the financial services authority (FSA), in charge of providing incentives for bankers to invest in "safe and sound" projects. The FSA can refuse to charter a bank at $t = 0$ if it does not satisfy certain regulatory conditions that will be specified later (essentially a capital adequacy requirement) and can also close a bank at $t = 1$ if it discovers the bank is insolvent. We abstract from agency conflicts between DIFs, CBs, and supervisors.[3]

At date $t = 0$, the bank raises the amount $D + E$ (deposits plus equity), pays the deposit insurance premium P, and invests I by making loans. At $t = 0$, the budget constraint of a bank is

$$I + P = D + E. \tag{3.1}$$

We assume that the supply of deposits is infinitely elastic at the (zero) riskless market rate. Equity is fixed. There is a perfectly competitive, risk-neutral, interbank market ready to lend any amount at fair rates from $t = 1$ to $t = 2$. There is no aggregate liquidity shortage. Investment is subject to constant returns to scale, a standard assumption in this literature (see, for example, Diamond and Dybvig 1983) that greatly simplifies the analysis, as will become clear later. The gross rate of return of the investment at $t = 2$ is $\tilde{R} = R_1$ in case of success and $\tilde{R} = R_0$ in case of failure, with $R_1 > 1 > R_0 > 0$.

A crucial element in our discussion will be whether or not supervision is efficient (i.e., insolvent banks detected and closed), and whether efficient closure rules can be implemented whereby insolvent banks—though not detected by supervisors—can be given incentives to declare bankruptcy at $t = 1$. We will consider three cases:

1. Efficient supervision (section 3.3): insolvent banks are detected and closed at $t = 1$.

---

[3] For an analysis of this issue, see Repullo (2000) and Kahn and Santos (2001).

2. Inefficient suspension and efficient closure rules (section 3.4): insolvent banks are not detected but are given incentives to declare bankruptcy at $t = 1$.

3. Regulatory forbearance (section 3.6): insolvent banks are not closed and gamble for resurrection by investing in inefficient projects in the hope of surviving.

3.2.2 Liquidity and Solvency Shocks

The state $k = S, L, N$ is privately observed by the banker. In state S (solvency shock), which occurs with probability β_S, the banker learns that his bank is insolvent, i.e., the probability of success of its investment at $t = 2$ is zero. In other words $\tilde{R} = R_0$ for sure. If state S does not occur, then the probability of success is p, but the bank can be hit by a liquidity shock (state L), which occurs with unconditional probability $(1 - \beta_S)\beta_L$. In state L, the bank is illiquid: it faces a deposit withdrawal that we assume to be proportional to bank assets, $\ell \equiv \lambda I$, with $0 < \lambda < 1$.[4] Even if liquidity is available at fair rates from date 1 to date 2, an illiquid bank that does not serve its deposit withdrawals at date 1 is forced to liquidate. The liquidation value of assets is $R_0 I$, the same as when the bank fails. Finally, with unconditional probability $(1 - \beta_S)\beta_N$ (with $\beta_N + \beta_L = 1$), the bank is in state N (no shock).[5]

Although banks may hold reserves at date 0, it is actually optimal for them not to do so for two reasons. First, there is no aggregate liquidity shock at date 1, and liquidity is available at fair rates.[6] Second, since the decision not to hold reserves is made when banks have no private information, it will not signal their type to seek liquidity at date 1.

3.2.3 Bankers' Incentives

The role of banks in our model is to channel funds to finance "safe and sound" projects. We model two types of actions that bankers can take in

---

[4]Alternatively, we could assume that withdrawals are proportional to deposits. This would introduce computational complexity without adding any insight.

[5]In reality, liquidity and solvency shocks are positively correlated whereas in our model a bank is either illiquid or insolvent. An alternative modeling assumption is that banks can be hit by a liquidity shock and a solvency shock at the same time. This would introduce a fourth possibility, where an insolvent bank may be illiquid. If this bank does not borrow λI, it is forced to close. If it borrows λI, then to stay in business it must use the loan to repay impatient depositors and thus cannot use it in the wasteful continuation of a project. Since nothing would change in our analysis as long as there is no aggregate shortage of liquidity, we maintain the assumption that there are three states of the world, i.e., the insolvent banks suffer no liquidity shock.

[6]When instead aggregate liquidity is scarce, reserve holdings become important (see, for example, Bhattacharya and Gale 1987).

this respect:

- screening projects at $t = 0$, i.e., choosing projects that have a reasonable probability of being successful; and

- monitoring projects at $t = 1$, i.e., ensuring that borrowers will fulfill their repayment obligations as much as they can.

Supervisors' actions (e.g., closing insolvent banks) as well as those of the central bank (e.g., providing emergency liquidity assistance) will affect bankers' profits and their incentives to screen and monitor their loans. Because of constant returns to scale, to determine these incentives it is sufficient to focus on the profit rates (per unit of investment) of banks in different states. Let $B_k^j \geqslant 0$ denote the expected profit rate[7] of the banker at date $t = 2$ after state $k = L, N$ and conditional on success $(j = 1)$ or failure $(j = 0)$. Similarly, let B_S denote the profit rate of the bankers in state S (in which case failure is certain). Limited liability implies that none of these profit rates can be negative. Notice that, since the $t = 2$ return is observable[8] and the bankers are risk neutral, it is optimal to set $B_k^0 = 0$ when $k = L, N$, i.e., when a solvent bank fails. This allows us to simplify the notation so that B_k^1 will be denoted simply B_k, $k = L, N$.[9]

The screening decision of the banker is modeled as follows. Exerting the screening effort at time $t = 0$ costs the banker e_0 per unit of investment and improves the quality of the pool of loan applicants which limits the probability of a solvency shock to β_S. Absent the screening effort, the probability of a solvency shock is $\beta_S + \Delta\beta$, where $\Delta\beta > 0$. The banker will exert the screening effort (which we assume to be efficient[10]) if and only if his *ex ante* expected profit rate from screening exceeds that without screening, namely if

$$\beta_S B_S + (1 - \beta_S)p(\beta_N B_N + \beta_L B_L) - e_0$$
$$\geqslant (\beta_S + \Delta\beta)B_S + (1 - \beta_S - \Delta\beta)p(\beta_N B_N + \beta_L B_L), \qquad (3.2)$$

which simplifies to

$$p(\beta_N B_N + \beta_L B_L) \geqslant \frac{e_0}{\Delta\beta} + B_S. \qquad (\text{MH}_0)$$

---

[7] The formulas for these profit rates will be developed later, as a function of the different institutional arrangements that we consider.

[8] Aghion et al. (1999) as well as Mitchell (2001) have shown that, if the returns are unobservable, banks may be able to extract an asymmetric information rent.

[9] Recall that in this paper we abstract from the analysis of contagion that may arise when a bank fails. Thus we assume that, when an insolvent bank is closed at $t = 1$ or a bank fails at $t = 2$, there are no repercussions on the banking system as a whole.

[10] This is satisfied if e_0 is small and $\Delta\beta$ is large; see the precise conditions given in equations (3.7) and (3.8).

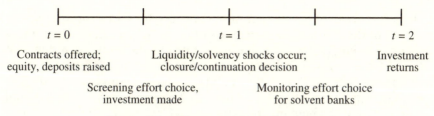

Figure 3.1. The sequence of the events.

We call this the moral hazard constraint at $t = 0$ (or screening constraint).

Similarly, the monitoring decision of the banker is modeled as follows. Exerting the monitoring effort at $t = 1$ (which we assume to be efficient[11]) costs the banker e_1 per unit of investment and ensures a probability of success p of the bank investment. Absent the monitoring effort, the probability of success is only $p(1 - \delta)$, with $0 < \delta < 1$. Monitoring effort increases the probability of success of banks' investments, because, for example, it limits borrowers' scope for value-reducing asset substitution and profit diversion.

The banker will exert the monitoring effort after state k ($k = L, N$) if and only if his expected profit rate from monitoring exceeds that without monitoring:

$$pB_k - e_1 \geqslant p(1 - \delta)B_k, \tag{3.3}$$

which simplifies to

$$B_k \geqslant \frac{e_1}{\delta p}. \tag{MH_1}$$

We call this the moral hazard constraint at $t = 1$ (or monitoring constraint).

The difference between the expected profit rate in case of solvency, $\beta_N B_N + \beta_L B_L$, and the expected profit rate in case of insolvency, B_S, is a measure of the strength of market discipline.

The sequence of the events is depicted in figure 3.1.

3.2.4 Prudential Regulation

In our model, prudential regulation is justified on the grounds that depositors cannot control the screening and monitoring activities of bankers. Regulation exists to ensure that bankers have appropriate incentives to do their job (i.e., exert screening and monitoring effort) and that the DIF does not lose money in expected terms.

---

[11] This is satisfied if e_1 is small and δ is large; see the precise conditions given in equations (3.7) and (3.8).

Regulation can be seen as a contract between the FSA (representing the interest of the DIF) and the bankers. This contract specifies I (how much a bank can lend), as well as the profit rates of the bankers in different states of the world, as a function of E (the equity of the bank) and the parameters characterizing investment returns and bankers' actions. The object of regulation is to set a contract that maximizes the expected total value added of the banking industry, i.e., the expected net present value (NPV) of investment returns subject to various incentive and participation constraints that we describe in what follows.

It is important to understand what the regulators can do that other agents cannot. Regulators have the power to set capital requirements, deposit insurance premiums, and lending rates for emergency loans provided by the LLR. These instruments allow the regulators to provide potentially different profit rates for banks as a function of their declared type. The regulators can also revoke the licenses of insolvent banks. Regulators have no information advantage with respect to other agents, and their resources come only from fairly priced deposit insurance. We will show how these instruments allow regulators to provide the right incentives to bankers. At this stage, we do not discuss implementation of an optimal contract between the FSA and the bankers. In particular, we do not yet specify how banks' liquidity needs are financed at $t = 1$.

The need to provide incentives to bankers lowers the income that can be paid to depositors and thus imposes a constraint on the depositors' participation. Indeed, the gross expected return $I\bar{R}$ on the project, where $\bar{R} \equiv \beta_S R_0 + (1 - \beta_S)(pR_1 + (1 - p)R_0)$ is the project's gross expected rate of return, must be distributed between the two types of claimholders: insured depositors and bankers. The insured depositors are entitled to a net payoff $D - P$; deposits D offer zero remuneration but are insured for a fair premium P. To provide the bankers with appropriate incentives, a minimum *ex ante* expected profit rate of

$$\bar{\pi} \equiv \beta_S B_S + p(\beta_L B_L + \beta_N B_N)(1 - \beta_S) \tag{3.4}$$

must be granted to them. For the project to be able to pay to all its claimholders, we therefore need

$$I\bar{R} \geqslant \bar{\pi}I + D - P. \tag{3.5}$$

Replacing $D - P$ from equation (3.1) in equation (3.5), the resulting investor participation constraint for outside investors at $t = 0$ is

$$I(\bar{R} - 1) \geqslant \bar{\pi}I - E. \tag{IP}$$

This constraint states that the expected net return on the bank's assets, i.e., the social surplus (left-hand side of the inequality (IP)), is at least equal to the expected increase in shareholder value (the right-hand side of inequality (IP)) or, equivalently, that the bank is not subsidized by outsiders.

We assume that at $t = 0$ the project has a positive expected NPV per unit of investment (i.e., $\bar{R} > 1$). This, in turn, implies that $pR_1 + (1 - p)R_0 > 1$; that is, an illiquid bank has a positive expected NPV from continuation.

Notice that constraint (IP) can be restated as a capital adequacy requirement,

$$\frac{E}{I} \geqslant K, \tag{3.6}$$

where $K \equiv \bar{\pi} + 1 - \bar{R}$ is the capital ratio. We assume that $\bar{R}$ is not too high ($\bar{R} < 1 + \bar{\pi}$) so that banks need capital (i.e., $K > 0$).

It is worth pointing out that this formulation introduces an endogenous opportunity cost of capital. Any increase in the aggregate amount of equity ΔE results in an increase in the size of banks and hence in an increase of the banking sector $\Delta I = \Delta E/K$, which generates an increase in the expected output $\Delta I(\bar{R} - 1)$.

3.3 Efficient Supervision: Detection and Closure of Insolvent Banks

To begin with, we examine the case where the shocks at $t = 1$ are public information: thus, insolvent banks are detected and closed at $t = 1$. This benchmark case corresponds to the ideal framework, where supervisors have perfect information about banks' shocks. In practice, regulators may not be able to detect and/or close insolvent banks, a point we examine in the next section.

The closure of an insolvent bank could nevertheless be obtained for some parameter constellation if the implementation of the efficient interbank lending structure leads banks to self-selection. If so, then the first best is achieved in spite of the lack of information regarding the shocks, a point we examine in section 3.3.3.

We introduce here the general structure of the problem of determining the optimal contract. The mathematical treatment will be the same in this section and in sections 3.4 and 3.6, where we consider the two other regulatory frameworks. Our approach will be to look for efficient allocation, i.e., to determine the monetary incentives for bankers to maximize the expected NPV of banks' investment under various regulatory frameworks, and then to introduce the institutional arrangements for implementing efficient allocation. As we will see in the sequel, central bank lending is the institutional arrangement for implementing the optimal allocation when supervision is not efficient and the CB can provide loans at better terms than the interbank market.

3.3.1   The Optimal Allocation when Supervision Is Efficient

Here we focus on the case where it is optimal to induce bankers to screen applicants at $t = 0$ and monitor them at $t = 1$. This is guaranteed by the conditions that the bank's expected NPV per unit of investment with (without) efforts at date 0 and at date 1 is positive (negative):

$$(\bar{R} - 1 - e_0 - (1 - \beta_S)e_1) > 0, \tag{3.7}$$

$$[(\beta_S + \Delta\beta)R_0 + (1 - \beta_S - \Delta\beta)(p(1 - \delta)R_1 + (1 - p(1 - \delta))R_0)] < 0. \tag{3.8}$$

Conditions (3.7) and (3.8) are satisfied if the costs of efforts e_0 and e_1 are small and if δ (the increase in the probability of success) and $\Delta\beta$ (the reduction in the probability of solvency) are large. In this case, the optimal allocation is obtained by maximizing the bank's expected NPV per unit of investment with efforts (left-hand side of equation (3.7)) under the participation constraint of investors (IP), the incentive-compatibility constraints for the banker, and the limited liability constraint (LL) for the banker. The constraint (LL) can be simply expressed as the requirement that the profit rate for the banker of an insolvent bank cannot be negative, $B_S \geqslant 0$.

Recall that constraint (IP) is equivalent to the capital adequacy requirement (3.6) and notice that I does not appear in the constraints (LL), (MH$_0$), or (MH$_1$) because of constant returns to scale. Therefore, the maximization of the expected NPV of banks' investment can be split into a two-stage problem. In the first stage we maximize the investment size subject to the binding capital requirement, namely we maximize I subject to $I = E/(\bar{\pi} + 1 - \bar{R})$, taking as given the *ex ante* expected profit rate $\bar{\pi}$.

In the second stage we choose the profit rates for the bankers in the states L, N, S to minimize the bankers' *ex ante* expected profit rate $\bar{\pi}$ under the limited liability and moral hazard constraints. Therefore, the optimal allocation can be found by solving the following program $(\wp^1)$:

$$\min_{B_L, B_N, B_S} \bar{\pi}$$

subject to:

$$B_S \geqslant 0, \tag{LL}$$

$$p(\beta_N B_N + \beta_L B_L) \geqslant \frac{e_0}{\Delta\beta} + B_S, \tag{MH$_0$}$$

$$B_k \geqslant \frac{e_1}{p\delta}, \quad k = L, N. \tag{MH$_1$}$$

The solution of $(\wp^1)$ is characterized in the following proposition.[12]

Proposition 3.1. *When supervision is efficient, the optimal allocation specifies a zero profit rate for insolvent banks (state S) and the same positive profit rate in the two other states L and N: $B_S = 0$; $B_N = B_L = \max(e_1/p\delta, e_0/p\Delta\beta)$.*

Proof. See the appendix (section 3.8).   □

3.3.2 Implementing Efficient Allocation

Let us now determine what institutional arrangements are needed in order to implement efficient allocation just characterized. First notice that $B_S = 0$ is obtained simply by closing the insolvent banks and fully expropriating their shareholders, as in a standard bankruptcy procedure. The second characteristic of the optimal allocation is that bankers obtain the same profit rate in the two remaining states, i.e., whether or not the bank experiences a liquidity shock ($B_N = B_L$). Since illiquid banks (state L) must borrow λI (in order to repay unexpected withdrawals at $t = 1$), their profit rate in case of success at $t = 2$ is

$$B_L = R_1 - \frac{(D - \lambda I) + \rho}{I}, \tag{3.9}$$

where $D - \lambda I$ represents the repayment to depositors who have not withdrawn at $t = 1$ and ρ is the repayment on the loan contracted at $t = 1$. Since we have normalized the riskless interest rate to zero, the quantity $\rho - \lambda I$ can be interpreted as the net cost of borrowing for the bank,

$$\rho - \lambda I = \sigma \lambda I, \tag{3.10}$$

where σ is the spread charged by the lender to the borrowing bank. Competition in the interbank market implies that this spread is zero if the interbank loan is collateralized but positive if there is credit risk.

By contrast, banks of type N do not have to borrow at $t = 1$, so their profit rate in case of success at $t = 2$ is

$$B_N = R_1 - \frac{D}{I}. \tag{3.11}$$

Using the relations (3.9)–(3.11), we see that $B_N - B_L = \sigma\lambda$.

Proposition 3.1 shows that efficiency requires that $B_N = B_L$; in other words, there can be no risk spread in the interbank market. This implies

---

[12] Observe that constraint (LL) can only bind in state S, since constraint (MH$_1$) implies that $B_k > 0$ for $k = L, N$.

that the repayment of interbank market loans must be fully guaranteed. Hence, we need to distinguish two conditions on the magnitude of the shocks. If the shocks are small with respect to the value of the assets that banks can pledge as collateral in the worst-case scenario ($\lambda < R_0$), then the implementation of the optimal allocation need not imply any direct involvement of the DIF, since interbank loans could be either senior to deposits or fully collateralized. Shocks are likely to be small if the time horizon involved is short. Thus, small shocks reflect the idea expressed by Padoa-Schioppa (1999) that "the probability that a modern bank is solvent, but illiquid, and at the same time lacks sufficient collateral to obtain regular central bank funding is...quite small." In the United States, for example, discount window loans on a typical day amount to a few hundred million dollars.[13]

If the shocks are large ($\lambda > R_0$), then loans cannot be fully collateralized. Thus, the optimal allocation cannot be implemented unless interbank loans are guaranteed, for example, by the DIF. Bailing out banks may cause losses and thus may require additional resources. These additional resources may come from the deposit insurance fund (thus increasing the DIF premium and lowering the size of the investment) or might involve taxpayer money if bank insolvency might cause contagion.

In reality, however, interbank loans are typically unsecured (Kane and Demirguc-Kunt 2001), for example, when depository institutions lend reserves to each other at overnight maturity. Why would an unsecured interbank market possibly lead to an inefficient allocation? The answer is that, when the interbank market loans are risky, B_L is reduced because of a credit-risk spread; that is, $B_L = B_N - \sigma\lambda$. However, owing to the monitoring moral hazard constraint, B_L cannot be smaller than $e_1/p\delta$. This means that B_N must be increased above this level, implying a reduction in the banks' lending capacity, an increase in the capital requirement, and a reduction in social surplus.[14]

The other tools for implementing efficient allocation are the capital ratio and the DIF premium. Bank maximization of I yields the optimal level of investment $\bar{I}$. After inserting $\bar{I}$ into the capital adequacy constraint (3.6), the capital ratio K is chosen to coincide with the optimum so that $E = \bar{K}\bar{I}$, where $\bar{K}$ denotes the capital ratio that solves (3.6) with

---

[13] However, they reached $46 billion on the day after the 9/11 terrorist attacks (Bartolini and Prati 2003).

[14] Strictly speaking, when $e_1/\delta < e_0/\Delta\beta$, program ($\wp^1$) has multiple solutions, of which some are compatible with a (small) spread. For simplicity we focus on the solution described in proposition 3.1.

equality. The actuarially fair deposit insurance premium is thus

$$P = [\beta_S + (1 - \beta_S)\beta_N(1 - p)][D - R_0\bar{I}]$$
$$+ [(1 - \beta_S)\beta_L(1 - p)][D - (R_0 + \lambda)\bar{I}]. \quad (3.12)$$

The bank's budget constraint at $t = 0$ (equation (3.1)) together with (3.12) determines the values of P and D.

3.3.3 Implementing Efficient Allocation under Adverse Selection

Theoretically, it should be possible to implement efficient allocation even in the presence of adverse selection. We briefly examine this possibility, for the sake of completeness. The main benefit of showing what happens in this case is that it allows us to establish forcefully that any reasonable framework for the analysis of the interbank market and the LLR must take into account the existence of the bankers' incentives to avoid closure and remain in business.

We remark that, when banks' types of shocks are not observable (adverse selection), it is still possible to implement efficient allocation as long as an insolvent bank cannot take actions that are detrimental to social welfare. This follows because returns on bank assets are observable. Thus, whenever a bank fails ($\tilde{R} = R_0$), the DIF is entitled to seize all its assets, implying $B_N^0 = B_L^0 = 0$ (as we have assumed) and $B_S = 0$; a secured interbank market, which implies $\sigma = 0$, will then lead to efficient allocation with $B_N = B_L$. In particular, no CB intervention for ELA is needed to implement efficient allocation.

The situation changes if we introduce the additional feature (which we believe to be realistic) that the managers of an insolvent bank have an incentive to remain in business, due to the possibility of either diverting assets from the bank or gambling for resurrection. This is what we investigate in the next section.

3.4 Efficient Closure

Rapid developments in technology and financial sophistication can impair the ability of regulators to maintain a safe and sound banking system (see, for example, Furfine 2001b). To capture this, we suppose from now on that insolvent banks cannot be detected by regulators and can attempt to gamble for resurrection (GFR). By this we mean that, at date 1, insolvent banks can borrow the same amount λI as illiquid banks and invest it without being detected. By assuming that insolvent and illiquid banks have the same liquidity demand, we make it easier for an insolvent bank to mimic an illiquid one; as a result, we give the regulators the harder case to handle. Recall that reserve management cannot be used to signal a bank's type.

We assume that this additional investment gives an insolvent bank a second chance, i.e., a positive (but small) probability of success $p_g \equiv \alpha p$ (with $0 < \alpha < 1$) for the bank's projects.[15] However, we assume that an insolvent bank that continues to invest destroys wealth; in other words, its reinvestment has a negative expected NPV, $p_g(R_1 - R_0) < \lambda$. In spite of this, managers of an insolvent bank may decide to use this reinvestment possibility in the hope that the bank recovers. We call this behavior "gambling for resurrection" by reference to the behavior of "zombie" Savings and Loan institutions during the U.S. S&L crisis in the 1980s.[16]

Providing bankers with incentives not to gamble for resurrection implies that bankers who declare bankruptcy at $t = 1$ are allowed to keep a positive profit. We interpret this as a bailout of the insolvent bank. The rate of profit B_S of the banker following a bailout, must be at least equal to the expected profit obtained from engaging in gambling for resurrection. An insolvent bank that gambles for resurrection obtains the same rate of profit in case of success as an L bank, B_L. However, an insolvent bank that gambles for resurrection must make an additional investment λI. Thus, the profit rate from gambling for resurrection in case of success is $B_L - \lambda$, and the expected profit rate is $p_g(B_L - \lambda)$. Hence, gambling for resurrection will be prevented if an insolvent bank obtains an expected profit rate at least equal to $p_g(B_L - \lambda)$, which introduces the new constraint

$$B_S \geqslant p_g(B_L - \lambda). \qquad \text{(GFR)}$$

As we show in the sequel the possibility of an insolvent bank gambling for resurrection creates an externality between the interbank market and the DIF.[17] Figure 3.2 summarizes the different possibilities in our model. The picture describes the events, the actions, and the returns when bankers exert effort to screen and to monitor and no early liquidation takes place.

---

[15]We could alternatively assume that the more the insolvent bank borrows and invests, the greater is the increase in its probability of success at date 2. Still it would be optimal for an insolvent bank to borrow exactly λI, because any different amount reveals its type.

[16]The negative expected NPV from continuation implies that managers would actually be better off by stealing the money outright at $t = 1$ if they could get away with it. Indeed, the negative expected NPV assumption is equivalent to $p_g R_1 + (1 - p_g)R_0 < \lambda + R_0$ so that stealing dominates gambling for resurrection. Akerlof and Romer (1993) document such looting behavior during the U.S. S&L crisis. Here we focus on GFR by assuming a large "cost of stealing": namely, such looters ultimately retain only a small fraction of what they steal, so that GFR is a more profitable behavior for bankers.

[17]We have chosen to model GFR as the main preoccupation of bank supervisors. We could have assumed instead that bank managers are able to engage in inefficient asset-substitution in order to expropriate value from the DIF. Our results would essentially carry over to this slightly different modeling assumption.

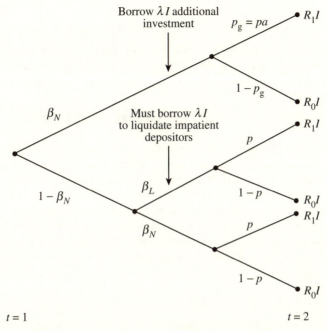

Figure 3.2. Events, actions, and returns. Notes: in the absence of a solvency shock, β_N is the probability of no shock for solvent banks; $\beta_L = 1 - \beta_N$ is the probability of a liquidity shock for solvent banks; R_1 is the investment return in case of success; R_0 is the investment return in case of failure; p is the probability of success for solvent banks; p_g is the probability of success for insolvent banks that gamble for resurrection; λ is the size of shock; I is the investment size.

3.4.1 Efficient Allocation with Orderly Closure

The most efficient way to avoid gambling for resurrection is for the FSA to provide the monetary incentives for managers of insolvent banks to spontaneously declare bankruptcy (see Aghion et al. 1999; Mitchell 2001). This means in practice that the FSA can organize an orderly closure procedure that discourages gambling for resurrection (or asset substitution). In contrast with the previous case of efficient supervision (where insolvent banks are detected and closed), bankers receive a strictly positive profit B_S even in the event of insolvency, which implies that their *ex ante* expected rate of profit is higher. But this implies, in turn, that a bank will face *ex ante* a higher capital requirement and will invest less: this is the social cost of inefficient supervision.

To find the optimal allocation, we proceed as in the case of efficient supervision (section 3.3.1). The *ex ante* expected profit rate of the

bankers is
$$\tilde{\pi} \equiv \beta_S B_S + p(\beta_L B_L + \beta_N B_N)(1 - \beta_S). \tag{3.13}$$

The binding capital adequacy requirement thus becomes $I = E/(\tilde{\pi} + 1 - \bar{R})$. Therefore, since E is given, to maximize I we look for the profit rates for the bankers in states L, N, S that minimize $\tilde{\pi}$. Namely, we solve the following program $(\wp^2)$:

$$\min_{B_L, B_N, B_S} \tilde{\pi} \qquad \text{subject to:} \quad \text{(LL), (MH}_0\text{), (MH}_1\text{), (GFR)}.$$

Before establishing the optimal allocation we have to impose conditions on the magnitude of the shock. Previously we distinguished two cases depending on whether or not the shock exceeds the bank's assets in the worst-case scenario. The presence of a GFR constraint introduces a new element: if the shock is large with respect to the cost of effort in relation to the increase of the probability of success that it induces ($\lambda > e_1/\delta p$), then the GFR constraint does not bind. Hence an insolvent bank will not find it convenient to gamble for resurrection, and the program $(\wp^2)$ has the same solutions as $(\wp^1)$. We therefore concentrate on the case $\lambda < e_1/\delta p$.

We now establish the following result.

Proposition 3.2. *If shocks are small ($\lambda < e_1/\delta p$), then $(\wp^2)$ has a unique solution. This solution is such that bankers who declare insolvency receive the minimum expected profit that prevents them from gambling for resurrection: $B_S = p_g(e_1/\delta p - \lambda) > 0$. The profit rates in the other states (L and N) depend on which moral hazard constraint binds.*

If the monitoring constraint binds (case (a), $e_1/\delta \geq e_0/\Delta\beta + B_S$), then bankers obtain the same profit rate whether or not they experience a liquidity shock: $B_N = B_L = e_1/p\delta$.

If, instead, the screening constraint binds (case (b), $e_1/\delta < e_0/\Delta\beta + B_S$), then the profit rate is higher for banks that do not experience a liquidity shock:

$$B_N = \frac{1}{p\beta_N}\left(\frac{e_0}{\Delta\beta} + B_S\right) - \frac{\beta_L}{\beta_N}\frac{e_1}{p\delta} > B_L = \frac{e_1}{p\delta}.$$

Proof. See the appendix.   □

Proposition 3.2 characterizes the optimal allocation when supervision is inefficient (i.e., when insolvent banks are not detected at $t = 1$), but the FSA (or the DIF) has the power to provide direct monetary incentives to the owner–managers of an insolvent bank who spontaneously declares bankruptcy at $t = 1$. In this way, gambling for resurrection is avoided.

In the next section we use the distinction between cases (a) and (b) to assess the potential role of the CB in implementing the optimal allocation identified previously when there is an interbank market that provides liquidity at fair rates at date 1.

3.5   Central Bank Lending

3.5.1   Central Bank Lending and the Interbank Market

We have established in proposition 3.2 that, when market discipline is weak and thus the main regulatory concern is to induce bankers to monitor their loans at date 1 (case (a)), there is no need to penalize a solvent but illiquid bank borrowing at date 1 ($B_N = B_L$). As a consequence, the implementation of efficient allocation is the same as when illiquid and insolvent banks can be identified (section 3.3). Provided that interbank market loans are either senior or fully collateralized, the optimal allocation can be implemented by the interbank market without any need for CB intervention.

A novel set of issues arises when market discipline is instead so strong that the monitoring moral hazard constraint is redundant (case (b)). The important problem here is inducing bankers to exert effort to screen loan applicants at date 0. To implement efficient allocation under these conditions, date 1 loans to any bank (including illiquid ones) will have to be set at a penalty rate, i.e., with a spread σ^* such that $B_N - B_L = \sigma^* \lambda$.

The need for a spread has two effects: it raises the issue of the feasibility of efficient allocation in the presence of an interbank market; and it limits the role of the CB to situations in which the interbank market spread is higher than that of the CB. The interbank market spread is determined by the condition of zero expected return, which we denote as $\sigma(\beta_S = 0)$, when the insolvent bank is bailed out.[18] Thus, only when the interbank spread and the optimal spread coincide ($\sigma(\beta_S = 0) = \sigma^*$) will efficient allocation be reached by the interbank market. In general, efficient allocation will not be reached, and we will have to consider two cases depending on whether (i) the optimal spread exceeds the interbank spread $\sigma^* > \sigma(\beta_S = 0)$ or (ii) the opposite inequality holds.

In the first case, $\sigma^* > \sigma(\beta_S = 0)$, it is impossible for the CB to provide ELA at the optimal penalty rate σ^*.[19] Thus, the potential role of the CB is limited to situations in which the optimal spread is lower than the interbank market spread, $\sigma^* < \sigma(\beta_S = 0)$. The presence of an interbank market limits the power of the FSA's incentive scheme to encourage bankers to exert screening efforts.

In summary, when the main type of moral hazard is monitoring (case (a)), a fully secured interbank market allows the implementation of efficient allocation. When, instead, the main source of moral hazard

---

[18]For the computations of the spreads σ^* and $\sigma(\beta_S = 0)$, see the appendix.

[19]Notice that the rationale for "lending at a penalty rate" is here completely different from the one in Bagehot. In our framework the issue of efficient reserves management does not arise. Lending at a penalty rate is desirable only to reduce the profits from GFR and hence the cost of bailing out banks.

is screening (case (b)), the interbank market should be unsecured and there may be a role for central bank lending.

3.5.2   The Operational Framework

Having established that the role of the CB is limited to situations in which screening loan applicants requires incentives and the interbank market spread, is higher than the optimal spread we now turn to the question of how the CB can implement efficient allocation and undercut the interbank market. The CB can lend at better terms than the market because it can make loans collateralized by banks' assets. However, collateralized loans are possible only if $\lambda < R_0$, the condition we focus on. When the magnitude of the shocks is such that $\lambda > R_0$, collateralized loans cannot be made and the optimal allocation cannot be implemented.

In many countries there is a legal requirement that CB loans must be collateralized, although what constitutes eligible collateral varies substantially. The rationale for collateralized loans is to avoid having the CB become creditor of a failing bank, which in turn may result in charges against the capital of the CB or conflicts of interest when the CB becomes creditor of a regulated entity (Delston and Campbell 2002). The CB thus has the advantage over the interbank market in that it can override the priority of the DIF claims. Gorton and Huang (2002a) argue precisely that governments can improve upon a coalition of banks in providing liquidity only because they have more power than private agents (e.g., they can seize assets). In practice, LLR operations are almost always the responsibility of the CB, whereas the DIF is usually managed by a public agency or by the banking industry itself (see Kahn and Santos 2001; Repullo 2000).

Kaufman (1991) and Goodfriend and Lacker (1999, p. 14) provide detailed evidence for the fact that, in the United States, lending by the Fed is in general collateralized and favored in bank-failure resolution with the FDIC assuming "the borrowing's bank indebtedness to the Fed in exchange for the collateral, relieving the Fed of the risk of falling collateral value." Of course, the risk is shifted onto the DIF.[20] In the Eurosystem all credit operations by the European System of Central Banks (ESCB) must be collateralized,[21] with the ESCB accepting a broader class of collateral than the Fed.

Under the ELA arrangements, LLR operations in the Eurosystem are conducted mainly at the level of the national central banks (NCBs), at the initiative of the NCBs and not of the ECB. NCBs can make collateralized

---

[20]See Sprague (1986, pp. 88–92) for an account of the resulting conflicts between Fed and FDIC.

[21]Article 18.1 of the ECB/ESCB statute (Issing et al. 2001).

loans up to a threshold without prior authorization from the ECB. Larger operations with a potential impact on money supply must be approved by the ECB. Since the costs and risks of ELA operations conducted autonomously by the NCBs are to be borne at the national level, NCBs have some leeway in relation to collateral policy as long as some national authority takes the risk.[22] Similarly, IMF loans enjoy a de facto preferred creditor status even though there is no legal basis for this condition.[23] In contrast, the Swiss National Bank follows the principle of providing assistance to the market as a whole instead of to individual banks (Kaufman 1991). In the United Kingdom no formal authority offers guidance to the provision of ELA by the Bank of England (see the Memorandum of Understanding 1997[24]), which on its side stresses the need to follow a discretionary rather than predictable approach.

3.5.3   The Terms of Central Bank Lending

The terms at which the CB must offer ELA in order to implement efficient allocation are directly deduced from proposition 3.2. Formally, we have the following proposition.

Proposition 3.3. *When loans can be collateralized* ($\lambda < R_0$) *if the screening constraint is binding, and if the optimal spread* σ^* *is lower than the interbank spread* $\sigma(\beta_S = 0)$, *then the CB can improve upon the unsecured interbank market solution by lending at a rate* σ^* *against good collateral.*

Several observations are in order. First, the possibility of ELA by the CB enables reaching efficient allocation by increasing the illiquid bank's profit rate up to its efficiency level. This is possible by using the discount-window facility and lending to illiquid banks at better terms than the market, so that they are not penalized by the high interbank market spreads. Second, there is a trade-off between lending to illiquid banks

---

[22]The operational procedures through which the two central banks lend money to banks for regular liquidity management have become more similar recently (Bartolini and Prati 2003), with the Fed converging toward a system of Lombard-type facility. First with the Special Lending Facility to address the Y2K issue and then at the beginning of 2003, the Fed has begun to make collateralized loans to banks on a no-questions-asked basis and at penalty rates over the target federal funds rate (Bartolini and Prati 2003), as opposed to rates 0.25–0.50 points below the fund rate over the previous ten years. Similarly, in the Eurosystem one of the main pillars of liquidity management is the Marginal Lending Facility, which banks can access at their own discretion to borrow reserves at overnight maturity from the Eurosystem at penalty rates (Issing et al. 2001).

[23]See Penalver (2004) for a discussion of the issue and a model of the IMF's preferred creditor status to mitigate financial crises.

[24]Memorandum of Understanding between HM Treasury, the Bank of England, and the FSA. (Available at www.bankofengland.co.uk/legislation/mou.pdf.)

at better terms and discouraging insolvent banks from gambling for resurrection. This trade-off and the interaction between regulation and liquidity provision are captured by the constraint $B_S \geqslant p_g(B_L - \lambda)$, which shows that B_L must be lowered in order to decrease the profit B_S left to insolvent banks. This is the condition that allows us to sort illiquid from insolvent banks. Indeed, an insolvent bank is less profitable than an illiquid bank for two reasons: it needs an additional investment λI and it succeeds with a lower probability, $p_g = \alpha p < p$. Thus, the insolvent bank cannot afford to borrow at the same interest rate as the illiquid bank. By charging a suitably high interest rate, the CB discourages an insolvent bank from borrowing.[25] Third, by requiring good collateral and therefore effectively overriding the priority of the DIF claims, the CB can lend at better terms than the interbank market. Note that the type of ELA envisioned here does not result in the use of taxpayer money but rather in a higher DIF premium that lowers the bank's size. Observing that a failing bank's assets are no longer $R_0 I$ but now $(R_0 - \lambda)I$ because the CB has priority over λI, the new DIF premium becomes

$$P = [\beta_S + (1 - \beta_S)\beta_N(1 - p)][D - R_0 I]$$

$$+ [(1 - \beta_S)\beta_L(1 - p)][D - (R_0 - \lambda + \lambda)I]. \qquad (3.15)$$

The premium in (3.15) exceeds that in (3.12), where gambling for resurrection is not an option, because I is smaller than in the case where the insolvent bank is detected. Fourth, we remark that a fully secured interbank market would here be inefficient. In case (b) the efficient solution requires a spread between B_N and B_L, $B_N = B_L + \lambda\sigma$; when $\sigma(\beta_S = 0) < \sigma^*$, banks generate a lower surplus with collateralized loans than with the optimal spread σ^*.

The conditions on the size of the shocks play an important role in establishing an ELA by the CB. Small shocks may pose no contagion threat but make gambling for resurrection attractive thus blurring the distinction between illiquid and insolvent banks. However, only when shocks are small can all loans be collateralized, which may allow the CB to implement efficient allocation. The provision of ELA by the CB may thus be justified even in the absence of contagion. This is not to say that ELA by the CB should be ruled out when there are contagion concerns. But when shocks are large, loans cannot be collateralized and hence efficient allocation cannot be implemented with additional resources needed to bail out insolvent banks.

---

[25] Observe that a bank of type N has no incentive to borrow λI from the CB and lend it again to the market at a higher rate because no bank would be ready to borrow directly at such a rate, which is higher than what they pay when they borrow directly from the CB.

Moreover, making explicit *ex ante* the rules of ELA from the central bank—and thus making explicit the profits that insolvent banks can receive if they accept an orderly closure—is an effective way to deal with moral hazard and gambling for resurrection. This is to be contrasted with two pieces of conventional wisdom about CB intervention. On the one hand we have the notion that "constructive ambiguity" with respect to the conduct of the CB in crisis situations would reduce the scope for moral hazard. On the other hand is the fear that a generous bailout policy hampers market discipline and generates moral hazard.

Our results show that this conventional wisdom may be oversimplified and identify the trade-off between the benefits of market discipline and the costs of gambling for resurrection. By explicitly modeling screening as well as moral hazard constraints and the possibility of gambling for resurrection, we account for a rich array of possible banker behaviors that generate complex interactions. It is true that guaranteeing a positive profit B_S to the bankers who spontaneously declare bankruptcy at $t = 1$ makes it more difficult for the FSA to prevent moral hazard at $t = 0$ and also imposes an additional cost on the DIF. However, since the expected profit rate of an insolvent bank is less than that of a solvent one ($B_S < \beta_L B_L + \beta_N B_N$), bankers have the correct *ex ante* incentive to exert effort at $t = 0$ to avoid being insolvent. Thus, B_S has to be sufficiently high to induce self-selection of an insolvent bank, and $\beta_L B_L + \beta_N B_N$ must be increased accordingly in order to keep intact the bankers' incentive to screen. For these reasons, the *ex ante* capital requirement must be increased. This has a cost in our model, since it implies that K increases in the capital requirement constraint, $KI \leqslant E$, and therefore that the volume of lending is reduced for a given level of equity.

Still, this is the most efficient way to prevent gambling for resurrection (or, more generally, asset substitution). Once insolvency has occurred, it would be inefficient (both *ex post* and *ex ante*) to impose penalties on the bank that spontaneously declares insolvency. From a policy point of view, this justifies a crisis resolution mechanism involving some kind of bailout of a failing bank. Such a mechanism has been advocated by Aghion et al. (1999), Mitchell (2001), and Gorton and Huang (2002a). However, there is an obvious criticism of such a mechanism: that it can lead to regulatory forbearance and possibly to corruption. If the FSA (or the DIF) has full discretion to distribute money to the owners-managers of banks, then organized frauds can be envisaged. This is why we examine in section 3.6 an alternative set of assumptions where such monetary transfers are ruled out.

3.5.4 When Is Central Bank Intervention Useful?

Proposition 3.3 gives two conditions that characterize the role for ELA by the central bank in implementing efficient allocation. These conditions require that the screening constraint be binding,

$$\frac{1-\alpha}{\delta}e_1 \leqslant \frac{e_0}{\Delta\beta} - \alpha p\lambda, \tag{3.16}$$

and that the interbank market spread be larger than the optimal spread; using equations (3.35) and (3.37) from the appendix yields

$$\frac{e_0}{\Delta\beta} - e_1\left(\frac{1-\alpha}{\delta}\right) + p\lambda(\beta_N - \alpha) < \lambda\beta_N. \tag{3.17}$$

After simple manipulations, we can see that these two constraints amount to

$$p < \frac{1}{\alpha\lambda}\left(\frac{e_0}{\Delta\beta} - e_1\left(\frac{1-\alpha}{\delta}\right)\right) < p + (1-p)\frac{\beta_N}{\alpha}. \tag{3.18}$$

This means that ELA by the CB is justified in our model only under very specific conditions: first, $e_0/\Delta\beta - e_1((1-\alpha)/\delta)$ must be positive, which means that the screening constraint has to dominate the monitoring constraint; second, β_N must be large, or rather the probability of a liquidity shock $(1-\beta_N)$ must be small,[26] which means that the use of the discount window has to be limited to exceptional circumstances; finally, p must be small, or rather the probability of bank failure $(1-p)$ must be high, which means that ELA is more likely to be needed in times of economic downturn or a banking crisis. Here β_S is irrelevant because the insolvent bank spontaneously declares bankruptcy.

The main conclusion of this section is that the role of the CB as LLR to implement the optimal allocation depends on several factors. First, a necessary condition for CB lending is inefficient supervision that fails to detect and close insolvent banks. A second requirement is that market discipline be so strong that the monitoring moral hazard constraint is redundant, yet scarce *ex ante* information makes it difficult to screen sound projects. Third, CB intervention is not needed during the expansionary phase of the cycle (p high). On the contrary, the CB is necessary to provide ELA when the economy as a whole is in crisis owing to the low probability of success of the investment (p low) and to high market spreads. Finally, the shock must be small with respect to the bank's assets so that CB loans can be collateralized.

---

[26]We also assume that α is so small that $\beta_N > \alpha$, in which case the third term in equation (3.18) decreases with p. This ensures that both conditions are satisfied when p is small enough.

3.6 Efficient Allocation in the Presence of Gambling for Resurrection

Offering a subsidy to bail out banks that are experiencing financial distress may pose difficulties for regulators. It may be difficult to prove that the money is well spent as it prevented banks from gambling for resurrection, which is not observed if the policy is successful. Regulatory forbearance may therefore result. This may happen, for example, if the supervisors do not have the discretion to distribute money to bankers and/or this is not feasible for political reasons. For these reasons in this section we investigate the case where gambling for resurrection cannot be avoided because the FSA is not allowed to bail out insolvent banks. We concentrate on the case $\lambda < R_0$.

Hence at $t = 1$, insolvent banks (which are not detected because supervisors are inefficient) have no incentive to declare bankruptcy and thus are not closed: they borrow λI at the same terms as illiquid banks and invest it with probability of success $p_g < p$. The interbank market is then plagued by adverse selection, which leads to a higher spread than in the case where gambling for resurrection can be prevented (see the appendix for the calculations).

However, efficient allocation is such that the profit rates of bankers in the different states are unchanged. For example, for an insolvent bank it is still equal to $B_S = p_g(B_L - \lambda)$, but the interpretation is different because this expected profit is now obtained by gambling for resurrection. The optimal incentive scheme for bankers is the same as in proposition 3.2; in particular, the *ex ante* expected profit rate of bankers is

$$\tilde{\pi} \equiv \beta_S B_S + p(\beta_L B_L + \beta_N B_N)(1 - \beta_S). \tag{3.19}$$

However, an insolvent bank that gambles for resurrection lowers the overall expected return from $\bar{R}$ to

$$\hat{R} = \beta_S[p_g R_1 + (1 - p_g)R_0 - \lambda] + (1 - \beta_S)[pR_1 + (1 - p)R_0]. \tag{3.20}$$

To find the optimal solution we proceed as in program $(\wp^2)$, observing that the binding capital adequacy requirement becomes

$$I(\hat{R} - 1) = \tilde{\pi}I - E, \tag{3.21}$$

where $\tilde{\pi}$ is found by solving program $(\wp^2)$. We immediately deduce the following proposition.

Proposition 3.4. *When gambling for resurrection cannot be prevented, the profit rates obtained by bankers in the optimal allocation are the same as in proposition 3.2. However, the overall net return on the bank's assets is lower and the market spread on interbank loans is higher.*

Several comments are in order. As in the case where gambling for resurrection could be prevented by efficient closure rules, efficient allocation requires that interbank loans not be collateralized. Therefore, we suppose from now on that interbank loans are junior (deposits are senior). The overall deposit insurance premium in the presence of gambling for resurrection is

$$P = [\beta_S(1 - p_g) + (1 - \beta_S)\beta_N(1 - p)][D - R_0 I]$$
$$+ [(1 - \beta_S)\beta_L(1 - p)][D - (R_0 + \lambda)I]. \quad (3.22)$$

We now compare the capital ratio and the investment level under orderly closure (section 3.5), K^*, I^*, and in the interbank market solution with gambling for resurrection, $\hat{K}, \hat{I}$. From the capital adequacy requirement constraints, we have

$$E = I^*(\tilde{\pi} - \bar{R} + 1) = I^* K^*, \quad (3.23)$$

$$E = \hat{I}(\tilde{\pi} - \hat{R} + 1) = \hat{I}\hat{K}. \quad (3.24)$$

Since $\hat{R} < \bar{R}$ and since the *ex ante* expected profit, $\tilde{\pi}$, for bankers is the same in the two supervisory regimes, it follows that $\hat{I} < I^*$ and $\hat{K} > K^*$. This highlights that the social cost of inefficient closure rules is a lower level of investment.

Comparing these results with those of section 3.5, we notice that the market spread there was $\sigma(\beta_S = 0)$, which is smaller than the interbank spread when gambling for resurrection cannot be prevented, $\sigma(\beta_S > 0)$ (see the appendix for the calculations). Thus it is more likely that the CB can improve matters when gambling for resurrection occurs. This in turn implies that the less efficient the supervision, the more likely that the CB has a role to play in ELA. To put it differently, forbearance by banking supervisors makes the ELA by the CB more likely to be needed.

As a consequence, the conclusions of proposition 3.3 carry over to an environment where gambling for resurrection cannot be prevented, provided that we replace $\sigma(\beta_S = 0)$ with $\sigma(\beta_S > 0)$. The interpretation, though, will be slightly different since now CB lending through the discount window will be justified not only for high β_N and low p but also for high β_S. This is because, in the absence of bailouts, the interbank market spread increases with the probability that a bank is insolvent. Collateralized CB loans would shift the losses onto the DIF, which would charge a higher premium than the one in (3.22) by the same argument of equation (3.15). Once again, the less efficient is bank supervision (the bigger is β_S in this case), the more important is the role of the CB.

If incentives for orderly closure are not provided, then separation of insolvent and illiquid banks does not take place, investment in the wasteful continuation of projects cannot be prevented, and the CB may end up lending to an insolvent bank as well.

3.7 Policy Implications and Conclusions

Our analysis allows us to make a number of policy recommendations. First, our study has implications for the optimal design of the interbank market. When market discipline operates well—because financial markets provide the information needed to monitor borrowers and the only source of bank moral hazard is *ex ante* (i.e., bankers must be given incentives to screen their loan applicants)—the interbank market must be unsecured and the LLR may intervene in order to limit the excessive liquidation of assets by illiquid banks. On the other hand, if market discipline is inoperative, and bank monitoring is crucial, then the LLR does not have any role and a secured interbank market can reach efficient allocation either through a repo market or by making the interbank market claims senior.

Second, there are fundamental externalities between the CB, interbank markets, and the banking supervisor. When supervision is not perfect, so that the insolvent bank cannot be detected, interbank spreads are high and there should be a central bank acting as an LLR. By contrast, if supervision is efficient, then interbank markets function well and the CB has only a limited role (if any) to play as a lender of last resort.

Third, although we have abstracted from agency conflicts between the CB, the banking supervisor, and the DIF, our model offers some indications about the optimal design of their functions. If the CB is not in charge of supervision (as in our model), then there is no fear of regulatory capture. Furthermore, the ability of the CB to shift losses from ELA onto the DIF strengthens the incentive of the supervisor to detect and close insolvent banks. Our policy recommendation is therefore to have an independent CB providing ELA under specific circumstances and a separate supervisor acting on behalf of the DIF that bears the losses in the case of any bank's failure.

A fourth implication, connected with the previous point, is that the analysis of the LLR intervention leads to a wider set of issues. The consistent design of an efficient market for liquidity should be based on the interaction between the following five policy instruments: interbank lending (secured or unsecured), closure policy, capital requirement, deposit insurance premiums, and ELA lending terms. These instruments, though controlled by different and independent institutions, should be designed in a consistent fashion.

Finally, conditions for access to ELA should be made known in advance to all interested parties, as already advocated in the "classical" view. This recommendation contrasts with the notion of "constructive ambiguity" often invoked to reduce the moral hazard allegedly associated with a CB safety net. On the contrary, making explicit *ex ante* that ELA will be structured to penalize insolvent banks ($B_S < \beta_L B_L + \beta_N B_N$) provides bankers with the strongest incentive to reduce the probability of insolvency.

To summarize, the traditional doctrine of the lender of last resort has been criticized on at least three important grounds. First, with modern interbank markets, it is not clear whether the CB still has a specific role to play in providing emergency liquidity assistance to individual banks in distress. Second, it is not always possible to distinguish clearly insolvent banks from illiquid banks. Third, the presence of a lender of last resort may generate moral hazard by the banks.

In this paper these three criticisms are taken into account. Moreover, we consider two different forms of moral hazard by banks—on the screening of applicants (before loans are granted), on the monitoring of borrowers (after loans are granted but before they have been repaid)—and we allow for gambling for resurrection by insolvent banks. Our model also explicitly incorporates efficient interbank markets that can provide emergency liquidity assistance to banks that either have sufficient collateral or are ready to pay competitive credit-market rates. Our main finding is that there is a potential role for ELA by the CB, but only when the following conditions are satisfied: supervision is inefficient, so that insolvent banks are not detected; it is very costly to screen sound firms; and interbank market spreads are high. These conditions are more likely to be satisfied during crisis periods. Our model thus offers a theory of ELA in crisis periods without having to assume hypothetical contagion effects. The main superiority of the CB over the interbank lenders stems from its ability to change the priority of claims and thereby lend at lower rates than the interbank market. If banks do not have sufficient collateral to post, then ELA requires additional resources, which strengthens the case for an integrated design of regulatory instruments and ELA.

In the end, unlike its "classical" predecessor, the LLR of the twenty-first century lies at the intersection of monetary policy, supervision and regulation of the banking industry, and organization of the interbank market. The issue is not what rules the LLR should follow but rather what architecture is best for providing liquidity to banks.

3.8 Appendix

Proof of Proposition 3.1. It is obviously optimal to set $B_S = 0$. Then program ($\wp^1$) reduces to

$$\min_{B_N, B_L} p(\beta_N B_N + \beta_L B_L)$$

subject to:

$$p(\beta_N B_N + \beta_L B_L) \geqslant \frac{e_0}{\Delta\beta}, \tag{3.25}$$

$$B_k \geqslant \frac{e_1}{p\delta}, \quad k = L, N. \tag{3.26}$$

The set of solutions depends on whether or not $e_0/\Delta\beta < e_1/\delta$. In the first case there is a unique solution: $B_L = B_N = e_1/p\delta$. In the second case, any feasible couple B_L, B_N such that the constraint (3.25) is binding is a solution. For simplicity we focus on the particular solution $B_L = B_N = e_0/p\Delta\beta$. □

Proof of proposition 3.2. Denote by y_i ($i = 1, 2, 3, 4$) the Lagrange multipliers of the constraints of program ($\wp^2$). The Lagrangian becomes

$$\Lambda = \tilde{\pi} - y_1\left(pB_N - \frac{e_1}{\delta}\right) - y_2\left(pB_L - \frac{e_1}{\delta}\right) - y_3[B_S - p_g(B_L - \lambda)]$$
$$- y_4\left[\beta_N pB_N + \beta_L pB_L - \left(\frac{e_0}{\Delta\beta} + B_S\right)\right]. \tag{3.27}$$

Thus

$$\frac{\partial\Lambda}{\partial B_N} = (1 - \beta_S)\beta_N - y_1 - y_4\beta_N = 0, \tag{3.28}$$

$$\frac{\partial\Lambda}{\partial B_L} = (1 - \beta_S)\beta_L - y_2 - y_4\beta_L + y_3\frac{p_g}{p} = 0, \tag{3.29}$$

$$\frac{\partial\Lambda}{\partial B_S} = \beta_S - y_3 + y_4 = 0. \tag{3.30}$$

Using the last equation, we obtain $y_3 \geqslant \beta_S > 0$.

From the first equation we have $y_1 = (1 - \beta_S - y_4)\beta_N \geqslant 0$, implying $y_4 \leqslant 1$. By the second equation $y_2 = (1 - \beta_S - y_4)\beta_L + y_3 p_g/p \geqslant 0$, which entails $y_2 > 0$ because $y_3 > 0$. Thus the corresponding inequalities are always binding:

$$B_L = \frac{e_1}{p\delta} \quad \text{and} \quad B_S = p_g\left[\frac{e_1}{\delta p} - \lambda\right]. \tag{3.31}$$

Therefore,

$$B_N = \max\left[\frac{e_1}{p\delta}, \frac{1}{p\beta_N}\left(\frac{e_0}{\Delta\beta} + B_S\right) - \frac{\beta_L}{\beta_N}B_L\right]. \tag{3.32}$$

In other words, there are two cases:

(a) $y_4 = 0$ and $y_1 > 0$. Here $B_N = e_1/p\delta = B_L$ and $B_S > 0$ since $\lambda < e_1/\delta p$ and $\rho = \ell$.

(b) $y_1 = 0$ and $y_4 = 1$. Here $p(\beta_N B_N + \beta_L B_L) = e_0/\Delta\beta + B_S$. This allows us to determine B_N ($B_N > B_L$) and $\rho > \ell$. Given

$$B_L = \frac{e_1}{p\delta}, \tag{3.33}$$

the condition $e_1/p\delta > 1/p\beta_N(e_0/\Delta\beta + B_S) - (\beta_L e_1)/(\beta_N \delta p)$ is equivalent to $e_1/\delta > e_0/\Delta\beta + B_S$, thus proving proposition 3.2 and determining

$$B_N = \frac{1}{p\beta_N}\left(\frac{e_0}{\Delta\beta} + p_g\left[\frac{e_1}{\delta p} - \lambda\right]\right) - \frac{\beta_L}{\beta_N}\frac{e_1}{p\delta}. \tag{3.34}$$

$\square$

3.8.1 Calculation of Interest Rate Spreads

Orderly closure. In case (b), $B_N > B_L$ implies that loans must be made with an interest rate spread σ^*, which can be computed from (3.34) and (3.33) as follows:

$$B_N - B_L = \sigma^*\lambda = \frac{1}{p\beta_N}\left(\frac{e_0}{\Delta\beta} + \frac{e_1}{\delta p}(p_g - p) - p_g\lambda\right). \tag{3.35}$$

The interbank market spread when loans are not fully collateralized is determined by the condition of zero expected return. Denoting by ρ the repayment on the loan λI, the condition of zero expected return in the case that insolvent banks are bailed out ($\beta_S = 0$) is

$$\rho p + (1 - p)R_0 = \lambda I, \tag{3.36}$$

implying a spread

$$\sigma(\beta_S = 0) = \frac{\rho}{\lambda I} - 1 = \frac{\lambda I - (1 - p)R_0}{p\lambda I} - 1. \tag{3.37}$$

Gambling for resurrection. Since $p_g < p$, the probability of repayment of an interbank loan when GFR cannot be prevented (p_{GFR}) is smaller than in the case in which GFR can be prevented (p):

$$p_{GFR} \equiv \frac{\beta_S p_g + (1 - \beta_S)\beta_L p}{\beta_S + (1 - \beta_S)\beta_L} < p. \tag{3.38}$$

Thus, the repayment ρ_{GFR} required at the equilibrium of the interbank market is obtained from the zero expected profit constraint,

$$\rho_{GFR} p_{GFR} + (1 - p_{GFR}) R_0 = \lambda I, \qquad (3.39)$$

implying a spread

$$\frac{\rho_{GFR}}{\lambda I} - 1 = \frac{\lambda I - (1 - p_{GFR}) R_0}{\lambda I p_{GFR}} - 1 \equiv \sigma(\beta_S > 0), \qquad (3.40)$$

which is increasing in β_S. When $p = p_g$, the market spread is independent of β_S; $\sigma(\beta_S > 0) = \sigma(\beta_S = 0)$. From (3.38) it follows that $\sigma(\beta_S > 0) > \sigma(\beta_S = 0)$.

References

Aghion, P., P. Bolton, and S. Fries. 1999. Optimal design of bank bailouts: the case of transition economies. *Journal of Institutional and Theoretical Economics* 155:51-70.

Akerlof, G., and P. M. Romer. 1993. Looting: the economic underworld of bankruptcy for profit. *Brooking Papers on Economic Activity* 2:1-60.

Allen, F., and D. Gale. 2000. Financial contagion. *Journal of Political Economy* 108:1-33.

Bagehot, W. 1873. *Lombard Street: A Description of the Money Market*. London: H. S. King.

Bartolini, L., and A. Prati. 2003. The execution of monetary policy: a tale of two central banks. Staff Report 165, Federal Reserve Bank of New York.

Bhattacharya, S., and D. Gale. 1987. Preference shocks, liquidity and central bank policy. In *New Approaches to Monetary Economics* (ed. W. Barnett and K. Singleton). Cambridge University Press.

De Bandt, O., and P. Hartmann. 2002. Systemic risk: a survey. In *Financial Crises, Contagion, and the Lender of Last Resort. A Reader* (ed. C. Goodhart and G. Illing). Oxford University Press.

Delston, R. S., and A. Campbell. 2002. Emergency liquidity financing by central banks: systemic protection or bank bailout? Working Paper, IMF Legal Department and IMF Institute Seminar on Current Developments in Monetary and Financial Law, May 7-17, 2002.

Diamond, D., and P. H. Dybvig. 1983. Bank runs, deposit insurance, and liquidity. *Journal of Political Economy* 91:401-19.

Flannery, M. J. 1996. Financial crises, payment systems problems, and discount window lending. *Journal of Money, Credit and Banking* 28(Part 2):804-24.

Freixas, X., C. Giannini, G. Hoggarth, and F. Soussa. 1999. Lender of last resort: a review of the literature. Financial Stability Review, Bank of England, Issue 7, pp. 151-67.

Furfine, C. H. 2001a. The reluctance to borrow from the Fed. *Economics Letters* 72:209-13.

Furfine, C. H. 2001b. Banks as monitors of other banks: evidence from the overnight Federal funds market. *Journal of Business* 74:33–57.

Goodfriend, M., and R. G. King. 1988. Financial deregulation, monetary policy, and central banking. In *Restructuring Banking and Financial Services in America* (ed. W. Haraf and R. M. Kushmeider). AEI Studies 481, Lanham, MD.

Goodfriend, M., and J. Lacker. 1999. Loan commitment and central bank lending. Federal Reserve Bank of Richmond, Working Paper 99-2.

Goodhart, C. 1987. Why do banks need a central bank? *Oxford Economic Papers* 39:75–89.

Gorton, G., and L. Huang. 2002a. Bank panics and the endogeneity of central banking. National Bureau of Economic Research, Working Paper 9102.

———. 2002b. Banking panics and the origin of central banking. National Bureau of Economic Research, Working Paper 9137.

Issing, O., V. Gaspar, I. Angeloni, and O. Tristiani. 2001. *Monetary Policy in the Euro Area*. Cambridge University Press.

Kahn, C. M., and J. A. C. Santos. 2001. Allocating bank regulatory powers: lender of last resort, deposit insurance and supervision. Bank for International Settlements, Working Paper 102.

Kane, E. J., and A. Demirguc-Kunt. 2001. Deposit insurance around the globe: where does it work? National Bureau of Economic Research, Working Paper 8493.

Kaufman, G. G. 1991. Lender of last resort: a contemporary perspective. *Journal of Financial Services Research* 5:95–110.

Mitchell, J. 2001. Bad debts and the cleaning of banks balance sheets: an application to transition economies. *Journal of Financial Intermediation* 10:1–27.

Padoa-Schioppa, T. 1999. EMU and banking supervision. *International Finance* 2:295–308.

Pagano, M., and T. Jappelli. 1993. Information sharing in credit markets. *Journal of Finance* 48:1693–718.

Penalver, A. 2004. The impact of the IMF preferred creditor status on crisis resolution. Bank of England, Working Paper, January.

Rajan, R. G., and L. Zingales. 2003. Banks and markets: the changing character of European finance. In *The Transformation of the European Financial System* (ed. V. Gaspar, P. Hartmann, and O. Sleijpen). European Central Bank.

Repullo, R. 2000. Who should act as a lender of last resort? An incomplete contract model. *Journal of Money, Credit and Banking* 32:580–605.

Sprague, I. H. 1986. *Bailout: An Insider's Account of Bank Failures and Rescues*. Basic Books.

PART 3
Prudential Regulation and the Management of Systemic Risk

Chapter Four

Macroeconomic Shocks and Banking Supervision

Jean-Charles Rochet

4.1 Introduction

The spectacular banking crises that many countries have experienced in the last twenty years (see, for example, Lindgren et al. (1996) for a list) have led several bankers, politicians, and economists to advocate increasing the pressure of market discipline on banks, as a complement to prudential regulation and supervision. They argue that the increased complexity of financial markets and banking activities have made traditional centralized regulation insufficient, either because it is too crude (like the Basel Accords of 1988) or too complex to be applicable (like the standardized approach proposed by the Basel Committee to account for market risks in the first revision of the Basel Accords). Moreover, the increase in competition, both among banks and with nonbanks, has made it impossible to maintain the status quo, where banks were protected from competition by regulators, in exchange for accepting some restrictions on their activities.

Subordinated debt (SD) proposals (e.g., Wall 1989; Gorton and Santomero 1990; Evanoff 1993; Calomiris 1998, 1999), whereby commercial banks would be required to issue a minimum amount of subordinated debt on a regular basis, have been put forward in order to implement such an increase in the pressure of market discipline. Indeed, if the bank is forced by regulation to issue SD on a regular basis, it will have incentives not to take too much risk since the cost of *issuing* new SD increases when the risk profile of the bank increases (direct market discipline). Similarly, if the capital adequacy requirement of the bank depends negatively on the secondary market price of its SD, the bank will have incentives to limit its risk of failure since the price of SD on *secondary markets* decreases when the risk of failure of the bank increases (indirect market discipline).

However, empirical evidence on the real effectiveness of market discipline is mixed.[1] In particular, Flannery and Sorescu (1996) argue that

---

[1] See, for example, Flannery (1998) and Sironi (2000) and the references therein.

market discipline can only work if absence of government intervention is anticipated. Moreover, the relative performances of market discipline versus supervision have not been analyzed in the context of macroeconomic shocks, the main trigger of banking crises. This is the line of research we examine here. We adapt the model of Holmström and Tirole (1997, 1998) to study in the simplest possible fashion the comparative roles of market discipline and centralized supervision in a context where banks can be hit by macroeconomic shocks.

Our results suggest that the main cause behind the poor management of banking crises may not be the "safety net" per se as argued by many economists, but instead the lack of commitment power of banking authorities, who are typically subject to political pressure. We show that the use of private monitors (market discipline) is a very imperfect means of solving this commitment problem. Instead, we argue in favor of establishing independent and accountable banking supervisors, as has been done for monetary authorities. We also suggest a differential regulatory treatment of banks according to their exposure to macroeconomic shocks. In particular, we argue that banks with a large exposure to macroshocks should be denied the access to emergency liquidity assistance by the central bank. By contrast, banks with a low exposure to macroshocks should have access to the lender of last resort but would face a capital ratio and a deposit insurance premium that increase with this exposure to macroshocks.

The plan of the rest of this article is as follows. In section 4.2, we briefly survey the academic literature on bank supervision and market discipline. In section 4.3, we develop a simple model of moral hazard in banking (inspired by Holmström and Tirole (1997)) that justifies the need for prudential regulation and/or market discipline. In section 4.4 we extend this model by introducing macroeconomic shocks and determine the optimal closure rule for banks in a situation of crisis. We also identify the source of regulatory forbearance: the lack of commitment power by political authorities. In section 4.5 we introduce market discipline and show that it does not solve the problem of regulatory forbearance. Finally, section 4.6 concludes by offering policy recommendations for reforming banking supervisory systems.

4.2   A Brief Survey of the Literature

Following the implementation of the first Basel Accord[2] (Basel Committee 1988), academic research has expended a great deal of effort

---

[2]Initially designed for internationally active banks of G10 countries, it has since been extended to a great number of countries.

in trying to assess the consequences of minimum capital standards on banks' behavior. For example, Furlong and Keeley (1989) show that value-maximizing banks tend to reduce risk taking after a capital requirement is imposed. Using a mean–variance framework, Kim and Santomero (1988) and Rochet (chapter 8) show that improperly chosen risk weights induce banks to select inefficient portfolios, and to undertake regulatory arbitrage activities which might paradoxically result in increased risk taking. These activities are analyzed in detail in Jones (2000).

Given these difficulties, banking regulators have tried to incorporate additional capital requirements for taking into account, for example, interest rate risk and market risk. After trying to impose a complex and ad hoc "standard approach," they have been forced to accept the idea that commercial banks use their own internal models (Value-at-Risk methods) that are validated *ex post* by regulators. Besanko and Kanatas (1993) and Boot and Greenbaum (1993) argue that increased capital requirements may reduce the monitoring incentives of banks and as a result decrease the quality of banks' assets. Blum and Hellwig (1995) study the macroeconomic implications of capital requirements and show that they tend to amplify business cycle fluctuations. Blum (1999) argues that, when dynamic effects are properly taken into account, increasing capital requirements also increase the value of future profits for banks and thus may paradoxically induce banks to take more risks.

Dewatripont and Tirole (1994) provide an incomplete contract approach to capital regulations. In their view, banking authorities are there to represent the interest of small, dispersed depositors who do not have the competence nor the incentives to monitor banks' assets. In their theory, capital requirements are an instrument for allocating control rights to the deposit insurance fund (or to the regulator) when things go badly. They criticize the Basel Accord for being too lenient during booms and too tough during recessions, since outside intervention only depends on the absolute performance of the bank (whereas they argue that it should only depend on its relative performance).

Hellman et al. (2000) argue in favor of reintroducing interest rate ceilings on deposits as a complementary instrument to capital requirements for mitigating moral hazard. By introducing these ceilings, the regulator increases the franchise value of the banks (even if these are not currently binding) which relaxes the moral hazard constraint. Similar ideas are put forward in Caminal and Matutes (2002). Furfine (2000) calibrates a dynamic model of bank behavior with moral hazard and argues that capital regulation strongly influences bank decision making. Milne and Whalley (1998), in a similar framework, argue that audit frequency by the supervisor can be a much more efficient tool for restraining moral hazard than capital requirements.

Many authors have advocated introducing market discipline (e.g., Calomiris 1998, 1999) but empirical evidence is ambiguous (Flannery and Sorescu 1996; Gorton and Santomero 1990). Several studies (Hannan and Hanweck 1988; Ellis and Flannery 1992; Cook and Spellman 1996) conclude that uninsured (and paradoxically even insured) deposits contain risk yields on premiums. The behavior of depositors during banking crises has also been studied. For example, Martinez Peria and Schmukler (2001) study the banking crises in Argentina, Chile, and Mexico in 1994–95 and show that depositors are able to distinguish the "bad" banks and that they "punish" them by withdrawing their deposits. Park and Peristiani (1998) also show that risky banks typically attract fewer depositors. However, d'Amato et al. (1998) find that macroshocks and contagion effects are also important in the explanation of banking crises. The impact of deposit insurance is less clear: Demirguc-Kunt and Detragiache (1997) find that explicit deposit insurance schemes tend to favor the occurrence of systemic risk. Cull (1998) finds that, since 1980, the countries that have established explicit deposit insurance schemes have had a lower increase in their financial depth[3] than the countries which did not. The main explanation they offer is that these deposit insurance schemes benefit from an implicit guarantee by the government, and insurance premiums do not reflect risks accurately. As a result, banks have a tendency to take very risky positions. However, when deposit insurance systems are adopted in a credible fashion (for example, after a crisis or during a period of stability), they tend to have the opposite effect of increasing financial depth.

4.3 A Simple Model of Prudential Regulation without Macroeconomic Shocks

In this section we introduce the benchmark model of banking regulation in the absence of macroeconomic shocks. We consider a static model with two dates ($t = 0, 1$) inspired by Holmström and Tirole[4] (1997), where banks are modeled as delegated monitors à la Diamond (1984). Banks collect a volume D of deposits from the public and invest them, together with their own funds E, in loans to private borrowers. The volume of loans granted by the bank is denoted by L. Since we focus on the role of banks as monitors of private borrowers, we take small depositors out of the picture by assuming that they are perfectly insured by a deposit insurance fund (DIF). We also neglect conflicts of interest inside the bank, i.e., between managers and shareholders. Thus, in the first version of the

---

[3] Financial depth is measured by the ratio M2/GDP.

[4] Holmström and Tirole study the financing needs of nonfinancial firms. We adapt their model to study the financing needs of banks.

model there are only two protagonists:[5] the "banker" (who represents the collective interests of the bank's managers and shareholders) and the DIF (which subrogates the collective interests of retail depositors). The budget constraint of the bank at date 0 is thus

$$D + E = L + P,$$

where P is the deposit insurance premium charged by the DIF. The lending technology has constant returns to scale.[6] This return is binomial: R (per unit) for success and zero for failure. All agents are risk neutral and do not discount future payments (alternatively, the interest rate is normalized to zero). Banking supervision is modeled as a contract between the banker and the DIF.[7] This contract stipulates the volume of loans L and the volume D of deposits that the bank can collect, the level of equity E being taken as given. The specificities of banking are thus captured by three assumptions:

- First we assume that $L > D$, which implies that some fraction of bank loans are financed by deposits.

- Second, we assume that the quality of loans is affected by an unobservable decision of the banker. He can either monitor the loans, in which case they have a "high" probability of repayment p, or "shirk," in which case the loans have a probability of repayment of only $p - \Delta p$. Shirking provides the banker with a private benefit with monetary equivalent B (per unit of investment).

- The social value of the bank exceeds the present value of its investments: we assume that, from the point of view of the economy[8] as a whole, the bank has an additional continuation value of $v \geqslant 0$ per unit of assets, which corresponds, for example, to public good aspects of the bank's activity such as the bank's role in the payments system[9] (Solow 1982).

---

[5]We later introduce sophisticated investors, who play the part of private monitors.

[6]Empirical evidence on the nature of returns to scale in the banking sector is mixed. Moreover, capital requirements are (for a given assets structure) roughly proportional to the size (assets volume) of the bank. Thus, assuming constant returns seems to be a reasonable approximation of reality.

[7]In fact, the contract is signed between the banker and the regulator, who is supposed to represent the interests of the DIF.

[8]There may also be a private continuation value, associated with the banker's non-transferable knowledge of borrowers (relationship banking as in Sharpe (1990) or Degryse and Van Cayseele (2000)). We do not discuss this aspect.

[9]This feature is not crucial: our results also hold when $v = 0$. However, in the next section it allows us to discuss the basic trade-off confronted by banking authorities during crises: rescuing insolvent banks and losing credibility or closing them and creating social disruption.

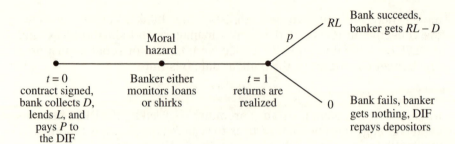

Figure 4.1. The time line of the model.

The time line of the model is summarized in figure 4.1.

At this stage, we need two assumptions on the parameters of our model.

Assumption 4.1. $(p - \Delta p)R + B + v < 1 < pR + v$.

Assumption 4.1 means that loans have a positive social value only when they are monitored. This assumption implies in particular that $R > B/\Delta p$.

Assumption 4.2. $p\left(R - \dfrac{B}{\Delta p}\right) < 1$.

As explained below, assumption 4.2 implies that banks need capital. If it was not satisfied, banks could be completely externally financed.

The optimal contract (L^*, D^*) maximizes expected social surplus under two constraints. The DIF has to break even and the banker must be given incentives to monitor the loans. Denoting by P the premium paid by the bank to the DIF, and using the budget constraint of the bank at date 0, we see that the DIF breaks even if and only if

$$P = D + E - L \geqslant (p - \Delta p)(1 - p)D$$

or

$$L \leqslant pD + E. \tag{4.1}$$

Similarly, the incentive-compatibility constraint is

$$P(RL - D) \geqslant (p - \Delta p)(RL - D) + BL,$$

which can be rewritten as

$$D \leqslant \left(R - \frac{B}{\Delta p}\right)L. \tag{4.2}$$

The optimal contract (L, D) is thus a solution of

$$
\begin{cases}
\max L[pR + v - 1], & \\
L \leqslant pD + E & (4.1), \\
D \leqslant \left(R - \dfrac{B}{\Delta p}\right)L & (4.2).
\end{cases}
$$

Proposition 4.1. *In the absence of macroeconomic shocks, the optimal organization of the banking sector can be implemented by a combination of two instruments:*

- *A deposit insurance system financed by (fair) risk-based premiums:*

$$
P = (1 - p)D.
$$

- *A capital adequacy requirement limiting banks' lending to a certain multiple of their equity:*

$$
L \leqslant \frac{E}{k}, \quad \text{where } k = p\frac{B}{\Delta p} - (pR - 1) > 0.
$$

Proof. The optimal organization of the banking sector is obtained by solving the above program. The solution is obtained by saturating the two constraints. In particular,

$$
D^* = \left(R - \frac{B}{\Delta p}\right)L^*.
$$

Plugging this into the other constraint, we obtain

$$
L^*\left[1 - \left(R - \frac{B}{\Delta p}\right)\right] = E.
$$

These two conditions characterize the optimal contract (D^*, L^*).

We now show that this contract can be implemented by actuarial deposit insurance premiums and a capital requirement $E/L \geqslant k$. Indeed, the shareholders' value equals

$$
S = p[RL - D],
$$

where $L = D + E - P = pD + E$ (since deposit insurance is actuarially priced).

Therefore, shareholders' value can also be written as

$$
S = (pR - 1)L + E,
$$

which is increasing in L. Thus if the bank is subject to a capital requirement $L \leqslant E/k$, shareholders will select the maximum possible volume of loans $L = E/k$. By choosing in turn the appropriate level for the capital ratio, i.e.,

$$k = p\frac{B}{\Delta p} - (pR - 1),$$

the bank regulator will implement the optimal allocation (D^*, L^*). $\quad\square$

Notice that this optimal allocation can also be implemented by a private arrangement between the DIF and the banker: the DIF offers a deposit insurance contract with a fair premium P and stipulates that the bank's assets L should not exceed E/k. The difference between private and public arrangements only appears if macroshocks are introduced. This is what we do in section 4.4.

4.4 How to Deal with Macroeconomic Shocks?

Protection of depositors is not the only preoccupation of bank supervisors: they also care about what may lead to the instability of the financial system as a whole (systemic risk). The theoretical literature has insisted a lot on a first cause of instability, namely bank runs, provoked by a sudden loss of confidence of depositors in the banks' safety. These bank runs were, for example, very common in the United States before the creation of the Fed. However, since the implementation of deposit insurance systems in most countries, such bank runs have become much less frequent, and banking authorities are now more concerned about systemic risk. One strand of the literature (e.g., chapters 5 and 7) has examined the possible mechanisms of contagion, i.e., propagation of one bank failure to other banks. We focus here on another source of systemic risk, namely *systematic* risk, generated by a common exposure of banks to macroeconomic shocks such as recessions, asset markets crashes, and the like. We introduce these macroshocks by assuming, as in Holmström and Tirole[10] (1998), that at an interim date $t = \frac{1}{2}$ each bank[11] suffers with some probability q from a liquidity shock: continuation can only occur if an additional amount of cash ρL is injected into the bank. We interpret this shock as resulting from a nondiversifiable event, e.g., a recession: the projects financed by the bank need a further injection of cash, otherwise they lose all value. We assume that the probability q is

---

[10]In Holmström and Tirole (1998) the cause of the liquidity shock can be microeconomic (i.e., diversifiable) or macroeconomic. We focus here on the second case.

[11]Holmström and Tirole (1998) do not consider banks but instead nonfinancial firms. Moreover, they take ρ to be a random variable, but assume it is identically distributed across firms. We assume instead that ρ is deterministic, but varies across banks.

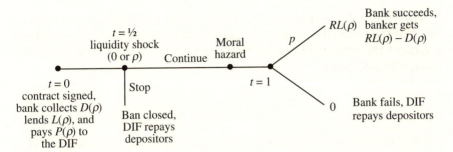

Figure 4.2. The time line in the presence of macroshocks.

sufficiently small for bank lending to remain profitable even if the risk of recession is taken into account. Specifically, we have the following assumption.

Assumption 4.3. $(1 - q)pR > 1$.

Notice that all banks are hit simultaneously but ρ differs across banks. This parameter ρ is known *ex ante* by the supervisor: it measures the bank's exposure to macroshocks.

The new time line is indicated by the figure 4.2.

Confronted with the possibility of such macroshocks, the regulators now have to consider the situation of the banking system as a whole. We assume that there is a continuum of banks, which for simplicity only differ through their exposure[12] ρ to macroshocks. ρ is distributed according to a continuous distribution with continuous distribution function F. $F(\hat{\rho})$ can thus be interpreted as the proportion of banks for which $\rho \leqslant \hat{\rho}$.

Since ρ, the macro-exposure of each bank, is known *ex ante* by the supervisors, the optimal regulation contract can be conditioned on it. Moreover, the supervisors may decide to close a bank at $t = \frac{1}{2}$ in the case of a recession, again conditionally on ρ. We denote by ρ the probability that the bank is allowed to continue in the case of recession. If a bank is closed, its assets are liquidated[13] and its depositors are compensated by the DIF. A regulation contract is described by a continuation probability $x(\rho)$, a volume of loans $L(\rho)$, and a volume of deposits $D(\rho)$. For the moment, we adopt a normative view point and solve for the (*ex ante*) optimal contract without specifying the way in which it is implemented (this is done in the next section).

---

[12]This exposure results, in fact, from policy decisions by banks, and therefore should be endogenized. We leave this for further research. In this paper, the distribution of ρ is taken as exogenous.

[13]For simplicity, we assume that the liquidation value of the bank's asset at $t = \frac{1}{2}$ is zero.

Since moral hazard takes place after the liquidity shock, it is easy to see that the optimal volume of deposits still corresponds to the maximal payment that can be obtained from bankers while preserving incentive compatibility, namely

$$D(\rho) = \left(R - \frac{B}{\Delta p}\right)L(\rho). \tag{4.3}$$

We rule out cross subsidies between banks or between the banking sector and the government. Thus, taking into account the expected cost of liquidity injections, the budget constraint of the bank at date 0 can then be written

$$L(\rho)\left[1 - \{1 - q + qx(\rho)\}p\left(R - \frac{B}{\Delta p}\right) + q\rho x(\rho)\right] = E. \tag{4.4}$$

This budget constraint takes into account the unconditional probability of continuation of the bank at $t = \frac{1}{2}$ (i.e., $1 - q + qx(\rho)$) and the liquidity injection needed in the case of a recession (i.e., $\rho x(\rho)$).

The social surplus W is the sum of two terms:

- the expected net surplus generated by bank lending,

- the social value of the banking system as a whole, captured by a function[14] V of the total assets $\bar{L}$ of the banks at the interim date $t = \frac{1}{2}$.

Therefore,

$$W = \int_0^{+\infty} \{(1 - q)qR + qx(\rho)(pR - \rho) - 1\}L(\rho)\,\mathrm{d}F + V(\bar{L}), \tag{4.5}$$

where

$$\bar{L} = \int_0^{+\infty} L(\rho)\{1 - q + qx(\rho)\}\,\mathrm{d}F. \tag{4.6}$$

The optimal regulatory contract is obtained by choosing $x(\cdot)$ and $L(\cdot)$ that maximize W under the budget constraint (4.4) of each bank.

Proposition 4.2. *In the presence of macroeconomic shocks, the optimal regulatory contract is characterized by a separation of banks into two categories:*

---

[14]This generalizes the constant v introduced in section 4.3 in the case of a single bank. In what follows, v is replaced by $V'(\bar{L})$, the marginal value of letting any given bank continue at $t = \frac{1}{2}$.

- *The banks for which $\rho \leqslant \rho^* = 1/(1-q)$ (small exposure to macroshocks) are rescued in the case of a crisis, but they are subject to a higher capital ratio (than in the absence of macroshocks). This capital ratio increases with their exposure ρ to macroshocks:*

$$k_1(\rho) = \frac{E}{L(\rho)} = 1 - p\left(R - \frac{B}{\Delta p}\right) + q\rho. \qquad (4.7)$$

- *The banks for which $\rho > \rho^*$ (large exposure to macroshocks) are closed in the case of a crisis and are subject to a flat capital ratio:*

$$k_0 = \frac{E}{L_0} = 1 - (1-q)p\left(R - \frac{B}{\Delta p}\right). \qquad (4.8)$$

Proof of proposition 4.2. Given that there is a separate budget constraint for each ρ (condition (4.4)), we can solve for $L(\rho)$ and maximize with respect to x the following quantity:

$$U(x,\rho) = \frac{(1 - q + qx)(pR + V'(\bar{L})) - qx\rho - 1}{1 - (1 - q + qx)p(R - B/\Delta p) + qx\rho}.$$

(E has been omitted because it only appears multiplicatively and therefore does not influence the optimal value of $x(\rho)$.) The expression of U can be simplified as follows:

$$U(x,p) = -1 + \frac{(1 - q + qx)(V'(\bar{L}) + pB/\Delta p)}{1 + qx\rho - (1 - q + qx)p(R - B/\Delta p)}$$

$$= -1 + \frac{V'(\bar{L}) + pB/\Delta p}{(1 + qx\rho)/(1 - q + qx) - p(R - B/\Delta p)}.$$

For a given ρ, this expression is monotonic in x: increasing if $\rho < 1/(1 - q)$, decreasing if $\rho > 1/(1 - q)$. Thus the optimal regulatory contract involves

$$x(\rho) = \begin{cases} 1 & \text{if } \rho \leqslant \dfrac{1}{1-q} \equiv \rho^*, \\ 0 & \text{if } \rho > \rho^*. \end{cases}$$

The corresponding capital ratios are deduced from constraint (4.4):

$$k(\rho) \equiv \frac{E}{L(\rho)} = 1 - \{1 - q + qx(\rho)\}p\left(R - \frac{B}{\Delta p}\right) + q\rho x(\rho),$$

by replacing $x(\rho)$ by its optimal value found above. $\qquad \square$

Proposition 4.2 adopts a normative viewpoint, i.e., it characterizes the optimal closure rule for banks in the presence of macroeconomic shocks. We now adopt a positive viewpoint and compare the optimal closure rule with the effective closure rules implied by two institutional arrangements: pure private contracting between the banks and the DIF on the one hand, and pure public supervision on the other hand.

Proposition 4.3. *A purely private organization of the banking sector leads to too many closures in the event of a recession: indeed, a bank is closed whenever*

$$\rho \leqslant \rho_0 = p\left(R - \frac{B}{\Delta p}\right) < \rho^*.$$

Proof. In the absence of a public intervention, the only way in which a bank can obtain liquidity at the interim date $t = \frac{1}{2}$ is by borrowing from other banks (or issuing new CDs). The maximum amount of cash that can be raised in the way is equal to the collateral value of the bank's assets, i.e., the maximal expected payment that can be obtained from bankers while preserving incentive compatibility:

$$\rho_0 \equiv p\left(R - \frac{B}{\Delta p}\right)L.$$

Assumption 4.2 states that $\rho_0 < 1$, which implies that $\rho_0 < \rho^* = 1/(1 - q)$. Therefore, all the banks with an intermediate exposure to macroshocks ($\rho \in \,]\rho_0, \rho^*[$) should be allowed to continue, but would be closed in the absence of a public intervention. $\qquad\Box$

Proposition 4.3 shows the need for the CB acting as an LLR: by providing liquidity assistance to the banks characterized by $\rho \in \,]\rho_0, \rho^*[$, the CB improves upon the purely private organization discussed in proposition 4.3. However, there is also a problem with public intervention. Indeed, once a bank has granted a certain volume of loans, its social continuation value is positive as long as $\rho < pR + V'(\bar{L}) \equiv \rho_1$, which is larger than $\rho^* = 1/(1 - q)$ by assumption 4.3. If the bank authorities are subject to political pressure, it will be impossible for them to limit liquidity assistance to the banks for which $\rho \leqslant \rho^*$, since it is *ex post* optimal to also let all the banks for which $\rho \in \,]\rho^*, \rho_1[$ continue. This not only implies too few closures (regulatory forbearance) but also overinvestment at $t = 0$, since bankers anticipate this forbearance. This is explained in the next proposition.

Proposition 4.4. *Prudential regulation by a public authority leads to forbearance: all banks for which $\rho \leqslant \rho_1$ receive liquidity support during* a recession. *In this case, the only thing regulatory authorities can do is to impose on these banks a flat capital ratio:*[15]

$$k_0 = 1 - (1 - q)p\left(R - \frac{B}{\Delta p}\right).$$

Comparing with the optimal contract characterized in proposition 4.2, we see that this leads to overinvestment by these banks, who thus exploit this anticipated regulatory forbearance.

Proof of proposition 4.4. We have already seen that it is *ex post* optimal for the government to provide liquidity assistance to all banks for which $\rho \leqslant \rho_1 = pR + V'(\bar{L})$ (positive social continuation value). When $\rho < \rho_0$ (solvent banks) this liquidity support is fully collateralized and the central bank does not lose any money. However, when $\rho \in]\rho_0, \rho_1]$, the central bank loses $(\rho - \rho_0)L$ in expectation, but seizes maximum income $(R - B/\Delta p)L = D$ in the case of success. From the DIF point of view the cost of deposit insurance becomes

$$[(1 - q)(1 - p) + q]D.$$

The associated capital ratio is

$$k_0 = \frac{E}{L} = 1 + \frac{P - D}{L} = 1 - (1 - q)p\left(R - \frac{B}{\Delta p}\right).$$

It is smaller than the efficient capital ratio characterized in proposition 4.2:

$$k_0 < k_1(\rho) = 1 - p\left(R - \frac{B}{\Delta p}\right) + q\rho.$$

This is because $\rho > \rho_0 = p(R - B/\Delta p)$. Thus there is overinvestment. Finally, notice that, from an *ex ante* view point, the marginal social value of loans made by a bank for which $\rho \in]\rho_0, \rho_1]$ is equal to $(\rho_1 - \rho)$, which is nonnegative. This means that it would be inefficient *ex ante* to restrict further the volume of credit granted by such banks. Thus the government cannot compensate for its lack of commitment power by an increase of capital ratios. $\square$

We see this as the fundamental problem faced by prudential supervision: public intervention is needed[16] in order to avoid too many bank

---

[15]Banks for which $\rho \leqslant \rho_0$ are subject to the same capital ratio as in proposition 4.2.

[16]Holmström and Tirole (1998) show that, when ρ corresponds to a diversifiable shock, private arrangements between firms and banks (namely private lines of credit) can be enough to implement the (second best) optimum. However, when there are macroshocks, public provision of liquidity is needed.

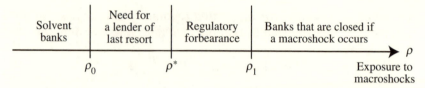

Figure 4.3. The fundamental problem faced by prudential supervision.

closures, but since governments are subject to commitment problems, public supervision alone leads to too few bank closures and overinvestment. By analogy with Dewatripont and Maskin (1995), we call this a soft budget constraint (SBC) phenomenon.[17] This problem is summarized by figure 4.3.

We discuss in section 4.6 a possible organization of banking supervision that could solve this problem. For the moment, we see how introducing market discipline by private investors modifies the picture.

4.5 Is Market Discipline Useful?

Proponents of market discipline for banks have argued that private investors might have to play a part complementary to public supervisors in the monitoring of commercial banks. In order to discuss the potential monitoring role of private investors, we now introduce an external monitor, who can reduce the unit private benefit of commercial bankers from B to $b < B$ by exerting a monitoring activity of unit cost y. The regulation contract has to stipulate the amount D_M that the external monitor is required to invest at $t = 0$ (interpreted as subordinated debt) and the repayment $R_M L$ he receives in the case of success.

The optimal regulation contract for a bank with a macro-exposure ρ is thus obtained by maximizing

$$W(\rho) = L\{(1 - q)\rho + qx(\rho_1 - \rho) - 1 - y\}. \tag{4.9}$$

The policy variables are $D \geqslant 0$, $L \geqslant 0$, $D_M \geqslant 0$, $R_M \geqslant 0$, and $x \in [0, 1]$. They have to satisfy the following constraints:

$$L[1 + qx\rho] - E - D_M \leqslant (1 - q + qx)pD, \tag{4.10}$$

$$\{(1 - q + qx)pR_M - y\}L \geqslant D_M, \tag{4.11}$$

$$R_M \geqslant y/\Delta p, \tag{4.12}$$

$$(R - R_M)L - D \geqslant bL/\Delta p, \tag{4.13}$$

where as before $\rho_1 = pR + V'(\bar{L})$.

---

[17]Notice, however, that the mechanism that underlies the SBC in Dewatripont and Maskin (1995) is different.

The objective function of this program is the net social surplus $W(\rho)$ produced by the bank, modified to take into account the cost of monitoring yL. Condition (4.10) is the breakeven constraint for the DIF, modified to take into account the amount D_M brought by market investors. Condition (4.11) is the participation constraint of these market investors. Conditions (4.12) and (4.13) are respectively the incentive-compatibility constraint of market investors and that of the banker.

Again all the constraints bind at the optimum. Thus,

$$R_M = \frac{y}{\Delta p}, \qquad D = \left(R - \frac{y+b}{\Delta p}\right)L, \qquad D_M = \left[(1-q+qx)p\frac{y}{\Delta p} - y\right]L.$$

Plugging this into the budget constraint (4.10), we see that the problem reduces to

$$\begin{cases} \max L\{(1-q)\rho_1 + qx(\rho_1 - \rho) - 1 - y\}, \\ \text{under the constraint} \\ L\left\{1 - (1-q+qx)p\left(R - \frac{b}{\Delta p}\right) + q\rho x + y\right\} \leqslant E. \end{cases}$$

The solution of this program is given in the next proposition.

Proposition 4.5. *The presence of external monitors increases the optimal closure threshold:*

$$\rho^*(y) = \frac{1+y}{1-q} > \rho^*.$$

In the absence of commitment power by the government, the effective closure threshold remains unchanged at ρ_1. Capital requirements are then reduced, due to the decrease in bank moral hazard, but the impact on social surplus is ambiguous.

Proof of proposition 4.5. Using the same reasoning as in the proof of proposition 4.2, the optimal $x(\rho)$ can be obtained by maximizing the expression,

$$U_1(x,\rho) = \frac{(1-q)\rho_1 + qx(\rho_1 - \rho) - 1 - y}{1 - (1-q+qx)p(R - B/\Delta p) + qx\rho - y},$$

which can be simplified into

$$U_1(x,\rho) = -1 + \frac{V'(\bar{L}) + pb/\Delta p}{(1 + qx\rho + y)/(1 - q + qx - p)(R - B/\Delta p)}.$$

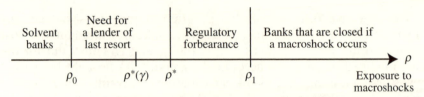

Figure 4.4. The impact of market discipline
(ρ^* is increased to $\rho^*(\gamma)$ but ρ_1 is unchanged).

For a given ρ, this expression is monotonic in x: increasing if

$$\rho < 1 + \frac{\gamma}{1-q},$$

decreasing if

$$\rho > 1 + \frac{\gamma}{1-q}.$$

Thus the optimal closure threshold is

$$\rho^*(\gamma) = 1 + \frac{\gamma}{1-q}.$$

However, if the government cannot commit, the effective closure threshold is still $\rho_1 = pR + V'(\bar{L})$. The capital requirement becomes

$$k_0' = 1 - (1-q)p\left(R - \frac{b}{\Delta p}\right) < k_0.$$

It is thus reduced by market discipline. However, since market discipline is costly, the overall impact on social welfare is ambiguous. □

The impact of market discipline is summarized in figure 4.4.

Therefore, if we compare it to the optimal contract with commitment, the use of an external monitor is not necessarily beneficial. More importantly, market discipline does not completely solve the commitment problem, except if the external monitor cannot exert pressure on politicians. Suppose indeed that the market debt D_M is held by foreign investors, as suggested in Calomiris (1999), and suppose that these foreign investors cannot lobby[18] the national regulator. In this case, the commitment problem of the latter will be reduced, since the *ex post* socially optimal continuation threshold will be reduced to $\rho_1' = \rho_1 - pR_F$, where R_F is the promised repayment to foreign investors in the case of

---

[18]This is probably questionable, given the internationalization of capital markets and the huge size of the major investors, who are typically multinational firms.

success. An adequate choice of R_F will give $\rho'_1 = \rho^*(y)$. Therefore, the main interest of using foreign investors as external monitors of national banks is to solve the commitment problem of the regulator. By pledging future income to outsiders (who cannot lobby political authorities), the regulator becomes tougher. However, the expected surplus is not necessarily increased, especially if foreign investors are characterized by high monitoring costs y and low monitoring effectiveness $B - b$.

An alternative solution to the commitment problem exists, which does not have all these drawbacks: requiring independency and accountability of banking supervisors, as has been done for monetary policy. We now conclude by examining how this reform could be organized, taking into account the need for an LLR.

4.6 Policy Recommendations for Macroprudential Regulation

We conclude this paper by offering some reflections on the ways in which the optimal contract characterized in section 4.4 can be implemented by an adequate design of the supervisory–regulatory system. As we saw in section 4.4, two crucial elements are needed:

- Intervention of the CB as an LLR for providing liquidity assistance, in the case of a recession, to the banks characterized by $\rho \leqslant \rho^*$.

- Preventing extension of this liquidity assistance to the banks characterized by $\rho^* < \rho \leqslant \rho_1$, for which *ex post* continuation value is positive (from a social point of view) but bailing them out would be welfare decreasing from an *ex ante* perspective.

We claim that these two elements can only be reconciled if the CB is made independent from political authorities, as has been done for monetary policy. To ensure accountability of the CB in its role as an LLR, a precise agenda has to be defined *ex ante*, namely providing liquidity assistance to a subset of banks (those for which $\rho \leqslant \rho^*$) that would be backed by the supervisors (or the DIF). To ensure that the DIF selects properly the banks that can be assisted, we require that the liquidity loans granted by the CB (acting as an LLR) would be backed by the DIF. In other words, those loans would be insured by the DIF: the CB would be completely protected against credit risk and no taxpayer money would be involved. The next proposition summarizes the proposed organization of the regulatory system.

Proposition 4.6. *The optimal contract (characterized in proposition 4.2) can be implemented by the following organization of the regulatory system:*

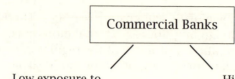

Commercial Banks

Low exposure to macroshocks ($\rho \leqslant \rho^*$)

High exposure to to macroshocks ($\rho > \rho^*$)

- Have access to emergency liquidity assistance by the central bank

- Pay a deposit insurance premium that increases with ρ:

$$P(\rho) = D\left(1 - p + pq\frac{\rho}{\rho_0}\right)$$

- Are subject to a capital requirement that increases with ρ:

$$k_1(\rho) = 1 - \rho_0 + q\rho$$

- Have no access to emergency liquidity assistance by the central bank

- Pay a flat deposit insurance:

$$P_0 = D(1 - p + pq)$$

- Are subject to a flat capital requirement:

$$k_0 = 1 - (1 - q)\rho_0$$

Figure 4.5. The optimal management of bank closures.

- *For each commercial bank, the supervisory authorities evaluate ρ, the bank's exposure to macroeconomic shocks, which determines the treatment of the bank by regulators.*

- *Banks with a small exposure, $\rho \leqslant \rho^*$, are backed by the DIF and, in the case of a macroshock, receive liquidity assistance by the CB. They face a capital adequacy requirement $k(\rho)$ and a deposit insurance premium $P(\rho)$ that increase with ρ:*

$$k(\rho) = 1 - p\left(R - \frac{b}{\Delta p}\right) + q\rho,$$

$$P(\rho) = D\left(1 - p + pq\frac{\rho}{\rho_0}\right).$$

Banks with a large exposure to macroshocks ($\rho > \rho^*$) are not backed by the DIF: they do not receive liquidity assistance by the CB. They face a capital requirement k_0 and a deposit insurance premium P_0 that do not depend on ρ:

$$k_0 = 1 - (1 - q)p\left(R - \frac{b}{\Delta p}\right),$$

$$P_0 = D(1 - p + pq).$$

The LLR activities of the CB are made independent from political powers: the CB exclusively provides liquidity assistance to the banks that are backed by supervisory authorities. Central bank loans are fully insured by the DIF.

This organization is summarized by figure 4.5.

References

D'Amato, L., E. Grubisik, and A. Powell. 1998. Contagion, bank fundamentals or macroeconomic shocks. Bank of Argentina Discussion Paper.

Basel Committee. 1988. International convergence of capital measurement and capital standards. Basel Committee on Banking Supervision 4 (July). Basel, Switzerland: Bank for International Settlements.

Besanko, D., and G. Kanatas. 1996. The regulation of bank capital: do capital standards promote bank safety? *Journal of Financial Intermediation* 5:160-83.

Blum, J. 1999. Do capital adequacy requirements reduce risk in banking? *Journal of Banking and Finance* 23:755-71.

Blum, J., and M. Hellwig. 1995. The macroeconomic implications of capital adequacy requirements for banks. *European Economic Review* 39:739-49.

Boot, A., and S. Greenbaum. 1993. Bank regulation, reputation and rents: theory and policy implications. In *Capital Markets and Financial Intermediation* (ed. C. Mayer and X. Vives). Cambridge University Press.

Calomiris, C. W. 1998. Blueprints for a new global financial architecture. (Available at www.house.gov/jec/imf/blueprint.htm.)

——. 1999. Building an incentive-compatible safety net. *Journal of Banking and Finance* 23:1499-519.

Caminal, R., and C. Matutes. 2002. Market power and banking failures. *International Journal of Industrial Organization* 20:1341-61.

Cook, D. O., and L. J. Spellman. 1996. Firm and guarantor risk, risk contagion and the interfirm spread among insured deposits. *Journal of Financial and Quantitative Analysis* 31:265-81.

Cull, R. 1998. The effect of deposit insurance on financial depth: a cross-country analysis. World Bank Working Paper Series 1875.

Degryse, H., and P. Van Cayseele. 2000. Relationship lending within a bank-based system: evidence from European small business data. *Journal of Financial Intermediation* 9:90-109.

Demirgüç-Kunt, A., and E. Detragiache. 1997. The determinants of banking crises: evidence from developed and developing countries. Policy Research Working Paper 1828. Washington, DC: The World Bank.

Dewatripont, M., and E. Maskin. 1995. Credit and efficiency in centralized and decentralized economies. *Review of Economic Studies* 62:541-55.

Dewatripont, M., and J. Tirole. 1994. *The Prudential Regulation of Banks*. Cambridge, MA: MIT Press.

Diamond, D. 1984. Financial intermediation and delegated monitoring. *Review of Economic Studies* 51:393–414.

Ellis, D., and M. Flannery. 1992. Does the debt market assess large banks' risk? *Journal of Monetary Economics* 30:481–502.

Evanoff, D. D. 1993. Preferred sources of market discipline. *Yale Journal of Regulation* 10:347–67.

Flannery, M. J. 1998. Using market information in prudential bank supervision: a review of the U.S. empirical evidence. *Journal of Money, Credit and Banking* 30:273–305.

Flannery, M. J., and S. M. Sorescu. 1996. Evidence of bank market discipline in subordinated debenture yields: 1983–1992. *Journal of Finance* 51:1347–77.

Furfine, C. 2000. Evidence on the response of US banks to changes in capital requirements. Working Paper 88. Basel, Switzerland: Bank for International Settlements.

Furlong, F., and M. Keeley. 1989. Bank capital regulation and risk taking: a note. *Journal of Banking and Finance* 13:883–91.

Gorton, G., and A. Santomero. 1990. Market discipline and bank subordinated debt. *Journal of Money, Credit and Banking* 22:119–28.

Goodfriend, M., and J. Lacker. 1999. Loan commitment and central bank lending. Federal Reserve Bank of Richmond, Working Paper 99-2.

Hannan, T. H., and G. A. Hanweck. 1988. Bank insolvency risk and the market for large certificates of deposit. *Journal of Money, Credit and Banking* 20:203–11.

Hellman, T. F., K. C. Murdock, and J. E. Stiglitz. 2000. Liberalization, moral hazard in banking, and prudential regulation: are capital requirements enough? *American Economic Review* 90:147–65.

Holmström, B., and J. Tirole. 1997. Financial intermediation, loanable funds, and the real sector. *Quarterly Journal of Economics* 112:663–92.

———. 1998. Private and public supply of liquidity. *Journal of Political Economy* 106:1–40.

Jones, D. J. 2000. Emerging problems with the Basel capital accord: regulatory capital arbitrage and related issues. *Journal of Banking and Finance* 21:491–507.

Kim, D., and A. Santomero. 1988. Risk in banking and capital regulation. *Journal of Finance* 43:1219–33.

Lindgren, C.-J., G. Garcia, and M. Saal. 1996. *Bank Soundness and Macroeconomic Policy.* Washington, DC: IMF.

Martinez Peria, M. S., and S. L. Schmukler. 2001. Do depositors punish banks for "bad" behavior? Market discipline, deposit insurance and banking crises. *Journal of Finance* 56:1029–51.

Milne, A., and E. Whalley. 1998. Bank capital regulation and incentives for risk taking. Discussion Paper, City University Business School, London, U.K.

Park, S., and S. Peristiani. 1998. Market discipline by thrift depositors. *Journal of Money, Credit and Banking* 26:439–59.

Sharpe, S. 1990. Asymmetric information, bank lending and implicit contracts: a stylized model of customer relationships. *Journal of Finance* 45:1069–85.

Sironi, A. 2000. An analysis of European bank SND issues and its implications
   for the design of a mandatory subordinated debt policy. *Journal of Financial
   Services Research* 19:233-66.

Solow, R. 1982. On the lender of last resort. In *Financial Crises: Theory, History
   and Policy* (ed. C. P. Kindleberger and J. P. Laffarge), pp. 237-48. Cambridge
   University Press.

Wall, L. D. 1989. A plan for reducing future deposit insurance losses: puttable
   subordinated debt. Federal Reserve Bank of Richmond *Economic Review*
   (July/August), pp. 2-17.

Chapter Five

Interbank Lending and Systemic Risk

Jean-Charles Rochet and Jean Tirole

Systemic risk refers to the propagation of an agent's economic distress to other agents linked to that agent through financial transactions. Systemic risk is a serious concern in manufacturing, where trade credit links producers through a chain of obligations,[1] and in the insurance industry through the institution of reinsurance. The anxiety about systemic risk is perhaps strongest among bank executives and regulators. For, banks' mutual claims, which, by abuse of terminology, we will gather under the generic name of "interbank loans" or "interbank transactions," have grown substantially in recent years. These include intraday debits on payment systems, overnight and term interbank lending in the Fed funds market or its equivalents, and contingent claims such as interest rate and exchange rate derivatives in OTC markets. To the extent that interbank loans are neither collateralized nor insured against, a bank's failure may trigger a chain of subsequent failures and therefore force the central bank to intervene to nip the contagion process in the bud. Indeed, it is widely believed by banking experts (and by interbank markets!) that industrialized countries adhere to a "too-big-to-fail" (TBTF) policy of protecting uninsured depositors of large insolvent banks, whose failure could propagate through the financial system, although authorities (rationally) refuse to corroborate this belief and like to refer to a policy of "constructive ambiguity" when discussing their willingness to intervene.[2] Interbank transactions also reduce the transparency of a bank's

---

[1]Trade credit has some specificities relative to, say, interbank lending. In particular, the value of collateral (the wares in trade credit) is usually much larger for the creditor (the supplier) than for other parties. Kiyotaki and Moore (1995) develop an interesting model of decentralized trade credit and study propagation in a chain of supplier–buyer relationships. The mechanics of their model (which is not based on peer monitoring) are different from those presented here. Also, Kiyotaki and Moore focus on propagation while, from our interbank lending slant, we are particularly concerned with the impact of interbank lending on solvency and liquidity ratios and on the compatibility between decentralized trading and centralized prudential control, and with the too-big-to-fail policy.

[2]While this work emphasizes contagion in the banking system through interbank transactions, financial distress may alternatively propagate through an informational

balance- and off-balance-sheet data and complicate the measurement of a bank's actual liquidity and solvency ratios for prudential purposes.

Systemic risk is a concern only in a decentralized environment in which banks incur credit risk in their mutual transactions. Banking regulators have various means at their disposal to prevent systemic risk. Traditionally, governments have implicitly insured most of the interbank claims by rescuing distressed banks through discount loans, the facilitation of purchase-and-assumptions, nationalizations, and so forth. It is, however, widely recognized that such policies do not provide proper incentives for interbank monitoring and may lead to substantial cross-subsidies from healthy banks to frail ones through a government-mediated mechanism. This concern about moral hazard has recently led regulators and politicians to consider ways of reducing the government's exposure to bank failures.

An alternative method of prevention of systemic risk would consist in *centralizing banks' liquidity management*. A case in point is a payment system in which the central bank acts as a counterparty and guarantees the finality of payments. To the extent that the central bank bears the credit risk if the sending bank defaults, the default cannot propagate to the receiving bank through the payment system. Similarly, the Fed funds market could be organized as an anonymous double auction (in which the central bank could participate to manage global liquidity), in which each bank would trade with the central bank rather than with other banks. The central bank would then have better control over interbank positions and would further prevent systemic risk on the interbank market. Last, bank transactions on derivative markets could be protected through sufficient collateral so that, again, banks would not grant each other credit. Whether the government is affected by a bank failure in a centralized system depends on the constraints it puts on banks, but, in any case, centralization, like insurance, eliminates systemic risk. Unsurprisingly, reformers tend to respond to the current concerns about systemic risk and moral hazard with projects emphasizing a reduction in interbank linkages, such as strict collateral requirements in settlement systems, qualitative reductions in the volume of interbank lending, and restrictions on banks' participation in derivative markets.

Unfortunately, reforms cannot currently be guided by a clear conceptual framework. Economic theorists have devoted little attention

---

channel. Namely, in a situation in which financial markets are imperfectly informed about the central bank's willingness to bail out failing banks, the central bank's refusal to support a troubled bank may signal that other banks may not be supported in the future either and may thus precipitate their collapse (although the collapse is likely to occur in practice through runs in the interbank market, the existence of interbank lending is not required for this argument).

to systemic risk.[3] The purpose of this paper is to provide a stylized framework in which some of the issues surrounding systemic risk can start being analyzed.[4] Our goal is to analyze whether one can build an articulate story for why the TBTF policy may exist in the first place, and to study how one might protect central banks while preserving the flexibility of the current interbank market.

The premise of our work is that the current system of interbank linkages suffers from its hybrid nature. On the one hand, banks engage in largely decentralized mutual lending. On the other hand, government intervention, voluntary or involuntary, destroys the very benefit of a decentralized system, namely, peer monitoring among banks. Consistency between goals and incentives could be restored in one of two ways. If one does not believe that the detailed information that banks have or may acquire about each other can be used fruitfully, or else that similar information can be acquired and utilized efficiently by regulatory authorities, then there is no particular reason to encourage decentralized interactions among banks.[5] Alternatively, one may argue that this reformist view of cutting interbank linkages amounts to throwing the baby out with the bathwater, and that one should preserve the current flexibility while improving banks' incentive to cross-monitor. This policy, to be successful, requires not only keeping banks formally responsible for their losses in interbank transactions, but also restoring the central bank's credible commitment not to intervene in most cases of bank distress. As we will see, this credibility cannot be taken for granted, and must build on a specific regulatory treatment of interbank transactions.

---

[3] The bank run literature initiated by Bryant (1980) and Diamond and Dybvig (1983) mostly focuses on the solvency of individual banks and leaves systemic risk aside for future research (in fact, both articles consider a single "representative" bank). Recently, several papers have analyzed the incentive constraints imposed by the possibility open to depositors to fake liquidity needs to take advantage of favorable reinvestment opportunities (Hellwig 1994; von Thadden 1994a,b) or to *ex ante* invest in profitable illiquid assets (Bhattacharya and Fulghieri 1994). The Bhattacharya and Fulghieri paper looks at an insurance mechanism among banks facing idiosyncratic shocks. As in Hellwig and von Thadden, private information about the realized idiosyncratic liquidity needs prevents the achievement of the optimal insurance allocation. While Bhattacharya and Fulghieri derive interbank contracting, they have no peer monitoring and thus the optimal private contract can be implemented through a centralized liquidity arrangement, in which the central bank acts as a counterparty to all transactions. So, systemic risk cannot arise. There is also a literature on peer monitoring in LDC credit relationships (see, for example, Armendariz 1995 and Stiglitz 1990). This literature does not study prudential regulation and systemic risk.

[4] Our model is in many respects a general model of systemic risk, and could be applied to other types of firms that lend to each other and need to monitor one another.

[5] There might be "political economy" considerations for why the centralization of liquidity management might be undesirable. We are, however, not aware of any explicit model along these lines.

To stress the point that a decentralized operation of interbank lending must be motivated by peer monitoring,[6] let us consider the following (alternative) plausible explanation of interbank lending. Some banks, perhaps due to their regional implantation, are good at collecting deposits, but have poor investment opportunities. In contrast, some other banks, such as the money center banks, have plenty of such opportunities or else are sufficiently large to afford the large fixed costs associated with complex derivative and other high-tech financial markets. It then seems natural for the former banks to lend to the latter. Yet, that a deposit-collecting bank should incur a loss when the borrowing bank defaults, as is implied by interbank lending, is not a foregone conclusion. If the relationship between the two banks involves a transfer of funds but no monitoring, the operation described above could be implemented in a more centralized way, which is probably better for prudential control. Namely, the deposit-collecting bank could pass the deposits on to the borrowing bank, while continuing to service them (in the same way a bank may continue to service mortgage loans it has securitized without recourse to other banks). The key difference with the interbank-loan institution is that the deposits made at the originating bank would, except to the eyes of the depositors, become deposits of the receiving bank. So, if the latter defaulted, losses would be borne by the deposit insurance fund, and not by the originating bank. We conclude that a mere specialization of banks into deposit-taking banks and actively investing banks by itself does not predict the existence of decentralized interbank lending.

Interbank loans are also subject to a debate in the prudential arena. International regulations currently require little capital for interbank lending. An interbank loan receives one-fifth of the weight of an industrial loan. Because capital requirements impose an 8% ratio of equity to risk weighted assets, only 1.6¢ of capital is required per $1 of interbank loan. Some observers would argue that this capital requirement is excessive in view of the track record of interbank loan reimbursements. This position, however, misses the point that this excellent historical record has been purchased at the price of government exposure and bank moral hazard. Indeed, in an improved system, in which banks would be made responsible for losses they incur on interbank transactions,

---

[6]There is ample evidence on the existence and relevance of peer monitoring in the banking industry. For example, in their study of the Suffolk system, Calomiris and Kahn (1996) show that this cooperative arrangement between New England banks to exchange each other's notes worked in effect as a disciplining device. For instance (p. 10), "The effectiveness of cooperative bank arrangements in preventing malfeasance by individual banks was enhanced by the collective banks' being able to 'blow the whistle' on an individual even before formal legal procedures could be initiated."

the latter would be riskier than they currently are and might be given a higher weight in the capital adequacy requirement. It might also be the case that formal quantitative restrictions (caps) would be imposed on interbank lending (as suggested by the reformers' position to limit interbank linkages).

The flip side of the coin is that, under effective interbank monitoring, debtors on the interbank market(s) are certified by their peers. The beneficiaries of (medium- or long-term) interbank loans might therefore be allowed lower capital ratios than banks that rely primarily on uninformed deposits for funds. Thus, with better incentives for monitoring, a fraction of (medium- and long-term) interbank borrowing could conceivably be included in the borrowing bank's regulatory capital, while this inclusion would make little sense in the current system. A peer-monitoring approach also explains why short-term loans, even uninsured, are poor substitutes for bank capital, as they allow lenders to escape responsibility for poor monitoring by liquidating their position.

A last policy issue is the question of the credibility of limited central bank involvement.[7] Interbank lending creates a "soft budget constraint" (SBC) when the borrowing bank is in distress and the lending bank is solvent provided one ignores its interbank activities.[8] For interbank loans to play their certification role, the lending bank must be held partly accountable for the borrowing bank's distress. This may, as we will see, imply closing the lending bank when it itself is solvent but near insolvency. In such cases, however, it is not "*ex post* optimal" for the central bank to adhere to the stated resolution method. The solvency of the lending bank leads to a rescue, which in turn conflicts with its *ex ante* incentives to monitor.

---

[7]For simplicity, this paper does not make a distinction between the deposit insurance fund, banking supervisors, and the several departments of the central bank.

[8]Interbank loans might conceivably impose another externality on the central bank. Increased indebtedness impairs incentives for good or prudent behavior and thus reduces the value of deposits, or, equivalently, increases the deposit insurance fund's liabilities. As usual, a lender (here, the lending bank) does not internalize the loss its loan inflicts on any other lender (here, the deposit insurance fund); this standard "multiprincipal externality" has been extensively studied in economics. (See, for example, Bernheim and Whinston (1986), Stole (1992), Martimort (1992), and, in a banking context, Bizer and DeMarzo (1992).) This externality, however, is limited by the existing regulatory regime. For, in the computation of the Cooke ratio, an increase in interbank borrowing does not affect the measurement of capital and risk weighted assets, and therefore, ceteris paribus, does not allow the borrowing bank to acquire assets other than Treasury and assimilated securities. (To be certain, current measures of capital do not continuously monitor interbank transactions (although, as we argue in Rochet and Tirole (chapter 6), there is a case for keeping track of bank's mutual net claims). There thus remains some "multiprincipal externality" of the lending bank on the deposit insurance fund.)

One of the key issues addressed in this paper is whether the rescue of the lending bank operates through a bailout of the borrowing bank, a move that we take to be the hallmark of the TBTF policy. Note that, despite its name, we deemphasize the concept of size in TBTF by simply viewing TBTF as a policy in which a borrowing bank bailout substitutes for direct assistance to its lenders. Because our viewpoint may surprise some readers, we ought to make some comments in this respect. First, it is clear that size per se cannot be the cause of TBTF; Drexel and the BCCI (which were allowed to fail) were large institutions whose failure created little risk of contagion as they were somewhat disconnected from the rest of the system. Second, even if one accepts our position, TBTF may not be a misnomer. As discussed above, large banks often borrow from smaller deposit-collecting banks, and thus there is a correlation between size and rescue operations. Third, the latter correlation may have alternative explanations; for instance, a political economy explanation may be that the failure of a large bank makes national headlines while that of small banks goes almost unnoticed in the media.

The paper is organized as follows. Section 5.1 sets up the benchmark situation of "autarky," in which banks do not monitor each other. That is, there is no interbank lending and liquidity markets might as well be centralized. The three-period autarky model is drawn from Holmström and Tirole (1995). Each bank must at date 0 hold liquid reserves in order to finance liquidity shocks at date 1. Once the liquidity shock is realized, there is still moral hazard in the bank. Returns accrue at date 2. The need for reserves is not obviated by the possibility of going to depositors or to the capital market to obtain more funds when the liquidity need occurs. So, banks must complement the possibility of diluting external claims by hoarding liquid securities or must count on credit facilities at the central bank. As we will see, in the optimal financial contract linking each bank and its lenders, the bank is subject to a liquidity requirement, proportional to the value of a bank's risky assets.

Section 5.2 considers optimal contracting in the presence of peer monitoring. To focus on the basic mechanics, it looks at the two-bank case in which one bank monitors the other. This generalization of the Holmström and Tirole model allows us to study how the borrowing bank's liquidity requirement should be affected by interbank lending and whether the borrowing bank's distress should propagate to the lending bank, possibly forcing the latter to shut down.

Section 5.2 focuses on (date-0) peer monitoring of date-1 performance. Concretely, this means that monitoring is aimed at encouraging the commercial activities of banks that will suffer low liquidity shocks. We show that the monitoree's survival decision and return are independent of the liquidity shock facing its monitor. This result implies that the decision of whether to close bank 1 is independent of whether this decision jeopardizes the survival of its monitor, bank 2. More concretely, the cost of rescuing bank 1 is independent of the existence of a monitor, as a bailout of bank 1 can be replaced by an equal-cost assistance loan to bank 2. So "too big to fail" is by no means a foregone conclusion.

Section 5.3 studies the robustness of the latter conclusion by looking at date-1 peer monitoring. There, the monitoring is aimed at encouraging the commercial activities of banks that will have low probabilities of poor returns (at date 2). We show that the banks' closure decisions are now interlinked because of the existence of economies of scope between monitoring and commercial activities. A bank is less likely to be allowed to fail if its failure jeopardizes the profitability of its lenders. We also show that even in an optimal prudential arrangement, propagation can occur. For example, starting from a situation in which no bank fails, a small increase in a bank's liquidity shock can trigger the closure of all banks. Section 5.4 summarizes the main insights and discusses avenues for research.

5.1 Benchmark: No Interbank Lending

5.1.1 The Model

The benchmark model is adapted from Holmström and Tirole (1995), to which we refer the reader for more detail. There are n banks, and three periods, $t = 0, 1, 2$. Banks and investors (depositors, consumers) are risk neutral with a time separable utility. That is, an agent with random consumption stream (c_0, c_1, c_2) has expected utility $E(c_0 + c_1 + c_2)$. Thus, the interest rate demanded by depositors is equal to zero.

A bank $i \in \{1, \ldots, n\}$ has access to a stochastic decreasing-returns-to-scale technology, which for an initial investment of size I_i (which can be interpreted as a portfolio of commercial loans, which we call a "project") costs $C(I_i)$ and returns RI_i if the "project" succeeds and 0 if it fails.[9] The cost function $C(\cdot)$ is increasing, strictly convex, and differentiable. (Equivalently the cost could be linear and the return in the case of success increasing and concave in investment.) The size of the investment I_i can be varied freely, subject only to financial constraints. The investment is made at date 0. At date 1, an additional, uncertain amount $\rho_i I_i > 0$ of cash is needed to carry on with the project. The *liquidity shock* ρ_i is distributed according to the cumulative distribution F, with a density

---

[9] The "project" stands for the bank's investments in loans or other illiquid assets. Our formulation implies that the bank is not perfectly diversified; otherwise, there would be no moral hazard (see Diamond 1984).

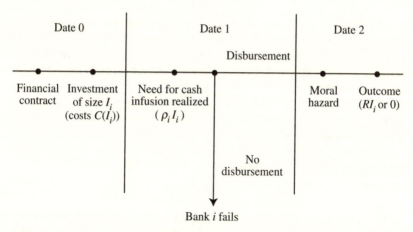

Figure 5.1.   The timing of events in the model.

function f. If $\rho_i I_i$ is not paid, the project terminates and yields nothing. If $\rho_i I_i$ is paid, the project continues and its payoff is realized at date 2.

Investment is subject to moral hazard in that the bank (a banking entrepreneur) privately chooses the probability p that the project succeeds. The bank can either "behave" or "shirk." One interpretation of this "effort choice" might be the intensity of the bank's monitoring of its commercial loans. If the bank behaves, the probability of success is p_H (high). If the bank shirks, the probability of success is p_L (low), where $p_H - p_L \equiv \Delta p > 0$, and it enjoys a private benefit, $BI_i > 0$, proportional to the level of its investment I_i. The private benefit to shirking might stand for insider lending or for the reduced monitoring effort. The firm makes the decision on p after the liquidity shock has been paid. If the project is abandoned, no decision on p needs to be made. We assume that it is optimal to provide incentives for the bank to behave.[10]

The timing of events is described in figure 5.1.

Bank i has a date-0 endowment of cash, A_i, and no endowments at dates 1 and 2. A_i is the bank's date-0 equity.[11] If the bank wants to invest $C(I_i) > A_i$, it will need to raise $C(I_i) - A_i$ from outside investors. For the moment, we assume that the initial investment level, the project outcome, and the liquidity shock are all verifiable (as we will see, nothing would change if only the banking entrepreneur observed the liquidity shock).

---

[10]This is the case, for example, if $B < (\Delta p)^2 R/p_H$. This condition guarantees that it is cheaper for outside claimholders to provide the banking entrepreneur with monetary incentives not to shirk.

[11]The identification of cash and equity is not a real restriction at date 0. Of course, these two notions differ after date 0.

Together with the scale I_i of the project, an allocation is characterized by a continuation rule at date 1 and a sharing rule for the proceeds of the investment. Because preferences are linear, the only relevant variables are the (interim) expected utility of bank i and of outside investors, conditionally on the realized liquidity shock ρ_i.[12] We denote these interim expected utilities by $U_i(\rho_i)$ and $V_i(\rho_i)$, respectively. The continuation rule is a function $\rho_i \to x_i(\rho_i) \in \{0,1\}$, with the interpretation that the project is continued when $x_i(\rho_i) = 1$ and stopped when $x_i(\rho_i) = 0$.

Feasibility requires that the sum of expected utilities not exceed expected investment proceeds, net of the liquidity shock:

$$U_i(\rho_i) + V_i(\rho_i) \leqslant x_i(\rho_i)[p_H R - \rho_i]I_i. \tag{5.1}$$

This constraint is binding in any optimal allocation (one could, for example, give more money to outside investors if it were not binding); we therefore have

$$V_i(\rho_i) \equiv x_i(\rho_i)[p_H R - \rho_i]I_i - U_i(\rho_i).$$

An allocation must also satisfy the following constraints:

$$(\Delta p)U_i(\rho_i) \geqslant x_i(\rho_i)[p_H B I_i], \quad i = 1,\ldots,n \tag{IC$_i$}$$

(incentive-compatibility constraint for bank i).

When $x_i(\rho_i) = 0$, constraint (IC$_i$) simply means that $U_i(\rho_i)$ cannot be negative (limited liability of the bank). When $x_i(\rho_i) = 1$, it means that the expected gain obtained by the bank by shirking is smaller than the increase in expected utility obtained by behaving (which increases the probability of success by Δp). Under risk neutrality, bank i receives R_i in the case of success and 0 otherwise. The moral hazard constraint in the case of continuation is $(\Delta p)R_i \geqslant BI_i$. Using $U_i(\rho_i) = p_H R_i$ then yields (IC$_i$).

An allocation is Pareto optimal if it maximizes a weighted sum of banks' and depositors' utilities under the constraints (5.1) and (IC$_i$) for $i = 1,\ldots,n$.[13] For simplicity, we take the weights (ν_i for bank i and λ for depositors) as exogenous. Note also that we give the same weight λ to all depositors. Thus Pareto optima are obtained by maximizing

$$L = \sum_i E[(\nu_1 - \lambda)U_i(\rho_i) + \lambda x_i(\rho_i)I_i(p_H R - \rho_i) + \lambda(A_i - C(I_i))]$$

---

[12] In the absence of interbank transactions, bank i's continuation decision, incentives, and utility should not depend on the other banks' liquidity shocks.

[13] We could also have introduced participation constraints as in the original model of Holmström and Tirole (1995). In effect, we would obtain similar formulas with endogenous welfare weights. To simplify the comparison with the case of interbank monitoring, we have taken exogenous weights.

under the moral hazard constraints (IC$_i$). Notice that λ has to exceed v_i for all i, otherwise the problem would have no solution (economically, a mere redistribution of wealth from depositors to bankers raises social welfare). Therefore, L is maximized for the smallest interim utilities satisfying (IC$_i$). Thus constraint (IC$_i$) is always binding:

$$U_i(\rho_i) = \begin{cases} p_H \dfrac{BI_i}{\Delta p} & \text{if } x_i(\rho_i) = 1, \\ 0 & \text{if } x_i(\rho_i) = 0. \end{cases} \tag{5.2}$$

If we now replace $U_i(\rho_i)$ by the value given by (5.2), the optimal $x_i(\cdot)$ and I_i can be obtained by maximizing

$$\frac{L}{\lambda} = \sum_i I_i E\left[\left\{\left(\frac{v_i}{\lambda} - 1\right)\frac{p_H B}{\Delta p} + (p_H R - \rho_i)\right\}x_i(\rho_i)\right] - \sum_i [C(I_i) - A_i].$$

Given ρ_i, the net present value (per unit of investment) of continuation thus equals the difference between $[p_H R - \rho_i]$ (the net return on investment) and $(1 - v_i/\lambda)p_H B/\Delta p$ (the net incentive cost). Therefore, the optimal continuation policy is characterized by a threshold liquidity shock ρ_i^A (where the superscript "A" stands for "autarky"), which is also independent of the level of equity:

$$x_i(\rho_i) = \begin{cases} 1 & \text{if } \rho_i \leqslant \rho_i^A, \\ 0 & \text{if } \rho_i > \rho_i^A, \end{cases}$$

where

$$\rho_i^A \equiv p_H\left(R - \frac{B}{\Delta p}\right) + \frac{v_i}{\lambda}\frac{p_H B}{\Delta p}. \tag{5.3}$$

This threshold represents the (interim) expected return on investment, net of incentive costs. Using this optimal continuation rule, the expression to be maximized becomes

$$\frac{L}{\lambda} = \sum_i \left\{I_i \int_0^{\rho_i^A} (\rho_i^A - \rho_i)f(\rho_i)\,d\rho_i - C(I_i) + A_I\right\}.$$

Finally, maximization with respect to I_i gives the optimal investment level I_i^A:

$$C'(I_i^A) = \int_0^{\rho_i^A} (\rho_i^A - \rho_i)f(\rho_i)\,d\rho_i = \int_0^{\rho_i^A} F(\rho_i)\,d\rho_i. \tag{5.4}$$

The integral in (5.4) can be interpreted as the (ex ante) expected return on investment net of the incentive cost and the liquidity shock.

Note from (5.3) that the optimal threshold satisfies $\rho_i^A < p_H R$, so that positive net present value reinvestments may not be optimal; that is, the logic of credit rationing and solvency requirements applies not only to the initial investment, but also to the reinvestment decision. More interestingly, let

$$\rho_0 \equiv p_H \left(R - \frac{B}{\Delta p} \right)$$

denote the expected per unit pledgeable income, that is, the maximal income that can be pledged to outsiders given the insiders' incompressible share. Note that the total value of the investors' claims on the bank is equal to $\rho_0 I_i$ (in the case of continuation). Condition (5.3) yields

$$\rho_i^A > \rho_0. \tag{5.5}$$

Condition (5.5) implies that the bank cannot withstand all shocks for which it should continue by just diluting its existing claims, that is, by leveraging itself up. This explains the need for hoarding liquid reserves.

5.1.2 Implementation

From the transposition of Holmström and Tirole (1995) to the banking sector, we know that the optimal allocation can be implemented in one of two ways, given that the bank needs to hoard at date 0 reserves in order to be able to withstand date-1 shocks above $\rho_0 I_i^A$.

Liquidity requirement. The bank can at date 0 borrow more than $C(I_i^A) - A_i$ and invest the residual amount in liquid assets such as Treasury bills, which it will be able to sell at date 1 in order to pay for the liquidity shock. For example, bank i can borrow $C(I_i^A) - A_i + \rho_0^A I_i^A$, agree to invest $\rho_0^A I_i^A$ in Treasury bills (or other liquid securities), and commit not to dilute existing claims at date 1. Alternatively, the bank can borrow only $C(I_i^A) - A_i + (\rho_i^A - \rho_0) I_i^A$, invest $(\rho_i^A - \rho_0) I_i^A$ in Treasury bills, but keep the option of leveraging itself up at date 1. Either way, it is important that the liquidity requirement be monitored by the investors (see Holmström and Tirole (1995) for details).

Credit line. Alternatively, the bank can borrow $C(I_i^A) - A_i$, but obtain a credit line (corresponding to the level of liquidity hoarding $(\rho_i^A - \rho_0) I_i^A$, assuming that dilution is allowed) from the central bank in exchange for an appropriate amount of equity or debt.

5.1.3 Positive NPV, Liquidity, and Solvency

We can now define the notions of (date-1) positive NPV, liquidity, and solvency. Bank i has *positive* NPV at date 1 if the expected return exceeds the liquidity shock it faces, that is, if and only if $p_H R \geqslant \rho_i$. To define a notion of liquidity, let $\mathcal{L}_i$ denote the bank's reserves, which are hoarded at date 0 and can be mobilized at date 1. $\mathcal{L}_i$ can represent, for example, the date-1 value of Treasury notes held by bank i plus the level of a credit line that bank i can draw upon at date 1. Bank i is *liquid* if its reserves exceed its liquidity shock, that is, if and only if $\mathcal{L}_i \geqslant \rho_i I_i$. It then does not need to contract new external financing in order to continue.

Last, we come to the notion of solvency. One possible definition is that bank i is solvent if, after efficient bargaining among the various stakeholders, the bank does not fail. As we will see, this definition can be given several interpretations depending on the control rights conferred upon the various stakeholders. First, we note that bank i is *solvent* if $\rho_i \leqslant \rho_0$, that is, if the value of outside claims on the bank exceeds the bank's liquidity shock. After efficient bargaining among the various stakeholders, a solvent bank is always rescued even if it has hoarded no liquidity. Note also that, in the absence of moral hazard ($B = 0$), $\rho_0 = p_H R$ and thus solvency coincides with positive NPV; but in general the agency cost introduces a wedge between the two concepts and a positive NPV bank need not be solvent.

Second, suppose that $\rho_0 < \rho_i < p_H R$ (for $\rho_i > p_H R$, bank i is always closed after efficient bargaining among the claimholders). Suppose that the bank has hoarded reserves $\mathcal{L}_i$ and that the banking entrepreneur has been previously given the right to use those reserves and to dilute a fraction α ($0 \leqslant \alpha \leqslant 1$) of outside claims to withstand liquidity shocks. Because $\rho_0 < \rho_i$, the community of outside claimholders would prefer to let the bank fail and therefore will not provide further credit. However, the banking entrepreneur is able to withstand the liquidity shock if $(\rho_i - \alpha\rho_0)I_i \leqslant \mathcal{L}_i$. We can talk about *solvency sustained by reserves and dilution rights* if this condition and $\rho_0 < \rho_i < p_H R$ are both satisfied. We see that whether the bank fails when $\rho_0 < \rho_i < p_H R$ depends on the control rights which have been conferred upon the bank.

Remark 5.1. In this paper we do not investigate whether the private sector is "liquidity self-sufficient," in that the aggregate liquidity needs can be covered by the holding of private securities (in which case Treasury securities provide no extra liquidity service and must be sold at par). The analysis in Holmström and Tirole (1995) implies two points. (i) In the absence of macroeconomic shock (there are a large number of banks facing independent liquidity shocks), the private sector is liquidity self-sufficient. However, banks' crossholdings of securities "dispatches" liquidity in an inefficient way, while a "liquidity bank" (such as the German Likobank) is able to achieve the social optimum. (ii) In the presence of macroeconomic shocks, the government has a role in creating and managing liquidity in the economy.

5.1.4   The Role of Banking Regulation in Our Framework

The optimal allocation described in sections 5.1.1 and 5.1.2 can be implemented through a contract between the bank and its investors specifying a liquidity requirement. In practice, however, depositors have very small individual incentives to participate in the design of the contract and to verify that the bank complies with its covenants. This free-rider problem creates a need for representation. In this paper, we follow Dewatripont and Tirole (1994) in viewing the role of (public or private) banking regulators as solving the depositors' collective action problem, and thus as writing and enforcing the banking contract that the bank would have signed with a rational representative depositor who would verify that her investments in the bank yield the market rate of interest. We will adhere to this view of regulation throughout the paper, even though we will allow regulatory authorities to face commitment problems in their role as protectors of depositors.

5.1.5   Modeling Interbank Monitoring

As we discussed, decentralized interbank transactions can be justified only on the ground that they contain privy information that banks hold about each other. Since the current incentives for mutual monitoring are poor, we must partly conjecture what monitoring would look like in a more incentive-compatible world. Following the literatures on moral hazard and adverse selection, there are two ways in which bank 2, say, can monitor bank 1. In the *moral hazard version*, bank 2 studies bank 1's activities and discloses information to the authorities, or else insists on improved management and use of derivatives or asset portfolio by bank 1 in order to grant an interbank loan. That is, bank 2 rules out some dimensions of potential mismanagement by bank 1 (this does not necessarily mean that all moral hazard in bank 1 is eradicated). In the *adverse selection version*, monitoring by bank 2 consists in acquiring information about bank 1's managerial ability or about the riskiness of its existing assets.

   Anecdotal evidence suggests that the adverse selection version is a better description of the *current* state of interbank monitoring. But there is no reason why the peer monitoring would not take the alternative form in a system in which banks would issue long-term, uninsured loans to each other.

As usual, the moral hazard and adverse selection description of monitoring give very similar results. We will here content ourselves with an exposition of the simpler moral hazard version. We have studied the adverse selection version in the case of two possible values for the liquidity shock of the borrowing bank. It is expositionally more complex since, under adverse selection, regulators may "screen" banks by offering menus of solvency and liquidity requirements, besides relying on peer monitoring to learn bank quality.

Monitoring will be described as in Holmström and Tirole (1997). It consists in identifying certain forms of misbehavior and therefore reducing the scope for moral hazard by the monitoree. More concretely, we will assume that monitoring shrinks the private benefit that the monitoree can enjoy by "shirking." Section 5.2 studies "date-0 monitoring" while section 5.3 focuses on "date-1 monitoring." Date-0 monitoring will consist in reducing (actually eliminating) the monitoree's incentive to mismanage in the short run (for instance, the monitor may check the monitoree's risk management system). In section 5.1 we assumed that the liquidity shocks were exogenous. We will in section 5.2 posit that the borrowing bank's liquidity shock follows some distribution and the bank enjoys no date-0 private benefit if the bank is monitored. If it is not monitored, the bank may be tempted to enjoy a private benefit between dates 0 and 1, which stochastically raises the liquidity shock. Last, date-1 monitoring will be described in section 5.3 as resulting in a reduction in the monitoree's private benefit of shirking between dates 1 and 2. The key distinction between date-0 and date-1 monitoring is that one takes place before and the other after the (date-1) closure decisions. Under date-0 monitoring, interbank linkages impact on the closure decisions in a *retrospective* way; namely, their object is to punish or reward monitors for their monitoring performance. As we will see, this implies that a bank's closure decision should not be influenced by the fragility of its lenders. However, SBC problems may appear. In contrast, the impact of date-1 monitoring should be *prospective*, and therefore a bank's closure decision may reflect the health of its monitors.

5.2 Date-0 Monitoring and Optimal Interbank Loans

5.2.1 The Two-Bank Case: Optimal Allocation with Peer Monitoring

In this section, we analyze in detail the simplest example of peer monitoring, that involving a borrowing bank (bank 1) and a lending bank (bank 2). In this situation, only one bank (bank 2) has an incentive to monitor the other bank.[14]

---

[14]In this section (and the next) we assume that the two banks do not interact on the product market. A bank meant to monitor a close competitor might want to shirk on its

We formalize monitoring in the following way. At private and unobservable cost cI_1 (proportional to the size I_1 of the investment of bank 1), bank 2 can reduce bank 1's private benefit of "shirking" on short-term management. Namely, if bank 2 incurs cI_1, bank 1 is unable to enjoy any private benefit by engaging in short-term mismanagement. The situation is then the same as that described in section 5.1 since we assumed there that the distribution of liquidity shocks was not subject to moral hazard. Let $F_1(\rho_1)$ denote the cumulative distribution of bank 1's liquidity shock when it is monitored, and let $f_1(\rho_1)$ denote the associated density (on $[0, \infty)$). On the other hand, if bank 2 does not monitor, that is, does not incur cI_1, bank 1's liquidity shock is distributed according to cumulative distribution $\tilde{F}_1(\rho_1)$ with density $\tilde{f}_1(\rho_1)$, where $F_1(\cdot)$ dominates $\tilde{F}_1(\cdot)$ in the sense of first-order stochastic dominance: $F_1(\rho_1) > \tilde{F}_1(\rho_1)$ for all $\rho_1 > 0$. The interpretation of this (stochastic) increase in the liquidity shock is that bank 1 is left free to engage in poor short-term management and enjoys a private benefit from this, that exceeds the loss in its monetary stake it incurs by generating higher liquidity shocks. We assume that the unit cost of monitoring, c, is small relative to the monitoree's private benefit of misbehaving, so that inducing monitoring by bank 2 is more efficient than not having monitoring and directly inducing bank 1 to behave. This assumption is natural given our goal of formalizing interbank monitoring. Last, we assume that bank 2 faces an exogenous liquidity shock ρ_2 distributed according to cumulative distribution function $F_2(\rho_2)$ with density $f_2(\rho_2)$ on $[0, \infty)$.

Let $\rho = (\rho_1, \rho_2)$ denote the vector of liquidity shocks encountered by the two banks at date 1. We maximize the same weighted sum of the welfares of banks 1 and 2 and their depositors as in the autarkic case,[15] subject to (i) the interim incentive constraints guaranteeing that the banks are diligent when they are not liquidated, and (ii) bank 2's *ex ante* incentive constraint, reflecting the fact that bank 2 chooses a privately optimal level of monitoring. We delay the discussion of the implementation of the optimum until section 5.2.2.

Let $E\{\cdot\}$ denote the expectation operator for the joint density $f_1(\rho_1) \times f_2(\rho_2)$, and let

$$\ell(\rho_1) \equiv \frac{f_1(\rho_1) - \tilde{f}_1(\rho_1)}{f_1(\rho_1)}$$

denote the likelihood ratio. As is usual, we assume that a lower liquidity shock "signals" a higher monitoring effort. That is, the likelihood ratio is decreasing in ρ_1 (this property implies the previously stated first-order stochastic dominance property).

---

monitoring duties solely to increase the probability of failure of the monitoree and thus to raise its market power.

[15] As before, we put the same weight on the welfare of depositors in both banks.

The optimum is a tuple described by $\{U_1(\rho), U_2(\rho), x_1(\rho), x_2(\rho)\}$ for each realization of ρ (where U_i and x_i denote, as in section 5.1, the interim utilities and the continuation probabilities), and investment levels I_1 and I_2, that solve program $(\mathcal{P})$, given by

$$\max L = \sum_{i=1}^{2} E[(v_i - \lambda)U_i(\rho) + \lambda x_i(\rho_i)I_i(p_{\mathrm{H}}R - \rho_i) + \lambda(A_i - C(I_i))] \quad (5.6)$$

subject to:

$$U_i(\rho) \geqslant x_i(\rho)p_{\mathrm{H}}\frac{BI_i}{\Delta p} \quad \text{for all } (i, \rho) \tag{IC$_i$}$$

and

$$E\{U_2(\rho)\ell(\rho_1)\} \geqslant cI_1. \tag{IC$_2'$}$$

Condition (IC$_2'$) is the incentive-compatibility condition ensuring that bank 2 monitors bank 1.[16]

One must also require that

$$x_i(\rho) = 1 \quad \text{for } \rho_i < \rho_0. \tag{5.7}$$

For, when bank i's liquidity shock is lower than the per-unit value ρ_0 of the bank, the bank is solvent (although perhaps illiquid, as we will see), and its liquidation is not credible. Investors have an incentive to dilute their claims on bank i in order to raise the cash needed to withstand the liquidity shock.

We did not explicitly impose the credibility constraint (5.7) in section 5.1 because it is redundant under autarky (recall that $\rho_i^{\mathrm{A}} > \rho_0$). As we saw, it is then never *ex ante* optimal to commit to shut down *ex post* a solvent bank. In contrast, under interbank monitoring one may want to "punish" bank 2 for a poor monitoring of bank 1 by liquidating bank 2 even when the latter is solvent. Such a liquidation policy is, however, not *ex post* optimal, and we assume that a financial reorganization then lets the bank continue. Imposing constraint (5.7) does not affect the qualitative results in this section, but will play an important role in our study of the SBC in section 5.2.3.

Maximizing program (5.6) subject to constraints (IC$_i$), (IC$_2'$), and (5.7) yields the following results, proved in the appendix.

---

[16]To see this, note that the left-hand side of (IC$_2'$) represents the gain in expected utility that bank 2 obtains by monitoring bank 1:

$$E\{U_2(\rho)\ell(\rho_1)\} = \int U_2(\rho_1, \rho_2)(f_1(\rho_1) - \tilde{f}_1(\rho_1))f_2(\rho_2)\,d\rho_1 d\rho_2.$$

- Bank 1's closure rule is the same as under autarky:

$$x_1(\rho) = 1 \quad \Longleftrightarrow \quad \rho_1 \leqslant \rho_1^* = \rho_1^A.$$

- The optimal investment level of bank 1 is determined by the equality between the net expected return on investment and its total marginal cost (direct cost + monitoring cost + incentive cost):

$$\int_0^{\rho_1^*} F_1(\rho_1) \, d\rho_1 = C'(I_1^*) + c\left(\frac{\nu_2 + \mu}{\lambda}\right),$$

where μ denotes the multiplier associated with constraint (IC$_2'$).

- Bank 2's closure rule depends on the performance of bank 1. More specifically, we have

$$x_2(\rho) = 1 \quad \Longleftrightarrow \quad \rho_2 \leqslant \rho_2^*(\rho_1) = \rho_0 + \frac{\max(0, \nu_2 + \mu\ell(\rho_1))}{\lambda} \frac{p_H B}{\Delta p}.$$

(To be complete, we actually need to assume $\rho_2^*(0) \leqslant p_H R$. This corresponds to an assumption of "restricted impact of interbank lending" that we discuss below.)

- Finally, the investment level of bank 2 is determined by a similar condition as under autarky, except that the closure rule for bank 2 is now stochastic:

$$E\left[\int_0^{\rho_2^*(\rho_1)} F_2(\rho_2) \, d\rho_2\right] = C'(I_2^*).$$

Let us describe now the consequences of these results, first for the borrowing bank and then for the lending bank.

- *Borrowing bank.* As one would expect, the study on the borrowing bank side is similar to that of the autarky case, for distribution $F_1(\rho_1)$. The following proposition and the next are proved in the appendix.

Proposition 5.1 (borrowing bank). *Under optimal interbank lending:*

(i) *the continuation decision and the welfare of the borrowing bank do not depend on the liquidity shock facing the lending bank;*

(ii) *the borrowing bank is closed less often than under autarky;*

(iii) *when the unit cost of monitoring, c, is small, the borrowing bank invests more than under autarky.*

Part (i) of proposition 5.1 is highly reminiscent of the sufficient statistic theorem of Holmström (1979) and Shavell (1979). Its simple implications will be drawn in section 5.2.2.

Part (ii) of proposition 5.1 comes from the fact that the liquidity threshold of the borrowing bank is the same as under autarky. Since the borrowing bank is now monitored, the distribution of liquidity shocks becomes F_1 instead of $\tilde{F}_1$, and the probability of closure decreases. The impact on investment (part (iii)) is less obvious, since the total cost of monitoring (direct cost + incentive cost) is proportional to I_1. However, in the limit case where $c = 0$ (costless monitoring) the incentive cost is also zero and bank 1 is clearly allowed to invest more than under autarky. Therefore, by continuity, this is also true for c small enough.

- *Lending bank.* To provide incentives for monitoring, the lending bank's stake must be linked to the borrowing bank's outcome, namely ρ_1. This linkage can be provided through two channels: bank 2's continuation decision and bank 2's reward. We will here restrict our attention to the case, which we will label "restricted impact of interbank monitoring," in which the linkage from the borrowing bank's liquidity shock to the lender's outcome operates solely through the continuation decision. That is, as in the autarky case, bank 2 never receives more than what is needed to preserve incentives (in a sense this means that bank 2 never has excess capital at date 1). The generalization of condition (5.3) of the autarky case for the lending bank then defines a contingent threshold $\rho_2^*(\rho_1)$ by

$$\rho_2^*(\rho_1) = p_H\left(R - \frac{B}{\Delta p}\right) + \frac{\max(0, v_2 + \mu \ell(\rho_1))}{\lambda} \frac{p_H B}{\Delta p}, \tag{5.8}$$

where μ is the shadow price of (IC_2'). "Restricted impact of interbank monitoring" is equivalent to the continuation decision for bank 2 never being *ex post* inefficient: $\rho_2^*(0) \leqslant p_H R$.[17]

Remark 5.2. When monitoring has a large impact on bank 1's shock or when the cost of monitoring is high, it becomes inefficient to reward bank 2 for low shocks solely through the continuation decision (the

---

[17] This is satisfied, for instance, if the unit cost of monitoring, c, is small (in which case μ is small) or if the likelihood ratio l (which is decreasing and equal to zero in expectation) does not vary much with ρ_1; this corresponds to the case in which monitoring is useful but does not affect drastically bank 1.

threshold defined in (5.8) then implies *ex post* inefficient continuation in some states of nature). It is then more efficient to reward bank 2 through direct monetary rewards as well (meaning, technically, that (IC_2') is not binding).[18]

Suppose that there is no SBC ($\rho_2^*(\rho_1) \geq \rho_0$ for all ρ_1). We will later discuss the SBC; let us rewrite bank 2's continuation decision as follows:

$$\rho_2 \geq \rho_2^*(\rho_1) \quad \Longleftrightarrow \quad \rho_2 + \rho_{21}(\rho_1) \geq \rho_2^A,$$

where

$$\rho_{21}(\rho_1) = -\frac{\mu}{\lambda}\ell(\rho_1)\frac{p_H B}{\Delta p}, \qquad \rho_2^A = \rho_0 + \frac{\nu_2}{\lambda}\frac{p_H B}{\Delta p}.$$

Notice that ρ_2^A is nothing but the autarky threshold (see equation (5.3)). But now this threshold is applied to the *overall liquidity shock* of bank 2, computed as the sum of ρ_2 and the "interbank liquidity shock" ρ_{21}. By construction, ρ_{21} has zero expectation. (This is one possible normalization of the interbank liquidity shock. We will provide another normalization in the next section.) $\rho_{21} > 0$ (which occurs for low ρ_1) can be interpreted as a realized profit generated by the interbank loan while $\rho_{21} < 0$ (which stems from a high ρ_1) corresponds to a loss on the interbank loan.

Proposition 5.2 (lending bank).

(i) *At the optimal allocation (and when the credibility constraint is not binding), the lending bank is liquidated whenever its overall liquidity shock $\rho_2 + \rho_{21}(\rho_1)$ exceeds the autarky threshold ρ_2^A. The interbank liquidity shock $\rho_{21}(\rho_1)$ is proportional to (minus) the likelihood ratio $\ell(\rho_1)$, and is therefore decreasing with ρ_1.*

(ii) *When the credibility constraint is not binding, the lending bank invests more than under autarky.*

It may seem strange that the lending bank is allowed to invest more in its own commercial activities. This is true only when the credibility constraint does not bind, and comes from a pure "option value." The interbank liquidity shock ρ_{21} amounts to adding a pure noise to the own liquidity shock ρ_2 of bank 2. Since the closure decision is made

---

[18]An awkward feature of the risk-neutrality-continuous-liquidity-shock model is that the monetary reward should take the form of a spike at $\rho_1 = 0$ in this case. As is well known there are various ways of obtaining smoother reward structures, for instance, by introducing risk aversion, or a constant likelihood ratio for small shocks, or else a "manipulability constraint" that the reward does not change discontinuously with the performance. As this is mainly a technical point, we will not pursue the analysis further.

after the realization of these two shocks, the expected net return on investment increases and the optimum investment level also increases. Another reason why part (ii) of proposition 5.2 is unlikely to be a robust conclusion (and therefore is interesting only because of its identifying an "option value" effect) is that the type of monitoring envisioned in this section does not embody a "reinforcement of moral hazard effect," that is, a deterioration of the moral hazard problem on commercial activities due to the presence of interbank activities. The outcome of monitoring is revealed *before* bank 2's moral hazard decision on its commercial loans. This limits the efficacy for bank 2 of shirking in both tasks, as shirking in the first is partly detected before the second can be undertaken (in *simultaneous* multitask finance problems with risk neutrality and limited liability, the binding moral hazard constraint is that the bank does not select to shirk on *all* tasks). In other words, the sequential timing implies that the moral hazard problem on interbank lending does not directly aggravate the moral hazard problem on commercial loans. Suppose by contrast that (i) the monitoring of commercial and interbank loans takes place simultaneously and (ii) the outcomes for the two activities are correlated, say, for macroeconomic reasons (this is to avoid diversification effects à la Diamond (1984), by which the widening of banking activities need not raise the need for regulatory capital). Then a minor reinterpretation of Holmström and Tirole (1997) shows that interbank loans *crowd out* commercial loans, that is, interbank loans require their own regulatory capital which must be subtracted from the capital available to sustain commercial loans.

5.2.2 Intuition and Implementation

The lending bank's closure decision should be linked with the performance of the borrowing bank. Bank 2's closure is more likely, the higher the liquidity shock faced by bank 1. The natural vehicle for this linkage is the credit risk on the interbank loan. We defined bank 2's *overall liquidity shock* (per unit of illiquid asset) as the sum of ρ_2 and the "interbank liquidity shock" ρ_{21}, which must correspond to the credit loss incurred at date 1 on the interbank market:

$$\hat{\rho}_2 \equiv \rho_2 + \rho_{21}.$$

The harder the liquidity shock hitting bank 1, the lower the value of the interbank loan and the higher the overall liquidity shock of bank 2.

While the qualitative features of the implementation of the optimum are clear, the exact details of this implementation depend on a number of institutional features.[19] In particular, one may entertain different

---

[19] Only a richer model could tell apart the various ways of implementing the optimum.

assumptions as to how small liquidity shocks are met by bank 1 (are its liquid assets sold or are claims on the bank diluted through issues of shares or increased leverage?), and as to the roles of priority on bank 1's second-period profit. So, we content ourselves with an example.

Example 5.1. Let us make the following assumptions:

(i) Each bank's liabilities are composed of inside equity (which cannot be diluted), outside equity, and debt claims (all debt claims are senior).

(ii) Bank i holds at date 0 liquid assets $\mathcal{L}_i$. Think of these assets as being interest-free Treasury bills (recall that the consumers' rate of time preference is normalized to be zero). These liquid assets are sold first to meet the liquidity shock; claims on the bank start being diluted when liquid assets no longer suffice to meet the shock. The dilution is then proportional to the claims' payoffs in the case of success.

To be able to withstand shocks up to $\rho_1^A I_1$, bank 1 must hold $\mathcal{L}_1 = (\rho_1^A - \rho_0)I_1$ in liquid assets. Let us next consider bank 2's holding of liquid assets. Let bank 2 hold $\mathcal{L}_2$ interest-free Treasury bills (with face value 1), as well as a nominal debt claim equal to $\beta\rho_0 I_1$ on bank 1. That is, the interbank loan entitles bank 2 to receive a fraction β of bank 1's second-period profit if bank 1 succeeds. When $\rho_1 \leqslant \rho_1^A$, the date -1 value of this interbank loan, V_{21}, is given by[20]

$$V_{21}(\rho_1) = \begin{cases} \beta\rho_0 I_1 & \text{if } \mathcal{L}_1 \geqslant \rho_1 I_1, \\ \beta[\rho_0 I_1 - (\rho_1 I_1 - \mathcal{L}_1)] = \beta(\rho_1^A - \rho_1)I_1 & \text{if } \mathcal{L}_1 \leqslant \rho_1 I_1, \end{cases}$$

where we make use of the proportional-dilution-of-claims assumption. When bank 1 has liquidity problems ($\mathcal{L}_1 \leqslant \rho_1 I_1$), then bank 2 incurs what we have called above an interbank liquidity shock:

$$\rho_{21} I_2 \equiv \beta\rho_0 I_1 - V_{21}(\rho_1) = \beta(\rho_1 I_1 - \mathcal{L}_1).$$

For $\rho_1 > \rho_1^A$, bank 1 fails at date 1 and $V_{21}(\rho_1) = 0$. Note that we adopt a normalization of ρ_{21} different from that in section 5.2.1. Here, the interbank liquidity shock is either zero or positive.

Bank 2 can securitize at date 1 its loan to bank 1 and obtain $V_{21}(\rho_1)$ if it needs to meet its own liquidity shock. So, bank 2's total reserves are equal to $\mathcal{L}_2 + V_{21}(\rho_1)$, and are nonincreasing in ρ_1. The interbank loan

---

[20] The excess liquidity, $\mathcal{L}_1 - \rho_1 I_1$, is then distributed at date 1 to outside shareholders, say.

just defined implements the optimum defined in proposition 5.2 if and only if

$$\mathcal{L}_2 + V_{21}(\rho_1) = [\rho_2^*(\rho_1) - \rho_0]I_2.$$

Thus, it implements the optimum if and only if the likelihood ratio (which, recall, defines $\rho_2^*(\cdot)$) satisfies this equality. Conversely, starting from a given likelihood ratio, one can build interbank claims that yield the optimum. Although the resulting interbank claim need not be a simple senior, unsecured debt claim as in this example, its qualitative features are similar to those of the example.

5.2.3 Soft Budget Constraints Do Not Imply Too Big to Fail

Conventional wisdom dictates that banks with large amounts of uninsured deposits cannot be allowed to fail when their failure would trigger a chain of bankruptcies (for example, sixty-six banks had uninsured deposits at Continental Illinois in excess of their capital when the latter was in distress in 1984). It is widely accepted that interbank lending puts the central bank in an awkward position of having to step in when a bank with large amounts of uninsured deposits is about to fail.

Our analysis of the SBC shows that it arises exactly in the circumstances that are perceived to create the TBTF conundrum, namely when the borrowing bank is in trouble (ρ_1 high) and the lending bank(s) are themselves fragile ($\rho_2 < \rho_0$, but high). One can also note that TBTF is itself an expression of an SBC, that is, of a policy that the central bank would like, but is unable, to commit to in order to create proper incentives. Indeed, TBTF depicts the case in which the undesirable rescue takes the specific form of bailing out the borrowing bank in order to save the lending banks, as opposed to letting the borrowing bank fail and rescuing the lending banks in other ways. The analysis of date-0 monitoring does not support the view that the borrowing bank should be kept alive.

Indeed, with date-0 monitoring, there is a compelling logic for why the closure decision should not necessarily be linked with the fate of the uninsured creditors. For, the central bank can let the borrowing bank fail while issuing emergency loans, guaranteeing uninsured deposits, exerting forbearance, or taking any other measure that prevents the contagion. Thus the central bank can opt for the cheapest of the two broad approaches (bail out versus closure and assistance to uninsured depositors), and not systematically rule out liquidation.

To stress this point, note that the key feature of monitoring as described here is that it is exerted *before* rescue decisions are made. If the monitor–monitoree relationship at that point of time is bygone (except for the resulting financial flows), then an unprofitable rescue cannot be undertaken. If it involves a net cost $X > 0$ to the outside claimholders altogether, a rescue that creates benefit $Y > 0$ for bank 2 costs $X + Y$ to the other holders of claims on bank 1. The latter are then better off offering Y to bank 2 and saving X by shutting bank 1 down.

Our second observation is that the presence of the credibility constraint (5.7) reduces the value of program ($\mathcal{P}$). Because the optimal policy is time consistent, and therefore the credibility constraint has no bite in the absence of interbank lending, interbank lending becomes less desirable when the central bank cannot commit not to bail out bank 2. Thus, it may be the case that the SBC leads banks to forgo interbank lending; equivalently, in the interpretation in which the central bank represents the interests of dispersed, free-riding depositors, the SBC may lead the central bank to prohibit interbank lending, when it would allow it if it could commit not to bail out bank 2. Conversely, it is never the case that the SBC makes interbank lending more desirable.

We summarize the observations made in this section in the following proposition.

Proposition 5.3 (central bank bailouts).

(i) *The central bank's inability to commit not to rescue a bank that incurs losses on the interbank market but is otherwise solvent may lead to the prohibition of interbank lending in cases where it would be allowed if the central bank's commitment were credible.*

(ii) *The SBC differs from TBTF, as the borrowing bank's closure decision is unrelated to the fragility of the lending bank. Central bank assistance to a solvent but failing lending bank operates through a direct assistance to that bank rather than through a bailout of the borrowing bank.*

5.3   Date-1 Monitoring, Too Big to Fail, and Bank Failure Propagations

Section 5.2 pointed out that TBTF is by no means a foregone conclusion. This section shows that TBTF policies resurface in the presence of economies of scope (à la Diamond (1984)) between monitoring and commercial activities. Such economies of scope exist when monitoring takes place at date 1 instead of date 0. The section also analyzes the possibility of propagation of bank failures.

5.3.1   A Symmetric Model of Date-1 Monitoring

So far, we have considered date-0 monitoring, which affects the monitoree's short-term performance, namely, the liquidity shock. We now slightly modify our setup by ignoring date-0 monitoring and by assuming instead that monitoring reduces the private benefit of date-1 shirking from BI to bI. The cost of monitoring is c per unit of investment; so the cost for the monitor is cI if the monitoree's investment is of size I. If the monitor does not incur cI, the monitoree shirks as long as his monetary incentive does not exceed BI; in contrast, in the presence of monitoring, the minimal monetary incentive that induces the monitoree to manage his commercial loans is only bI.

For simplicity, we consider a symmetric model with n equally endowed banks ($i = 1,\ldots,n$) located on a circle, where bank i is supposed to monitor bank $i - 1$ (with the convention that $0 = n$). We assume that B is large enough so that it is never optimal to leave one bank unmonitored. "Closing" bank i at the interim date $t = 1$ (which will occur if its liquidity shock ρ_i is large enough) means in fact a liquidation of its investment (commercial activity), but monitoring of bank $i-1$ can still be performed. (One can then think of bank i as a deposit-taking bank which must monitor whom it lends to in the money market.) When such a *downsizing* occurs (or when both banks' commercial activities are shut down), we denote it by $x_i = 0$. When $x_i = 1$, on the contrary, bank i is allowed to continue its commercial activities (that is, withstand liquidity shock ρ_i and operate I_i). Denoting (as before) by $U_i(\rho)$ the interim payoff of bank i (as a function of the vector $\rho = (\rho_1,\ldots,\rho_n)$ of all liquidity shocks), we can write the incentive-compatibility constraints as follows:

$$(p_H - p_L)U_i(\rho) \geqslant p_H c I_{i-1} \tag{5.9}$$

when $x_i = 0$ and $x_{i-1} = 1$,

$$(p_H - p_L)U_i(\rho) \geqslant p_H b I_i \tag{5.10}$$

when $x_i = 1$ and $x_{i-1} = 0$, and finally

$$(p_H^2 - p_L^2)U_i(\rho) \geqslant p_H(b I_i + c I_{i-1}) \tag{5.11}$$

when $x_i = x_{i-1} = 1$. Indeed, when both bank i and bank $i - 1$ are allowed to maintain their commercial activities, risk neutrality implies that the most efficient way to provide bank i with the correct incentives is to punish it when either its investment or the investment of bank $i - 1$ is unsuccessful (in which case bank i gets a zero return). It is only when both investments are successful that bank i receives a positive return. Therefore, condition (5.11) expresses the fact that the expected utility gain of bank i exceeds the private benefit of misbehaving in commercial activities (bI_i) plus the cost of monitoring bank $i - 1$ (cI_{i-1}).

5.3.2   The Nature of the Economies of Scope between Interbank and Commercial Activities

The economies of scope are easily detected by comparing (5.11) with (5.9) and (5.10): if we denote $p_H - p_L$ by Δp and $p_H/(p_H + p_L)$ by y (which is therefore less than 1), the minimum rent to be given to bank i to behave in both activities is

$$U_i(\rho) = \frac{p_H^2}{p_H^2 - p_L^2}(bI_i + cI_{i-1}) = \frac{yp_H}{\Delta p}(bI_i + cI_{i-1}). \qquad (11')$$

Therefore, the minimum rent that induces bank i to monitor both its commercial activities and bank $i-1$ is less than the sum of the minimum rents that correspond to separate activities:

$$U_i(\rho) = \frac{p_H}{\Delta p}(bI_i) \qquad (10')$$

for commercial activities alone, and

$$U_i(\rho) = \frac{p_H}{\Delta p}(cI_{i-1}) \qquad (9')$$

for interbank monitoring alone. Multiplying these three expressions by the relevant probabilities of continuation and combining them, we obtain a condition on the minimum *ex ante* utility of bank i, which depends on the probabilities x_i and x_{i-1} that the commercial activities of banks i and $i - 1$ are maintained at $t = 1$:

$$E[U_i] \geqslant \frac{p_H}{\Delta p}E[y(bI_i + cI_{i-1})x_ix_{i-1} + cI_{i-1}x_{i-1}(1-x_i) + bI_ix_i(1-x_{i-1})],$$

which can also be written

$$E[U_i] \geqslant \frac{p_H}{\Delta p}\{bI_iE(x_i - (1-y)x_ix_{i-1}) + cI_{i-1}E(x_{i-1} - (1-y)x_ix_{i-1})\}.$$

$$(5.12)$$

Note that $1 - y = p_L/(p_H + p_L)$ is a simple measure of the economies of scope.[21]

---

[21] See Cerasi and Daltung (1994) for a richer study of the costs and benefits of the diversification of a bank's monitoring activities.

5.3.3 Characterization of Pareto-Optima

Pareto-Optima allocations can be obtained by maximizing a weighted sum of the banks' and depositors' utilities, under the incentive-compatibility constraints[22]:

$$\max L = \sum_{i=1}^{n} (v_i - \lambda) E[U_i] + \lambda \sum_{i=1}^{n} (E[x_i(p_H R - \rho_i)]I_i - C(I_i)) + \lambda \sum_{i=1}^{n} A_i$$

subject to, for all i,

$$E[U_i] \geqslant \frac{p_H}{\Delta p} \{ b I_i E[x_i - (1-y)x_i x_{i-1}] + c I_{i-1} E[x_{i+1} - (1-y)x_i x_{i-1}] \}.$$
$$(\text{IC}_i)$$

The welfare weight of the depositors, λ, strictly exceeds v_i for all i (otherwise the utility of at least one bank would be infinite), and so (IC_i) is binding. Therefore, we can replace $E[U_i]$ by the right-hand side of (IC_i) and obtain a simpler expression of the Lagrangian:

$$L = \sum_{i=1}^{n} (v_i - \lambda) \frac{p_H}{\Delta p} \{ b I_i E[x_i - (1-y)x_i x_{i-1}]$$
$$+ c I_{i-1} E[x_{i-1} - (1-y)x_i x_{i-1}] \}$$
$$+ \lambda \sum_{i=1}^{n} (E[x_i(p_H R - \rho_i)]I_i - C(I_i)) + \lambda \sum_{i=1}^{n} A_i.$$

In contrast with the case of date-0 monitoring, the Lagrangian is no longer separable in the x_is. The closure decisions for the n banks are now intertwined. More specifically, for a given realization $\rho = (\rho_1, \ldots, \rho_n)$ of liquidity shocks, the optimal $x = (x_1, \ldots, x_n)$ is obtained by maximizing the following expression:

$$H(x, \rho) = \sum_{i=1}^{n} (v_i - \lambda) \frac{p_H}{\Delta p} \{ b I_i (x_i - (1-y)x_i x_{i-1})$$
$$+ c I_{i-1}(x_{i-1} - (1-y)x_i x_{i-1}) \}$$
$$+ \sum_{i=1}^{n} \lambda I_i x_i (p_H R - \rho_i),$$

which can also be written in a more compact form as

$$H(x, \rho) = \sum_{i=1}^{n} u_i x_i + \sum_{i=1}^{n} v_i x_i x_{i-1} \tag{5.13}$$

---

[22]Because there is no date-0 incentive problem in this section, it is not optimal to contract at date 0 on inefficient date-1 closure decisions, and therefore we need not add the credibility constraint (5.7).

with

$$u_i \equiv I_i \left\{ \lambda(p_H R - \rho_i) - (\lambda - v_i)\frac{p_H b}{\Delta p} - (\lambda - v_{i+1})\frac{p_H c}{\Delta p} \right\}$$

and

$$v_i \equiv (1 - y)\frac{p_H}{\Delta p}(\lambda - v_i)\{bI_i + cI_{i-1}\} > 0.$$

Therefore, bank i's commercial activities are shut down at the optimum if and only if

$$\frac{\partial H}{\partial x_i} = u_i + v_i x_{i-1} + v_{i+1} x_{i+1} \leqslant 0. \tag{5.14}$$

Since v_i is positive for all i, this is less likely (other things being equal) when $x_{i+1} = 1$ or $x_{i-1} = 1$.

Proposition 5.4 (local interdependency). *A bank's commercial activities are less likely to be liquidated if its "neighbors" are not.*

Note that H satisfies the single crossing property in (x_i, ρ_i):

$$\frac{\partial^2 H}{\partial x_i \partial \rho_i} = -\lambda I_i < 0 \quad \text{for all } i.$$

Also, H is supermodular in the vector of control variables x:

$$\frac{\partial^2 H}{\partial x_i \partial \rho_i} \geqslant 0 \quad \text{for all } i, j \text{ (with equality if } |i - j| \neq 1).$$

Therefore, we can apply the monotone comparative statics result of Milgrom and Shannon (1994, theorem 4) and obtain the following proposition.

Proposition 5.5 (global interdependency). *For all i and j, bank i is more likely to be liquidated ($x_i = 0$) if the liquidity shock ρ_j facing bank j increases.*

5.3.4 Too Big to Fail and Systemic Risk

An interesting consequence of the global interdependency (proposition 5.5) is that it can lead to some (efficient) propagation of bank failures. We content ourselves with a simple example. Let us recall the expression of H:

$$H(x, \rho) = \sum_{i=1}^{n} u_i x_i + \sum_{i=1}^{n} v_i x_i x_{i-1}.$$

We demonstrate the existence of situations (that is, particular realizations of ρ) in which H has (exactly) two maxima: $x^* = (0,\dots,0)$ and $x^{**} = (1,\dots,1)$. In such situations, by the comparative statics results obtained above, a slightly higher liquidity shock for any of the banks will imply a complete breakdown of the banking system ($x^* = (0,\dots,0)$), whereas a slightly lower liquidity shock for any of the banks would on the contrary entail no failure at all ($x^* = (1,\dots,1)$). We interpret this as showing the existence of unstable situations where the failure of a single bank can propagate to the entire banking system.

Proposition 5.6 (propagation). *For some values of ρ, H has exactly two maxima: $x^* = (0,\dots,0)$ and $x^{**} = (1,\dots,1)$. Thus a small increase in a bank's liquidity shock may imply the closure of the entire banking system.*

Proof. We only give an example for $n = 3$. Recall that v_1, v_2, v_3 are given positive numbers, while u_i depends linearly on ρ_i. Therefore we have to find u_1, u_2, u_3 such that

$$0 = u_1 + u_2 + u_3 + v_1 + v_2 + v_3 \tag{5.15}$$

and

$$0 \geqslant \max(u_1, u_2, u_3, u_1 + u_2 + v_2, u_2 + u_3 + v_3, u_1 + u_3 + v_1). \tag{5.16}$$

Now (5.15) implies, in particular, that

$$u_1 + u_2 + v_2 = -[u_3 + v_1 + v_3],$$

which has to be nonpositive by (5.16). Therefore,

$$-(v_1 + v_3) \leqslant u_3 \leqslant 0.$$

Similarly, the conditions on u_1 and u_2 are

$$-(v_1 + v_2) \leqslant u_1 \leqslant 0, \qquad -(v_2 + v_3) \leqslant u_2 \leqslant 0.$$

It is obvious that these constraints are jointly compatible with (5.15). $\square$

5.4 Conclusion

We have investigated whether the flexibility afforded by decentralized interbank transactions can be made consistent with protecting the central bank against undesired rescue operations. We first argued that the flexibility must correspond to effective peer monitoring; otherwise, centralizing the payment system, the Fed funds market, and other markets in which banks currently have bilateral exposures would result in an equally efficient allocation of liquidity among banks and would facilitate prudential control.

Our preliminary insights for capital adequacy requirements are as follows. (i) Provided lenders can be made accountable for poor monitoring, interbank lending certifies the borrowing banks, which may in some circumstances be able to count some of their interbank liabilities as regulatory capital. (ii) Lender accountability requires interbank loans to be medium- or long-term loans, so lenders cannot fly by night and escape their monitoring obligations. Accountability is weakened when the central bank cannot commit not to rescue an otherwise solvent bank whose survival is jeopardized by bad interbank loans.

We also established a distinction between the soft budget constraint and too big to fail. The SBC takes the form of TBTF when central bank assistance to a solvent but failing lending bank operates through a bailout of the borrowing bank rather than through direct assistance to the lending bank. Perhaps surprisingly, we found that TBTF never occurs in the absence of returns to scope between commercial and interbank activities. On the other hand, if such returns to scope exist, the fates of banks are inexorably linked; so, a bank's trouble may permeate the entire banking system even though, in an optimal regulatory framework, domino effects can be nipped in the bud by guarantees and sufficient collateral.

Some readers may not view economies of scope as the only, or even the main, cause of TBTF. Alternative, although more complex, theories of TBTF are worth exploring. In fact, the logic emphasized in the paper of comparing the costs of alternative failure resolution methods, as compelling as it is, may well overstate the likelihood of direct lending-bank assistance relative to borrowing-bank bailout. Suppose a bank is about to fail and thereby create difficulties for some of the banks which loaned to it. Our model predicts that, in this situation, the central bank will assist only those lenders who are solvent but about to fail because of their interbank shortfall, and this at the smallest possible level of assistance. This reasoning, however, ignores transaction costs. To operate the selective rescue, the central bank must have a clear picture of (i) mutual positions, (ii) priority rules in bankruptcy (which, incidentally, are still somewhat ill-defined in netting systems), and (iii) solvent banks' needed cash infusion. While computers have substantially improved information about these dimensions of the rescue decision, the central bank must still exercise difficult judgment in a short time span in order to operate this selective rescue properly. It might then be simpler for the central bank to bail out the failing bank.

This and many other fascinating questions lie outside the scope of this paper, whose main objectives have been to build a formal framework in which analysis of interbank lending and systemic risk can begin, and to derive some first insights.

5.5 Appendix: Solution of Program ($\mathcal{P}$)

The Lagrangian of program (5.8) can be written

$$L = E[U_1(\rho)(\nu_1 - \lambda_1 + \mu_1(\rho))] + E[U_2(\rho)(\nu_2 - \lambda_2 + \mu_2(\rho) + \mu\ell(\rho_1))]$$
$$+ \sum_i \left\{ I_i E\left(x_i(\rho)\left[\lambda(p_H R - \rho_i) - \mu_i(\rho)\frac{p_H B}{\Delta p}\right]\right) \right.$$
$$\left. - \lambda C(I_i) - (\nu_2 + \mu)c I_1\right\},$$

where $\mu_i(\rho)$ and μ denote, respectively, the multipliers associated with constraints (IC$_i$) and (IC$_2'$). $x_i(\rho)$ is also required to satisfy condition (5.7). The differentiation of L_1 with respect to $U_1(\rho)$ and $U_2(\rho)$ gives

$$\mu_1(\rho) = \lambda_1 - \nu_1 \geqslant 0 \quad \text{and} \quad \mu_2(\rho) = \lambda_2 - \nu_2 - \mu\ell(\rho_1) \geqslant 0.$$

This implies that (IC$_i$) is binding for all i and ρ, except maybe when $\ell(\rho_1)$ is maximum. In other words, the incentive-compatibility constraints (IC$_i$) are always binding, except for low values of ρ_1, where $U_2(\rho)$ may be strictly above $x_2(\rho)p_H B I_2/\Delta p$. When the likelihood ratio ℓ does not vary too much with ρ_1, on the contrary, (IC$_i$) binds everywhere. This corresponds to the case of "restricted impact of interbank monitoring," on which we focus. Maximizing L_1 with respect to $x_i(\rho)$ gives

$$x_i(\rho) = 1 \quad \Longleftrightarrow \quad \rho_i \leqslant p_H R - \frac{\mu_i(\rho)}{\lambda_i}\frac{p_H B}{\Delta p} \equiv \rho_i^*(\rho), \qquad (5.17)$$

as long as $\rho_i^*(\rho) \geqslant \rho_0$.

Replacing $\mu_i(\rho)$ by its value for $i = 1, 2$, we obtain that ρ_i^* is constant (the same as in autarky) and that ρ_2^* only depends on ρ_1:

$$\rho_1^* = \rho_0 + \frac{\nu_1}{\lambda_1}\frac{p_H B}{\Delta p} = \rho_1^A, \qquad (5.18)$$

$$\rho_2^*(\rho_1) = \rho_0 + \frac{\nu_2 + \mu\ell(\rho_1)}{\lambda_2}\frac{p_H B}{\Delta p}. \qquad (5.19)$$

Maximizing L_1 with respect to I_1 yields

$$\frac{\partial L_1}{\partial I_1} = 0 = \lambda_1\{E[x_1(\rho)(\rho_1^* - \rho_1)] - (\nu_2 + \mu) - C'(I_1^*)\}.$$

Now (5.18) implies that the credibility constraint never binds for bank 1; therefore the above condition can be simplified:

$$\int_0^{\rho_1^*} F_1(\rho_1)\,d\rho_1 = E[(\rho_1^* - \rho_1)_+] = C'(I_1^*) + c\frac{v_2 + \mu}{\lambda}. \quad (5.20)$$

Finally, maximizing L with respect to I_2 gives

$$\frac{\partial L}{\partial I_2} = 0 = \lambda\{E[x_2(\rho)(\rho_2^*(\rho_1) - \rho_2)] - C'(I_2^*)\}. \quad (5.21)$$

For large values of ρ_1, the credibility constraint may be binding:

$$x_2(\rho) = 1 \quad \Longleftrightarrow \quad \rho_2 \leqslant \max(\rho_0, \rho_2^*(\rho_1)).$$

Condition (5.21) therefore becomes

$$\int_0^{+\infty} \left(\int_0^{\max(\rho_0, \rho_2^*(\rho_1))} (\rho_2^*(\rho_1) - \rho_2) f_2(\rho_2)\,d\rho_2 \right) f_1(\rho_1)\,d\rho_1 = C'(I_2^*).$$
$$(5.22)$$

Proof of proposition 5.1. By (5.18), the optimal threshold ρ_1^* is the same as under autarky (this is because the welfare weights v_i and λ are exogenous):

$$\rho_1^* = \rho_1^A = \rho_0 + \frac{v_1}{\lambda}\frac{p_H B}{\Delta p}.$$

Now, since $\tilde{F}_1$ dominates F_1 in the sense of first-order stochastic dominance, we have

$$F_1(\rho_1^*) \geqslant \tilde{F}_1(\rho_1^A),$$

which means that the borrowing bank is indeed closed less often than under autarky.

As far as investment is concerned, we start by examining the limit case $c = 0$. In that case the autarkic closure rule is feasible, since, by the independence of liquidity shocks,

$$E[U_2^A(\rho_2)\ell(\rho_1)] = E[U_2^A(\rho_2)]E[\ell(\rho_1)] = 0.$$

This implies that $\mu = 0$ and that the investment under peer monitoring, given by

$$C'(I_1^*) = \int_0^{\rho_1^*} F_1(\rho_1)\,d\rho_1,$$

is larger than the investment under autarky, given by

$$C'(I_1^A) = \int_0^{\rho_1^A} \tilde{F}_1(\rho_1)\,d\rho_1.$$

By continuity, this remains true for small c. $\qquad\qquad\qquad\qquad\square$

Proof of proposition 5.2. Part (i) has already been proved in the text. To prove (ii), let us define an auxiliary function:

$$V(\hat{\rho}) \equiv \int_0^{\hat{\rho}} (\hat{\rho} - \rho) \, dF_2(\rho) = \int_0^{\hat{\rho}} F_2(\rho) \, d\rho.$$

This function is convex; therefore by Jensen's lemma,

$$E[V(\rho_2^*(\rho_1))] \geqslant V(\rho_2^A), \tag{5.23}$$

where we have used the fact that

$$E(\ell(\rho_1)) = 0,$$

which implies that $E[\rho_2^*(\rho_1)) = \rho_2^A$.

Now the left-hand side of (5.23) is equal to $C'(I_2^*)$ (when the credibility constraint does not bind), whereas its right-hand side is just $C'(I_2^A)$. Since C' is an increasing function we have established that

$$I_2^* \geqslant I_2^A.$$

$\square$

References

Armendariz, B. 1995. On the design of a credit agreement with peer monitoring. Mimeo, London School of Economics.

Bhattacharya, S., and P. Fulghieri. 1994. Uncertain liquidity and interbank contracting. *Economics Letters* 44:287–94.

Bernheim, D., and M. Whinston. 1986. Common agency. *Econometrica* 54:923–42.

Bizer, D., and P. DeMarzo. 1992. Sequential banking. *Journal of Political Economy* 100:41–61.

Bryant, J. 1980. A model of reserves, bank runs and deposit insurance. *Journal of Banking and Finance* 4:335–44.

Calomiris, C. W., and C. M. Kahn. 1996. The efficiency of self-regulated payment systems: learning from the Suffolk system. *Journal of Money, Credit and Banking* 28(Part 2):766–97.

Cerasi, V., and S. Daltung. 1994. The optimal size of a bank: costs and benefits of diversification. Mimeo, IGIER, Milan, and Sveriges Riksbank, Stockholm.

Dewatripont, M., and J. Tirole. 1994. *The Prudential Regulation of Banks.* Cambridge, MA: MIT Press.

Diamond, D. 1984. Financial intermediation and delegated monitoring. *Review of Economic Studies* 51:393–414.

Diamond, D., and P. H. Dybvig. 1983. Bank runs, deposit insurance, and liquidity. *Journal of Political Economy* 91:401–19.

Hellwig, M. 1994. Liquidity provision, banking and the allocation of interest rate risk. *European Economic Review* 38:1363–89.

Holmström, B. 1979. Moral hazard and observability. *Bell Journal of Economics* 10:74–91.

Holmström, B., and J. Tirole. 1995. Private and public supply of liquidity. Mimeo, MIT and IDEI.

———. 1997. Financial intermediation, loanable funds, and the real sector. *Quarterly Journal of Economics* 112:663–92.

Kiyotaki, N., and J. Moore. 1997. Credit chains. Mimeo, London School of Economics.

Martimort, D. 1992. Multiprincipaux avec anti-sélection. *Annales d'Economie et de Statistique* 28:1–38.

Milgrom, P., and C. Shannon. 1994. Monotone comparative statics. *Econometrica* 62:157–80.

Shavell, S. 1979. Risk sharing and incentives in the principal–agent relationship. *Bell Journal of Economics* 10:55–73.

Stiglitz, J. 1990. Peer monitoring and credit markets. *World Bank Economic Review* 4:351–66.

Stole, L. 1992. Mechanism design under common agency. Mimeo, MIT.

Von Thadden, E. L. 1994a. Optimal liquidity provision and dynamic incentive compatibility. Mimeo, Basel.

———. 1994b. The term-structure of investment and the banks' insurance function. Mimeo, Basel.

Chapter Six

Controlling Risk in Payment Systems

Jean-Charles Rochet and Jean Tirole

Over the past twenty years the growing integration of financial markets, the development of new financial instruments, and the advance of computer technology have all contributed to a remarkable growth of financial activity in the main industrialized countries. One of the most significant consequences of this growth has been the unprecedented increase in the volume of trade on the large-value interbank payment systems (see table 6.1), which itself has resulted in a massive increase in intraday overdrafts on those systems (see table 6.2).

The central banks of the large industrialized countries, concerned with the risks that this growth was creating for their banking systems, have been studying the risks of interbank payment systems, work that has borne fruit with the Angell Report (Basel Committee 1989) and the Lamfalussy Report (Basel Committee 1990) both under the aegis of the Bank for International Settlements (BIS), and the Padoa-Schioppa Report (European Community 1992) under the aegis of the EC.

Of particular concern is the organization of interbank large-value transfer systems. Banks have traditionally concluded among themselves multilateral netting arrangements which settle at discrete time intervals. This is the modern form of clearinghouses, which still operate for small-value transfers. These arrangements ("clearing or net settlement systems") are designed to reduce the need for settlement balances and to reduce the number of portfolio adjustments. On the other hand, central banks worry about the settlement lags and implicit overdrafts associated with net systems and tend to favor "real time" or "continuous gross systems" for large-value interbank transfers. Whereas in a net system a payment is cleared with the settlement of the balance to the settlement agent (typically at the end of the day), in a gross system payment orders are examined one after the other in real time. If the sender's account has a sufficient funds balance, the order is executed irrevocably. If not, it is in principle canceled. Such cancelations, however, are costly. To make them less frequent, two mechanisms are used: the settlement agent can grant participants intraday overdrafts; and unexecuted orders can go into a queue, with an "optimization" enabling the highest number of waiting

Table 6.1. Daily payment flows (billions USD).

Payment systems		1980	1985	1990
United States	Fedwire	192	436	796
	CHIPS	148	314	885
Japan	BOJ-NET	—	—	1,031
	FEYSS	4	32	203
	Zengin	5	12	52
	CB Chèque	23	46	134
Great Britain	Town Clearing	44	47	37
	CHAPS	—	12	135
Germany	Daily Clearing	N.a.	N.a.	214
	EAF	—	N.a.	62
France	Chambre de compensation	N.a.	N.a.	89
	SAGITTAIRE	—	N.a.	26

Source: Goodhart and Schoenmaker (1993); n.a., not available.

Table 6.2. Maximum intraday overdrafts in the United States (billions USD).

Payment systems	September 1988	October 1990	April 1993
Fedwire	55	71	74
CHIPS	45	52	52

Source: Goodhart and Schoenmaker (1993).

orders to be carried out when sufficient funds are available. The gross payment principle is of concern to the commercial banks, who fear that they will have to shoulder not only collateral demands but also higher risks than in a system based on netting.

Our purposes are to review and analyze the different risks incurred by the participants in interbank large-value payment systems in order to perform a comparative study of the main interbank payment systems in operation in large industrialized countries, to identify the key ingredients of interbank payment systems and to analyze those ingredients in the light of economic theory. Finally, we develop an analytical framework encompassing existing systems and suggesting alternative organizations of the payment system.

The design of a payment system must meet several goals. Within the banking sector, the payment system must promote efficient financial management and responsibility at an individual level, and facilitate the early detection of bank insolvency. The payment system should also limit the risk that a single bank's troubles[1] propagate to other banks. The payment system must more generally enable risk control for the entire banking system.[2]

The paper is organized as follows. Section 6.1 describes the key elements of payment systems in the abstract. Section 6.2 reminds the reader of the three dominant paradigms, as illustrated by CHIPS, Fedwire, and the Swiss Interbank Clearing System (SIC). Section 6.3 highlights a few insights that an economic approach can bring to the study of payment systems. Section 6.4 introduces the analytical framework of section 6.5 through a discussion of the costs and benefits of interbank transactions. Section 6.5 develops a general analytical framework that encompasses the existing payment systems as special cases. Section 6.6 concludes.

6.1 Taxonomy of Payment Systems

6.1.1 Different Types of Risk

The main risks incurred in trading systems are credit risk, liquidity risk, operational risk, and systemic risk. Let us recall the definitions suggested by the BIS committees (Committee on Payment and Settlement Systems and Committee on Interbank Netting Systems) and used also by Parkinson et al. (1992). *Credit risk* refers to the risk of a transaction not being realized at full value. A *liquidity risk* is the risk of a settlement not being realized at the desired time but at an unspecified time in the future. Though the difference between those two risks is fundamental,

---

[1] We emphasize economic difficulties faced by a bank. Such difficulties can also result from a purely technological problem. As an illustration one can cite the computer problem the Bank of New York experienced in November 1985. Following a computer breakdown—the computer dealing with sales of government securities was refusing both to deliver the securities and to collect the funds owed to the bank—the bank found itself with an overdraft of $22.6 billion. The Fed accepted to cover it in exchange of guarantees of $36 billion. The San Francisco earthquake (1989) and the complete electricity breakdown in New York City's financial district (1990) are further examples of the potentially major risks banks may encounter.

[2] The risks attached to economic and financial crises are considerable. Be it in the United States (with the Savings and Loan collapse, the cost of which has been grossly estimated at $1,000 per inhabitant, and with the widespread crisis in the commercial banking sector with over one thousand bankruptcies in the 1980s), in Latin America (with the liquidation of 20% of Argentinean banks between 1980 and 1982, the closure of five of the largest Brazilian savings banks in April and May 1984, the forced nationalization of a large part of the banking sector in Chile and Mexico in the early 1980s), in Japan (with the housing market and stock market crisis), or in Scandinavia with the recent banking crisis (for example, three of the largest Norwegian banks were recently rescued from bankruptcy by the government), examples of such dramatic crises abound. All episodes have led to substantial concern over systemic risk and large-scale state intervention.

it is not always possible to differentiate them straightaway when there is a payment incident.[3]

Operational risks relate to computers and telecommunication systems breakdowns. As was discussed in the Bank of New York example in footnote 1, such breakdowns can have considerable consequences. Operational risks have an impact on liquidity and credit risks for at least two reasons: they increase the settlement lag, and de facto in certain cases the settlement risk if the bank in question has a nonnegligible failure probability. They also alter the possibility for the banks to control the solvency of their counterparties.

In its most widely used sense, *systemic risk* designates the risk that serious solvency and liquidity problems within one or several banks jeopardize the stability of the entire banking system (or of the marketplace). However, the BIS committees have often adopted a wider definition, which also includes the risk that payment problems encountered by a system participant might spread to a limited number of other participants. It is therefore useful to clarify the different aspects of a systemic risk.

6.1.2 The Meaning of Systemic Risk

The notion of systemic risk covers several distinct phenomena:

1. *Widespread liquidity problems stemming from unwinding in a net system or from a gross system gridlock.*[4] This is the most widely used

---

[3]To illustrate the credit and/or liquidity risks that may arise during interbank payments, let us take as a reference the case of two banks A and B (where A is in difficulty) and look at three situations:

- A sends a payment message to B, to be credited to the account of one of B's clients. B can wait for the successful close of the transaction before crediting its client's account, in which case it does not incur any risk. If it credits the account immediately and without recourse, it incurs a credit risk.

- A sends a payment message to B for B's own account (for example, to repay an interbank loan) and B lends the same funds straightaway. In that case B incurs a liquidity risk. True enough, B still has to take into account the risk that A will not repay the loan, should the payment message not be finalized, but the credit risk exists anyway. The point is that B anticipates the confirmation of A's repayment and is thus led into a second transaction which, if A's payment is not finalized, will propel B into searching for liquid assets.

- B lends to A, a classic credit risk.

See Borio and Van den Bergh (1993) for a broader discussion of payment system risks.

[4]In a net system, unwinding refers to the cancelation of all payment orders sent to and received by a failing bank during the day of its failure. Gridlock refers to a coordination failure in a gross system, where banks delay their payment orders until they themselves receive incoming orders.

definition in discussions of payment systems, but probably also the least important. In fact, the spreading of liquidity problems from one bank to other banks has in practice almost always been avoided (for example, there has never been any unwinding in net systems).

2. *Propagation of failures through interbank lending.* When banks are linked to each other through large transactions in the Fed funds and other markets, the failure of one of them may trigger a domino effect in the financial system (a theoretical model of propagation is studied in chapter 5).

3. *Macroeconomic risks having an effect on several banks.* This kind of systemic risk affects, for example, securities markets (by provoking a generalized fall in prices as in the 1987 crash (see Bernanke 1990)) and also the other settlement systems. The fall in real estate prices is another example of a macroeconomic risk.

4. *Learning-related contagion.* The idea here is that the failure of a bank is informative about the possible failure of other banks and can thus induce depositors and creditors to withdraw their funds. The information can concern either the health of the banks or (perhaps more importantly in a world where runs are chiefly runs on the interbank market) the preferences of the central bank: the news that a bank has failed suggests that other banks with similar assets could also fail, a piece of information that provokes a run; if it is uncertain whether the central bank is willing to protect the uninsured creditors of a bank, the central bank's nonintervention, when a particular bank is in trouble, can trigger a run on others.

6.1.3 The Dimensions of Payment System Design

In reality there are many types of payment systems rather than just two (gross and net). The main distinctions are as follows:[5]

(a) How are the messages processed? There are basically three existing paradigms with respect to the finality of payment orders:

- net processing (usually with decentralized management of credit risk and sharing out of that risk amongst participants, for example, CHIPS in the United States);

---

[5] There are other potential dividing lines among payment systems, such as the degree of disclosure of positions. In many systems such as Fedwire, SIC, and CHAPS, receiving banks are informed only when the payment is accepted by, say, the central bank. But more information can be revealed; for example, SIC participants can view the backlog of all payments they are destined to receive. More disclosure occurs when payment messages are sent simultaneously to, say, the central bank and to the receiving bank. See Summers (1994) for a discussion. The access conditions also differ across payment systems.

- gross processing with intervention of the settlement agent—who can be private but who more often than not is the central bank—as a counterparty to every transaction (for example, Fedwire in the United States);

- direct gross processing, without counterparty (for example, SIC in Switzerland).

The difference between the last two systems stems from the possibility of intraday overdrafts if the settlement agent permits it. Similarly, a gross system without counterparty but with queue optimization is not unlike a net system operating several times a day. A polar example of queue management is SIC, where orders are processed strictly on the FIFO mode (first in first out).[6] The only possibility offered to participants is to cancel pending payments orders. So queue management must occur through cancelation of a payment order and reentry into it. The queuing mechanism in SIC has no netting capabilities.

(b) How are losses shared in the case of failure? In the case of a bank's failure, losses are shared by everyone taking part in the system to a varying degree:

- the state, through either the central bank or the Treasury;[7]

- the settlement agent as a legal entity (e.g., the clearinghouse);

- the financial market in its entirety (this is the case of a solidarity mechanism organized by the central bank or the banking industry in which the surviving banks cover the losses of a defaulting bank proportionally to their capitalization);

- the bank's creditors;

- the bank's customers who initiated the payment orders (if such recourse is legally possible);

- the bank's shareholders;

- the depositors.

---

[6]The new version of SIC, SIC2, allows participants to attach a priority code to a payment message. The FIFO rule still applies within a priority level (Vital 1994).

[7]In the United States the Fed, when it uses collaterals posted by the banks to cover losses it had to sustain, de facto carries those losses forward onto the Deposit Insurance Fund (the FDIC), that is, the U.S. Treasury.

The loss allocation rules are fundamental: (i) these rules determine which participants in the system are called to monitor the banks; (ii) these rules clearly have an influence on the possibility of bank crises spreading and therefore on systemic risk.

Loss-sharing rules impact on the previous distinction among payment systems based on the execution of payment orders. In particular, there can in fact be a legal difference between a gross system without counter-party but with queue optimization and a net system operating several times a day. With the gross system, a bank may face a credit risk with another bank equal to the gross value of the transfer it is due. On the other hand, with a net system the risk usually accounts only for the net value. Let us illustrate this point with a fictional example of mutual debts reimbursement. Let us imagine that bank A transfers $100 to bank B which must then transfer $120 back to A, a sum corresponding to another transaction of interbank lending. If bank B cannot transfer the $120, bank A in principle loses the lot in a gross system. However, in a net system, the first transfer is canceled during the end-of-day unwinding and bank A's loss is only $20. A net system therefore means that bank A gets priority over bank B's other creditors. Net processing, whether by a receiver or by a clearing system, is likely to reduce the risk of solvency problems spreading from one bank to other banks. The losses are spread to other economic agents, especially the state, and can thus reduce systemic risk (as is noted in the Lamfalussy report).

Admittedly, this reasoning overestimates the increase in risk borne by the banks in a gross system relative to a net system, for two reasons. First, in a gross system bank A is still owed $120 by bank B. It is therefore possible for it to recover some of the monies during receivership. In fact, if the receiver decided to prioritize bank A and grant it the one hundred transferred dollars without ado, the sole difference with a net system would reside in the liquidity risk on the $100, which would only exist with a gross system; that is, bank A would receive the $100 with a long delay (and perhaps without interest, in which case there would be a credit risk as well) and would have to borrow in the meantime. Conversely, the legal status of unwinding is ill-defined. The legal system could refuse to do any netting of reciprocal debts and thus consider each debt one by one. In this case banks could be given less priority than the other creditors of a defaulting bank than is suggested by the above example.

In all cases, loss-sharing rules must be consistent with existing bankruptcy laws or legal precedents. We have already noted that the priority given by a clearing system to the bank creditors of a defaulting bank might not be granted, since it neglects the other creditors. Similarly, the "zero-hour rule" stipulates that in bankruptcy cases all payments made on bankruptcy day are rescinded retroactively.

(c) Protection methods. Overdrafts can be constrained either by ceilings or by price incentives. The price method is illustrated by Fedwire in the United States, which has been charging for intraday overdrafts since April 1994. Charging leads to reactions (see, for example, Gilbert 1989; Humphrey 1984, 1986, 1987; Hancock and Wilcox 1996) so as to reduce overdrafts (at least for healthy banks; see below). Banks can resort to bypass (by using CHIPS, of course, but also with bilateral netting or with novation agreements); to term borrowing on the interbank market or rollovers; to the development of an intraday interbank market; to passing the charge onto the clients (such as securities firms); or to delaying the payment orders as long as possible.

Quantitative instruments (which, incidentally, are subject to some of the responses described above) are more pervasive. They include the following:

- Collateral requirements, in the spirit of credit balances at a banking correspondent, or of stock market margin calls. These collaterals can comprise reserves (usually nonremunerated and therefore of a very low volume) and securities remunerated at market rate, whose cost, more complex to assess, is an opportunity cost representing the yield difference between a less liquid, and therefore more remunerative, investment and an investment in securities pledged as collaterals. This opportunity cost, therefore, depends on both the general conditions of the market (liquidity premium) and the regulatory arrangements: delimitation of the set of all securities that can be pledged as collaterals, and the importance of administrative costs.

- Ceilings or limits of bilateral overdrafts, possibly negotiated in a decentralized way, as with CHIPS, where there is also an overall limit (multilateral or net debit cap; see section 6.2.1) on the overall overdraft of one participant versus others. (Moreover, in the case of several systems operating in parallel, global caps can be defined on the entire system.)

6.2   Three Illustrations

We now describe three markedly different systems. Section 6.5 of the paper will locate these three systems within our general analytical framework.

6.2.1   A Net System: CHIPS

The Clearinghouse Interbank Payment System (CHIPS) was created in 1970. It links electronically 21 American and 113 foreign banks operating on the American market. At the end of 1990, daily transactions on CHIPS represented approximately $885 billion, with a significant proportion of international transactions.[8] Since its inception, CHIPS has operated with explicit intraday overdrafts.[9] Each participant starts the day with a nil position and regularizes its end-of-day net position with a Fedwire order before closing. Payments have been executed on the same day since 1981.

The protection of CHIPS and CHIPS participants against a bank's default has operated as follows since 1990.[10] Bilateral net credit limits are defined by the participants in a decentralized way. They are chosen daily by each bank for each of its potential debtors (they can naturally be negotiated bilaterally), and can be modified at any time within the day. The sender net debit cap is then calculated as 5% of the total net credit limit granted by the other participants, and limits the amount that any one participant can owe to the entire CHIPS system.[11] The loss-sharing rule is "the survivors pay," i.e., losses would be shared out among the surviving institutions and covered by the collaterals (in securities) previously demanded from the various participants. More precisely, should bank A default, every other participant would be due to bring in at 6.30 p.m. a contribution proportional to the highest bilateral ceiling that it gave bank A during the day. The total sum of those contributions (additional settlement obligations or ASOs) is equal to

---

[8]The 1995 levels of transaction were $1.2 trillion per day on CHIPS versus $800 billion per day on Fedwire (Richards 1995). The new daylight overdraft fees charged since April 1994 by Fedwire (which coincided with enhanced risk control measures on CHIPS) do not seem to have triggered a noticeable shift of activity from Fedwire to CHIPS (Summers 1994).

[9]Strictly speaking, CHIPS cannot have overdrafts. The correct term is "net debit position."

[10]According to the rules in force until 1990 it was expected that a bankruptcy on CHIPS would entail the unwinding of all transactions implicating the defaulting bank. Humphrey (1986) has made several simulations on the consequences of a defaulting participant. The hypothesis he adopted was that only institutions faced with losses superior to their capital fail to honor their obligations. These simulations indicate that such a bankruptcy would have affected nearly half of the participants and one-third of the transactions. That is, payments of at least $300 billion would have been canceled, which seems to underline that such systemic risk is not to be neglected. Let us note, however, that similar simulations made more recently for the Italian system (Angelini and Giannini 1993) gave notably lower systemic risks. In all cases such simulations must be looked at with great caution. The criterion (losses higher than capital) is rather arbitrary, since it does not take into account the liquidity of a bank's assets, nor the possibility of interbank lending. Moreover, Humphrey's study was completed using data collected before CHIPS had installed global and bilateral ceilings. Finally, in real life, formal rules of revocation would probably not be applied anyway.

[11]From 1986 until 1991, i.e., until just after CHIPS adopted loss-sharing procedures, banks were subject to a "cross-system cap" relative to their cumulative position on CHIPS and Fedwire.

bank A's credit balance. Participants are also due to make a collateral deposit (Treasury bills, bonds, or notes) equal at least to its highest ASO, i.e., its biggest contribution, should any participant default. As we shall formally demonstrate in section 6.5, CHIPS is thus self-protected against the failure of any of its participants alone. In the case of several institutions defaulting simultaneously, rules are more complex and self-protection is not complete. The reader is referred to the Federal Reserve Bank of New York introductory paper on CHIPS (1991) for more details.

6.2.2 A Gross System with Counterparty:[12] Fedwire

Fedwire is an old system, since it was created simultaneously with the Federal Reserve Banks on November 16, 1914. Fedwire is very open since it regroups nearly eleven thousand banks today; it operates on a gross payment mode where transactions are irrevocable. The Fedwire settlement agent, the Fed itself, guarantees a successful close to the transactions.

Intraday overdrafts on Fedwire have traditionally been large, an average $55 billion in September 1988 (see Clair 1991, p. 123) compared with the $45 billion total debit position on CHIPS, and the Fed's past efforts to reduce them had not been very successful (Clair 1991, pp. 127–28; Hancock and Wilcox 1996). One of the reasons is the high overdraft ceiling on Fedwire. Another is that until 1991, book entry securities transactions were not posted in the Fedwire ceiling so that they would not bear on the functioning of the U.S. Treasury bond market or on the running of open market trading. As a result, 60% of overdrafts on Fedwire were excluded from ceilings calculations (Federal Reserve Bank of New York 1989). This anomaly was corrected in 1991.

Intraday overdrafts on Fedwire used to be free. Today, overdraft facilities are still free of charge, but their utilization is priced (in contrast, standard credit lines carry both facility and utilization fees). In April 1994, daylight overdrafts started carrying a charge of ten basis points (0.10%) of average per-minute daylight overdraft, less a deductible amount equal to 10% of the institution's risk-based capital. The daylight overdraft fee was raised to fifteen basis points in April 1995. (It may be useful to remember that in net payment systems, intraday overdrafts do not appear explicitly and are therefore necessarily free.) The Fedwire daylight overdraft fees produced a dramatic decline in overdrafts. Both the peak overdrafts and the average per-minute overdrafts fell by approximately 40% in the six months following the introduction of fees.

---

[12]Strictly speaking, the Federal Reserve is not a counterparty to transactions over Fedwire. The situation is therefore different (from the legal viewpoint) from that of a futures or options clearinghouse, which is indeed the legal counterparty to all transactions.

The fees have also triggered a couple of institutional changes (Richards 1995; Summers 1994; Hancock and Wilcox 1996).[13] On the other hand, for most institutions, the net debit caps seem to be the more relevant factor constraining daylight overdrafts (Richards 1995).[14]

It is interesting to compare Fedwire with futures or options clearing-houses. These systems have a lot in common. Gorton (1985) argues that the Fed's creation was more a rationalization of the American clearing-houses than a real reform. As with the Fed, clearinghouse staff are in charge of monitoring; participants are not supposed to monitor each other.[15] Finally, clearinghouses ensure that all transactions are brought to a successful close. Yet there remain some important differences:

- There is in principle no insurance mechanism originating from the central bank (lender of last resort) in the case of a clearinghouse.

- The clearinghouses are self-protected by margin calls (comparable to collaterals) and by the existence of limits on intraday price varia-tions. Although theoretically the systemic risk is nil, clearinghouses must be capitalized, since they may suffer losses stemming from a delay between margin calls and price changes and the possible nonresponse to a margin call; credit lines with banks further reduce the risk of their insolvency.

6.2.3 CHIPS and Fedwire: Cooperation and Competition

Theoretically, these two systems are potential competitors. Practically, the markets are relatively segmented (see table 6.3): CHIPS specializes in international transactions which, in 1987, represented in volume 82% of its payments (unlike Fedwire, CHIPS is compatible with SWIFT[16]). In

---

[13]Hancock and Wilcox find that the increase in the fee from zero to ten basis points has reduced the average daily maximum overdraft on Fedwire by $85 billion and the amount of aggregate overdrafts at any time during the day by $40 billion. Some institutions have installed automated systems for managing and queuing payments they send. Large banks have also started passing charges on to some of their customers, and peaks of securities overdrafts have moved earlier in the day.

[14]There are other signs that the fees charged by Fedwire are moderate. No intraday fund market has yet developed (although quotes on interbank overnight funds start depending on the time of the day at which funds are sent or received (see Summers 1994)). Last, there does not seem to have been a significant shift in the value of payment activity to later in the day (Summers 1994).

[15]A notable exception in the clearinghouse group is CHIPS, which is very decentralized (for other recent exceptions for OTC transactions, see Parkinson et al. (1992, p. 23)).

[16]SWIFT is an international network (operated by a cooperative organization created and owned by commercial banks) which facilitates the exchange of payments and other financial messages between financial institutions.

Table 6.3. Transactions by survey category by
wire system (daily amounts in millions of dollars).

	CHIPS			
Types of transaction	Number of transactions	%	Dollar amount	%
Securities purchase/ redemption/ financing	32	1.2	930	1.7
Bank loan	44	1.6	1,001	1.8
Federal funds	10	0.4	146	0.3
Commercial and misc.	131	4.7	4,702	8.4
Settlement	130	4.7	7,140	12.8
Eurodollar placements	659	23.7	18,259	33.0
Foreign exchange	1,773	63.8	23,476	42.0
Totals	2,779	100.0	55,652	100.0

	Fedwire			
Types of transaction	Number of transactions	%	Dollar amount	%
Securities purchase/ redemption/ financing	990	32.6	27,717	24.8
Bank loan	79	2.6	2,340	2.1
Federal funds	888	29.2	39,709	35.5
Commercial and misc.	540	17.8	18,762	16.8
Settlement	228	7.5	11,735	10.5
Eurodollar placements	289	9.5	11,200	10.0
Foreign exchange	27	0.9	245	0.2
Totals	3,041	100.0	111,708	100.0

Source: Federal Reserve Bank of New York (1987).

fact, according to a Federal Reserve Bank of New York study (1987), 99%
of international transactions were routed via CHIPS; moreover, 70% of
international transactions on Fedwire were occurring after the 4.30 p.m.
closure of CHIPS. On the other hand, Fedwire had the quasimonopoly of
federal funds transfers (99.6%) and of securities transactions (96.8%). In

1990, daily transactions were $638 billion for Fedwire and $622 billion for CHIPS.

Nevertheless, the potential competition is considerable. Furthermore, the two systems are inexorably linked. Since CHIPS net positions settle on Fedwire it may seem difficult to isolate a payment default on CHIPS from a payment default on Fedwire. Moreover, the banks can choose between the two payment systems. The control of positions by the Fed must therefore take place simultaneously on both systems, unless CHIPS is completely self-protected (which is not quite the case, since there is a possibility of simultaneous default of several institutions).

A third observation is that the technology of payment systems has a very high fixed cost and a very low marginal cost (for the clearinghouse). A situation of perfect competition with transactions charges at marginal cost would inevitably lead to losses on both systems, a situation which could probably be sustained by the public system for a while, but which might eliminate the private system.[17]

6.2.4   A Gross System without Counterparty: SIC

SIC (Swiss Interbank Clearing) was set up jointly by a group of Swiss commercial banks and the SNB (Swiss National Bank).[18] It came into service in June 1987. It works on a gross payment mode, with a twenty-two-hour-a-day settlement period and without overdraft facilities from the central bank.[19] However, banks participating in SIC must have an account with the SNB, so as to settle their transactions on SIC. These accounts are different from the master accounts that manage the commercial banks' reserves with the SNB. The banks (who have real time access to all the transactions concerning their account) can therefore freely allocate their liquid assets between their two accounts, knowing well that any payment order on SIC that is not fully covered will not be carried out. In that case the order goes onto a waiting list and is carried out on the FIFO mode as soon as there are sufficient funds. Should an order not have been carried out at "cut-off one" (currently, 3 p.m.), it is canceled

---

[17]Incidentally, note that the two systems currently have very different pricing rules: discounts on CHIPS and proportional charges on Fedwire according to the number of transactions. In fact, CHIPS has a complex fee schedule, involving both the sender and the receiver, which provides incentives for banks to follow technical standards that facilitate automated processing, and to originate large volumes. We thank Bruce Summers for drawing our attention to this point.

[18]For a detailed analysis of SIC, the reader is referred to Vital and Mengle (1988) and Vital (1994).

[19]The SIC infrastructure (hardware, software, network) is owned by Telekurs AG, a company jointly owned by the Swiss banks, and is exclusively operated by the central bank.

Table 6.4. Participation, volume, and value of payments on SIC
(June 10 to December 31, 1987).

	1987*	1988	1989
Number of participants	95	157	163
(end of period)			
Number of payments			
Daily average	32,348	127,296	223,467
Peak day	72,029	318,816	437,910
Annual total	4,722,841	32,333,203	56,135,513
Value of payments (billions SF)			
Daily average	77	99	120
Peak day	133	203	250
Annual total	11,163	25,183	30,020
Value of payments (billions USD)			
Daily average	52	68	73
Peak day	89	139	153
Annual total	7,492	17,202	18,350
Average payment (SF)	2,363,619	778,858	534,772
Approximate amount of largest			
payments (millions SF)	800	800	800

Source: Vital (1990, p. 6).

and has to be presented again on the following day. Immediately after cut-off one, only the orders corresponding to regularization payments (payments between SIC participants) are taken into account for same-day settlement. Participants with a deficit thus have one hour to find sufficient funds to regularize their position. If they do not succeed in regularizing their position at cut-off two (4 p.m.), the participants can draw on (expensive) collateralized credit lines preestablished with the SNB, and the SNB can come to the rescue of participants undergoing technical problems.

Significant data relating to SIC can be found in tables 6.4 and 6.5. Since January 1988 the SNB has notably done away with mandatory reserves. Consequently, the average amount of reserves outstanding held by SIC participants has gone down from approximately SF7.5 billion to SF2.4 billion in 1990, while the average daily turnover (circulation speed) has increased from SF12 to SF48 billion (SF80 on peak days). Yet the system is working rather well in spite of the low reserve levels and the absence of a genuine intraday interbank market. First, the banks sort the payments. They start with the low-value and finish with the high-value payments (which otherwise could block the system). They also split the high-value payments (amounts over SF100 million) into smaller chunks. This

Table 6.5. SIC payments by payment size, 1989.

Payment size (SF)	Percent of total	
	Volume	Value
1–4,999	79.5	0.2
5,000–999,999	16.1	2.2
1 million and more	4.4	97.6

Source: Vital (1990, p. 7).

presorting helps to reduce the necessary reserves. And, third, charging penalizes late input and late settlement of payment orders (Vital 1990, p. 14), which further encourages presorting.[20] Because high-value payments go onto a waiting list, as if in a batch, the Swiss system shares some features with a net system.[21]

6.3 An Economic Approach to Payment Systems

6.3.1 Even in a Payment System, the Primitive Problem Is that of Solvency, Not of Liquidity

Let us consider an imaginary world where all banks are solvent. Then, as soon as some basic markets exist, the payment system is irrelevant, as a bank in need of money can find it almost instantaneously.

- True enough, an ill-conceived system (for example, without an interbank market or an outside supplier of liquid assets) could create artificial synchronization problems. But banks and central banks are sophisticated actors who understand those questions well. The fact that unwinding in a net system and SIC-type gross system gridlock can arise from *artificial* liquidity problems created by the system is well-understood.

- Another possible objection to the irrelevance of the payment system with solvent banks is that a gross system enables intraday charging while a net system does not. Economic theory can, of course, only agree with the idea of charging an intraday interest rate (a commodity at 11 a.m. is not the same thing as a commodity at 3 p.m.). This question, however, seems to us rather minor. What

---

[20]There is also some netting of foreign exchange transactions between two big banks, with the corresponding Swiss franc payments settled via SIC on a gross basis.

[21]We refer to Vital (1994) for a description of the timing of payments in volume and value.

will the transaction costs be in an economy where industrial and commercial actors start drawing up their delivery contracts in terms of hours and minutes rather than days? Will these transaction costs not exceed the economic loss associated with the absence of the intraday credit market?

To our mind, the *serious* problems of liquidity are those associated with solvency. The chief problem is one of monitoring, detection, and intervention vis-à-vis troubled banks. Only after having discussed this question can we possibly tackle the implications for the organization of payment systems.

We must note that solvency issues are longer-term questions.[22] This does not mean that liquidity questions are secondary, quite the contrary: as banks are often forewarned of their clients' solvency problems when they are asked for a credit line extension or for a complementary loan, by the same token, banks' liquidity problems play the (imperfect) role of *signal* for the banking authorities.

6.3.2   Is Monitoring a Natural Monopoly?

Bank monitoring entails the collection of all relevant information concerning a bank. This information can be relatively objective, such as the bank's net position on a payment system, its liquidity ratio, or the updating of its balance sheet. It is also often quite subjective (but nevertheless very useful), such as the probability of reimbursement of certain loans granted by the bank, the correlation of the risks (for example, the interest and exchange rate risks) it is facing, or the central bank's willingness to lend, should the said bank be in distress. Information acquisition is expensive and information is a public good: once it has been collected it can be used by all (for example, a rating can be communicated to all at a negligible cost). The *technical* optimum therefore consists in having one monitor only (natural monopoly).

The nature of the natural monopoly of information collection must be seen in its broadest sense. Some economic agents, due to their privileged relationship with a bank, may have easier access than others to certain relevant elements of information about that bank, but may have more difficult access to other elements. A natural monopoly means that it is technically more efficient not to multiply the agents collecting the same particular piece of information, but to organize things in such a way

---

[22]For example, according to Todd (1991), S&L's historical insolvency criterion is the absence of complete reimbursement for sixty days. The central bank often anticipates bank failures before they actually happen; intraday surprises are rare. In fact, as is noted in the well-known U.S. Treasury report (1991, p. X-2), most failed American banks had previously been assessed as being undercapitalized.

that each piece of information is collected by the agent whose cost of information acquisition is the lowest.

These are the natural monitors of a bank:

- the central bank (banking supervisors, payment services, or the Reserve Bank Operations Division) or other government agencies (deposit insurance fund, Securities and Exchange Commission, etc.);

- a clearinghouse;

- the other banks;

- (for a small bank) a larger bank acting as a correspondent;

- the auditor;

- a stock or claimholder (for example, a private insurance company that insures deposits and has control rights, or a big shareholder);

- a rating agency;

- the clients of the bank.

It is important to understand that, for several reasons, *the (purely technical) natural monopoly character of monitoring does not, from an economic viewpoint, imply the existence of a sole lender.*

First, the lending institution, in view of the size of its own capital, may not necessarily be able to finance the totality of the loans for which it is the sole monitor, although it can act as a leader and attract other funds by committing its own capital (see, for example, Holmström and Tirole 1997).

Second, monitoring is an expensive activity for the lender and therefore also for the borrower. A trustworthy borrower will thus prefer to borrow from lenders exercising a lighter kind of monitoring, as the latter are cheaper. Thus firms with high net worth (Hoshi et al. 1993) or reputational capital (Diamond 1991) can use the bond market. The analogy for banks is that well-capitalized or reputable banks be subject to light monitoring on the interbank market.

Third, that the borrower might become too dependent on the sole lender has called into question the technical vision of a natural monopoly in monitoring. This idea was developed in the context of the bank–client relationship (see, for example, Rajan 1992), but it can also be applied to the situation where the borrower is a bank. Consider a firm that has a relationship with only one bank ("main bank"). Over time, the bank acquires private information about the firm and thus some superiority over other potential lenders; later on it will be able to demand stringent terms from the firm. Of course, other lenders will then be able to offer the firm more advantageous terms, but they will be reluctant to do so because of the well-known "winner's curse" phenomenon. A new lender succeeds in providing the firm with a loan when the main bank has access to private pessimistic information and thus seeks to disengage itself. In other words, the new lender tends to take over precisely when the firm's prospects are poor. (There are certain analogies between a firm's fear of a main bank's future power and the fear of commercial banks vis-à-vis the central bank as a sole interlocutor.) The alternative is to deal with at least two banks. While monitoring duplication makes this solution onerous today, the increase in competition will protect the firm from future abuse.

6.3.3   The Necessity of an Adequacy between the Role and the Incentives of the Monitor

It is clear that monitors must have proper incentives to monitor. There must exist both a stake and a means of intervention. Intervention can be classified using Hirschman's (1970) classic distinction between "voice" (active intervention) and "exit" (passive intervention).

On the one hand, the monitor can force the bank's management to reorient its policy by imposing overdraft ceilings, solvency requirements, a recapitalization or a risk-taking reduction (regulator), or by directly taking part in certain important aspects of the bank's management (shareholders).

On the other hand, the monitor can disengage himself in the same way that a clearinghouse can exclude one of its members.[23]

6.3.4   Limiting the Overdrafts: Price or Quantities?

The two main ways to limit overdrafts are to charge interest on intraday overdrafts and to set quantitative limits (caps). The economist's prime instinct is to recommend that commodities and services be priced at a level close to their costs.[24] This would justify the charging of intraday overdrafts, especially when they expose the central bank (or settlement agent or other counterparties) to a credit risk. However, we have been warned by economic theory and banking practice against a naive use of prices in situations where information is incomplete. Just as bankers are

---

[23]The case of a rating agency is slightly different. What is at stake is the rating agency's reputation rather than direct monetary incentives; the intervention method is the disclosure of information to other actors.

[24]Some authors such as Angell (1991) and Faulhaber et al. (1990) have supported the idea that intraday overdraft charges should play a prime role.

not content with charging their clients debit interests but also put a limit on their overdrafts, the central bank or the settlement agent should not content themselves with tariffing banks' overdrafts. It may be useful to see why.

Moral hazard problems. Overdraft charges and, in particular, charges that increase with the level of overdrafts (or decrease with the bank's level of equity capital) increase a troubled bank's difficulties. This reinforces the natural propensity of such banks to choose high-risk strategies. Naturally, tariffing overdrafts may play a dissuasive role and induce banks to reduce their overdrafts, but it is easy to demonstrate that it could also have the opposite effect. That is, the overdraft demand can grow with the rate of interest they are charged! Overdraft charging increases failure probability and may thus encourage the bank to increase its overdraft and take further risk to try "to save its skin" (see Dewatripont and Tirole (1994, chapter 13) for more details).

Adverse selection problems. Tariffing can also create adverse selection problems for the lender. Indeed, an interest rate increase tends to eliminate the banks with low *nonobservable* risk and to select those with high *nonobservable* risk. This is due to the fact that the probability of a high-risk bank reimbursing an overdraft is low. The rate increase will therefore have a lesser effect than with a low-risk bank that knows that it will repay its overdraft. (This reasoning has given birth to credit rationing theory (see, for example, Jaffee and Russell 1976; Stiglitz and Weiss 1981).)

Thus, capping overdrafts or, equivalently, demanding sufficient collateral seems a reasonable response to moral hazard and adverse selection problems. It should be noted, though, that demanding much collateral seriously curtails the banks' transformation role (inducing some "narrow banking") and relatedly creates difficulties for small and medium-sized firms (through a "credit crunch").

6.3.5 Externalities between Payment Systems

This section looks at the costs and benefits of the coexistence of several payment systems. We first consider complementary and then substitute systems.

(a) Externalities between Complementary Systems

Two systems are complementary if there is between them a clear division in the sharing of operations. For example, one system may have a monopoly on the payment of securities transactions while another manages the other payments. We have seen that Fedwire and CHIPS can be described as complementary for the time being, although they are in fact likely to become more substitutable in the future.

Externalities can be found even between complementary systems.

Supervision of a private settlement agent. As systems overflow into one another into what is a pyramid of payment systems, problems in one system can have repercussions on another. In practice, the final settlement usually takes place in the system managed by the central bank (for example, CHIPS in Fedwire) and the propagation risk between systems disappears.

One must, however, accept the existence of an externality. A clearinghouse could let its members take risks (especially correlated risks) and rely on the central bank in case of difficulties. It therefore seems legitimate for the central bank to ask to verify (1) the position of the participants of the private clearinghouse, (2) the health of the clearinghouse itself, and (3) the existence of clear risk-sharing rules.

Verification of (1) amounts to saying that the central bank needs the information of the clearinghouse to supervise its participants; (2) and (3) stem from the idea that the clearinghouse itself is a financial intermediary that needs to satisfy capital adequacy.

Coordination between systems. The separated management of systems, even when complementary, can be inconvenient.

It is inefficient to impose overdraft ceilings and collateral requirements *without coordination.* (Note that we are now beginning to see cross-margining agreements (for example, between the Options Clearing Corporation and the Chicago Mercantile Exchange) that share the collaterals as well as any profit or loss in the computation of margin requirements (see Parkinson et al. 1992).) First, a bank might have large credit positions on one system and debit ones on another, though its net position on both systems together is balanced. It could then be faced with artificial liquidity problems on the system where it is in debit. This is similar to what could happen on security markets. For example, in the United States, a financial intermediary could buy stock options and then sell the same securities on the cash market or on credit on two different clearinghouses.

Second, even for a bank which is in debit on all systems, there is little chance that systems independently choose a socially correct level of collateral. For example, if on different systems the risks are independent, the individual protection of each system then neglects diversification. The quantity of collateral necessary to protect satisfactorily n coordinated systems is much smaller than n times the quantity of collateral necessary to protect one system only.

Relatedly, it is probably a good thing that systems, even complementary ones, manage together the liquidity crises of a bank. After all, payment systems can be considered as potential lenders to the bank. As such they can play the hot potato game, that is, get into a run so as to offload their losses onto other systems when the bank is in trouble. This run can take the form of increased demands for collateral or, relatedly, of reductions of the unsecured overdraft ceilings. We must remember that systems can then become too strict in terms of bank control and that ideally one should be able to renegotiate debts to obtain better coordination.[25] However, in view of the very short operational time span of payment systems this renegotiation may be difficult to achieve.

(b) Substitute Systems: Regulation of Competition

For the time being there seems to be relatively little competition between payment systems. Yet competition is likely to grow and will involve prices (for example, tariff differences between Fedwire and CHIPS), the system's reliability, opening times (note that the Federal Reserve Board decided in February 1994 to expand its operating hours to eighteen hours a day, from 12:30 a.m. to 6:30 p.m., beginning in 1997, presumably in order to enter the international payments market), participation costs (securities requirements, net versus gross, ceiling levels), and the system's ease of use.

Of course, the different components of competition do not have the same impact. For example, as long as prices must track the marginal costs of payment transfers, they cannot have a determining role in the choice of a system for the transfer of high-value payments. In that case, ceiling levels and collateral requirements are more crucial determinants of market shares.

The advantages of competition. As always, competition creates incentives for efficiency and better service, in particular through comparison with competitors ("yardstick competition"). Furthermore, competition

---

[25]Let us illustrate this point with the following simplistic example where two systems coexist: system 1 (public) and system 2 (private). A bank needs an overdraft or a credit equal to 3 on system 2. If it gets the credit, its assets will be worth 10 with probability $\frac{1}{2}$. Otherwise they will be worth 0. The social optimum is to grant the overdraft because $\frac{1}{2} \cdot 10 > 3$. Let us now suppose that system 1 holds senior debt, value 6, from the bank (for example, via the deposit insurance fund, which, for the purpose of illustration, we assume to be senior). *In the absence of concerted action*, system 2 will not grant the overdraft, because the most it will ever get from the bank is $(10 - 6) = 4$, or an expectation of 2. This is the classic phenomenon of debt overhang according to which each lender is loath to lend as it does not internalize the positive externality of its loan on already existing debts held by other lenders. It is therefore necessary, either to *renegotiate* system 1's debt or to induce system 1 to authorize an overdraft itself.

protects participants somewhat against possibly abusive requirements of a monopolistic operator.

The disadvantages of competition. Disadvantages specific to substitute systems must be added to those, already listed, of complementary systems:

- *Duplication of substitute systems.* This duplication might be avoided if one system operated a single support and gave access to all competing systems. One would have to make sure that access is equitable (as with Computer Reservations Systems). Alternatively, one can avoid duplication by having the single, common support operated by a third party (as with the dismantling of AT&T).

- *Predation.* A system can enter into fierce competition (low prices, low collateral requirements, high ceilings, etc.) in order to make a competing private system lose money and stop it from trading. Less extremely, the incentive to build a network can also result in relentless competition for market shares, insofar as the participants perceive the costs of switching payment system. This latter possibility is relevant to the understanding of competition in regulatory laxity between financial markets. This is particularly important in the case of mixed systems, that is, when one of them is managed by the central bank.[26]

---

[26]On that point it is interesting to note that in the United States, there are two constraints on Fedwire. (1) The Monetary Control Act imposes a long-term cost and revenue matching (global) constraint for the priced services of the Federal Reserve (see the Fed press release of March 26, 1990). For the moment, there is a further constraint, self-imposed by the Federal Reserve Board, that production costs be recovered by product line and not only on average (see Summers 1991). If the experience of other industries (such as telecommunications) is of any relevance, this self-imposed constraint may be loosened with the advent of competition among payment systems. Namely, the allocation of fixed costs among product lines poses certain problems when facing competition on certain segments. The fixed costs of installing and managing the system are large. Fixed costs allocation is an accounting device that has very little to do with economic reality. Moreover, it is difficult to define prices and marginal costs on those markets. First, prices are net, taking into account the costs to the bank of depositing collateral and of using other systems when caps are reached. Second, those net prices are not the same for everyone since self-protection methods are not the same for every bank. Finally, and relatedly, the marginal cost of a transaction for the system depends on the threat this transaction poses it. Thus, it is difficult to equalize prices and average costs on payments simply with accounting rules. There is also an upstream debate about optimum prices (average cost or Ramsey price, marginal cost, other rule) that we shall omit here. (2) The Board is forced to perform an analysis of "competitive impact." In other words, it is accepted that the Fed could have a dominant position. It must, however, avoid abusing its dominant position when making choices with regards to Fedwire.

6.4   Centralization versus Decentralization

We now turn to the analytical contribution of the paper, namely, the specification of alternative and more general rules for controlling risks in payment systems. This section introduces the formal framework developed in section 6.5. To make reasoning easier, we shall begin with the extreme case where the central bank is the only monitor, and then we shall introduce the possibility of interbank loans (intraday and overnight), implying mutual monitoring by the commercial banks.

6.4.1   The Extreme Case of the Central Bank as the Only Monitor

First, let us consider the extreme case where centralized monitoring is desirable. Since in this case banks are not supposed to monitor each other, it is logical that interbank loans be insured and that the central bank suffer all failure costs. In exchange, the central bank must have the means to monitor and intervene. The central bank is then the banks' banker in the strongest sense of the word. Everything is as if interbank transactions were prohibited and the central bank acted as a counterparty to all transactions.

This is only a benchmark, which will serve as an intermediary step in our argument. However, the paradigm described here is more than a pure invention. Centralized monitoring systems do exist, with some differences. For instance, the settlement agent in a clearinghouse for options or futures markets acts as a counterparty to all transactions; the participants do not have any bilateral position (which is equivalent to having bilateral positions insured by the settlement agent on condition that the latter be aware of those bilateral positions) and are not supposed to monitor each other. The settlement agent is the sole monitor and is entitled to reduce overdrafts, demand collateral, exclude a participant, etc. (There are two differences with the paradigm envisaged here: the clearinghouse has an explicit budgetary constraint and there are complementary systems, so that any failure puts several systems at risk.) Closer to our paradigm is the case where interbank loans (especially to the large banks) are implicitly insured. For example, even though certain interbank loans do not get reimbursed in case of failure, our paradigm can be considered as a rough approximation of a number of existing systems.

It is then easy to see that the concept of intraday overdrafts is much too restrictive, as they represent only part of the risk banks are inflicting on the central bank; furthermore, if constraints are imposed on those intraday overdrafts, they may be partly replaced by interbank loans with various maturities. Within that paradigm, the central bank must therefore monitor the "generalized overdraft" continuously.

The proper measurement of this generalized overdraft (denoted by $-\Delta_i(t)$ in the next section) lies beyond the limited scope of this study. It might, for example, include the intraday overdraft, the net position on the interbank market, and the positions to be unwound on the derivatives markets.

The advantages of a centralized system are that institutions conform to the monitoring-is-a-natural-monopoly idea (there are no externalities between lenders or between payment systems), and that there is no systemic risk, since interbank "loans" are insured.

The disadvantages of a centralized system are contingent on the extent of regulatory discretion:

- Either generalized overdraft ceilings are based on *objective* or *uniform* criteria (for example, level of equity capital as in the United States). In that case, the system lacks flexibility because it does not use the finer subjective information on bank solvency. Objective measures are often accounting measures, slow at reflecting new information and not taking into account, or only slightly, such information as the market value or the correlation of assets. On that point, one may remember that bankers must often assess whether it is opportune to give further credit to their clients. At an interbank level, this point underlines the importance of subjective information.

- Or the central bank is authorized to adjust *discretionarily* the generalized overdraft caps that may in particular depend on its assessment of the health of each bank. This solution increases regulatory flexibility and may enable stronger banks to increase their authorized overdrafts. The drawbacks of discretionary regulation are well-known: possibility of favoritism or capture (the possibility of capture also exists when there is a uniform rule, but it is easier to detect than in the case of specific rules for each single bank) and risk of a "soft-budget constraint" for banks.

- Finally, banks could either be dependent on the central bank's decisions or play a game of clandestine and inefficient bypass.

Suppose now we accept the idea of a relatively nondiscretionary regulation, thus based only on objective information (this is in the spirit of the Basel agreements on solvency regulation). One could nonetheless make use of subjective (fine) information without providing the central bank with discretion. For instance, a private settlement agent or the other banks could act as monitors and use fine information, provided they have proper incentives. Thus, uninsured interbank loans or overdrafts authorized by a settlement agent use fine information (although not necessarily in an optimal way, since there are externalities on the other lenders, including the deposit-insurance system if there is one).

6.4.2 Adding Interbank Loans and Banks' Mutual Monitoring

One way to reflect fine information is to authorize loans on the interbank and monetary markets *on top of* the central bank capped overdrafts. Those loans *must not be insured* if they are to reflect decentralized information efficiently. This possibility is particularly appealing to the large commercial banks, which in the United States or in France tend to be net borrowers. (Allen et al. (1989) show that the money center banks are net borrowers on the (unsecured[27]) Fed Funds Market; small banks, however, are net lenders on this market while they go to the (secured) repurchase agreements market when they need money.)

There are two possible interpretations of this situation, interpretations that have very different implications as to the desirability of aggregating unsecured loans with overdrafts. First, it may be that larger banks represent a *lower risk* and thus can borrow without collateral. The fine information about a bank's good health is then reflected in an overdraft-plus-interbank-loans aggregate level of borrowing higher than for other banks. This is all quite healthy.

On the other hand, it may also be that large banks find it easier to borrow because it is assumed that their debts are insured de facto: they are "too big to fail." (As an example, sixty-six banks had noninsured deposits with the Continental Illinois Bank superior to their own equity capital (net worth) when the bank failed in 1984. It was difficult for the authorities not to react. And in fact, in most countries, governments step in to avoid or minimize the consequences of a large bank's failure. The recent Scandinavian experience is a further illustration of that point.) In that case, such loans do not in any way reflect the fine information on the good health of the bank.

Here again we are finding two essential elements of the debate: healthy banks are legitimately concerned with managing their borrowings with sufficient flexibility, and the central bank is equally rightly concerned about being forced to bring in funds (to avoid failures spreading) that it has no desire to release.

---

[27] In 1986, only 3.48–32.72% of the deposits at the six largest New York clearinghouse banks were insured (Todd 1991).

6.5   An Analytical Framework

6.5.1   Description

The objectives stated in the previous section—flexibility for the banks and control by the central bank—need not be incompatible. The trust that banks have in each other can, even on a single system, be expressed (as on CHIPS) through *bilateral overdraft ceilings*. These ceilings can be added to the debit ceiling agreed upon by the other lender, the central bank, in order to create flexibility; then the net balances corresponding to the overdrafts and mutual lending operations should not be insured by the central bank, so as to induce mutual monitoring.

To reduce the risk that the central bank be forced to step in to avoid a propagation, bilateral caps could also be *subjected to a rule limiting spillovers*. An example of such a rule is given by the constraint:

$$\frac{\text{BC}_{ji}}{\text{NW}_j} \leqslant f(S_i),$$

where BC_{ji} is the bilateral cap granted by bank j to bank i, NW_j represents j's net worth (or equity), S_i is a measure of i's solvency (either its solvency ratio, or a rating, or an aggregate of such measures), and $f(S_i)$ is an increasing function of S_i. Such a rule only transposes and adapts to the short term the restrictions against large risks included in international solvency regulations (those restrictions against large risks, included in the Basel agreements, are not specific to interbank loans and are designed to overcome the lack of portfolio risk measures in the definition of the Cooke ratio, rather than to address the too-big-to-fail issue). Clearly the idea is to limit the lending bank's losses relative to its net worth (equity capital) so that it does not get into difficulties should the borrowing bank fail. The constraint on the maximum intraday overdraft cap could in fact be less rigid than that on overnight or longer-term loans, in order to reflect the high uncertainty about the arrival time of payments during the day.

Because of the very short time to reach agreement, overdraft authorizations and interbank overnight loans, contrary to long-term loans, do not usually include covenants limiting the borrower's total indebtedness. Global caps are (imperfect) substitutes for such missing covenants. One can also imagine that global caps be made contingent on bilateral caps (as on CHIPS) so as to reflect the fine information, and possibly the bank's equity (net worth). In such a system, the global cap for the net interbank balance of bank i is given by

$$\text{GC}_i = g\left(\sum_{j \neq i} \text{BC}_{ji}, S_i \right),$$

where g is an increasing function of its two variables.

Let us now clarify those ideas by taking the case of intraday trading in a continuous time settlement system. A "day" begins at time 0, when the central bank and the banks fix bilateral caps. Bank i receives caps BC_{0i} from the central bank and BC_{ji} from bank j ($j = 1, \ldots, n, j \neq i$). One could consider the case where, as on CHIPS, those ceilings can be adjusted during the day, but we are taking them as constant to simplify the presentation. In the same way, we are simplifying the presentation by ignoring global cap constraints. Let t be any time during the day. We shall note the following points:

- $\Delta_{ij}(t)$ is the cumulative net balance from 0 to t of the payment orders from j to i, that is, the sum of payments already sent from j to i less the sum of payments already sent from i to j. $\Delta_{ij}(t)$ is therefore positive if i is in credit versus j. Likewise, $\Delta_{i0}(t)$ represents the net cumulative balance of bank i vis-à-vis the central bank (where the central bank is here treated like the other banks and not as a settlement agent acting as a counterparty). $\Delta_{i0}(t)$ is positive if bank i has a surplus vis-à-vis the central bank.

- $\Delta_i(t) = \Delta_{i0}(t) + \sum_{j \neq i} \Delta_{ij}(t)$ is the global net cumulative position of bank i.

To fully understand the link between those variables it is useful to refer to existing systems (later we shall give a full description of the constraints on those systems). For example, CHIPS keeps track of the bilateral positions $\Delta_{ij}(t)$ (on top of the global position). On the other hand, in a system such as Fedwire, where the settlement agent acts as a counterparty to all payments, the only position to be entered is the global position $\Delta_i(t)$.

We shall now review the different characteristics of the system just described: payments finality, bilateral cap constraints, and loss sharing. Anticipating a little, we can consider the bilateral cap BC_{ji} as a kind of credit line granted by j to i in "*commercial currency*." As we shall see, this concept is very much like a bilateral cap granted in a CHIPS-like net system (hence the notation), with the differences that it provides more flexibility (by getting rid of the necessity of a "double coincidence of wants," as is detailed below) and that it can coexist on a single system with an overdraft facility granted by the central bank.

(a) Execution of Payments

Suppose that at time t bank i wants to transfer p to another bank. If

$$[\Delta_i(t) - p] + \left[BC_{0i} + \sum_{j \neq i} BC_{ji} \right] \geq 0, \tag{6.1}$$

the payment goes through and is final. Otherwise it is rejected (in which case bank i would probably not even have sent it, since it can find out if (6.1) will be met in a continuous time settlement system). In order to interpret condition (6.1), let us note that $[p - \Delta_i(t)]$ is the net deficit of bank i toward the system, if the payment is executed. This net deficit must therefore be lower than the sum of the overdraft authorized by the central bank (BC_{0i}) and by the commercial banks (BC_{ji}).

(b) Constraints on Bilateral Caps

The credit line granted to j by i must satisfy

$$BC_{ji} \leqslant BC_{ji}^{\max},$$

where

$$BC_{ji}^{\max} = f(S_i)NW_j, \tag{6.2}$$

according to our previous discussion.

(c) Loss Sharing

Suppose that bank i is declared bankrupt at time t. The payment system must absorb its deficit $[-\Delta_i(t)]$ and bank j sustains a loss proportional to the ceiling it granted bank i,

$$L_j = \frac{BC_{ji}}{BC_{0i} + \sum_{k \neq i} BC_{ki}}[-\Delta_i(t)], \tag{6.3}$$

and similarly for the central bank. The total loss is then covered, enabling the payment system to carry on working. Let us note that condition (6.1) implies that, at every moment t,

$$\Delta_i(t) + \left[BC_{0i} + \sum_{j \neq i} BC_{ji} \right] \geqslant 0,$$

and therefore

$$L_j \leqslant BC_{ji}.$$

A bank cannot incur a loss superior to the ceiling it granted the failing bank. We are leaving aside the issue relating to bank j's payment of its obligation. Two of the possible solutions are the use of collaterals previously supplied by bank j (as on CHIPS, see below) and the granting of liquidity loans by the central bank to bank j as a function of the latter's obligation.

6.5.2 Comparison with Existing Systems

This section aims to clarify the constraints affecting several systems.

SIC. The Swiss system can be characterized by the fact that all upper bounds on the bilateral caps, and therefore the bilateral caps themselves, are nil:

$$BC_{0i}^{max} = BC_{ji}^{max} = 0. \tag{2SIC}$$

As a consequence, the condition of finality of a payment p from bank i to another bank becomes

$$\Delta_i(t) - p \geqslant 0. \tag{1SIC}$$

That is, bank i must have sufficient funds on its account with the settlement agent to make the payment.

CHIPS. CHIPS being a net system with no central bank participation, we have

$$BC_{0i}^{max} = 0$$

and

$$BC_{ji}^{max} = +\infty. \tag{2CHIPS}$$

(This does not mean, of course, that bilateral credit limits on CHIPS are infinite. They are constrained by the amount of collateral deposited by the banks (see below).)

Whether a payment from i to j is final does not depend on the global position of bank i on CHIPS, but rather on the bilateral position. The payment becomes final if

$$[\Delta_{ij}(t) - p] + BC_{ji} \geqslant 0. \tag{1CHIPS}$$

Suppose now that bank i fails at time t. Bank i's global net position is then

$$\tilde{\Delta}_i(t) = \sum_{j \neq i} \Delta_{ij}(t),$$

which only differs from the expression previously used, insofar as the central bank does not have a position on CHIPS. ($-\tilde{\Delta}_i(t)$ is called "net-net debit balance.") Bank j's loss (called additional settlement obligation or ASO) is then given by the equivalent of equation (6.3):

$$L_j = \frac{BC_{ji}}{\sum_{k \neq i} BC_{ki}} [-\tilde{\Delta}_i(t)]. \tag{3CHIPS}$$

CHIPS's essential difference with the system described in section 6.5.1 is the tighter constraint imposed by CHIPS on payments (compare (6.1) and (1CHIPS)). On CHIPS, as long as bank j grants a sufficient bilateral "overdraft facility" to bank i, bank i can send payments to bank j even if bank i is in substantial global debit of commercial currency; on the other hand, it cannot use this overdraft to make a payment to a bank k which would not have granted an overdraft to i.[28] In the absence of complex multilateral arrangements, CHIPS therefore imposes that the mutual payment structure more or less coincides with the authorized bilateral overdrafts structure. CHIPS is therefore relatively constraining. An overdraft on CHIPS can be compared with a loan issued by one country to another under the condition that the borrowing country must use the loan to buy goods and services from the lending country. We suggest eliminating the need for a "double coincidence of wants" and thinking in terms of global credit lines.

Let us conclude this discussion of CHIPS with two further points. First, bilateral caps on CHIPS can be changed during the day. The BC_{ji} in equation (3CHIPS) need to be understood as the maximum caps granted during the day. Second, bank j must deposit enough collateral to settle its highest commitment without resorting to borrowing. Thus bank j deposits a quantity of *collateral* CO_j in Treasury notes equal to at least

$$CO_j = 5\% \max_i BC_{ji} \qquad (6.4)$$

(once more, BC_{ji} must be interpreted as the cap granted by j to i).

Furthermore, there is a cap on each bank's debit position, that is to say,

$$-\tilde{\Delta}_i(t) \leqslant 5\% \left[\sum_{k \neq i} BC_{kj} \right]. \qquad (6.5)$$

(The right-hand side of this inequality is known as the "net sender debit cap.") CHIPS's self-protection in the case of an isolated bank failure stems from the fact that the same coefficient (5%) is applied to the calculation of collateral (condition (6.4)) and to the debit cap (condition (6.5)). Indeed, let us suppose that bank i fails: the sum of the losses to be covered is thus $-\tilde{\Delta}_i(t)$, and the contribution asked from bank j is given by equation (3CHIPS):

$$L_j = \frac{BC_{ji}}{\sum_{k \neq i} BC_{ki}} [-\tilde{\Delta}_i(t)].$$

---

[28]In theory, it is conceivable that some indirect arrangement could be designed so as to enable bank i to make a payment to bank k: bank i could make a payment to bank j, who, having an untapped overdraft facility (defined by the bilateral net debit cap) with bank l, could make a payment to that bank, etc., so that at the end of the chain bank k receives the payment. This possibly long chain of payments seems to require a complex multilateral contract (which is all the more unrealistic in that the time scale is quite short in payment systems).

But bank i's debit is limited by condition (6.5), which we can also write as follows:

$$\frac{-\tilde{\Delta}_i(t)}{\sum_{k \neq i} BC_{ki}} \leqslant 5\%.$$

Consequently, the contribution asked from j is itself bounded above:

$$L_j \leqslant 5\% \times BC_{ji}.$$

And condition (6.4) implies that

$$L_j \leqslant CO_j,$$

which means that losses are covered by the collateral. We shall not be going into the details of the more complex rules applicable in the case of simultaneous failures of several banks.

To conclude this discussion of CHIPS, we note that a second difference with the paradigm of section 6.5.1 is the full protection of CHIPS against a default by a single bank. Such strict collateralization makes sense for a subordinate system like CHIPS that clears on the central bank system. Our single-system paradigm can allow for more general and flexible rules that do not necessarily require full protection, and yet impose some safeguards on imprudent interbank lending. In this respect, the paradigm of section 6.5.1 is closer to Fedwire in spirit.

Fedwire. On Fedwire, the settlement agent is a counterparty to every transaction and banks do not grant each other mutual overdrafts. Thus, we have

$$BC_{ji}^{\max} = 0.$$

The central bank, on the other hand, authorizes an overdraft for bank i. The finality condition of a payment p (the analogue of (6.1)) is then

$$[\Delta_{i0}(t) - p] + BC_{0i} \geqslant 0, \qquad \text{(1Fedwire)}$$

where $\Delta_{i0}(t)$ is bank i's net position vis-à-vis Fedwire.[29]

---

[29]Our framework can also accommodate the policy set by the Board of Governors in 1985, which asked each institution to voluntarily adopt a cap (verified *ex post* by the Fed) to limit the overdraft it incurs on large-dollar systems. Mathematically,

$$BC_{0i} = BC_{0i}^{\max} = \alpha(\hat{S}_i)NW_j, \qquad \text{(2Fedwire)}$$

where the hat over the solvency variable designates the solvency declared by the bank itself to the Fed, an announcement probably more truthful when bank i is not in distress. (By contrast, we assumed in our formula (6.2) that the regulator could observe (in real time) the true solvency parameter S_i.)

6.5.3 Discussion

Our formal approach unifies and authorizes a comparison of the different payment systems. Moreover, it facilitates an evaluation of the constraints that would weigh on systems trying to combine the advantages of existing systems and to achieve better the following objectives: systemic risk prevention, wide access to the network, flexibility of the interbank loans system, and discrimination among banks on the basis of their true solvency. It should be emphasized that the central bank can continue using its privileged supervisory information to protect itself against insolvent banks or, conversely, to allow a bank to continue to participate in the payment system. Thus, the functions provided by Fedwire-type gross settlement systems and by multilateral netting systems can be improved and made more transparent while coexisting on a single, continuous-time settlement system.

Our conception of intraday lines of credit would operate in a different way than one based on bilateral net debit caps. Currently, on CHIPS, bank j takes into account the bilateral flow of payments when choosing its bilateral net debit cap vis-à-vis bank i. It regards the bilateral net debit cap as enabling a timely receipt of payment orders due to itself and its customers from bank i. And bilateral credit extension between banks is free.

Our intraday credit lines follow a different and much more familiar logic. We view bilateral exposures as reflecting bilateral trust and thus interbank monitoring. Trust is directly related to the borrowing bank's overall health and is conceptually much less related to the specific pattern of bilateral payment flows. An obvious implication of this credit line view is that the lending bank should be responsible in the case of default of the borrowing bank.[30] Lending therefore should be costly, which in turn implies that intraday credit lines should be rewarded through payments from the borrowing bank. Such payments would presumably be facility as well as utilization fees, but the specificities are to be left to institutions, which can use their experience with credit lines for corporate borrowers when designing credit lines for other banks. In fact, it is likely that our system would evolve to a situation in the spirit of

---

The authorized overdraft BC_{0i} serves as a ceiling on Fedwire and was used until 1991 as a global cap on Fedwire plus CHIPS. To be more precise, if bank i was in deficit on CHIPS ($\tilde{\Delta}_i(t) < 0$), the ceiling was then a ceiling on Fedwire only, as in (1Fedwire).

If, on the other hand, bank i had a surplus on CHIPS ($\tilde{\Delta}_i(t) \geqslant 0$), the finality condition became

$$[\Delta_i(t) - p] + BC_{0i} \geqslant 0, \qquad\qquad (1\text{Fedwire}')$$

where $\Delta_i(t) = \Delta_{i0}(t) + \tilde{\Delta}I(T)$.

[30]See chapter 5 for a theoretical analysis of interbank lending and systemic risk.

correspondent banking, which is where, for any i, only a small number of the BC_{ji}s are nonzero.

Not only should this conceptual framework shed new light on the subject, but it should also enable an in-depth examination of new questions. Should a net session be introduced at the start of the day to clear all transfers resulting from previous contracts between banks and therefore perfectly foreseeable operations (overnight interbank loans, swap agreements, etc.)? How should central bank overdrafts (the BC_{0i}) be fixed? Should they be contractually linked to ratings, to a solvency measure, or to the bilateral caps (the BC_{ji})? Should bilateral caps be modifiable during the day? All these questions deserve to be examined more closely.

6.6   Conclusion

The design of payment systems should reflect several preoccupations, such as the efficacy of prudential control, the protection of the central bank against the necessity to intervene to avoid systemic risk, the smooth running of the payment system, reasonable collateral requirements, and an efficient use of high-quality information on the health of the banks. Whether specific systems (net, gross, or mixed systems) are likely to achieve these objectives in turn hinges on who pays in the case of failure, who monitors, and who can intervene. In particular, the coexistence of two or more payment systems can have certain advantages, but it calls for a close coordination between those systems. On the other hand, a single system can provide the same functions as several systems, provided it offers a menu of options to its users.

We also argued that liquidity and solvency issues cannot be dissociated. On that point we regret the compartmentalization of the research done on prudential rules and payment systems. Beyond the necessary integration of these two fields, we also think that conceptually the traditional thinking about prudential systems can shed, after some adjustment, new light on the desirable organization of payment systems. Conversely, research on prudential regulation has perhaps ignored liquidity issues too often.

The contribution of this paper has been twofold. It has discussed how standard arguments of industrial organization and corporate finance could be used to shed light on alternative organizations of the payment system. And it has provided an analytical framework encompassing existing systems and suggesting a new organization that combines the benefits of centralized and decentralized arrangements.

This analytical framework has suggested the possibility of safeguarding the flexibility of interbank mutual overdraft facilities while improving current systems through three measures:

(i) a reinterpretation of bilateral debit caps as bilateral credit lines, so as to escape the rigidity of the "double coincidence of wants";

(ii) the use of a broader definition of mutual overdraft facilities between banks; and

(iii) the centralization of the bilateral credit lines and transactions in a gross payment system, so as to allow the central bank to better monitor positions and to avoid being forced to intervene to prevent systemic risk.

It would thus seem that the respective benefits of current net and gross systems could be combined, and further benefits could be added.

We hope that despite the preliminary stage of some of our conclusions, this paper can shed new light on the in-depth work on payment systems already undertaken by the banking profession.

References

Allen, L., S. Peristiani, and A. Saunders. 1989. Bank size, collateral, and net purchase behavior in the Federal funds market: empirical evidence. *Journal of Business* 62:501–16.

Angelini P., and C. Giannini. 1993. On the economics of interbank payment systems. Banca d'Italia, Temi di Discussione 193.

Angell, W. 1991. A proposal to rely on market interest rates on intraday funds to reduce payment system risk. In *Governing Banking's Future* (ed. C. England), chapter 10. Boston, MA: Kluwer.

Basel Committee. 1989. Report on netting schemes (Angell Report). Committee on Payment and Settlement Systems 2. Basel, Switzerland: Bank for International Settlements.

———. 1990. Report of the Committee on Interbank Netting Schemes of the central banks of the Group of Ten countries (Lamfalussy Report). Committee on Payment and Settlement Systems 4. Basel, Switzerland: Bank for International Settlements.

Bernanke, B. S. 1990. Clearing and settlement during the crash. *Review of Financial Studies* 3:133–51.

Borio, C. E. V., and P. Van den Bergh. 1993. The nature and management of payment system risks: an international perspective. Economic Paper 36. Basel, Switzerland: Bank for International Settlements.

Clair, R. 1991. Daily overdrafts: who really bears the risk? *Governing Banking's Future* (ed. C. England), chapter 17, pp. 117–41. Boston, MA: Kluwer.

Dewatripont, M., and J. Tirole. 1994. *The Prudential Regulation of Banks*. Cambridge, MA: MIT Press.

Diamond, D. 1991. Monitoring and reputation: the choice between bank loans and directly placed debt. *Journal of Political Economy* 99:689–721.

European Community. 1992. Issues of common concern to EC central banks in the field of payment systems (Padoa-Schioppa Report). Ad Hoc Working Group on EC Payment Systems, September.

Faulhaber, G. R., A. Phillips, and A. M. Santomero. 1990. Payment risk, network risk, and the role of the Fed. In *The U.S. Payment System: Efficiency, Risk and the Role of the Fed* (ed. D. Humphrey), pp. 197–246. Boston, MA: Kluwer.

Federal Reserve Bank of New York. 1987. A study of large-dollar payment flows through CHIPS and Fedwire.

——. 1989. The Federal Reserve wire transfer network.

——. 1991. The clearinghouse interbank payments system.

Gilbert, R. A. 1989. Payments system risk: what is it and what will happen if we try to reduce it? Federal Reserve Bank of St. Louis, Jan/Feb, pp. 1–17.

Goodhart, C., and D. Schoenmaker. 1993. Institutional separation between supervisory and monetary authorities. Mimeo, London School of Economics.

Gorton, G. 1985. Clearinghouses and the origin of central banking in the United States. *Journal of Economic History* 45:277–83.

Hancock, D., and J. A. Wilcox. 1996. Intraday bank reserve management: the effects of caps and fees on daylight overdrafts. *Journal of Money, Credit and Banking* 28(Part 2):870–908.

Hirschman, A. 1970. *Exit, Voice and Loyalty.* Cambridge, MA: Harvard University Press.

Holmström, B., and J. Tirole. 1997. Financial intermediation, loanable funds, and the real sector. *Quarterly Journal of Economics* 112:663–92.

Hoshi, T., A. Kashyap, and D. Scharfstein. 1993. The choice between public and private debt: an analysis of post-regulation corporate financing in Japan. National Bureau of Economic Research Working Paper.

Humphrey, D. H. 1984. The U.S. payment system: costs, pricing, competition and risk. Monograph Series in Finance and Economics, New York University, numbers 1 and 2, pp. 1–135.

——. 1986. Payments finality and risk of settlement failure. In *Technology and the Regulation of Financial Markets* (ed. A. Saunders and L. J. White), chapter 8, pp. 97–120. Lexington, MA: Lexington Books.

——. 1987. Payments system risk, market failure, and public policy. In *Electronic Funds Transfers and Payments: The Public Policy Issues* (ed. E. H. Solomon), chapter 4. Boston, MA: Kluwer.

Jaffee, D., and T. Russell. 1976. Imperfect information, uncertainty and credit rationing. *Quarterly Journal of Economics* 90:651–66.

Parkinson, P., A. Gilbert, E. Gollob, and L. Hargraves. 1992. Clearance and settlement in U.S. securities markets. Board of Governors of the Federal Reserve System Staff Study 163, March.

Rajan, R. 1992. Insiders and outsiders: the choice between informed and arm's length debt. *Journal of Finance* 47:1367–400.

Richards, H. 1995. Daylight overdraft fees and the Federal Reserve's payment system risk policy. *Federal Reserve Bulletin*, pp. 1065–77.

Stiglitz, J., and A. Weiss. 1981. Credit rationing in markets with imperfect information. *American Economic Review* 71:393–410.

Summers, B. J. 1991. Clearing and payment systems: the role of the central bank. *Federal Reserve Bulletin* (February), pp. 81–90.

——. 1994. Risk management in national payment systems. Paper given at Structural Changes in Financial Markets: Trends and Prospects. OECD.

Todd, W. 1991. Banks are not special: the Federal safety net and banking power. In *Governing Banking's Future* (ed. C. England), chapter 6, pp. 79–105. Boston, MA: Kluwer.

Vital, C. 1990. Swiss Interbank Clearing: further experience with a queuing mechanism to control payment system risk. Prepared for the Global Funds Transfer Conference, New York, February.

——. 1994. An appraisal of the Swiss Interbank Clearing System SIC. Paper presented at the EFMA Conference on Payment Systems, Brussels, May 27.

Vital, C., and D. L. Mengle. 1988. SIC: Switzerland's new electronic interbank payment system. Federal Reserve Bank of Richmond, pp. 12–27.

Chapter Seven

Systemic Risk, Interbank Relations, and the Central Bank

Xavier Freixas, Bruno M. Parigi, and Jean-Charles Rochet

The possibility of a systemic crisis affecting the major financial markets has raised regulatory concern all over the world. Whatever the origin of a financial crisis, it is the responsibility of the regulatory body to provide adequate fire walls for the crisis not to spill over to other institutions. In this paper we explore the possibilities of contagion from one institution to another that can stem from the existence of a network of financial contracts. These contracts are essentially generated from three types of operations: the payments system, the interbank market, and the market for derivatives.[1] Since these contracts are essential to the financial intermediaries' function of providing liquidity and risk sharing to their clients, the regulating authorities have to set patterns for central bank intervention when confronted with a systemic shock. In recent years, the 1987 stock market crash, the Savings and Loan crisis, the Mexican, Asian, and Russian crises, and the crisis of the Long Term Capital Management hedge fund have all shown the importance of the intervention of the central banks and of the international financial institutions in affecting the extent, contagion, patterns, and consequences of the crises.[2]

---

[1] There is ample empirical evidence on financial contagion. For a survey see de Bandt and Hartmann (2002). Kaufman (1994) reviews empirical studies that measure the adverse effects on banks' equity returns of default of a major bank and of a sovereign borrower or unexpected increases in loan-loss provisions announced by major banks. Others have studied contagion through the flow of deposits (Saunders and Wilson 1996) and using historical data (Gorton 1988; Schoenmaker 1996; Calomiris and Mason 1997). Whatever the methodology, these studies support the view that pure panic contagion is rare. Far more common is contagion through perceived correlations in bank asset returns (particularly among banks of similar size and/or geographical location).

[2] A well-known episode of near financial gridlock where a coordinating role was played by the central bank is represented by the series of events the day after the stock crash of 1987. Brimmer (1989, pp. 14–15) writes that "On the morning of October 20, 1987, when stock and commodity markets opened, dozens of brokerage firms and their banks had extended credit on behalf of customers to meet margin calls, and they had not received balancing payments through the clearing and settlement systems.... As margin calls mounted, money center banks (especially those in New York, Chicago, and San Francisco)

In contrast to the importance of these issues, theory has not succeeded yet in providing a convenient framework for analyzing systemic risk so as to derive how the interbank markets and the payments system should be structured and what should be the role of the lender of last resort (LLR).

A good illustration of the wedge between theory and reality is provided by the deposits shift that followed the distress of Bank of Credit and Commerce International (BCCI). In July 1991, the closure of BCCI in the United Kingdom made depositors with smaller banks switch their funds to the safe haven of the big banks, the so-called "flight to quality" (Reid 1991). Theoretically, this should not have had any effect, because big banks should have immediately lent again these funds in the interbank market and the small banks could have borrowed them. Yet the reality was different: the Bank of England had to step in to encourage the large clearers to help those hit by the trend. Some packages had to be agreed (as the £200 million to the National Home Loans mortgage lender), thus supplementing the failing invisible hand of the market. So far theory has not been able to explain why the intervention of the LLR in this type of event was important.

Our motivation for analyzing a model of systemic risk stems from both the lack of a theoretical setup and the lack of consensus on the way the LLR should intervene. In this paper we analyze interbank networks, focusing on possible liquidity shortages and on the coordinating role of the financial authorities—which we refer to as the central bank for short—in avoiding and solving them. To do so we construct a model of the payment flows that allows us to capture in a simple fashion the propagation of financial crises in an environment where both liquidity shocks and solvency shocks affect financial intermediaries that fund long-term investments with demand deposits.

We introduce liquidity demand endogenously by assuming that depositors are uncertain about where they have to consume. This provides the need for a payments system or an interbank market.[3] In this way we

---

were faced with greatly increased demand for loans by securities firms. With an eye on their capital ratios and given their diminished taste for risk, a number of these banks became increasingly reluctant to lend, even to clearly creditworthy individual investors and brokerage firms.... To forestall a freeze in the clearing and settlement systems, Federal Reserve officials (particularly those from the Board and the Federal Reserve Bank of New York) urged key money center banks to maintain and to expand loans to their creditworthy brokerage firm customers."

[3]Payment needs arising from agents' spatial separation with limited commitment and default possibilities were first analyzed in Townsend (1987). For the main theoretical issues related to systemic risk in payment systems, see Berger et al. (1996) and Flannery (1996); for an analysis of peer monitoring on the interbank market, see chapter 5; and for an analysis of the main institutional aspects, see Summers (1994).

extend the model of Freixas and Parigi (1998) to more than two banks, to different specifications of travel patterns and consumers' preferences. The focus of the two papers is different. Freixas and Parigi consider the trade-off between gross and net payments systems. In the current paper we concentrate instead on systemwide financial fragility and central bank policy issues. This paper is also related to Freeman (1996a,b). In Freeman, demand for liquidity is driven by the mismatch between supply and demand of goods by spatially separated agents that want to consume the good of the other location, at different times. If agents' travel patterns are not perfectly synchronized, a centrally accessible institution (e.g., a clearinghouse) may arise to provide means of payments. This allows the clearing of the debt issued by the agents to back their demand. In our paper liquidity demand instead arises from the strategies of agents with respect to the coordination of their actions.

Our main findings are, first, that, under normal conditions, a system of interbank credit lines reduces the cost of holding liquid assets. However, the combination of interbank credit and the payments system makes the banking system prone to experience (speculative) gridlocks, even if all banks are solvent. If the depositors in one location, wishing to consume in other locations, believe that there will not be enough resources for their consumption at the location of destination, their best response is to withdraw their deposits at the home location. This triggers the early liquidation of the investment at the home location, which, by backward induction, makes it optimal for the depositors in other locations to do the same.

Second, the structure of financial flows affects the stability of the banking system with respect to solvency shocks. On the one hand, interbank connections enhance the "resiliency" of the system to withstand the insolvency of a particular bank, because a proportion of the losses on one bank's portfolio is transferred to other banks through the interbank agreements. On the other hand, this network of cross-liabilities may allow an insolvent bank to continue operating through the implicit subsidy generated by the interbank credit lines, thus weakening the incentives to close inefficient banks.

Third, the central bank has a role to play as a "crisis manager." When all banks are solvent, the central bank's role to prevent a speculative gridlock is simply to act as a coordinating device. By guaranteeing the credit lines of all banks, the central bank eliminates any incentive for early liquidation. This entails no cost for the central bank since its guarantees are never used in equilibrium. When instead one bank is insolvent because of poor returns on its investment, the central bank has a role in the orderly closure of this bank. When a bank is to be liquidated, the central bank has to organize the bypass of this defaulting bank in the payment network and provide liquidity to the banks that depend on this defaulting bank. Furthermore, since the interbank market may loosen market discipline, there is a role for supervision with the regulatory agency having the right to close down a bank even if this bank is not confronted with any liquidity problem.

Fourth, when depositors have asymmetric payments needs across space, the role of the locations where many depositors want to access their wealth (money center locations) becomes crucial for the stability of the entire banking system. We characterize the too-big-to-fail (TBTF) approach often followed by central banks in dealing with the financial distress of money center banks, i.e., banks occupying key positions in the interbank network system.

The results of our paper are closely related to those of Allen and Gale (2000), where financial connections arise endogenously between banks located in different regions. In our work interregional financial connections arise because depositors face uncertainty about the location where they need to consume. In Allen and Gale financial connections instead arise as a form of insurance: when liquidity preference shocks are imperfectly correlated across regions, cross-holdings of deposits by banks redistribute the liquidity in the economy. These links, however, expose the system to the possibility of a small liquidity shock in one location spreading to the rest of the economy. Despite the apparent similarities between the two models and the related conclusions pointing at the relevance of the structure of financial flows, it is worth noticing that in our paper we focus instead on the implications for the stability of the system when one bank may be insolvent.

This paper is organized as follows. In section 7.1 we set up our basic model of an interbank network. In section 7.2 we describe the coordination problems that may arise even when all banks are solvent. In section 7.3 we analyze the "resiliency" of the system when one bank is insolvent. In section 7.4 we investigate whether the closure of one bank triggers the liquidation of others, and we show under which conditions the intervention of the central bank is needed to prevent a domino or contagion effect. Section 7.5 provides an example of asymmetric travel patterns and its implications for central bank intervention. Section 7.6 discusses the policy implications, offers some concluding remarks, and points to possible extensions.

7.1   The Model

7.1.1   Basic Setup

We consider an economy with one good and N locations with exactly one bank[4] in each location. There is a continuum of risk-neutral consumers of equal mass (normalized to one) in each location. There are three periods: $t = 0, 1, 2$. The good can be either stored from one period to the next or invested. Each consumer is endowed with one unit of the good at $t = 0$. Consumers cannot invest directly but must deposit their endowment in the bank of their location, which stores it or invests it for future consumption. Consumption takes place at $t = 2$ only. The storage technology yields the riskless interest rate which we normalize at 0. The investment of bank i yields a gross return R_i at $t = 2$, for each unit invested at $t = 0$ and not liquidated at $t = 1$. At $t = 0$ the bank optimally chooses the fraction of deposits to store or invest. The deposit contract specifies the amount c_1 received by depositors if they withdraw at $t = 1$, and their bank is solvent. At $t = 2$, remaining depositors share the returns of the remaining assets equally. To finance withdrawals at $t = 1$ the bank uses the stored good, and, for the part in excess, liquidates a fraction of the investment. Each unit of investment liquidated at $t = 1$ gives only α units of the good (with $\alpha \leqslant 1$).

We extend this model by introducing a spatial dimension: a fraction $\lambda > 0$ of the depositors (we call them the *travelers*) must consume at $t = 2$ in other locations. The remaining $(1 - \lambda)$ depositors (the *nontravelers*) consume at $t = 2$ in the home location. So in our model consumers are uncertain about *where* they need to consume.

Our model is in the spirit of Diamond and Dybvig's (1983) model (hereafter DD) but with a different interpretation. In DD, risk-averse consumers are subject to a preference shock as to *when* they need to consume. The bank provides insurance by allowing them to withdraw at $t = 1$ but exposes itself to the risk of bank runs since it funds an illiquid investment with demand deposits. Our model corresponds to a simplified version of DD where the patient consumers must consume at home or in the other location(s) and the proportion of impatient consumers is arbitrarily small. This allows us to concentrate on the issue of payments across locations without analyzing intertemporal insurance. Our focus is on the coordination of the consumers in the various locations, and not on the time-coordination of the consumers at the same location.[5]

---

[4]This unique bank can be interpreted as a mutual bank, in the sense that it does not have any capital and acts in the best interest of its customers.

[5]The demandable deposit feature of the contract in this model does not rely necessarily on intertemporal insurance but may have alternative rationales. For example,

Since we analyze interbank credit, the good should be interpreted as cash (i.e., central bank money). Cash is a liability of the central bank that can be moved at no cost, but only by the central bank.[6]

If we interpret our model in terms of payment systems, the sequence of events takes place within a 24-hour period. Then we could interpret $t = 0$ as the beginning of the day, $t = 1$ as intraday, $t = 2$ as overnight, and the liquidation cost $(1 - \alpha)$ as the cost of (fire) selling monetary instruments in an illiquid intraday market.[7]

We assume that R_i is publicly observable at $t = 1$. In a multiperiod version of our model, R_i would be interpreted as a signal on bank i's solvency that could provoke withdrawals by depositors or liquidation by the central bank at $t = 1$ (intraday). For simplicity, we adopt a two-period model, and we assume here that the bank is liquidated anyway, either at $t = 1$ or at $t = 2$. Notice that even if R_i is publicly observed at $t = 1$ (we make this assumption to abstract from asymmetric information problems), it is not verifiable by a third party at $t = 1$ (only ex post, at $t = 2$). Therefore, the deposit contract cannot be fully conditioned on R_i. More specifically, the amount c_1 received for a withdrawal at $t = 1$ can just depend on the only verifiable information at $t = 1$, namely the closure decision. We denote by D_0 this contractual amount[8] in the case where the bank is not closed at $t = 1$. On the other hand, whenever the bank is closed (whether at $t = 1$ or at $t = 2$) its depositors equally share its assets (see assumptions 7.1 and 7.2 below).

In order to be more explicit, it is worth examining the characteristics of the optimal deposit contract in the DD model when the proportion

---

Calomiris and Khan (1991) suggest that the right to withdraw on demand, accompanied by a sequential service constraint, gives informed depositors a credible threat in case of misuse of funds by the bank.

[6]Models in the tradition of DD have typically left the characteristics of the one good in the economy in the mist. This is all right in a microeconomic setup, but the model has monetary implications that lead to a different interpretation depending on whether the good is money or not. In particular, if the good is not money but, for example, wheat, then Wallace's (1988) criticism applies. In other words, if the good was interpreted as wheat, we would have to justify why the central bank was endowed with a superior transportation technology. As we assume the good to be money, it is the fact that commercial banks use central bank money to settle their transactions that gives the central bank the monopoly of issuing cash. Therefore, the possibility to transfer money from one location to another corresponds to the ability to create and destroy money. Note also that interpreting the good as cash implies that currency crises, which are often associated with systemic risk, are left out of our analysis. This is so because "cash" is then limited by the level of reserves of the central bank.

[7]Since banks specialize in lending to information-sensitive customers, $1 - \alpha$ can also be interpreted as the cost of selling loans in the presence of a lemons' problem.

[8]This amount results from ex ante optimal contracting decisions that could be solved explicitly. For conciseness, we take D_0 as given. Note that, if R_i were verifiable, D_0 could be contingent on it and the risk of contagion could be fully eliminated.

of early diers tends to zero. This provides a useful benchmark for measuring the exposure of the interbank system to market discipline in our multibank model. Let μ denote the proportion of early diers and u be the Von Neumann–Morgenstern utility function of depositors, with $u' > 0$ and $u'' < 0$. The optimal deposit contract (c_1, c_2) maximizes $\mu u(c_1) + (1-\mu)u(c_2)$ under the constraint $\mu c_1 + (1-\mu)c_2/R = 1$. Together with the budget constraint, this optimal contract is characterized by the first-order condition

$$u'(c_1) = Ru'(c_2). \tag{7.1}$$

When μ tends to zero, it is easy to see that c_2 tends to R and that c_1 tends to $D_0 = u'^{-1}(Ru'(R))$. Since $R > 1$ and u' is decreasing, we see immediately that $D_0 < R$. Therefore, if the bank is known to be solvent, no depositor has interest to withdraw unilaterally before he or she actually needs the money.

7.1.2   General Formulation of Consumption across Space

Travel patterns, that is, which depositor travels and to which location, are exogenously determined by nature at $t = 1$ and privately revealed to each depositor. They result from depositors' payment needs arising from other aspects of their economic activities. For each depositor initially at location i, nature determines whether he or she travels and in which location j he or she will consume at $t = 2$.[9] To consume at $t = 2$ at location j ($i \neq j$) the travelers at location i can withdraw at $t = 1$ and carry the cash by themselves from location i to location j. The implicit cost of transferring the cash across space is the foregone investment return.[10] This motivates the introduction of credit lines between banks to minimize the amount of good not invested. The credit line granted by bank j to bank i gives the depositors of bank i going to bank j the right to have their deposits transferred to location j and obtain their consumption at $t = 2$ as a share of the assets at bank j at date $t = 2$.

A way to visualize the credit line granted by bank j to bank i is to think that consumers located at i arrive in location j at $t = 2$ with a check written on bank i and credited to an account at bank j. Bank i, in turn, gives credit lines to one or more banks as specified below.[11] At $t = 2$ the banks compensate their claims and transfer the corresponding

---

[9]More generally, depositors receive shocks to their preferences that determine their demand for the good indexed by a particular location.

[10]We could also add an explicit cost of "traveling with the cash" (i.e., bypassing the payments system). It would not affect our results.

[11]For a similar characterization of credit chains in the context of trading arrangements, see Kiyotaki and Moore (1997).

amount of the good across space. The technology to transfer the good at $t = 2$ is available for trades between banks only.

To make explicit the values of the assets and the liabilities resulting from interbank relations, we adopt the simplest sharing rule, as expressed in the following assumption.

Assumption 7.1. *All the liabilities of a bank have the same priority at $t = 2$.*

This rule defines how to divide a bank's assets at $t = 2$ among the claimholders. It implies that credit lines are honored in proportion to the amount of the assets of the bank at date $t = 2$. In particular, if D_i is the *ex post* value of a (unit of) deposit in bank i, then $D_i = $ (Bank$_i$ total assets)/(Bank$_i$ total liabilities). This assumption also implies that the banks cannot determine the location of origin of the depositors; thus depositors become anonymous and the banks cannot discriminate among them. Note that more complex priority rules could be more efficient in the resolution of liquidity crises. However, we assume that they are not feasible in our context: this is a reduced-form assumption aiming at capturing the limitations of the information that is available in interbank networks. An additional assumption is needed to describe what happens when a bank is closed at $t = 1$.

Assumption 7.2. *If a bank is closed at $t = 1$, its assets are shared between its own depositors only.*

Assumption 7.2 simply means that when the bank is closed at time $t = 1$, only its depositors have a claim on its assets. Bank closure at time 1 may come from a decision of the regulator or from the withdrawals of all depositors. Assumption 7.2 implies that when a bank is closed at time 1, it is deleted from the interbank network.

Let π_{ij} be the measure of depositors from location i consuming at location j, where i can take any value including j, and let t_{ij} be the proportion of travelers going from location i to j, $j \neq i$ (by definition, $t_{ii} = 0$). The matrix Π that defines where consumers go and in which proportions is related to the matrix T of travel patterns by

$$\Pi \equiv (1 - \lambda)I + \lambda T, \tag{7.2}$$

where $\Pi = (\pi_{ij})_{ij}$, I is the identity matrix, and $T = (t_{ij})_{ij}$. This specification allows us to parametrize independently two features of the payment system: λ captures the intensity of interbank flows and the matrix T captures the structure of these flows. By definition, we have for all i, $\sum_j \pi_{ij} = 1$. For the sake of simplicity, unless otherwise specified (see section 7.5), we will impose the following additional restrictions.

Assumption 7.3. *For all j, $\sum_i \pi_{ij} = 1$.*

In this way we discard the supply and demand imbalances at a specific location as the cause of a disruption in the payments system or in the interbank market. Because of the complexity of the transfers involved in an arbitrary matrix Π, we will illustrate our findings in two symptomatic cases:

- In the first one $t_{ij} = 1$ if $j = i + 1$ and $t_{ij} = 0$ otherwise, with the notational convention that $N + 1 \equiv 1$. To visualize this case it is convenient to think that the consumers are located around a circle, as in Salop's (1979) model. All travelers from i go to location $i+1$, the clockwise adjacent location, where they must consume at $t = 2$. The payments structure implied by this travel pattern generates what we define as *credit chain interbank funding*, when the bank at location $i + 1$ provides credit to the incoming depositors from location i.

- In the second travel pattern $t_{ij} = 1/(N-1)$ with $i \neq j$. Each couple of banks swaps $\lambda/(N-1)$ customers so that at time $t = 2$ at location j there are $\lambda/(N-1)$ travelers from each of the other $(N-1)$ locations. We will refer to this perfectly isotropic case as the *diversified lending case*.[12]

With *credit chain interbank funding*, credit flows in the direction opposite to travel. With *diversified lending*, every bank gives credit lines uniformly to all other $N-1$ banks. In terms of payments mechanisms, the interbank credit described above can be interpreted as a compensation scheme (net system) or a real-time gross system (RTGS) with multilateral credit lines.

Let us now introduce the players of the game, namely the N banks and their depositors. At $t = 0$ banks decide whether to extend each other credit lines. In the absence of credit lines, all travelers have to withdraw at $t = 1$, which reduces the quantity that each bank can invest: this is what we call the *autarkic situation*. On the other hand, in the general case with credit lines, the value of final consumption at $t = 2$ is determined by a noncooperative game played by the banks' depositors. At $t = 1$ each depositor located at i and consuming at location j simultaneously and without coordination determines the fraction x_{ij} of his or her deposit to maintain in the bank. Accordingly, the percentage of investment remaining at location j where he or she must consume is

$$X_j \equiv \max\left[1 - \sum_k \pi_{jk}(1 - x_{jk})\frac{D_0}{\alpha}, 0\right]. \tag{7.3}$$

---

[12] The structure of the payment flows in the credit chain interbank funding and in the diversified lending is very similar to that studied by Allen and Gale (2000).

Because of assumption 7.1, the final consumption of depositors (i, j) results from a combination of a withdrawal at time $t = 1$ in bank i (i.e., $(1 - x_{ij})D_0$) plus a proportion x_{ij} of the value at $t = 2$ of a deposit D_j in bank j. To determine the possible equilibria of the depositors' game, we have to compare D_0 with the (endogenous) values of the deposits $D_1, \ldots, D_N$ in all the banks at $t = 2$. Now, to determine D_i, consider the balance sheet equation for bank i at $t = 2$:

$$X_i R_i + \sum_j \pi_{ji} x_{ji} D_j = \left(\sum_j \pi_{ji} x_{ji} + \sum_j \pi_{ij} x_{ij} \right) D_i, \qquad (7.4)$$

where the left-hand (right-hand) side represents the assets (liabilities) of bank i, $X_i R_i$ is the return on its investment, $\sum_j \pi_{ji} x_{ji} D_j$ are the credits due from other banks, $(\sum_j \pi_{ji} x_{ji}) D_i$ are the debts with other banks, and $\sum_j \pi_{ji} x_{ji} D_i$ are its deposits. Notice that assumption 7.2 implies that the above equation does not apply when bank i is closed at $t = 1$. In this case $X_i = D_i = 0$.

The optimal behavior of each depositor (i, j) is $x_{ij} = 1 \Leftrightarrow D_j \geqslant D_0$, $\forall i, j$. Since it depends only on j, we denote by x^j the common value of the x_{ij}, where $x^j = 1$ if $D_j > D_0$ and $x^j = 0$ otherwise. This allows a simplification of (7.4):

$$X_i R_i + \left(\sum_j \pi_{ji} D_j \right) x^i = \left[\left(\sum_j \pi_{ji} \right) x^i + \sum_j \pi_{ij} x^j \right] D_i. \qquad (7.5)$$

We establish the following notation: Π' is the transpose of $\Pi = (\pi_{ij})_{i,j}$, $D = (D_1, \ldots, D_N)'$, and $R = (R_1, \ldots, R_N)'$. For a given strategy vector $(x_{ij})_{i,j}$ one can compute the assets in place at bank i (X_i) and the return on a deposit at bank i (D_i). Then we check whether the strategies are optimal:

$$x_{ij}^* = \begin{cases} 1 & \text{if } D_j > D_0, \\ 0 & \text{if } D_j < D_0. \end{cases} \qquad (7.6)$$

Any fixed point of this algorithm (i.e., $x_{ij}^* \equiv x_{ij}$) is an equilibrium of our game.

When the mechanism of interbank credit functions smoothly, $x_{ij} \equiv 1$ for all (i, j) and depositors' welfare is greater than in the autarkic situation. This is because interbank credit lines allow each bank to keep a lower amount of liquid reserves and to invest more. However, the system is also more fragile. As we show in the following sections, the noncooperative game played by depositors has other equilibria than $x_{ij} \equiv 1$.

7.2   Pure Coordination Problems

We first analyze the equilibria of the game when all deposits are invested at $t = 1$, investment returns are certain, and all banks are solvent, so that the only issue is the coordination among depositors. Disregarding the mixed strategy equilibria where depositors are indifferent between withdrawing their deposits and transferring them to the recipient banks, we obtain our first result.

Proposition 7.1. *We assume that $R_i > D_0$ for all i (which implies that all banks are solvent). There are at least two pure strategy equilibria:* (i) *the inefficient bank run allocation, where $x^* = 0$ (speculative gridlock equilibrium), and* (ii) *efficient allocation, where $x^* = 1$ (credit line equilibrium).*

Proof. See the appendix (section 7.7).   □

Several comments are in order. In the credit line equilibrium there is no liquidation, while in the speculative gridlock equilibrium all the banks' assets are liquidated. Since liquidation is costly and all banks are solvent, the credit line equilibrium dominates the speculative gridlock equilibrium as well as any other equilibrium where some liquidation takes place. The speculative gridlock equilibrium arises as a result of a coordination failure like in DD. If depositors rationally anticipated at $t = 0$ a speculative gridlock equilibrium, they would prefer the autarkic situation.

In the credit line equilibrium with diversified lending, bank i extends credit lines to all the other banks and receives credit lines from them. In equilibrium the debt arising from bank i's depositors at $t = 2$ using bank i's credit lines with the other banks is repaid at $t = 2$ by bank i serving the depositors from the other banks. It is precisely because the behavior of one bank's depositors is affected by the expectation of what the depositors going to the same location will do that this equilibrium is vulnerable to a coordination failure. If the depositors in a sufficiently large number of banks believe that they will be denied consumption at the location where they have to consume, it is optimal for them to liquidate their investment, which makes it optimal for the depositors in all other banks to do the same. The speculative gridlock equilibrium is related to the notion of the domino effect that may arise in payments systems as a result of the settlement failure of some participant. Still, it may occur here even if all banks are solvent. Note that banks do not play any strategic role: only depositors play strategically.

From the efficiency viewpoint, when all the banks are solvent the credit line equilibrium dominates autarky which in turn dominates the speculative gridlock equilibrium.[13] Hence there is a trade-off between a risky interbank market based on interbank credit and a safe payment mechanism which foregoes investment opportunities.[14]

Both the gridlock and the credit line equilibria involve the use of credit lines. In both equilibria banks extend and honor credit lines up to the amount of their $t = 2$ resources. In the speculative gridlock equilibrium it is not the banks that do not honor the credit lines, but rather the depositors, who, by forcing the liquidation of the investment, reduce the amount of resources available at $t = 2$.

There is a clear parallel between these two equilibria in our economy with N locations and the equilibria in a one-location DD model. These results are also related to the papers by Bhattacharya and Gale (1987) and Bhattacharya and Fulghieri (1994) that consider N-location DD economies without geographic risks.

The credit line equilibrium can be implemented in several ways: through a compensation system where credits are netted, by an RTGS system with multilateral or bilateral credit lines, through lending by the central bank, and through deposit insurance.

In this basic version of the model, in the event of a gridlock, every bank is *solvent* though *illiquid*. Thus no difficulty in distinguishing between insolvent and illiquid banks arises for the central bank.[15] The central bank has a simple coordinating role as an LLR in guaranteeing private-sector credit lines or in providing fiat money, both backed by the authority of the Treasury to tax the return on the investment.[16]

Similarly, by guaranteeing the value of deposits at the consumption locations, deposit insurance eliminates any incentive for the depositors to protect themselves by liquidating the investment, thus making it optimal for banks to extend credit to each other.

Like deposit insurance, which is never used in equilibrium in the DD model, the coordination role of the central bank costs no resources

---

[13]When $\alpha = 1$ the last two are equivalent. The cost of the gridlock equilibrium is proportional to $1 - \alpha$. Notice that autarky is equivalent to a payment system with fully collateralized credit lines like TARGET (Trans-European Automated Real-Time Gross Settlement Express Transfer), the payment system designed to handle transactions in the Euro area.

[14]For an analysis of this trade-off in a related setting, see Freixas and Parigi (1998). However, even an RTGS like the European system TARGET is not immune to a systemic crisis. As Garber (1998) points out, if there is a risk that a currency will leave the Euro currency area, the very infrastructure of TARGET, where national central banks of the participating countries extend unlimited daily credit to each other, provides the perfect mechanism to mount speculative attacks on the system.

[15]For an analysis of this issue, see the companion paper by Freixas et al. (chapter 3).

[16]For example, in the Canadian electronic system for the clearing and settlement of large-value payments the central bank guarantees intraday credit lines (Freedman and Goodlet 1998).

(excluding moral hazard issues), since in equilibrium it will not be necessary for the central bank to intervene. However, in a richer model credit line guarantees and deposit insurance would not have the same effect. In fact, unlike credit lines guarantees, deposit insurance penalizes the managers of distressed banks, and might offer better incentives to managers to monitor each other.

7.3   Resiliency and Market Discipline in the Interbank System

In the next two sections we tackle the issue of the impact of the insolvency of one bank on the rest of the system. In this section we investigate under which conditions the losses of one bank can be absorbed by the other banks without provoking withdrawals by depositors (this is what we call resiliency) and what are the implications in terms of market discipline. In the next section we consider the issue of contagion. That is, we investigate whether the closure of an insolvent bank generates a chain reaction causing the liquidation of solvent banks.

In order to model the possibility of insolvency in a simple way, we make the extreme assumption that the return R_i on the investment at location i can be either $R \geqslant D_0$ or 0. If $R = 0$, bank i is insolvent, in which case it is efficient to liquidate it, absent contagion issues. For the remainder of this paper we assume that the probability of $R = 0$ is so low that it is optimal for the banks to invest all deposits at $t = 0$.[17] Returns are publicly observable at $t = 1$ but verifiable only at $t = 2$ so that no contract can be made contingent on these returns. Notice that by assumption 7.1 the public information that bank 1 is insolvent cannot be used by the other banks to distinguish and discriminate against the depositors of the insolvent bank. The efficient allocation of resources requires that banks be liquidated if and only if they are insolvent:

$$X_i = \begin{cases} 0 & \text{if } R_i = 0, \\ 1 & \text{if } R_i = R. \end{cases} \tag{7.7}$$

Whether this efficient closure rule is a Nash equilibrium of the noncooperative game between depositors will depend on the structure of the interbank payment system. To illustrate this, we focus on the case in which one bank (say, bank 1) is insolvent, and we investigate under which conditions $x = (1,\dots,1)$ is still an equilibrium, i.e., under which conditions $D_i \geqslant D_0$ for all i. When $x = (1,\dots,1)$ and $R_1 = 0$ the balance

---

[17]For a large probability of failure, it is optimal to use the storage technology only.

sheet equations (7.5) give

$$D = (2I - \Pi')^{-1} \begin{pmatrix} 0 \\ R \\ \vdots \\ R \end{pmatrix} = R(2I - \Pi')^{-1} \begin{pmatrix} 0 \\ 1 \\ \vdots \\ 1 \end{pmatrix}. \tag{7.8}$$

From (7.8) we define by y the minimum of the components of the vector

$$(2I - \Pi')^{-1} \begin{pmatrix} 0 \\ 1 \\ \vdots \\ 1 \end{pmatrix}. \tag{7.9}$$

We establish the following proposition:

Proposition 7.2 (resiliency and market discipline). *When $R_1 = 0$, a necessary condition for $x = (1, \ldots, 1)$ to be an equilibrium is that the smallest value of time $t = 2$ deposits (Ry), which depends on the structure of interbank payment flows, exceeds D_0.*

Proof. From (7.8) and the definition of y we see that $D_i \geqslant D_0$ for all i if and only if $y \geqslant D_0/R$. $\qquad \square$

Several comments are in order. Proposition 7.2 highlights an important aspect of the tension between efficiency and stability of the interbank system. On the one hand, it establishes the conditions under which the system can absorb the losses of one bank without any deposit withdrawal. Resiliency, however, entails the cost of forbearance of the insolvent bank. On the other hand, it establishes the conditions under which $x = (1, \ldots, 1)$ is no longer an equilibrium. If a bank is known at $t = 1$ to be insolvent, depositors may withdraw and withdrawals may not be confined to the insolvent bank; hence market discipline entails the cost of possibly excessive liquidation. We interpret y as a measure of the exposure of the interbank system as a whole to market discipline when one bank is insolvent.[18]

We now study how y varies with λ (the proportion of travelers) and N (the number of locations) in the two cases of credit chain and diversified lending.

---

[18]As a benchmark consider again the limit of the DD optimal contract when the proportion of early diers tends to zero. If we compute D_0 when $u(c) = c^{1-a}/(1 - a)$ (CRRA utility function), from (7.1) we have $D_0/R = R^{-a}$, which is decreasing in R. Therefore, more profitable assets decrease the exposure of the bank to market discipline.

Proposition 7.3. *Both in the credit chain case and in the diversified lend-ing case, y increases with λ and N; i.e., when the proportion of travelers increases or the number of banks increases, the system becomes less exposed to market discipline.*

Proof. See the appendix (section 7.7).   □

When the number of banks increases, the insolvency of one bank has a lower impact on the value of the deposits in the other banks. Similarly, an increase in the fraction of travelers has the effect of spreading on the other banks a larger fraction of the loss due to the insolvency of one bank. This seems quite intuitive for the diversified lending case, since the banks hold more diversified portfolios of loans. The novelty is that this result also holds true for the credit chain case where banks have the possibility to pass part of their losses to other banks through the interbank market.

We now compare the two systems for given values of λ and N. We then compare the exposure to market discipline of the credit chain and the diversified lending structures.

Proposition 7.4. *In the case of the insolvency of one bank, the system is more exposed to market discipline under diversified lending than under credit chains; i.e., $y^{\text{cre}} > y^{\text{div}}$.*

Proof. See the appendix (section 7.7).   □

Proposition 7.4 may appear counterintuitive since diversification is usually associated with the ability to spread losses. The result depends on the proportion of the losses on its own portfolio that the insolvent bank is able to transfer to other banks through the payments system. In a diversified lending there is more diversification so that solvent banks exchange a larger fraction of their claims. As a consequence, in a diversified lending the insolvent bank is able to pass over to the solvent banks a smaller fraction of its losses.

The case with three banks ($N = 3$) and where everybody travels ($λ = 1$) provides a good illustration. In a diversified lending system the balance sheet equations (7.5) become

$$D_i = \tfrac{1}{2}[R_i + \tfrac{1}{2}(D_{i-1} + D_{i+1})], \quad i = 1, 2, 3. \tag{7.10}$$

This means that if bank 1 is insolvent (i.e., $R_1 = 0$), depositors at banks 2 and 3 get an equal share of total surplus, while bank 1 depositors receive 50% less. After easy computations, we find that bank 1 depositors receive $\tfrac{2}{5}R$, or equivalently bank 1 is able to pass $\tfrac{3}{5}$ of its losses to the solvent banks whose depositors end up receiving $\tfrac{4}{5}R$.

Consider now the case of credit chains. Still assuming $\lambda = 1$, the balance sheet equations give

$$D_i = \tfrac{1}{2}[R_i + D_{i+1}], \quad i = 1, 2, 3. \tag{7.11}$$

We can compute the losses experienced by each bank (with respect to the promised returns R) and it is a simple exercise to check that the only solution is

$$D_1 = \tfrac{3}{7}R, \quad D_3 = \tfrac{5}{7}R, \quad D_2 = \tfrac{6}{7}R. \tag{7.12}$$

Therefore, bank 1 is able to pass on a higher share of its losses than in the diversified lending case, which explains the lower exposure of the interbank system to market discipline in the credit chain system.

The results of this section highlight another side of interbank markets in addition to their role in redistributing liquidity efficiently, as studied by Bhattacharya and Gale (1987). Interbank connections enhance the "resiliency" of the system to withstand the insolvency of a particular bank. However, this network of cross-liabilities may loosen market discipline and allow an insolvent bank to continue operating through the implicit subsidy generated by the interbank credit lines. This loosening of market discipline is the rationale for a more active role for monitoring and supervision with the regulatory agency having the right to close down a bank in spite of the absence of any liquidity crisis at that bank.

The effect of a central bank's guarantee on interbank credit lines would be that $x = (1, \ldots, 1)$ is always an equilibrium, even if one bank is insolvent. The stability of the banking system would be preserved at the cost of forbearance of inefficient banks.

7.4 Closure-Triggered Contagion Risk

7.4.1 Efficiency versus Contagion Risk

We now turn to the other side of the relationship between efficiency and stability of the banking system, and investigate under which conditions the closure at time $t = 1$ of an insolvent bank does not trigger the liquidation of solvent banks in a contagion fashion. Suppose indeed that bank k is closed at $t = 1$. Assumption 7.2 implies that $X_k = 0$ and $D_k = 0$. Closing bank k at $t = 1$ has two consequences. First, we have an *unwinding* of the positions of bank k since $\pi_{ki}D_k$ assets and $\pi_{ki}D_i$ liabilities disappear from the balance sheet of bank k. In a richer setting this is equivalent to a situation in which the other banks have reneged on their credit lines toward bank k, possibly as a result of the arrival of negative signals on its return. Second, a proportion π_{ik} of travelers going to location k will be *forced to withdraw early* the amount $\pi_{ik}D_0$ and bank

i will have to liquidate the amount $\pi_{ik}D_0/\alpha$. If $\pi_{ik}D_0/\alpha$ is sufficiently large, bank i is closed at $t = 1$; otherwise the cost at $t = 2$ of the early liquidation is $\pi_{ik}((D_0/\alpha)R - D_i)$.

Notice that if $\pi_{ik}D_0/\alpha \geqslant 1$, then $X_i = 0$, i.e., bank i is liquidated simply because there are too many depositors going from location i to location k. The type of contagion that takes place here is of a purely mechanical nature stemming simply from the direct effect of inefficient liquidation. Since this case is straightforward let us instead concentrate on the other case, namely $\pi_{ik}D_0/\alpha < 1$. Because of unwinding and forced early withdrawal, the full general case is more complex. Since $x^k = 0$, we have to suppress all that concerns bank k from the equations (7.5). We obtain

$$X_{i(k)}R_i + \sum_{j\neq k} \pi_{ji}D_j x^i = \left(\sum_{j\neq k} \pi_{ij}x^j + \sum_{j\neq k} \pi_{ji}x^i\right)D_i, \qquad (7.13)$$

where

$$X_{i(k)} = \max\left[1 - \pi_{ik}\frac{D_0}{\alpha} - \sum_{j\neq k} \pi_{ji}(1 - x^j)\frac{D_0}{\alpha}, 0\right]. \qquad (7.14)$$

We now have to check whether $x_{ij} \equiv 1$ for all $i, j \neq k$ can correspond to an equilibrium. In this case, $X_{i(k)} = \max[1 - \pi_{ik}D_0/\alpha, 0]$ and system (7.13) becomes

$$R_i = \left(\sum_{j\neq k} \frac{\pi_{ij} + \pi_{ji}}{X_{i(k)}}\right)D_i - \sum_{j\neq k} \frac{\pi_{ji}}{X_{i(k)}}D_j. \qquad (7.15)$$

Since by assumption $R_i \equiv R$ for all $i \neq k$, (7.15) becomes

$$\left(1 - \pi_{ik}\frac{D_0}{\alpha}\right)R + \sum_{j\neq k} \pi_{ji}D_j = (2 - \pi_{ik} - \pi_{ki})D_i. \qquad (7.16)$$

This allows us to establish a result analogous to proposition 7.2.

Proposition 7.5 (contagion risk). *There is a critical value of the smallest time $t = 2$ deposits below which the closure of a bank causes the liquidation of at least one other bank. This critical value is lower in the credit chain case than in the diversified lending case. The diversified lending structure is always stable when the number N of banks is large enough, whereas N has no impact on the stability of the credit chain structure.*

Proof. This follows the same structure as the proof of proposition 7.2.
Denoting by M_k the inverse of the matrix defined by system (7.16),
stability is equivalent to

$$\begin{pmatrix} D_1 \\ \vdots \\ D_N \end{pmatrix} = RM_k \begin{pmatrix} 1 \\ \vdots \\ 1 \end{pmatrix} > D_0 \begin{pmatrix} 1 \\ \vdots \\ 1 \end{pmatrix}. \tag{7.17}$$

One can see that all the elements of M_k are nonnegative,[19] thus stability
obtains if and only if $D_0/R \leqslant \psi_k$, where ψ_k denotes the minimum of the
components

$$M_k \begin{pmatrix} 1 \\ \vdots \\ 1 \end{pmatrix}.$$

The computation of ψ_k is cumbersome in the general case but easy in
our benchmark examples (where, because of symmetry, k does not play
any role). One finds

$$\Psi_{cre} = 1 - \lambda\left(\frac{D_0}{\alpha} - 1\right) \quad \text{and} \quad \Psi_{div} = 1 - \lambda\left(\frac{D_0/\alpha - 1}{N - 1 - \lambda}\right) \tag{7.18}$$

in the credit chain example and in the diversified lending case, respectively. It is immediate from these formulas that $\Psi_{cre} < \Psi_{div}$ (for $N \geqslant 2$)
and that Ψ_{div} tends to 1 when N tends to infinity while Ψ_{cre} is independent
of N.   □

7.4.2 Comparison with Allen and Gale (2000)

It is useful to compare our results with those of Allen and Gale (2000).
Proposition 7.2 establishes that systemic crises may arise for fundamental reasons, as in Allen and Gale. However, the focus of the two
papers is different. Allen and Gale are concerned with the stability of the
system with respect to liquidity shocks arising from the random number
of consumers that need liquidity early in the absence of aggregate
uncertainty. They show that the system is less stable when the interbank
market is incomplete (in the sense that banks are allowed to cross-hold
deposits only in a credit chain fashion) than when the interbank market
is complete (in the sense that banks are allowed to cross-hold deposits
in a diversified lending fashion).

In our paper interbank links instead arise from consumers' geographic
uncertainty and we focus on the implications of the insolvency of one

---

[19]The fact that the matrix M_k has nonnegative elements follows from a property of
diagonal dominant matrices (see, for example, Takayama 1985, p. 385).

bank in terms of market discipline and the stability of the system. In particular in proposition 7.4 we show how the structure of interbank links allows the losses of one bank to be spread over other banks. We show that a diversified lending system is more exposed to market discipline (i.e., less resilient) than a credit chain system because in the latter the insolvent bank is able to transfer a larger fraction of its losses to other banks, thus reducing the incentives for its own depositors to withdraw. In proposition 7.5 we are concerned with the stability of the system with respect to contagion risk triggered by the efficient liquidation at time $t = 1$ of the insolvent bank.

7.5 Too-Big-to-Fail and Money Center Banks

Regulators have often adopted a too-big-to-fail (TBTF) approach in dealing with financially distressed money center banks and large financial institutions.[20] One of the reasons is the fear of the repercussions that the liquidation of a money center bank might have on the corresponding banks that channel payments through it. Our general formulation of the payments needs, where the flow of depositors going to the various locations is asymmetric, offers a simple way to model this case and to capture some of the features of the TBTF policy. We interpret the TBTF policy as designed to rescue banks which occupy key positions in the interbank network, rather than banks simply with large size.[21]

Consider, for example, the case where there are three locations ($N = 3$). Locations 2 and 3 are peripheral locations and location 1 is a money center location. All the travelers of locations 2 and 3 must consume at location 1, and one-half of the travelers of location 1 consume at location 2 and the other half at location 3. That is, $t_{12} = t_{13} = \frac{1}{2}$ and $t_{21} = t_{31} = 1$, $t_{23} = t_{32} = 0$.[22] This implies that

$$X_1 = \max\left\{1 - \frac{D_0}{\alpha}\left[1 - (1 - \lambda)x^1 - \lambda\left(\frac{x^2 + x^3}{2}\right); 0\right]\right\} \tag{7.19}$$

and

$$
\begin{aligned}
X_2 &= \max\left\{1 - \frac{D_0}{\alpha}[1 - (1 - \lambda)x^2 - \lambda x^1]; 0\right\}, \\
X_3 &= \max\left\{1 - \frac{D_0}{\alpha}[1 - (1 - \lambda)x^3 - \lambda x^1]; 0\right\}.
\end{aligned}
\tag{7.20}
$$

---

[20] See, for example, the intervention of the monetary authorities in the Continental Illinois debacle in 1984 and, to some extent, in arranging the private-sector rescue of Long Term Capital Management.

[21] The failure of Barings in 1996 is an example of the crisis of a large financial institution that did not create systemic risk.

[22] Note that we now abandon assumption 7.3 (the symmetry assumption).

Suppose now that one of these banks (and only one) is insolvent (this is known at $t = 1$). The next proposition illustrates how the closure of a bank with a key position in the interbank market may trigger a systemic crisis.

Proposition 7.6.

(i) If $\lambda > \mu = \alpha(1/D_0 - 1/R)$, the liquidation of bank 1 triggers the liquidation of all other banks (too-big-to-fail).

(ii) If $\lambda > 2\alpha/D_0$, liquidation of bank 2 or bank 3 does not trigger the liquidation of either of the other two banks.

Proof. To prove (i) notice that if bank 1 is closed then $X_1 = 0$ and $x^1 = 0$. Then $D_2 = X_2R = (1 - (D_0/\alpha)\lambda)R$. Thus $x^2 = 0$ if $(1 - (D_0/\alpha)\lambda)R < D_0 \Leftrightarrow \lambda > \alpha(1/D_0 - 1/R)$. To prove (ii) notice that if bank 2 is closed then $x^2 = 0$. If $(1, 0, 1)$ is an equilibrium, when $D_0\lambda/\alpha < 2$ the balance sheet equations become

$$
\left.
\begin{aligned}
D_1\left(1 - \frac{\lambda}{2}\frac{D_0}{\alpha} + \lambda\right) &= \left(1 - \frac{D_0}{\alpha}\frac{\lambda}{2}\right)R_1 + \lambda D_3, \\
D_3\left(1 + \frac{\lambda}{2}\right) &= R_3 + \frac{\lambda}{2}D_1.
\end{aligned}
\right\}
\tag{7.21}
$$

If $R_3 = R_1 = R$, this yields $D_3 = D_1 = R$. This implies that $x = (1, 0, 1)$ is an equilibrium whenever $D_0\lambda/\alpha < 2$. $\square$

Our last result concerns the optimal attitude of the central bank when the money center bank becomes insolvent ($R_1 = 0$). When D_0/R is low, no intervention is needed. When D_0/R is large, the central bank has to inject liquidity. More precisely, we have the following proposition.

Proposition 7.7. When $R_1 = 0$, $x = (1, 1, 1)$ is an equilibrium if D_0/R is sufficiently low (no central bank intervention is needed). In the other case, the cost of bailout increases with D_0/R.

Proof. When $R_1 = 0$, $x = (1, 1, 1)$ can be an equilibrium if

$$
D > D_0 \begin{pmatrix} 1 \\ \vdots \\ 1 \end{pmatrix}.
$$

When $x = (1, 1, 1)$, the balance sheet equations (7.5) become

$$
R_1 + (D_2 + D_3) = 3D_1, \tag{7.22}
$$

$$
R_2 + \tfrac{1}{2}D_1 = \tfrac{3}{2}D_2, \qquad R_3 + \tfrac{1}{2} = \tfrac{3}{2}D_3. \tag{7.23}
$$

Table 7.1. Summary of central bank interventions.

Problem	Type of central bank intervention	Costs	Results
Speculative gridlock	Coordinating role of central bank • guarantee credit lines • deposit insurance	Never used in equilibrium; no cost apart from moral hazard	Proposition 7.1
Insolvency in a resilient interbank market	*Ex ante* monitoring and supervision	Imperfect monitoring leads to forbearance and moral hazard	Proposition 7.2
Insolvency leading to contagion	Orderly closure of insolvent bank and arrangement of credit lines to bypass it	No cost, apart from moral hazard and money center banks; in the case of money center banks it may be too costly or even impossible to organize orderly closure	Proposition 7.5; Proposition 7.6
	Bailout	Transfer of taxpayer money	Proposition 7.7

Solving (7.22) and (7.20) when $R_1 = 0$, $R_2 = R_3 = R$ yields $D_1 = \frac{4}{7}R$, $D_2 = D_3 = \frac{6}{7}R$, which is an equilibrium if and only if $D_0/R < \frac{4}{7}$. The cost of bailout is 0 if and only if $D_0/R < \frac{4}{7}$, it is $D_0 - \frac{4}{7}R$ if and only if $\frac{4}{7} < D_0/R < \frac{6}{7}$. When $D_0/R > \frac{6}{7}$, the central bank also has to inject liquidity in the solvent banks. The total cost to the central bank becomes $3D_0 - \frac{16}{7}R$. $\qquad\square$

7.6 Discussions and Conclusions

We have constructed a model of the banking system where liquidity needs arise from consumers' uncertainty about where they need to consume. Our basic insight is that the interbank market allows the minimization of the amount of resources held in low-return liquid assets. However, interbank links expose the system to the possibility that a number of inefficient outcomes arise: the excessive liquidation of productive investment as a result of coordination failures among depositors; the reduced incentive to liquidate insolvent banks because of the implicit subsidies offered by the payments networks; and the inefficient liquidation of solvent banks because of the contagion effect stemming from one insolvent bank.

7.6.1   Policy Implications

We use this rich setup to derive a set of policy implications (summarized in table 7.1) with respect to the interventions of the central bank.

First, the interbank market may not yield efficient allocation of resources because of possible coordination failures that may generate a "gridlock" equilibrium. The central bank thus has a natural coordination role to play which consists of implicitly guaranteeing the access to liquidity of individual banks. If the banking system as a whole is solvent, the cost of this intervention is negligible and its distortionary effects may stem only from moral hazard issues (proposition 7.1).

Second, if one bank is insolvent, the central bank faces a much more complex trade-off between efficiency and stability. Market forces will not necessarily force the closure of insolvent banks. Indeed, the resiliency of the interbank market allows it to cope with liquidity shocks by providing implicit insurance, which weakens market discipline (proposition 7.2). The central bank therefore has the responsibility to provide *ex ante* monitoring of individual banks. However, it is the responsibility of the central bank to handle systemic repercussions that may be caused by the closure of insolvent banks (proposition 7.5). In this case two courses of action are available: orderly closure or bailout of insolvent banks. Given the interbank links, the closure of an insolvent bank must be accompanied by the provision of central bank liquidity to the counterparts of the closed bank.[23] This is what we call orderly closure. Assuming that this is possible, theoretically it entails no costs apart from moral hazard. However, the orderly closure might simply not be feasible for money center banks (proposition 7.6) in which case the central bank has no choice but to bail out the insolvent institution, with the obvious moral hazard implications of the TBTF policy.

Our model can be extended in various directions, some of which are discussed below.

7.6.2   Imperfect Information on Banks' Returns

In reality, both the central bank and the depositors have only imperfect signals on the solvency of commercial banks (although the central bank's signals are hopefully more precise). Therefore, the central bank will have to act knowing that with some probability it will be lending to (guaranteeing the credit lines of) insolvent institutions and with some probability it will be denying credit to solvent institutions. Also, depositors may run on all the banks which have generated a bad signal.

---

[23] For instance, in the credit chain case, if bank k is closed the central bank can borrow from bank $k - 1$ and lend to bank $k + 1$, thus allowing the interbank arrangements to function smoothly.

The consequences are different depending on the structure of the interbank market. In the credit chain case, the central bank will have to intervene to provide credit with a higher probability than in the diversified lending case. Therefore in the credit chain case the central bank has a higher probability of ending up financing insolvent banks. *Ex ante*, therefore, the central bank intervention is much more expensive in the credit chain case, so that in this case a fully collateralized payments system may be preferred.

7.6.3 Payments among Different Countries

Systemic risk is often related to the spreading of a financial crisis from one country to another. Our basic model can be extended to consider various countries instead of locations within the same country. When depositors belong to different countries, travel patterns that generate a consumption need in another location have the natural interpretation of demand of goods of other countries, i.e., import demand. Goods of the other country can be purchased through currency (like in autarky in the basic model) or through a credit line system whereby the imports of a country are financed by its exports. Our results extend to the model with different countries but the role of the monetary authority is somewhat different. While in our setup the lending ability of the domestic monetary authority was backed by its taxation power, the lending ability of an international financial organization is ultimately backed by its capital. Hence the resources at its disposal are limited and in the case of aggregate uncertainty its ability to guarantee banks' credit lines is limited.[24]

7.7 Appendix: Proof of Proposition 7.1

Notation

Define

$$M(\lambda) \equiv [2I - \Pi']^{-1} = [(1 + \lambda)I - \lambda T']^{-1}$$

$$= \frac{1}{1 + \lambda}\left[I - \frac{\lambda}{1 + \lambda}T'\right]^{-1}, \tag{7.24}$$

where I is the identity matrix. We first need a technical lemma.

Lemma 7.1. *All the elements of $M(\lambda)$ are nonnegative: $m_{ij}(\lambda) \geqslant 0$ for all i, j. Moreover, for all i, $\sum_j m_{ij}(\lambda) = 1$. As a consequence, if $R_i > D_0$*

---

[24]See the role of the IMF in the 1997 Asian crises and the 1998 Russian crisis.

for all i, then

$$M(\lambda)R > D_0 \begin{pmatrix} 1 \\ \vdots \\ 1 \end{pmatrix}. \tag{7.25}$$

Proof. $M(\lambda) = (2I - \Pi')^{-1}$. Since Π' is a Markov matrix (because of assumption 7.3), all its eigenvalues are in the unit disk and $M(\lambda)$ can be developed into a power series:

$$M(\lambda) = \tfrac{1}{2}(I - \tfrac{1}{2}\Pi')^{-1} = \sum_{k=0}^{+\infty} \frac{\Pi'^k}{2^{k+1}}. \tag{7.26}$$

This implies that $M(\lambda)$ has positive elements. Moreover,

$$\begin{pmatrix} 1 \\ \vdots \\ 1 \end{pmatrix}$$

being an eigenvector of Π' (for the eigenvalue 1), it is also an eigenvector for $M(\lambda)$.   □

Proof of proposition 7.1. (i) Because of assumption 7.2, $D_i = 0$ when $x_{ij} = 0$ for all j. Therefore, $x_{ij}^* \equiv 0$ is always an equilibrium.

(ii) $x^j = 1 \Rightarrow X_j = 1$. Using the assumption that $\sum_j \pi_{ji} = 1$, equation (7.5) becomes

$$2D = R + \Pi'D. \tag{7.27}$$

For $x^j = 1$ to be an equilibrium for all j, it must be

$$D = [2I - \Pi']^{-1}R = M(\lambda)R \geqslant D_0 \begin{pmatrix} 1 \\ \vdots \\ 1 \end{pmatrix}. \tag{7.28}$$

This is an immediate consequence of the above lemma, which implies that $x = (1, \ldots, 1)$ is always an equilibrium when all banks are solvent. There are no other equilibria when $\alpha = D_0$. Indeed, if $x^i = 0$, then equation (7.5) implies that $X_i = 0$ or $D_i = R_i$. But X_i cannot be zero (unless all x^j are also zero) and $D_i = R_i > D_0$ contradicts the equilibrium condition. Notice, however, that when $\alpha < D_0$, X_i can be zero even if some of the x^j are positive, which implies that other equilibria may exist.   □

Before establishing proposition 7.3, we have to compute the expression of matrix $M(\lambda)$ in the two cases of credit chain and diversified lending.

Consider the credit chain case first, where the matrix T is given by

$$T = \begin{pmatrix} 0 & 1 & 0 & \cdots & 0 \\ & & \cdots & & \\ & & & \cdots & \\ 0 & \cdots & & 0 & 1 \\ 1 & 0 & \cdots & 0 & 0 \end{pmatrix}. \qquad (7.29)$$

Therefore $T'^N = I$, so that $T'^k = T'^{k+N} = T'^{k+2N} = \cdots$. Now

$$M(\lambda) = \left(\frac{1}{1+\lambda}\right) \sum_{k=0}^{\infty} (\theta T')^k, \qquad (7.30)$$

where $\lambda/(1+\lambda) \equiv \theta$. Let $\Theta \equiv \{1 + \theta + \theta^N + \theta^{2N} \cdots\}$. Thus

$$M(\lambda) \equiv \frac{\Theta}{1+\lambda}[I + \theta T' + (\theta T')^2 + \cdots + (\theta T')^{N-1}] = \frac{1-\theta}{1-\theta^N}A, \quad (7.31)$$

where

$$A \equiv [I + \theta T' + \cdots + (\theta T')^{N-1}]$$

$$= \begin{pmatrix} 1 & \theta^{N-1} & \cdots & \cdots & \theta^2 & \theta \\ \theta & 1 & \theta^{N-1} & \cdots & \cdots & \theta^2 \\ \cdots & \cdots & \cdots & \cdots & \cdots & \cdots \\ \cdots & \cdots & \cdots & \cdots & \cdots & \cdots \\ \cdots & \cdots & \cdots & \cdots & 1 & \theta^{N-1} \\ \theta^{N-1} & \cdots & \cdots & \theta^2 & \theta & 1 \end{pmatrix}. \qquad (7.32)$$

Consider now the diversified lending case, where the matrix T is given by

$$T = \frac{1}{N-1} \begin{pmatrix} 0 & 1 & \cdots & \cdots & 1 \\ 1 & 0 & 1 & \cdots & 1 \\ \cdots & \cdots & \cdots & \cdots & \cdots \\ 1 & \cdots & 1 & 0 & 1 \\ 1 & \cdots & \cdots & 1 & 0 \end{pmatrix}. \qquad (7.33)$$

It follows that $T = T'$. Now

$$M(\lambda) = \frac{1}{1+\lambda}\left[I - \frac{\lambda}{1+\lambda}T'\right]^{-1} = (1-\theta) \sum_{k=0}^{\infty} (\theta T')^k.$$

Notice that

$$T'^2 = \frac{1}{N-1}I + \frac{N-2}{N-1}T',$$

$$T'^3 = \frac{1}{N-1}T' + \frac{N-2}{N-1}T'^2 = \frac{1}{N-1}T' + \frac{N-2}{N-1}\left[\frac{1}{N-1}I + \frac{N-2}{N-1}T'\right].$$

Finally,

$$T'^3 = \frac{N-2}{(N-1)^2}I + \left[1 - \frac{N-2}{(N-1)^2}\right]T'. \tag{7.34}$$

Recursively, we obtain

$$T'^k = \beta_k I + (1 - \beta_k)T', \tag{7.35}$$

where

$$\beta_k = \frac{1}{N}\left[1 - \left(\frac{-1}{N-1}\right)^{k-1}\right]. \tag{7.36}$$

Therefore,

$$M(\lambda) = (1 - \theta)\sum_{k=0}^{\infty}(\theta T')^k = (1 - \theta)\sum_{k=0}^{\infty}[\theta^k \beta_k I + \theta^k (1 - \beta_k)T']. \tag{7.37}$$

Proof of proposition 7.3. If

$$R = \begin{pmatrix} 0 \\ R \\ \vdots \\ R \end{pmatrix},$$

the necessary condition for $x = (1,\dots,1)$ to be an equilibrium becomes

$$D = M(\lambda)R = M(\lambda)\begin{pmatrix} 0 \\ R \\ \vdots \\ R \end{pmatrix} \geqslant D_0. \tag{7.38}$$

In the credit chain case equation (7.32) implies that the first row of condition (7.38) becomes

$$\frac{1-\theta}{1-\theta^N}(\theta^{N-1} + \cdots + \theta)R \geqslant D_0 \tag{7.39}$$

or

$$\frac{D_0}{R} \leqslant 1 - \frac{1}{1 + \theta + \cdots + \theta^{N-1}} \equiv y_N^{\text{cre}}. \tag{7.40}$$

It is easy to see that y_N^{cre} increases in N and in θ (and therefore in y). Notice that $y_\infty^{\mathrm{cre}} = \theta$.

Under diversified lending, $M(\lambda)$ is given by (7.37). Checking the first row of (7.38) and dividing by R yields

$$\frac{D_1}{R} = (1 - \theta) \sum_{k=1}^{\infty} \left[\theta^k (1 - \beta_k) \frac{N-1}{N-1} \right] \equiv y_N^{\mathrm{div}} \geqslant \frac{D_0}{R}. \tag{7.41}$$

Using

$$\beta_k = \frac{1}{N} \left[1 - \left(\frac{-1}{N-1} \right)^{k-1} \right], \tag{7.42}$$

equation (7.41) becomes

$$y_N^{\mathrm{div}} = (1 - \theta) \sum_{k=1}^{\infty} \theta^k \left(1 - \frac{1}{N} \left[1 - \left(\frac{-1}{N-1} \right)^{k-1} \right] \right) \tag{7.43}$$

or

$$N y_N^{\mathrm{div}} = (1 - \theta) \left[(N - 1) \sum_{k=1}^{\infty} \theta^k + \sum_{k=1}^{\infty} \theta^k \left(\frac{-1}{N-1} \right)^{k-1} \right]. \tag{7.44}$$

Since

$$(1 - \theta) \sum_{k=1}^{\infty} \theta^k = \frac{(1 - \theta)\theta}{(1 - \theta)} = \theta \tag{7.45}$$

and

$$\begin{aligned} (1 - \theta) \sum_{k=1}^{\infty} \theta^k \left(\frac{-1}{N-1} \right)^{k-1} &= \theta(1 - \theta) \sum_{k=0}^{\infty} \theta^k \left(\frac{-1}{N-1} \right)^{k} \\ &= \frac{\theta(1 - \theta)}{1 + \theta/(N-1)} = \frac{(N-1)\theta(1 - \theta)}{N - 1 + \theta}, \end{aligned} \tag{7.46}$$

equation (7.44) becomes

$$\begin{aligned} N y_N^{\mathrm{div}} &= (N - 1)\theta + \frac{(N-1)\theta(1 - \theta)}{N - 1 + \theta} \\ &= \frac{(N-1)\theta[N - 1 + \theta + 1 - \theta]}{N - 1 + \theta}, \end{aligned} \tag{7.47}$$

from which

$$y_N^{\mathrm{div}} = \frac{(N-1)\theta}{N - 1 + \theta} = \frac{1}{1/\theta + 1/(N-1)}. \tag{7.48}$$

Recalling that $\theta = \lambda/(1 + \lambda)$, we see that y_N^{div} increases with λ and N, and that $y_\infty^{\mathrm{div}} = \theta$. $\quad\square$

Proof of proposition 7.4. Comparing y_N^{div} and y_N^{cre} we obtain

$$\frac{y_N^{\text{div}}}{\theta} = \frac{N-1}{N-1+\theta} = \frac{1}{1+\theta/(N-1)} \tag{7.49}$$

and

$$\frac{y_N^{\text{cre}}}{\theta} = \frac{1-\theta^{N-1}}{1-\theta^N} = \frac{1+\theta+\theta^2+\theta^3+\cdots+\theta^{N-2}}{1+\theta+\theta^2+\theta^3+\cdots+\theta^{N-1}}$$

$$= \frac{1}{1+\theta^{N-1}/(1+\theta+\theta^2+\theta^3+\cdots+\theta^{N-2})}. \tag{7.50}$$

Since $\theta^{N-2} < \theta^{N-3} < \theta^{N-4} < \cdots$, then

$$\frac{\theta^{N-2}}{1+\theta+\theta^2+\theta^3+\cdots+\theta^{N-2}} < \frac{1}{N-1}. \tag{7.51}$$

Thus

$$\frac{\theta^{N-1}}{1+\theta+\theta^2+\theta^3+\cdots+\theta^{N-2}} < \frac{\theta}{N-1} \quad \Longrightarrow \quad \frac{y_N^{\text{cre}}}{\theta} > \frac{y_N^{\text{div}}}{\theta}. \tag{7.52}$$

$\square$

References

Allen, F., and D. Gale. 2000. Financial contagion. *Journal of Political Economy* 108:1–33.

Berger, A. N., D. Hancock, and J. C. Marquardt. 1996. A framework for analyzing efficiency, risks, costs, and innovations in the payments systems. *Journal of Money, Credit and Banking* 28(Part 2):696–732.

Bhattacharya, S., and P. Fulghieri. 1994. Uncertain liquidity and interbank contracting. *Economics Letters* 44:287–94.

Bhattacharya, S., and D. Gale. 1987. Preference shocks, liquidity and central bank policy. In *New Approaches to Monetary Economics* (ed. W. Barnett and K. Singleton). Cambridge University Press.

Brimmer, A. F. 1989. Distinguished lecture on economics in government: central banking and systemic risks in capital markets. *Journal of Economic Perspectives* 3:3–16.

Calomiris, C. W., and C. Khan. 1991. The role of demandable debt in structuring optimal banking arrangements. *American Economic Review* 81:497–513.

Calomiris, C. W., and J. R. Mason. 1997. Contagion and bank failures during the Great Depression: the June 1932 Chicago banking panic. *American Economic Review* 87:863–83.

De Bandt, O., and P. Hartmann. 2002. Systemic risk: a survey. In *Financial Crises, Contagion, and the Lender of Last Resort. A Reader* (ed. C. Goodhart and G. Illing). Oxford University Press.

Diamond, D., and P. H. Dybvig. 1983. Bank runs, deposit insurance, and liquidity. *Journal of Political Economy* 91:401–19.

Flannery, M. J. 1996. Financial crises, payment systems problems, and discount window lending. *Journal of Money, Credit and Banking* 28(Part 2):804–24.

Freedman, C., and C. Goodlet. 1998. The Canadian payments systems: recent developments in structure and regulation. In *Payments Systems in the Global Economy: Risks and Opportunities, Proceedings of the 34th Annual Conference on Bank Structure and Competition*. Federal Reserve Bank of Chicago.

Freeman, S. 1996a. Clearinghouse banks and banknote over-issue. *Journal of Monetary Economics* 38:101–15.

———. 1996b. The payment system, liquidity, and rediscounting. *American Economic Review* 86:1126–38.

Freixas, X., and B. Parigi. 1998. Contagion and efficiency in gross and net payment systems. *Journal of Financial Intermediation* 7:3–31.

Garber, P. M. 1998. Notes on the role of TARGET in a stage III crisis. National Bureau of Economic Research Working Paper 6619.

Gorton, G. 1988. Banking panics and business cycles. *Oxford Economic Papers* 40:751–81.

Kaufman, G. 1994. Bank contagion: a review of the theory and evidence. *Journal of Financial Services Research* 8:123–50.

Kiyotaki, N., and J. Moore. 1997. Credit chains. Mimeo, London School of Economics.

Reid, M. 1991. Flight to quality. *Banking World*, September.

Salop, S. 1979. Monopolistic competition with outside goods. *Bell Journal of Economics* 10:141–56.

Saunders, A., and B. Wilson. 1996. Contagious bank runs: evidence from the 1929–1933 period. *Journal of Financial Intermediation* 5:409–23.

Schoenmaker, D. 1996. Contagion risk in banking. LSE Financial Markets Group, Discussion Paper 239.

Summers, B. J. (ed.). 1994. *The Payment System, Design, Management, and Supervision*. Washington, DC: IMF.

Takayama, A. 1985. *Mathematical Economics*, 2nd edn. Cambridge University Press.

Townsend, R. M. 1987. Economic organization with limited communication. *American Economic Review* 77:954–71.

Wallace, N. 1988. Another attempt to explain an illiquid banking system: the Diamond–Dybvig model with sequential service taken seriously. *Quarterly Review of the Federal Reserve Bank of Minneapolis* 12:3–16.

PART 4

Solvency Regulations

Chapter Eight

Capital Requirements and the Behavior of Commercial Banks

Jean-Charles Rochet

8.1 Introduction

This paper is motivated by the adoption at the European Community level of a new capital requirement for commercial banks. This reform (fully effective from January 1993) is in fact closely inspired by a similar regulation (the so-called Cooke ratio) adopted earlier (December 1987) by the Bank of International Settlements.

I try to examine here what economic theory can tell us about such regulations, and more specifically:

- Why do they exist in the first place?

- Are they indeed a good way to limit the risk of failure of commercial banks?

- What effects can be expected on the behavior of these banks?

In fact, the above questions have already been examined, notably by U.S. economists who have used essentially two competing sets of assumptions. In the first setup, financial markets are supposed to be complete and depositors are perfectly informed about the failure risks of banks. Then the Modigliani–Miller indeterminacy principle applies and the market values of banks are independent of the structure of their assets portfolio, as well as their capital to assets ratio. However, when a bankruptcy cost is introduced, as in Kareken and Wallace (1978), it is found that unregulated banks would spontaneously choose their assets portfolio in such a way that failure does not occur. The reason is market discipline: since capital markets are supposed to be efficient and banks' creditors (including depositors) are supposed to be perfectly informed, any increase in the banks' riskiness would immediately be reflected in the rates of return demanded by stockholders and depositors. It is only when a deposit insurance scheme is introduced that this market discipline is corrupted and the banks' decisions become distorted. This is a classical "moral-hazard" argument: depositors have no more incentives to monitor the investment behavior of their banks since they are (a priori) insured against failures.

However, all this comes from the mispricing of deposit insurance: even when it is provided by a formal insurance company, like the Federal Deposit Insurance Corporation (FDIC) in the United States, its price is not computed on an actuarial basis. Indeed the insurance premiums only depend on the volume of deposits, and not on asset composition or capital ratios. As a consequence these premiums are not related to the failure probabilities of banks. But if we accept the assumption of complete, efficient capital markets, there is no need for regulating banks' capital:

- If depositors are fully informed, banks spontaneously choose efficient portfolios and deposit insurance is useless.

- If depositors are not fully informed (but the regulator is), they should be protected by a deposit insurance scheme funded by actuarially fair premiums. The only remaining difficulty is then technical: we have to find a reasonably simple way to compute these premiums (a solution to this problem is offered in Kerfriden and Rochet (1993)).

On the other hand, it is hard to believe that a deep understanding of the banking sector can be obtained within the setup of complete contingent markets, essentially because of the already mentioned Modigliani-Miller indeterminacy principle. This principle implies that, except for bankruptcy cost considerations, banks are completely indifferent about their assets portfolio and capital ratios. Therefore, we have to turn to an incomplete markets setting. The problem then comes from the absence of a theoretically sound objective function for firms in general, and banks in particular. Consequently, an alternative set of assumptions has been adopted by a second strand of the literature, notably Koehn and Santomero (1980) and Kim and Santomero (1988). It is adapted from the portfolio model of Pyle (1971) and Hart and Jaffee (1974). Banks are supposed to behave as competitive portfolio managers, in the sense that first they take prices (and yields) as given, and second they choose the composition of their balance sheets (including liabilities) so as to maximize the expectation of some (ad hoc) utility function of the bank's financial net worth. The results obtained by Koehn and Santomero (1980) and Kim and Santomero (1988) are essentially the following:

- Imposing a capital regulation will in general lead banks not only to reduce the total volume of their risky portfolio, but also to recompose it in such a way that their assets allocation becomes inefficient.

- As a consequence it is quite possible that the failure probability of some banks may increase (!) when the capital regulation is imposed. Nevertheless, it is possible to compute "theoretically correct risk weights" such that these adverse effects are eliminated.

However, there are two features of the Pyle–Hart–Jaffee model which are difficult to justify here:

- First, equity capital is treated in the same way as other securities: banks are assumed to be able to buy and sell their own stocks at a given exogenous price, which is in particular independent of the investment behavior of the bank. This is hard to reconcile with the fact that the returns to the bank's stockholders clearly depend on the bank's investment policy.

- Second, banks behave as if they were fully liable! In other words, although the regulation under study is precisely motivated by the default risk of commercial banks, this is not taken into account by the banks themselves.

Thus I do essentially two things in this paper:

- I reexamine the conclusions of Koehn and Santomero (1980) and Kim and Santomero (1988) in a model where a bank's equity capital is fixed, at least in the short run. Their main result, namely that the adoption of a capital requirement will not necessarily entail a diminution of the banks' risk of default, is shown to also be valid in our context, where it is simpler to understand. I also provide a very simple recommendation for computing "correct" risk weights: to make them proportional to the systematic risks (the betas) of the assets.

- I take into account limited liability and I show that it modifies in a substantial way the banks' behavior toward risk. Under certain circumstances, banks may become risk-lovers. Imposing a minimum capital is then necessary to prevent them from choosing very inefficient portfolios. A solvency ratio alone, even with correct risk weights, would not be sufficient.

The paper is organized as follows. The model is presented in section 8.2. Section 8.3 is dedicated to the behavior of banks in the complete markets setup. The portfolio model is introduced in section 8.4, and the behavior of banks without capital requirements is examined in section 8.5. Capital requirements are introduced in section 8.6, and limited liability in section 8.7. Section 8.8 contains some concluding remarks, and mathematical proofs are gathered in two appendixes.

8.2   The Model

It is a static model with only two dates: $t = 0$, where the bank chooses the composition of its portfolio; and $t = 1$, where all assets and liabilities are liquidated. There are only two liabilities: equity capital K_0 and deposits D. In most of the paper, K_0 is exogenously fixed but D is chosen by the bank, taking into account the total cost (operating costs + interest paid to depositors + possibly, deposit insurance premiums) $C(D)$ of these deposits. This cost function depends on the institutional framework (which will be discussed below) as well as on the competitive position of the bank on the deposit market (existence or size of a branch network) The marginal cost of deposits, $C'(D)$, is supposed to be strictly increasing, continuous, with $C'(+\infty) = +\infty$. On the asset side, the bank is allowed to invest any amount x_i on security i ($i = 0, \ldots, N$), taking as given the random returns $\tilde{R}_i$ on these securities. Security zero is supposed to be riskless (R_0 is deterministic). The accounting equations giving the total of the balance sheet are easily obtained:

$$\sum_{i=0}^{N} x_i = D + K_0 \qquad \text{(at } t = 0\text{)},$$

$$\sum_{i=0}^{N} x_i(1 + \tilde{R}_i) = D + C(D) + \tilde{K}_1 \quad \text{(at } t = 1\text{)}.$$

$\tilde{K}_1$, the final net worth of the bank, can easily be expressed in terms of the risky portfolio $x = (x_1, \ldots, x_N)$ and D, which we will take as decision variables:

$$\tilde{K}_1 = \sum_{j=1}^{N} x_i\tilde{\rho}_i + (R_0 D - C(D)) + K_0(1 + R_0), \qquad (8.1)$$

where $\tilde{\rho}_i = \tilde{R}_i - \tilde{R}_0$ denotes the excess return on security i.

For the moment, we assume that financial markets are complete in the Arrow-Debreu sense, and equally accessible to all agents. Thus it is possible to compute the equilibrium price S_0 at date 0 of any security S, characterized by its random liquidation value $S(\omega)$, where ω represents the state of the world at date 1 and belongs to some probability space $(\Omega, \mathcal{A}, \pi)$. In order to avoid technicalities we assume for the moment that Ω is finite and we denote by $(p(\omega))_{\omega \in \Omega}$ the vector of Arrow-Debreu contingent prices. We then have

$$S_0 = \sum_{\omega \in \Omega} p(\omega)\tilde{S}(\omega).$$

In particular, for all $i = 0, \ldots, N$, we have

$$1 = \sum_{\omega \in \Omega} p(\omega)(1 + \tilde{R}_i(\omega)) \tag{8.2}$$

and notably

$$\frac{1}{1 + R_0} = \sum_{\omega \in \Omega} p(\omega). \tag{8.3}$$

Thus, for all $i = 1, \ldots, N$,

$$0 = \sum_{\omega \in \Omega} p(\omega)\tilde{\rho}_i(\omega). \tag{8.4}$$

We are now in a position to compare the decisions of banks under different institutional arrangements, assuming that each bank tries to maximize its market value $\mathcal{V}$:

$$\mathcal{V} = \sum_{\omega \in \Omega} p(\omega) \max(0, \tilde{K}_1(\omega)), \tag{8.5}$$

where $\max(0, \cdot)$ appears because of limited liability and

$$\tilde{K}_1(\omega) = \sum_{i=1}^{N} x_i \tilde{\rho}_i(\omega) + [R_0 D - C(D)] + K_0(1 + R_0).$$

8.3 The Behavior of Banks in the Complete Markets Setup

Following Merton (1977), several authors (e.g., Kareken and Wallace 1978; Sharpe 1978; Dothan and Williams 1980) have used option pricing formulas for computing the net present value of the subsidy implicitly provided by the deposit insurance system to commercial banks. The two crucial assumptions of this approach (namely that option prices can always be computed and that banks maximize the net present value of their capital) can only be justified when financial markets are complete. The purpose of this section is to analyze directly the behavior of banks in such a complete markets setup. This will illustrate the limits of this approach for modeling the banking system. We now characterize this behavior of banks under alternative institutional arrangements.

8.3.1 Without Deposit Insurance

If depositors are fully informed, they will require an interest rate R_D that takes into account the possibility of failure. Therefore, there is no need for a deposit insurance scheme. If we neglect for a moment the payments services provided by deposits, we must have

$$D = \sum_{w \in \Omega} p(w) \min\left[D(1 + R_D), (D + K_0)(1 + R_0) + \sum_{i=1}^{N} x_i \tilde{\rho}_i(w)\right]. \quad (8.6)$$

It is clear in particular that R_D depends on $x = (x_1, \ldots, x_N)$, D, and K_0. Moreover, $C(D)$ is just equal to $R_D D$ and we can rearrange equation (8.5) to get

$$V + D\frac{1 + R_D}{1 + R_0}$$

$$= \sum_{w \in \Omega} p(w) \max\left[D(1 + R_D), (D + K_0)(1 + R_0) + \sum_{i=1}^{N} x_i \tilde{\rho}_i(w)\right].$$

Adding this to (8.6), we obtain

$$V + D\left(1 + \frac{1 + R_D}{1 + R_0}\right)$$

$$= \sum_{w \in \Omega} p(w)\left[D(1 + R_D), (D + K_0)(1 + R_0) + \sum_{i=1}^{N} x_i \tilde{\rho}_i(w)\right].$$

Using equation (8.2) we get

$$V + D\left(1 + \frac{1 + R_D}{1 + R_0}\right) = D\left(1 + \frac{1 + R_D}{1 + R_0}\right) + K_0.$$

Finally,

$$V = K_0 \quad (8.7)$$

and we are back to the Modigliani–Miller indeterminacy principle: the market value of the bank is completely independent of any of its actions. If we introduce a reorganization cost g supported by the bank in the case of failure, as in Kareken and Wallace (1978), then (8.7) becomes

$$V = K_0\left(\sum_{w \in \Omega_F} p(w)\right)g,$$

where Ω_F denotes the set of states of nature in which the bank fails. V is then maximum for any choice of x and D that prevents this failure, i.e., such that $\Omega_F = \varnothing$.

8.3.2 With Deposit Insurance but No Capital Requirement

From now on, depositors are assumed to be imperfectly informed on the banks' activities, which justifies implementation of a deposit insurance scheme. We will suppose that this scheme provides full insurance for all deposits and is funded through proportional insurance premiums:

$$P = kD, \quad k > 0.$$

We also take into account the payments services provided by the banks in association with deposits. They have a unit cost y but in counterpart depositors are ready to accept interest rates R_D lower than R_0. More specifically, there is an (inverse) supply function $R_D(D)$ (with $R'_D > 0$ and $R_D(+\infty) = R_0$) and the bank is supposed to behave as a (local) monopoly on the deposit market. The cost function is then

$$C(D) = (R_D(D) + y + k)D.$$

Again, the market value of the bank can be written as

$$V = \sum_{w \in \Omega} p(w) \max(0, K_0, (1 + R_0) + DR_0 - C(D) + \langle x, \tilde{p}(w) \rangle). \quad (8.8)$$

But in contrast with the case without deposit insurance, $C(D)$ is now independent of x and K_0. We have to solve

$$\left. \begin{array}{l} \max_{x,D} V, \\[2mm] x_i \geqslant 0, \quad i = 1, \ldots, N, \\[2mm] \sum_{i=1}^{N} x_i \leqslant K_0 + D. \end{array} \right\} \quad (\mathcal{P}_1)$$

Proposition 8.1. *We assume complete contingent markets, full deposit insurance with premiums depending only on deposits, and no capital requirement. Then the bank specializes on a unique, risky asset.*

Proof. It is a straightforward consequence of the remark that formula (8.5) implies that V is a convex function of x. Thus, D being fixed, $(\mathcal{P}_1)$ amounts to maximize a *convex* function on a convex polytope. Its solution is obtained for one of its extreme points $x^0, x^1, \ldots, x^N$ characterized by

$$x^0 = 0 \quad \text{and} \quad \begin{cases} x_i^j = 0 & \text{if } i \neq j, \ i = 1, \ldots, N, \\[2mm] x_j^j = K_0 + D & (\text{or } x_0^j = 0). \end{cases}$$

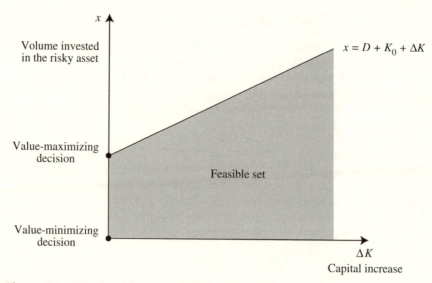

Figure 8.1. The feasible set and the bank's optimal decision with value-maximizing banks, fixed-rate deposit insurance, and no capital requirement (case $N = 1$).

Each of these extreme points corresponds to a specialization of the bank's portfolio on a unique asset j. It remains to prove that this cannot be the riskless asset $j = 0$. For that purpose, it is enough to remark that

$$\frac{\partial \mathcal{V}}{\partial x_i}(x^0) = \sum_{\omega \in \Omega} p(\omega) \tilde{\rho}_i(\omega), \quad i = 1, \ldots, N.$$

Therefore, x_0 corresponds to the minimum of $\mathcal{V}$ on the feasible set.

Let us remark in passing that, as soon as the probability of failure is positive, the volume of deposits chosen by the bank is also inefficient. The bank attracts more deposits than a full liability bank would. □

In this setup, it is also easy to study the decision of increasing the bank's capital. For that purpose, we need to define two new variables: a retention coefficient τ (i.e., the proportion of the stock that remains in the hands of initial stockholders) and the amount ΔK collected at $t = 0$ from new stockholders. Because of our complete markets assumptions, these two variables are linked by the following equation:

$$\Delta K = (1 - \tau) \sum_{\omega \in \Omega} p(\omega) \max(0, \tilde{K}_1(\omega)), \tag{8.9}$$

where the new expression of the final net worth of the bank, $\tilde{K}_1(w)$, is

$$\tilde{K}_1(w) = \sum_{i=1}^{N} x_i \tilde{\rho}(w) + (R_0 D - C(D)) + (K_0 + \Delta K)(1 + R_0). \qquad (8.10)$$

The objective function of the initial stockholders is

$$V = \tau \sum_{w \in \Omega} p(w) \max(0, \tilde{K}_1(w)).$$

Because of (8.10) it can also be written as

$$V = \sum_{w \in \Omega} p(w) \max(0, \tilde{K}_1(w)) - \Delta K.$$

The program to be solved is now

$$\left. \begin{array}{c} \max V, \\ x \in \mathbb{R}_+^N, \quad \Delta K \geqslant 0, \\ \sum_{i=1}^{N} x_i \leqslant D + K_0 + \Delta K \end{array} \right\} \qquad (\mathcal{P}_2)$$

(see figure 8.1).

Proposition 8.2. *Under the assumptions of proposition 8.1, the bank will not choose to increase its capital:* $\Delta K^* = 0$. *The solutions of* $(\mathcal{P}_1)$ *and* $(\mathcal{P}_2)$ *are the same: specialization on a unique, risky asset.*

Proof. Again, V is convex with respect to $(x, \Delta K)$. Moreover, it is non-increasing with respect to ΔK:

$$\frac{\partial V}{\partial(\Delta K)} = \sum_{w \in \Omega_{NF}} p(w)(1 + R_0) - 1 \leqslant 0 \quad \text{(because of (8.3))},$$

where Ω_{NF} is the set of "no-failure" states.

Since the solution of $(\mathcal{P}_2)$ is an extreme point of the feasible set only two cases are possible:

- $\Delta K = 0$, and we are back to problem $(\mathcal{P}_1)$;

- $\Delta K > 0$ and all other constraints are binding, which is impossible since $D + K_0 > 0$.

□

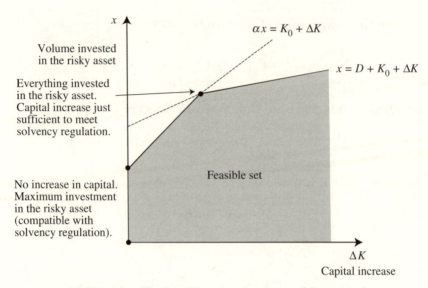

Figure 8.2. The feasible set and two possible optimal decisions when a solvency ratio is introduced (case $N = 1$).

8.3.3   With Deposit Insurance and Capital Requirements

Now we introduce a capital requirement, taking the following form:

$$\langle \alpha, x \rangle = \sum_{i=1}^{N} \alpha_i x_i \leqslant K_0 + \Delta K_0,$$

where $\alpha_i > 0$ is to be interpreted as the "risk weight" of security i. The decision problem of the bank becomes

$$\left. \begin{aligned} & \max \mathcal{V}, \\ & x \in \mathbb{R}^N_+, \quad \Delta K \geqslant 0, \\ & \sum_{i=1}^{N} x_i \leqslant D + K_0 + \Delta K, \\ & \sum_{i=1}^{N} \alpha_i x_i \leqslant K_0 + \Delta K \end{aligned} \right\} \tag{$\mathcal{P}_3$}$$

(see figure 8.2).

Proposition 8.3. *Under the assumptions of proposition 8.1, except that a capital requirement is introduced, three cases are possible for the bank's optimal behavior:*

(1) *No increase of capital* ($\Delta K = 0$): *maximum investment on a unique risky asset* ($x := 0$ for $i \neq j$, $x_j^* = \min(D + K_0, K_0/\alpha_j)$), *the rest (if any) being invested in the riskless asset.*

(2) *Complete specialization on a unique, risky asset* ($x_i^* = 0$ for $i \neq j$, $x_j^* = D + K_0 + \Delta K$); *capital increase just sufficient for meeting the capital requirement.*

(3) *No increase of capital* ($\Delta K = 0$): *specialization on two risky assets* j, k ($x_i^* = 0$ for $i \neq j, k$) *in such a way that the capital requirement binds.*

Proof. Again, it is a straightforward consequence of the convexity of $\mathcal{V}$ with respect to $(x, \Delta K)$ and the fact that $\mathcal{V}$ is nondecreasing in ΔK. Three cases are possible.

- $\Delta K = 0$, and there exists j such that

$$x_i^* = 0 \quad \text{for } i \neq j,$$
$$x_j^* = \min\left(D + K_0, \frac{K_0}{\alpha_j}\right).$$

- $\Delta K = 0$, $x_i^* = 0$ for $i \neq j, k$:

$$x_j^* + x_k^* = D + K_0,$$
$$\alpha_j x_j^* + \alpha_k x_K^* = K_0.$$

- $\Delta K > 0$: then there exists j such that

$$x_i^* = 0 \quad \text{for } i \neq j,$$
$$x_j^* = D + K_0 + \Delta K = \frac{K_0 + \Delta K}{\alpha_j}.$$

$\square$

It is clear then that, if we believe in the complete markets assumption, a capital requirement is a very inefficient tool for limiting the risk taken by banks. Moreover, it entails severe reallocations of assets since in most cases it is optimal for banks to specialize in at most two risky assets. On the other hand, there is a very simple solution to our problem (if we assume that the regulator is able to monitor the investment decisions of the bank), namely to charge an "actuarially fair" premium for deposit insurance. This premium is defined by

$$P^* = \sum_{\omega \in \Omega} p(\omega) \max(0, -\tilde{K}_1(\omega)). \qquad (8.11)$$

Instead of adding the insurance premium to the cost of deposits, we are now going to subtract it from the objective function of the bank, which becomes

$$\mathcal{V} = \sum_{\omega \in \Omega} p(\omega) \max(0, \tilde{K}_1(\omega)) - \Delta K - P^*.$$

Because of equation (8.11), we also have

$$\mathcal{V} = \sum_{\omega \in \Omega} p(\omega) \tilde{K}_1(\omega) - \Delta K,$$

$$= \sum_{\omega \in \Omega} p(\omega)[\langle x, \tilde{\rho}(\omega) \rangle + R_0 D - C(D) + (K_0 + \Delta K)(1 + R_0)] - \Delta K.$$

Finally, using (8.3) and (8.4), this simplifies to

$$\mathcal{V} = K_0 + \frac{R_0 D - C(D)}{1 + R_0}. \qquad (8.12)$$

Proposition 8.4. *Under the assumptions of proposition 8.1, except that insurance premiums are computed on an actuarial basis, the bank is indifferent to its asset portfolio x and capital increases ΔK. As a consequence, capital requirements are useless.*

Proof. Obvious from equation (8.12).   □

8.4 The Portfolio Model

Since the complete market setup is rather disappointing for studying capital regulations, we turn to the incomplete markets case. However, things become extremely intricate, unless we adopt several stringent assumptions.

Assumption 8.1. *The bank behaves as a portfolio manager, i.e., it tries to maximize the expectations of $u(\tilde{K}_1)$, where u is a (Von Neumann–Morgenstern) utility function (with $u' > 0$, $u'' < 0$).*

The justification for this assumption is the well-known difficulty of defining a theoretically sound objective function for firms in an incomplete markets setting.

Assumption 8.2. *Equity capital is fixed ($\Delta K = 0$).*

This is a departure from previous papers on the subject (Kahane 1977; Koehn and Santomero 1980; Kim and Santomero 1988), who made the same assumption as Hart and Jaffee (1974). There is an exogenous price for equity capital, and the bank chooses ΔK in a competitive fashion. Since we are concerned with failure possibilities, it does not seem reasonable to assume that the price of capital is independent of the investment policy of the bank. However, again because of our incomplete markets assumption, it is not easy to specify a reasonable way in which the price of capital depends on x, ΔK, and D. Therefore, we were forced to adopt assumption 8.2.

In order to simplify the analysis we are finally going to make a technical assumption.

Assumption 8.3. *The vector $\tilde{\rho} = (\tilde{\rho}_i, \ldots, \tilde{\rho}_N)$ is Gaussian, with mean $\rho = (\rho_i, \ldots, \rho_N)$ and nonsingular variance-covariance matrix V.*

A well-known consequence of this assumption is that we can restrict ourselves to a mean-variance analysis.

Proposition 8.5. *Under assumptions 8.1-8.3, the objective function and the default probability of the bank only depend on*

$$\mu = E(\tilde{K}_1) = \langle x, p \rangle + R_0 D - C(D) + K_0(1 + R_0),$$

$$\sigma^2 = \langle x, Vx \rangle.$$

More specifically,

$$Eu(\tilde{K}_1) + U(\mu, \sigma),$$

where U is concave in $U(\mu, \sigma)$, increasing in μ, decreasing in σ, and

$$\Pr[\tilde{K}_0 < 0] = N(-\mu/\sigma),$$

where N denotes the standard Gaussian cumulative.

Proof. Assumption 8.3 implies that $\tilde{K}_1$ is Gaussian of mean μ and variance σ^2. Therefore,

$$Eu(\tilde{K}_1) = \int u(\sigma y + \mu)\, dN(y) = U(\mu, \sigma);$$

u being increasing, so is the mapping $\mu \to u(\mu + \sigma y)$ (for all y), which implies that U is increasing in μ; u being concave, so is the mapping $(\mu, \sigma) \to u(\mu + \sigma y)$ (for all y), which implies that U is concave in (μ, σ). Finally, by symmetry of N, we can write

$$U(\mu, \sigma) = \int_0^{+\infty} \{u(-\sigma y + \mu) + u(\sigma y + \mu)\}\, dN(y);$$

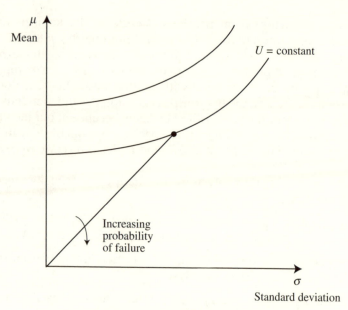

Figure 8.3. Indifference curves and failure probability of a full liability bank in the portfolio model.

u being concave, the mapping $\sigma \rightarrow u(\mu + \sigma y) + u(\mu - \sigma y)$ is decreasing (for all $y > 0$), and thus U is decreasing in σ.

Finally,

$$P(\tilde{K}_1 < 0) = P\left[\frac{\tilde{K}_1 - \mu}{\sigma} < -\frac{\mu}{\sigma}\right] = N\left(-\frac{\mu}{\sigma}\right),$$

which is a decreasing function of μ and an increasing function of σ. ☐

See figure 8.3.

8.5 The Behavior of Banks in the Portfolio Model without Capital Requirements

In order to solve the bank's decision problem, we are going to use proposition 8.5 and first characterize the feasible set in terms of means and variances. Before that, let us determine the optimal quantity of deposits D^*. Since we have ignored liquidity considerations (i.e., we assumed deterministic deposits) and since U is increasing in μ, D^* is simply determined by the condition

$$C'(D^*) = R_0.$$

In the case where the bank would only invest in the riskless asset (and choose $x = 0$), its final net worth would be nonrandom and equal to

$$K = R_0 D^* - C(D^*) + K_0(1 + R_0).$$

This quantity, which we call "corrected net worth," incorporates the intermediation margin obtained by the bank in the deposit activity. The magnitude of this margin may be very different across countries, because it depends in particular on the (possible) regulations of deposit rates and the degrees of competition for deposits. Similarly, the magnitude of this term may be very different across banks in the same country, because different banks may have very different cost functions. In some countries, it is clearly nonnegligible. Let us remark incidentally that this intermediation margin introduces a relation between the deposit and assets activities of the bank, even though the riskless asset is inelastic. This has to be contrasted with Klein (1971).

Let us now turn to the portfolio choice, by first characterizing the "feasible set" (in terms of means and variances) for an unregulated bank of corrected net worth K. For the sake of simplicity, we will suppose that the "borrowing constraint" ($x_0 \geqslant 0$) is not binding:

$$A_0(K) \overset{\text{def}}{=} \{(\mu, \sigma), \exists x \in \mathbb{R}_+^N, \mu + K + \langle x, \rho \rangle, \sigma^2 = \langle x, Vx \rangle\}.$$

By proposition 8.5, our problem is equivalent to

$$\left. \begin{aligned} &\max U(\mu, \sigma), \\ &(\sigma, \mu) \in A_0(K). \end{aligned} \right\} \qquad (\mathcal{P}')$$

Since U is increasing in μ, the solution of $(\mathcal{P}')$ will always belong to the "efficient set":

$$A_0^+(K) = \{(\sigma, \mu) \in A_0(K), \forall \mu' > \mu(\sigma, \mu') \notin A_0(K)\}.$$

As is well-known, $A_0^+(K)$ is a straight line. This is illustrated in figure 8.4.

Lemma 8.1. $A_0^+(K) = \{(\sigma, \mu), \mu - K = \lambda \sigma)\}$, where λ is a positive constant.

Proof. See the appendix (section 8.9). □

Remark 8.1. Thus the no-short-sales requirement ($x \in \mathbb{R}_+^N$) does not modify the traditional results of the CAPM: all banks choose portfolios collinear to x^*. At equilibrium, x^* is thus proportional to the market portfolio x^M. If the same no-short-sales requirements apply to all investors in the economy, then $X_i^M > 0$ for all i (otherwise security i is

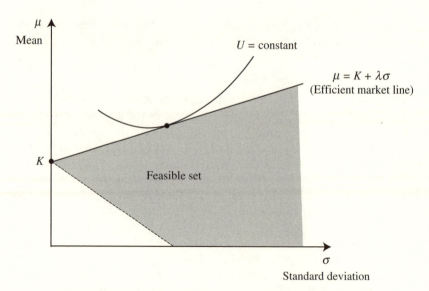

Figure 8.4. The feasible set and the optimal decision of
a utility-maximizing bank, with full liability and no capital requirement.

not traded). *Ex post*, the no-short-sales requirements are nonbinding and
we are back to the CAPM:

$$x^* = \frac{V^{-1}\rho}{\langle \rho, V^{-1}\rho \rangle} \quad \text{and} \quad \lambda = \langle \rho, V^{-1}\rho \rangle^{1/2}.$$

In particular the vector ρ of mean excess return is proportional to the
vector $\beta = Vx$ of the covariances with the market portfolio return.

In this very simple mean–variance world, a good indicator of default
risk is given by the following "adjusted" capital ratio:

$$\text{CR} = \frac{K}{\langle \alpha, X \rangle}.$$

This is indeed a consequence of the following proposition.

Proposition 8.6. *Under assumptions 8.1–8.3 and when capital is not
regulated, the default probability of a bank is a decreasing function of
its adjusted capital ratio.*

Proof. It is easily deduced from the fact that all banks choose risky
portfolios with the same composition. Let $x(K)$ be the optimal risky
portfolio for a bank having an "adjusted net worth" equal to K. By the
arguments above we know that

$$x(K) = \sigma(K)x^{\text{M}},$$

where x^M is the market portfolio, normalized in such a way that it has a unit variance (i.e., $x^M = V^{-1}\rho/\sigma$). $\sigma(K)$ is a nonnegative constant, equal to the standard deviation of the argument maximum of $(\mathcal{P})$. It is the maximum of $\sigma \to U(K + \lambda\sigma, \sigma)$ and, in particular, the mean return on $x(K)$ equals

$$\mu(K) = K + \lambda\sigma(K).$$

As a consequence,

$$CR(K)^{-1} = \frac{\langle \alpha, X(K) \rangle}{K} = \frac{\sigma(K)}{K}\langle \alpha, X_M \rangle$$

and

$$Pr(\tilde{K}_1 < 0) = N\left(-\frac{\mu(K)}{K}\right) = N\left(-1 - \lambda\frac{\sigma(K)}{K}\right)$$

$$= N\left(-1 - \lambda\frac{\lambda\langle \alpha, X_M \rangle}{CR(K)}\right).$$

Since $\lambda > 0$, and N is increasing, the proof is complete. $\qquad\square$

Proposition 8.6 may seem a good justification for capital requirements. *Independently* of the choice of risk weights $\alpha_1, \dots, \alpha_N$, but provided that the numerator of the ratio is adjusted to incorporate intermediation profits on deposits, the capital ratio is an increasing function of the default risk. The trouble is that as soon as the capital requirement is imposed, the banks' behavior changes and proposition 8.6 ceases to be true. This will be the subject of the next section.

As a conclusion to the present section, we examine the dependence of the default risk of an unregulated bank on its (corrected) net worth. Is $CR(K)$ a monotonic function of K? In other words, if no capital regulation were imposed, would the more capitalized banks be more or less risky than the less capitalized ones? It turns out that the answer to this question depends on the properties of the utility function u. More specifically, we have the following proposition.

Proposition 8.7. *If the Arrow–Pratt relative index of risk aversion $-xu''(x)/u'(x)$ is decreasing (respectively increasing), then the default probability of an unregulated bank is an increasing (respectively decreasing) function of its "adjusted" net worth K.*

Proof. By proposition 8.6, the default probability of an unregulated bank is an increasing function of

$$\tau(K) = \frac{\sigma(K)}{K},$$

where $\tau(K)$ is the solution to $\max_\tau Eu[K(1 + \tau \tilde{R}_M)]$ and $\tilde{R}_M$ is the random return of the market portfolio. By well-known results of Arrow (1974) and Pratt (1964), if $-(xu''(x))/(u'(x))$ is monotonic, then $\tau(K)$ is monotonic in the other direction.   □

As a consequence of proposition 8.7, the most frequently used specifications of Von Neumann–Morgenstern utility functions, namely exponential and isoelastic functions, lead to a default probability that is, respectively, a decreasing and a constant function of K.

8.6   Introducing Capital Requirements into the Portfolio Model

In order to concentrate on one distortion at a time, we will assume that the capital regulation requires the adjusted capital ratio to be less than 1. Or, equivalently, we neglect the intermediation margin $K - K_0$. The new feasible set is now restricted to

$$A_1(K) = \{(\sigma,\mu),\ \exists x \in \mathbb{R}_+^N,\ \mu - K = \langle x, \rho \rangle,\ \langle x, Vx \rangle = \sigma^2,\ \langle \alpha, x, \rangle \leqslant K\}.$$

As before, let us denote by $A_1^1(K)$ the "efficient set under regulation," i.e., the upper contour of $A_1(K)$.

Proposition 8.8. *In general the efficient set under regulation is composed of a subset of the "market line" $A_0^+(K)$ and a nondecreasing curve (a portion of hyperbola). In the particular case when the risk weights α_i are proportional to the systematic risks β_i or to the mean excess returns ρ_i, this portion of hyperbola degenerates into a horizontal line.*

Proof. See the appendix (section 8.9).   □

Proposition 8.8 shows that the consequences of imposing a capital requirement are very different according to the value of the risk weights α_i. If these weights are "market-based," in the sense that the vector α is proportional to the vector β of systematic risks, then the new efficient set is a strict subset of the market line. All banks continue to choose an efficient portfolio. Those which are constrained by the regulation choose a less risky portfolio than before. This is illustrated in figure 8.6. As a consequence, their default probability decreases.

On the other hand, if the risk weights are not "market-based," the adoption of the capital regulation has two consequences: for those banks which are constrained, the total "size" of the risky portfolio (as measured by $\langle \alpha, x \rangle$) decreases, but the portfolio is reshuffled, by investing more in those assets i for which ρ_i/α_i is highest, and investing less in the other assets. The total effect on the failure probability is ambiguous. As

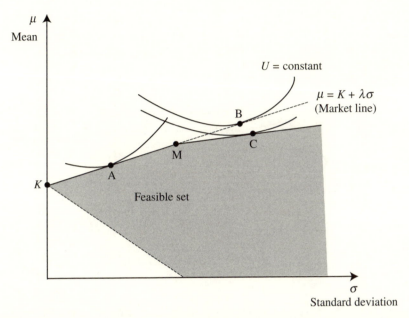

Figure 8.5. The feasible set and the optimal decisions of utility-maximizing banks (with full liability) when there is a capital requirement with arbitrary risk weights. A, choice of an unconstrained bank; B, previous choice of a constrained bank; C, new choice of the same bank. In this example the failure probability of the constrained bank has increased after the imposition of the capital requirement.

shown by the example given in the appendix (section 8.10), it may very well increase in some cases, the reshuffling effect dominating the "size" effect. This is illustrated in figure 8.5. A similar result has been obtained before in Kim and Santomero (1988).

As a conclusion to this section, let us examine the following question: which banks are going to be constrained by the capital regulation? The answer is again related to the monotonicity of the relative index of risk aversion.

Proposition 8.9. *If the relative index of risk aversion* $-(xu''(x))/(u'(x))$ *is decreasing (increasing), the banks with the highest (lowest) net worth will be constrained by the capital regulation.*

Proof. A bank is constrained by the capital regulation if and only if the portfolio chosen in the unregulated case has a variance greater than $\bar{\sigma}^2 = \langle \rho, V^{-1}\rho \rangle / \langle \alpha, V^{-1}\rho \rangle^2$. The result then follows from proposition 8.7. $\square$

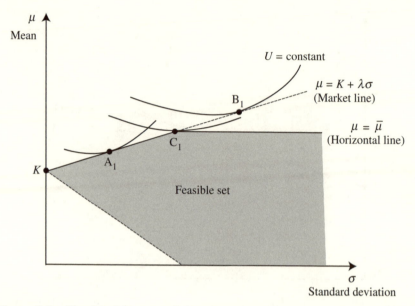

Figure 8.6. The feasible set and the optimal decisions of utility-maximizing banks (with full liability) when there is a capital requirement with correct risk weight. A, choice of an unconstrained bank; B, previous choice of a constrained bank; C, new choice of the same bank. Note that the failure probability of the constrained bank has decreased and that it still chooses an efficient portfolio.

8.7 Introducing Limited Liability into the Portfolio Model

As remarked by Keeley and Furlong (1990), it is ironic that the very source of the problem under study, namely the limited liability of banks, has so far been neglected in the portfolio model. When it is taken into account, the objective function of the bank becomes

$$W(\mu,\sigma) = \int_{-\mu/\sigma}^{\infty} u(\mu + \sigma y)\, dN(y) - CN\left(-\frac{\mu}{\sigma}\right),$$

where $C \geqslant 0$ represents a (fixed) bankruptcy cost and u has been normalized in such a way that

$$u(0) = 0.$$

Let us remark that our normality assumption implies that the bank's utility still depends on (μ,σ) and not on the truncated moments of $\tilde{K}$. However, the properties of W will differ markedly from the utility function under full liability, given by

$$U(\mu,\sigma) = \int_{-\infty}^{+\infty} u(\mu + \sigma y)\, dN(y).$$

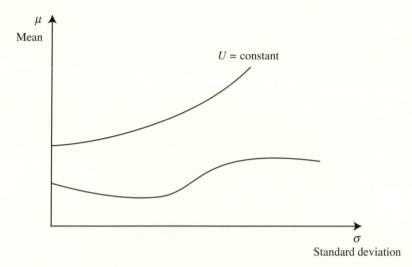

Figure 8.7. The shape of the bank's
indifference curves under limited liability.

It is easy to see that, like U, W is an increasing function of μ. However, unlike U, W is neither necessarily increasing nor concave with respect to σ.

In fact, our first result asserts that if the absolute index of risk aversion is bounded above, then

- for small μ and large σ, W is increasing in σ (the bank exhibits locally a risk-loving behavior!);

- W is not everywhere quasiconcave.

Proposition 8.10. *We assume that*

$$-\frac{u''(x)}{u'(x)} \leqslant a \quad \text{for all } x.$$

Then, if

$$\mu a\left[1 + \frac{aC}{u'(\mu)}\right] < 1,$$

we have

$$\lim_{\sigma \to +\infty} \frac{\partial W}{\partial \sigma}(\mu, \sigma) = 0^+.$$

As a consequence, for σ large enough, W is increasing in σ. Moreover, W is not everywhere quasiconcave.

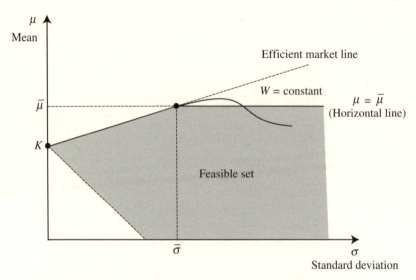

Figure 8.8. Portfolio choice with limited liability and "correctly weighted" solvency ratio but no minimum capital.

Proof. See the appendix (section 8.9).   □

The shape of the indifference curves in the (μ, σ)-plane is given by figure 8.7.

We are now in a position to study the portfolio choice of a limited liability bank. For simplicity, from now on we are going to take $C = 0$. Let us begin with the unregulated case. Since W is increasing in μ, we can limit ourselves to $A_0^+(K) = \{(\mu, \sigma) / \mu = K + \lambda\sigma\}$. In order to find the maximum of W on $A_0^+(K)$, we have to study the auxiliary function

$$\omega(\sigma) = W(K + \lambda\sigma, \sigma).$$

Proposition 8.11. *We assume that* $-(u''(x))/(u'(x)) \leqslant a$ *for all* x *and that* $C = 0$. *For all* $K < 1/a$, $\omega(\sigma)$ *is increasing with* σ. *Therefore its supremum is attained for* $\sigma = +\infty$.

Proof. See the appendix (section 8.9).   □

Of course, proposition 8.11 does not mean that a bank with too few own funds would choose an "infinitely risky portfolio." Indeed, we have neglected nonnegativity constraints on asset choices. Therefore, even in the unregulated case, only a portion of the market line is in fact attainable. When nonnegativity constraints start to be binding, the efficient set becomes a hyperbola similar to the one we found in the

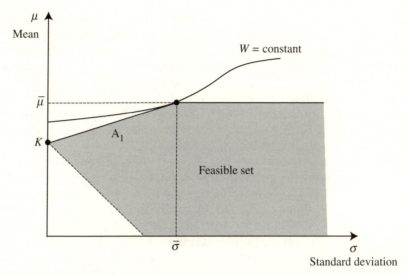

Figure 8.9. Portfolio choice with limited liability, "correctly weighted" solvency ratio, and minimum capital R.

regulated case. The correct interpretation of proposition 8.11 is that, for $K < 1/a$, the bank will choose a very "extreme" portfolio with (at least partial) specialization on some assets. The convexity of preferences due to limited liability eventually dominates risk aversion.

Although we do not provide a full characterization of the behavior of a limited liability bank, propositions 8.10 and 8.11 together have an interesting consequence. Even with correct risk weights, a capital ratio may not be enough to induce an efficient portfolio choice of the bank. This is explained by figure 8.8.

When K is small enough, W is increasing on the efficient market line but it may happen that $W(\bar{\mu}, \sigma)$ becomes larger than $W(\bar{\mu}, \bar{\sigma})$ for σ large enough. Consequently, and in contradistinction with the full liability case, the bank would not choose $(\bar{\mu}, \bar{\sigma})$. As a consequence it may be necessary to impose an additional regulation in the form of a minimal capital level $\tilde{K}$ as suggested by figure 8.9.

8.8 Conclusion

Of course one should not take too literally all the conclusions of the very abstract and reducing model presented in the paper. However, we have clarified several elements of the polemic between value-maximizing models and utility-maximizing models.

If we accept the assumption of complete contingent markets (the only correct way to justify value-maximizing behavior), then it is true that under fixed-rate deposit insurance, absence of capital regulations would lead to a very risky behavior of commercial banks. However, capital regulations (at least of the usual type) are a very poor instrument for controlling the risk of banks: they give incentives for choosing "extreme" asset allocations, and are relatively inefficient for reducing the risk of bank failures. The correct instrument consists in using "actuarial" pricing of deposit insurance, which implies computing risk-related premiums. A pricing formula incorporating interest rate risk is obtained in a companion paper (Kerfriden and Rochet 1993).

On the other hand, if we take into account incompleteness of financial markets and adopt the portfolio model (utility-maximizing banks), the correct choice of risk weights in the solvency ratio becomes crucial. If these risk weights are related to credit risk alone (as is the case for the Cooke ratio and its twin brother, the EU ratio), this may again induce very inefficient asset allocations by banks. We suggest instead the adoption of "market-based" risk weights, i.e., weights proportional to the systematic risks of these assets, measured by their market betas. However, contrarily to previous papers using the portfolio model, we do not neglect the limited liability of the banks under study. We show that it implies that insufficiently capitalized banks may exhibit risk-loving behaviors. As a consequence it may be necessary to impose a minimum capital level as an additional regulation.

It may seem unrealistic to suggest the adoption of "market-based" risk weights for bank loans, which constitute a large proportion of banks' assets and are a priori nonmarketable. However, the success of the securitization activity in the United States has shifted the border between marketable and nonmarketable assets. Moreover, once nonsystematic risk has been diversified there is not much of a difference between a pool of loans and a government bond. However, further research is needed to correctly account for the asymmetric information aspects of the banking activity.

8.9 Appendix

8.9.1 Proof of Lemma 8.1

By the projection theorem, the function $\langle x, Vx \rangle$ (which equals $\|Bx\|^2$, where B denotes the "square-root" of V, i.e., the unique symmetric positive definite matrix such that ${}^t BB = V$) has a unique minimum x^* on the convex set

$$C = \{x \in \mathbb{R}_+^N, \langle x, \rho \rangle = 1\}.$$

Thus

$$A_0^+(K) \cap \{\mu = 1\} = \{(\lambda, 1)\},$$

where
$$\lambda = \langle x^*, Vx^* \rangle > 0.$$

By homogeneity of the definition of $A_0(K)$, we obtain

$$A_0^+(K) = \{(\sigma, \mu), \mu - K = \lambda\sigma\}.$$

8.9.2 Proof of Proposition 8.8

For arbitrary $\mu \geqslant K$ we have to solve

$$\min\langle x, Vx \rangle \quad \text{for } x \in \mathbb{R}_+^N, \text{ such that } \langle \rho, x \rangle = \mu - K, \langle \alpha, x \rangle \leqslant K. \quad (\mathcal{P}'')$$

When the second constraint is not binding, we are back to our initial problem. The solution of $(\mathcal{P}'')$ is

$$x = (\mu - K)x^*, \quad \text{where } x^* = \frac{V^{-1}\rho}{\langle \rho, V^{-1}\rho \rangle}.$$

This is feasible if and only if

$$\langle \alpha, x \rangle = (\mu - K)\frac{\langle \alpha, V^{-1}\rho \rangle}{\langle \rho, V^{-1}\rho \rangle} \leqslant K. \quad (8.13)$$

In that case,

$$\sigma = \langle x, Vx \rangle^{1/2} = \frac{\mu - K}{\langle \rho, V^{-1}\rho \rangle^{1/2}} = \frac{\mu - K}{\lambda}.$$

In particular, if $\langle \alpha, V^{-1}\rho \rangle \leqslant 0$, condition (8.13) is always satisfied for $\mu \geqslant K$ and the capital requirement is ineffective. This case is completely uninteresting. Therefore, we may assume that $\langle \alpha, V^{-1}\rho \rangle > 0$.

When the second constraint is binding, we have to distinguish between two cases.

Case 8.1 ($\exists h > 0, \alpha = h\rho$). Then the feasible set of problem $(\mathcal{P}'')$ is nonempty when
$$\mu - K \leqslant K/h.$$

As a consequence,

$$A_1^+(K) \subset \left\{(\sigma, \mu), \mu - K = \min\left(\lambda\sigma, \frac{K}{h}\right)\right\}.$$

When α is positive, $A_1(K)$ is in fact a triangle.

Case 8.2 (α and ρ are linearly independent). The Lagrangian of $(\mathcal{P}'')$ can be written as

$$\mathcal{L} = \langle x, Vx \rangle - 2v_1 \langle \rho, x \rangle - 2v_2 \langle \alpha, x \rangle,$$

and the first-order condition gives

$$Vx = v_1\rho + v_2\alpha,$$

where v_1, v_2 are determined by

$$\langle \rho, x \rangle = \mu - K \quad \text{and} \quad \langle \alpha, x \rangle = K.$$

In other words,

$$v = \begin{pmatrix} v_1 \\ v_2 \end{pmatrix} = M^{-1} \begin{pmatrix} \mu - K \\ K \end{pmatrix},$$

where

$$M = \begin{pmatrix} \langle \rho, V^{-1}\rho \rangle & \langle \rho, V^{-1}\alpha \rangle \\ \langle \alpha, V^{-1}\rho \rangle & \langle \alpha, V^{-1}\alpha \rangle \end{pmatrix} \quad \text{is positive definite.}$$

Consequently,

$$\sigma^2 = \langle x, Vx \rangle = v_1\langle \rho, x \rangle + v_2\langle \alpha, x \rangle = (\mu - K)v_1 + v_2 K$$
$$= (\mu - K)^2 r + 2(\mu - K)Ks + tK^2, \tag{8.14}$$

where

$$M^{-1} = \begin{pmatrix} r & s \\ s & t \end{pmatrix} \quad \text{is such that } \Delta = rt - s^2 > 0 \text{ and } s < 0$$

(because $\langle \alpha, V^{-1}\rho \rangle > 0$).

Since M^{-1} is positive definitive, (8.14) is the equation of a hyperbola. x is indeed the solution to $(\mathcal{P}'')$ if and only if $v_2 \leqslant 0$, which is equivalent to

$$\mu - K \geqslant -\frac{tK}{s}\frac{\langle \rho, V^{-1}\rho \rangle}{\langle \alpha, V^{-1}\rho \rangle}K.$$

Finally, we obtain

$$A_1^+(K) \subset (\sigma, \mu), \quad \mu - K = \begin{cases} \lambda\sigma, & \sigma \leqslant \bar{\sigma}K, \\ \dfrac{K}{r}\left[-s + \sqrt{\dfrac{r\sigma^2}{K^2} - \Delta}\right], & \sigma > \bar{\sigma}K, \end{cases}$$

where

$$\bar{\sigma} = -\frac{t}{s\lambda} = \frac{(\rho, V^{-1}\rho)^{1/2}}{\langle \alpha, V^{-1}\rho \rangle}.$$

8.9.3   Proof of Proposition 8.10

$$\frac{\partial W}{\partial \sigma}(\mu, \sigma) = \int_{-\mu/\sigma}^{+\infty} y u'(\mu + y\sigma) \, dN(y) - \frac{C\mu}{\sigma^2} f\left(\frac{\mu}{\sigma}\right).$$

Since

$$\frac{u''(x)}{u'(x)} \leqslant a,$$

$e^{ax} u'(x)$ is an increasing function of x, which implies that

$$\forall y \quad y u'(\mu + y\sigma) \geqslant y u'(\mu) e^{-ay\sigma}.$$

Thus,

$$\frac{\partial W}{\partial \sigma}(\mu, \sigma) \geqslant y u'(\mu) \int_{-\mu/\sigma}^{+\infty} y e^{-ay\sigma} f(y) \, dy - \frac{C\mu}{\sigma^2} f\left(\frac{\mu}{\sigma}\right).$$

After straightforward computations the right-hand side can be transformed as follows:

$$\frac{\partial W}{\partial \sigma}(\mu, \sigma) \geqslant f\left(\frac{\mu}{\sigma}\right) \left[\left\{ 1 - a\sigma A\left(\frac{\mu}{\sigma} - a\sigma\right) \right\} u'(\mu) - \frac{C\mu}{\sigma^2} \right],$$

where we have introduced the auxiliary function

$$A(t) = \frac{N(t)}{f(t)},$$

which is such that

$$A'(t) = 1 + tA(t).$$

Similarly,

$$f'(t) = -t f(t).$$

We need a technical lemma.

Lemma 8.2. $\forall t \; A(t) \leqslant -1/t + 1/t^3$; moreover, when $t \to +\infty$, these two functions are equivalent.

Using this lemma, we obtain

$$\frac{\partial W}{\partial \sigma} \geqslant f\left(\frac{\mu}{\sigma}\right) u'(\mu) \left[1 - \frac{C\mu}{u'(\mu)\sigma^2} + \frac{1}{(\mu/a\sigma^2) - 1} - \frac{(1/a\sigma)^2}{((\mu/a\sigma^2) - 1)^3} \right].$$

Denoting the term between brackets by $\psi(a)$, we have

$$\psi(a) = 1 - \frac{1}{1 - (\mu/a\sigma^2)} - \frac{C\mu}{u'(\mu)\sigma^2} + \frac{1}{a^2\sigma^2(1 - (\mu/a\sigma^2))^3}$$

$$= \frac{1}{\sigma^2} \left[-\frac{\mu/a}{1 - \mu/a\sigma^2} - \frac{C\mu}{u'(\mu)} + \frac{1}{a^2(1 - (\mu/a\sigma^2))^3} \right]$$

and

$$\lim_{\sigma \to +\infty} \sigma^2 \psi(\sigma) = \frac{1}{a^2} - \frac{\mu}{a} - \frac{C\mu}{u'(\mu)}.$$

Thus if $\mu a(1 + (aC/u'(\mu))) < 1$, $\partial W/\partial \sigma$ is positive for σ large enough. Since $\partial W/\partial \sigma$ is negative for σ small enough, W cannot be quasiconcave with respect to σ.

Proof of lemma 8.2.

$$A(t) = \int_{-\infty}^{t} \exp \tfrac{1}{2}(t^2 - x^2) \, dt.$$

Let

$$s = \exp \tfrac{1}{2}(t^2 - x^2) \quad \text{or} \quad x = -\sqrt{t^2 - 2 \ln s},$$

$$A(t) = \int_{0}^{1} \frac{ds}{\sqrt{t^2 - 2 \ln s}}.$$

Let $B(t) = t^2(tA(t) + 1)$ and

$$\phi(s, t) = \frac{-2 \ln s}{(1 - (2 \ln s)/t^2) + \sqrt{1 - (2 \ln s)/t^2}},$$

$$B(t) = \int_{0}^{1} t^2 \left\{ 1 - \frac{1}{\sqrt{1 - (2 \ln s)/t^2}} \right\} ds,$$

$$B(t) = \int_{0}^{1} \phi(s, t) \, ds.$$

For all $s \in [0, 1]$, $t \to \phi(s, t)$ is increasing. Moreover,

$$\lim_{t \to +\infty} \phi(s, t) = -\ln s.$$

By Lebesgue's monotone convergence theorem

$$\inf_{t} B(t) = \lim_{t \to -\infty} B(t) = -\int_{0}^{1} \ln s \, ds = 1$$

and the proof is completed.   □

8.9.4 Proof of Proposition 8.11

$$w'(\sigma) = \lambda \frac{\partial W}{\partial \mu} + \frac{\partial W}{\partial \sigma}$$

$$= \int_{-\mu/\sigma}^{+\infty} (\lambda + y) u'(\mu + \sigma y) \, dN(y).$$

Using the fact that $x \to e^{ax}u'(x)$ is increasing, we have

$$\forall y \quad (\lambda + y)u'(\mu + \sigma y) \geqslant (\lambda + y)u'(\mu - \sigma\lambda)e^{-a\sigma(y+\lambda)}.$$

Thus

$$w'(\sigma) \geqslant u'(\mu - \sigma\lambda)e^{+a(\mu-\sigma\lambda)}\int_{-\mu/\sigma}^{+\infty}(\lambda + y)e^{-a(\mu+\sigma y)}\,dN(y).$$

After straightforward computations the right-hand side can be expressed as follows:

$$w'(\sigma) \geqslant u'(\mu - \sigma\lambda)e^{+a(\mu-\sigma\lambda)}f\left(\lambda + \frac{K}{\sigma}\right)\left[1 + (\lambda - a\sigma)A\left(\mu + \frac{K}{\sigma} - a\sigma\right)\right].$$

Let us consider the auxiliary function

$$H(\sigma) = 1 + (\lambda - a\sigma)A\left(\lambda + \frac{K}{\sigma} - a\sigma\right).$$

We have

$$\lim_{\sigma \to +\infty} H(\sigma) = +\infty.$$

We are going to prove that the graph of H crosses the horizontal axis at most once, by showing that

$$\forall \sigma > 0 \quad H(\sigma) = 0 \Rightarrow H'(\sigma) < 0.$$

A straightforward computation indeed gives

$$H'(\sigma) = -A\left(\lambda + \frac{K}{\sigma} - a\sigma\right)\left[a + \left(a + \frac{K}{\sigma^2}\right)(\lambda - a\sigma)\left(\lambda + \frac{K}{\sigma} - a\sigma\right)\right]$$
$$- (\lambda - a\sigma)\left(a + \frac{K}{\sigma^2}\right).$$

Thus

$$H(\sigma) = 0 \Rightarrow -A\left(\lambda + \frac{K}{\sigma} - a\sigma\right) = \frac{1}{\lambda - a\sigma} < 0$$
$$\Rightarrow H'(\sigma) = \frac{1}{\lambda - a\sigma}\left[a + \frac{K}{\sigma}\left(a + \frac{K}{\sigma^2}\right)\right] < 0.$$

By the technical lemma already used in the proof of proposition 8.10, we know that

$$\lim_{t \to -\infty}(t^2 + t^3 A(t)) = 1;$$

consequently,

$$\lim_{t \to +\infty} \sigma^2 H(\sigma) = \lim_{t \to -\infty} \frac{\sigma^2(t)}{t^2}\left[t^2 + \left(t - \frac{K}{\sigma(t)}\right)t^2 A(t)\right],$$

where

$$\sigma(t) = \sigma \iff t = \lambda + \frac{K}{\sigma} - a\sigma.$$

In particular,

$$\lim_{t \to +\infty} \frac{\sigma^2(t)}{t^2} = \frac{1}{a^2}.$$

Thus

$$\lim_{\sigma \to +\infty} \sigma^2 H(\sigma) = \frac{1}{a^2}\left[1 + aK \lim_{t \to -\infty} t A(t)\right] = \frac{1 - aK}{a^2}.$$

Thus, when $K < 1/a$, $\liminf_{\sigma \to +\infty} w'(\sigma) \geqslant 0$ and w is increasing.

8.10   An Example of an Increase in the Default Probability Consecutive to the Adoption of the Capital Requirement

We take an exponential specification: $u(x) = (1/a)(1 - e^{-ax})$, where $a > 0$.

   In that case we have

$$U(\mu, \sigma) = u(\mu - \tfrac{1}{2}a\sigma^2).$$

The portfolio chosen in the unregulated case is such that

$$\mu_0 = K + \lambda\sigma_0,$$

where σ_0 solves

$$\max_{\sigma}(\lambda\sigma - \tfrac{1}{2}a\sigma^2).$$

That is,

$$\sigma_0 = \frac{\lambda}{a} \quad \text{and} \quad \mu_0 = K + \frac{\lambda^2}{a}.$$

When the capital requirement is introduced, and the bank is indeed constrained, the portfolio it chooses has a mean return μ_1 that maximizes

$$\mu - \tfrac{1}{2}a[(\mu - K)^2 r + 2(\mu - K)Ks + tK^2],$$

that is,

$$\mu_1 = K + \frac{1}{r}\left[\frac{1}{a} - Ks\right] \quad \text{and} \quad \sigma_1^2 = tK^2 + \frac{1}{r}\left[\frac{1}{a^2} - K^2 s^2\right].$$

When $a \to 0$ we have

$$\frac{\mu_0}{\sigma_0} \sim \lambda \quad \text{and} \quad \frac{\mu_1}{\sigma_1} \sim \frac{1}{\sqrt{r}}.$$

But

$$\lambda^2 = \langle \rho, V^{-1}\rho \rangle = \frac{t}{\Delta} = \frac{t}{rt - s^2} > \frac{1}{r}.$$

Consequently, when the parameter a is small enough, $\mu_1/\sigma_1 < \mu_0/\sigma_0$, and the failure probability of the bank increases when the capital requirement is adopted.

References

Arrow, K. J. 1974. *Essays in the Theory of Risk-Bearing.* Amsterdam: North-Holland.

Dothan, U., and J. Williams. 1980. Banks, bankruptcy and public regulation. *Journal of Banking and Finance* 4:65–88.

Hart, O. D., and D. M. Jaffee. 1974. On the application of portfolio theory to depository financial intermediaries. *Review of Economic Studies* 41:129–47.

Kahane, Y. 1977. Capital adequacy and the regulation of financial intermediaries. *Journal of Banking and Finance* 2:207–17.

Kareken, J. H., and N. Wallace. 1978. Deposit insurance and bank regulation: a partial equilibrium exposition. *Journal of Business* 51:413–38.

Keeley, M. C., and F. T. Furlong. 1990. A reexamination of mean–variance analysis of bank capital regulation. *Journal of Banking and Finance* 14:69–84.

Kerfriden, C., and J.-C. Rochet. 1993. Measuring interest rate risk of financial institutions. *Geneva Papers on Risk and Insurance Theory* 18(2):111–30.

Kim, D., and A. M. Santomero. 1988. Risk in banking and capital regulation. *Journal of Finance* 43:1219–33.

Klein, M. A. 1971. A theory of the banking firm. *Journal of Money, Credit and Banking* 3:205–18.

Koehn, H., and A. M. Santomero. 1980. Regulation of bank capital and portfolio risk. *Journal of Finance* 35:1235–44.

Merton, R. C. 1977. An analytical derivation of the cost of deposit insurance and loan guarantees: an application of modern option theory. *Journal of Banking and Finance* 1:3–11.

Pratt, J. 1964. Risk aversion in the small and in the large. *Econometrica* 2:122–36.

Pyle, D. 1971. On the theory of financial intermediation. *Journal of Finance* 26:734–47.

Sharpe, W. F. 1978. Bank capital adequacy, deposit insurance and security values. *Journal of Financial and Quantitative Analysis* 13:701–18.

Chapter Nine

Rebalancing the Three Pillars of Basel II

Jean-Charles Rochet

9.1 Introduction

The ongoing reform of the Basel Accord is supposed to rely on three "pillars": a new capital ratio, supervisory review, and market discipline. But even a cursory look at the proposals of the Basel Committee on Banking Supervision reveals a certain degree of imbalance between these three pillars. Indeed, the Basel Committee (2003) gives a lot of attention (132 pages) to the refinements of the risk weights in the new capital ratio, but it is much less precise about the other pillars (16 pages on pillar 2 and 15 pages on pillar 3).[1]

Even though the initial capital ratio (Basel Committee 1988) has been severely criticized for being too crude and opening the door to regulatory arbitrage,[2] it seems strange to insist so much on the importance of supervisory review[3] and market discipline as necessary complements to capital requirements while remaining silent on the precise ways[4] this complementarity can work in practice. One possible reason for this imbalance is a gap in the theoretical literature. As far as I know, there is no tractable model that allows a simultaneous analysis of the impact of solvency regulations, supervisory action, and market discipline on the behavior of commercial banks.

This paper aims to fill that gap by providing a simple framework for analyzing the interactions between the three pillars of Basel II. We start by offering a critical assessment of the academic literature on the

---

[1]This imbalance is also reflected in the comments on Basel II; see Saidenberg and Schuermann (2003) for an assessment.

[2]See, for example, Santos (1996) and Jones (2000). The alleged role of risk-based capital ratios in the "credit crunch" of the early 1990s is discussed in Bernanke and Lown (1991), Berger and Udell (1994), Peek and Rosengren (1995), and Thakor (1996).

[3]For example, the Basel Committee (2003) insists on the need to "enable early supervisory intervention if capital does not provide a sufficient buffer against risk."

[4]In particular, despite the existence of very precise proposals by U.S. economists (Calomiris 1998; Evanoff and Wall 2000; see also the discussion in Bliss 2001) for mandatory subordinated debt, these proposals are not discussed in the Basel II project.

three pillars,[5] and argue that none of the existing models allows for a satisfactory integration of these pillars. We therefore develop in section 9.3 a new formal model that tries to incorporate the most important criticisms of existing theoretical models of bank regulation. Section 9.4 shows that minimum capital ratios can be justified by a classical agency problem, à la Holmström (1979), between bankers and regulators, even in the absence of mispriced deposit insurance. We demonstrate in section 9.5 that, under restrictive conditions, these capital requirements can be reduced if banks are mandated to issue subordinated debt on a regular basis (direct market discipline). Finally, section 9.6 explores the interactions between market discipline and supervisory action and shows that they are complementary rather than substitutes.

9.2   The Three Pillars in the Academic Literature

Most of the academic literature on Basel I concentrates on the credit crunch of the early 1990s[6] and on the distortions of banks' asset allocation generated by the wedge between the market assessment of banks' asset risks and its regulatory counterpart in Basel I. Several theoretical articles (see, for example, chapter 8; Koehn and Santomero 1980; Kim and Santomero 1988; Furlong and Keeley 1990; Thakor 1996) use static portfolio models to explain these distortions. In such models, appropriately designed capital requirements could be used to correct the incentives of bank shareholders to take excessive risks, due to the mispricing of deposit insurance or simply to the limited liability option. Using a different approach, Froot and Stein (1998) model the buffer role of bank capital in absorbing liquidity risks. They determine the capital structure that maximizes the bank's value when there are no audits or deposit insurance.

Yet, as pointed out by Hellwig (1998) and Blum (1999), static models fail to capture important effects of capital requirements. The empirical literature (see, for example, Hancock et al. 1995; Furfine 2001) has tried to calibrate dynamic models of bank behavior in order to study these intertemporal effects. However, none of these papers has studied the interactions of capital requirements with supervisory action[7] and market discipline.

---

[5]Reviews of this literature can be found in Thakor (1996), Jackson et al. (1999), and Santos (2000).

[6]Discussions of this issue can be found in Berger and Udell (1994), Thakor (1996), Jackson et al. (1999), and Santos (2000).

[7]However, Peek and Rosengren (1995) provide empirical evidence of the impact of increased supervision on bank lending decisions.

The literature on continuous time models of bank behavior was initiated by Merton (1977). Assuming an exogenous closure date, he shows that the fair price of deposit insurance can be computed as a European put option. Merton (1978) extends this framework by considering random audits and endogenous closure dates.[8]

Merton's seminal contributions have been extended in several directions, in particular:

- Fries et al. (1997) introduce deposit withdrawal risk and study the impact of banks' closure policies on the fair pricing of deposit insurance;

- Bhattacharya et al. (2002) study closure rules that can be contingent on the level of risk taken by banks; and

- Levonian (2001) introduces subordinated debt in Merton's (1977) model and studies its impact on bankers' incentives for risk taking.

9.3 A Formal Model

Our model aims to take seriously most of the criticisms of previous models of bank regulation while remaining tractable.[9]

First, it is a dynamic model, because static models necessarily miss important consequences of bank solvency regulations.[10] The simplest dynamic models are in discrete time, like those of Calem and Rob (1996) or Buchinsky and Yosha (1997), but they typically do not yield closed-form solutions and entail the use of numerical simulations. For transparency, we instead use a continuous time model, à la Merton (1977, 1978), which requires using diffusion calculus but is ultimately revealed to be more tractable. Following Merton, we therefore assume that the (economic) value A_t of a bank's assets at date t follows a diffusion process:

$$\frac{dA}{A} = \mu\, dt + \sigma\, dW, \tag{9.1}$$

[8]Merton (1977, 1978) assumes that bank assets are traded on financial markets (in order to use the arbitrage pricing methodology), which implies that the social value of banks is independent of their liability structure.

[9]The model is a variant of the one used by Décamps et al. (chapter 10), who also analyze the interactions between the three pillars of Basel II.

[10]The main problem is that, in a static model, solvency regulations have an impact only when they are binding. However, the great majority of banks today have much more capital than the regulatory minimum (this was not the case in 1988). Hence, it is difficult to explain the impact of a capital ratio in today's world by using a static model. For other critiques, see Blum (1999).

where dW is the increment of a Wiener process and μ and σ are the drift and volatility of asset value. For simplicity, we assume that all investors are risk neutral[11] and discount the future at a constant rate $r > \mu$. The bank's assets continuously generate an instantaneous cash flow $x_t = \beta A_t$, where $\beta > 0$ is the constant payout rate.[12]

We depart from the complete frictionless markets assumption made by Merton (1977, 1978)[13] and many of his followers, since this assumption implies that the social value of banks is independent of their liability structure, a hardly acceptable feature if one wants to study the consequences of solvency regulations for banks. Following Gennotte and Pyle (1991), we assume instead that banks create value by monitoring borrowers, and thus acquire private information about these borrowers. The counterpart to this private information is that the resale value of a bank's assets (typically, in case of liquidation) is only a fraction λA (with $\lambda < 1$) of the economic value A of these assets.[14]

We also assume that the monitoring of borrowers has a fixed-cost component,[15] equivalent to a flow cost ry per unit of time (its present value is therefore y). From a social perspective, a bank should thus be closed when its asset value falls below some threshold A_L (the liquidation threshold). The social value of the bank, denoted $V(A)$, equals the expected present value of future cash flows $x_t = \beta A_t$, net of monitoring costs ry, until the stopping time τ_L (the first time t that the bank hits the liquidation threshold A_L), when the bank is liquidated and its assets are resold at price λA_L. As shown in the appendix, this social value equals

$$V(A) = (A - y) + \{y - (1 - \lambda)A_L\}\left(\frac{A}{A_L}\right)^{-a}, \qquad (9.2)$$

where a is the positive root of the quadratic equation

$$\tfrac{1}{2}\sigma^2 x(x + 1) - \mu x = r. \qquad (9.3)$$

---

[11] Small depositors are risk averse but they are fully insured and do not play an active role in our model. In any case, risk neutrality is not crucial for our results, but it simplifies the analysis. We could assume alternatively that all investors use the same risk-adjusted measure for evaluating risky cash flows.

[12] Because of risk neutrality, the expected net present value of these cash flows (conditional on the information available at date t) has to coincide with A_t, which is equivalent to the condition $\beta = r - \mu$.

[13] In Merton (1978), there are audit costs but no liquidation costs due to the resale of banks' assets, as we have here. As a result, social surplus is unaffected by liquidation decisions.

[14] A similar assumption is made in the corporate finance literature (Leland 1994; Leland and Toft 1996; Fries et al. 1997), but $(1 - \lambda)$ is interpreted as a "physical" liquidation cost. Here, it is a cost due to the opacity of bank assets.

[15] A proportional cost of monitoring, if any, can be subtracted with the drift in equation (9.1).

Note that this total value is composed of two terms:

- the value A of its assets, net of monitoring costs y, and

- the option value associated with the (irreversible) closure decision.

As in the real options literature (see, for example, Dixit and Pindyck 1994), the social value of the bank is maximized for a threshold A_L that is below the breakeven threshold $A_0 = y/(1 - \lambda)$. More specifically, the level of A_L that maximizes the social value of the bank (notice that this level is independent of A, and thus is time consistent) is what we call the first-best closure threshold:

$$A_{FB} = \frac{a}{a + 1} \frac{y}{1 - \lambda}. \tag{9.4}$$

Thus, our model captures an important feature of real-life banking systems:[16] even in the absence of moral hazard, government subsidies, and the like, the failure rate of banks cannot be zero. The socially optimal failure rate takes into account the embedded real option: given that bank closures are irreversible (and entail a real cost, due to the imperfect resaleability of banks' assets), it is optimal to let banks operate (up to a certain point) below the breakeven level, defined by the condition $A_0 - y = \lambda A_0$, in the hope that they recover. In more concrete terms, the fact that the resolution of bank failures costs money (*ex post*) to the deposit insurance fund (DIF) does not necessarily imply some kind of inefficiency. This feature is illustrated in figure 9.1.[17]

So far, we have introduced only one of the two important features of banking: the opacity of banks' assets,[18] which implies that they have to be monitored and cannot be resold at full value. We now introduce the second feature: the bulk of a bank's liabilities consists of retail

---

[16]Of course, our desire to get closed-form solutions limits our model to one state variable only. This means that we cannot address important questions such as the way banks allocate their assets among different classes of risks and the hoarding of liquid assets as another buffer against risk. The first topic is addressed by the vast literature on risk-weighted ratios (chapter 8; Koehn and Santomero 1980; Kim and Santomero 1988; Furlong and Keeley 1990; Thakor 1996). The second topic is addressed in Milne and Whalley (2001).

[17]Notice that the first-best social value of the bank is a convex function of asset value. However, when agency problems are taken into account, and make the liquidation threshold become greater than A_0, the value function becomes concave, and thus exhibits risk aversion.

[18]Morgan (2002) provides indirect empirical evidence on this opacity by comparing the frequency of disagreements among bond ratings agencies over the values of firms across sectors of activity. He shows that these disagreements are much more frequent, all else being equal, for banks and insurance companies than for other sectors of the economy.

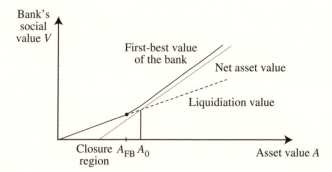

Figure 9.1. The real option embedded in a bank's social value.

deposits D, fully insured by a DIF and paying interest rD. The DIF is financed by a premium P paid at discrete dates. We assume that this premium is fair (so we rule out systematic subsidies from the DIF to the banks) but cannot be revised by continuous readjustments. The academic literature has focused a lot on the "moral hazard" problem created by the put-option feature of deposit insurance. It has been extensively argued that this feature, and more generally the limited liability of bank shareholders, gives these shareholders incentives to take excessive risks, especially when banks are insufficiently capitalized. We focus here on a different agency problem, also created by limited liability, but of a different nature: bankers[19] may not have enough incentives to monitor their assets when their value becomes too small.[20] We assume that when monitoring stops (we say that the banker "shirks"), the quality of bank assets deteriorates,[21] and the dynamics of asset value become

$$\frac{\mathrm{d}A}{A} = (\mu - \Delta\mu)\,\mathrm{d}t + \sigma\,\mathrm{d}W, \tag{9.5}$$

where $\Delta\mu > 0$. Equation (9.5) indicates that the shirking/monitoring decision impacts only the expected profitability of the bank's assets and not the risk. Most of the academic literature has considered the polar case in which μ is unchanged but σ increases by moral hazard (the asset-substitution problem). Which specification is more appropriate is

---

[19]We assume that bank managers act in the best interest of shareholders. It would also be interesting, but presumably difficult, to introduce an agency problem between managers and shareholders.

[20]Bliss (2001) argues that this agency problem may be fundamental: "Poor (apparently irrational) investments are as problematic as excessively risky projects (with positive risk-adjusted returns). Evidence suggests that poor investments are likely to be the major explanation for banks getting into trouble."

[21]We assume that this deterioration—that is, $\Delta\mu$ in equation (9.5)—is so large that shirking is never optimal from a social viewpoint.

an empirical question.[22] In Décamps et al. (chapter 10), we consider the general case in which both μ and σ are altered by the banker's decision.

In the absence of shirking, the value of the bank's equity is given by a simple formula in the spirit of equation (9.2) (see the appendix for all mathematical derivations):

$$E(A) = A - D - y + (D + y - A_L)\left(\frac{A}{A_L}\right)^{-a}. \tag{9.6}$$

As in Merton (1977, 1978), the value of the bank's equity is the sum of two terms:

- the value of assets A net of debt (deposits) D (and of the monitoring cost, which does not appear in Merton (1974)), and

- the value of the limited liability option.

However, as in Merton (1978) but in contrast to Merton (1977), the value of the limited liability option is not of the Black–Scholes type (it is actually simpler). This is because it can be exercised at any time, which corresponds to a down-and-out barrier option, instead of at a fixed date, which corresponds to a European option. In Merton (1978), the closure option can be exercised only after an audit by the supervisor. Here we assume that, thanks to the information revealed by the market (indirect market discipline), closure can occur at any time.

A_L is now chosen by shareholders so as to maximize equity value. The corresponding threshold is

$$A_E = \frac{a}{a + 1}(D + y). \tag{9.7}$$

At this threshold, the marginal value of equity is zero: $E'(A_E) = 0$ (smooth-pasting condition). Shirking is optimal for bankers whenever their expected instantaneous loss from shirking, $AE'(A)\Delta\mu$, becomes less than the instantaneous monitoring cost yr. Since $E'(A_E) = 0$, this has to be true for some interval $[A_E, A_S]$.

Proposition 9.1. *When the cost of monitoring y/D (per unit of deposits) is smaller than $(a + 1)/(\lambda a) - 1$, there is a conflict of interest between shareholders and the DIF: insufficiently capitalized banks shirk.*

---

[22]In the appendix to his paper, Bliss (2001) convincingly argues that the asset-substitution problem might have been overemphasized. He reviews several empirical articles that conclude that bank failures are often provoked by "bad investments" rather than "bad luck" (and excessive risk taking).

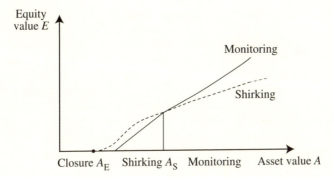

Figure 9.2. The possibility of insufficiently capitalized banks shirking.

Interestingly, there are parameter values for which the agency problem does not matter: when y/D is large (greater than $(a + 1)/(\lambda a) - 1$), shareholders decide to close the bank before the shirking constraint becomes binding. However, when y/D is smaller than this threshold, there is a conflict of interest, even in the absence of mispriced deposit insurance. It is similar to the conflict of interest between bondholders and shareholders of undercapitalized firms.

Figure 9.2 represents the typical pattern of the value of the bank's equity E as a function of the value A of its assets in the case where deposits are fully insured (and therefore depositors have no incentives to withdraw) but the bank is left unregulated. The closure threshold A_E (below which the bank declares bankruptcy[23]) and the shirking threshold A_S (below which the bank shirks) are chosen by bankers so as to maximize the value of equity. The reason why shirking is sometimes preferred by shareholders (in the intermediate region $A_E \leqslant A \leqslant A_S$) even though it is socially inefficient is not the deposit insurance option (as is the case for asset-substitution problems, where typically $y = \Delta\mu = 0$, $\Delta\sigma^2 = 0$), but rather the agency problem between the bank and the deposit insurance fund. Indeed, the cost of monitoring is entirely borne by the bank, but the bank collects only a fraction of the benefits of monitoring. When these benefits are small, the banker prefers to shirk. As we describe in the next section, this can be prevented by imposing a minimum capital ratio.

---

[23] Following Leland (1994), we assume that shareholders are not cash constrained. In Décamps et al. (chapter 10), we examine the alternative case in which bankruptcy is precipitated by the bank's liquidity problems. Note that when there is shirking, the value of A_E is no longer given by equation (9.7).

9.4 Justifying the Minimum Capital Ratio

In our model, the justification for a minimum capital ratio is not an asset-substitution problem (as in the vast majority of academic papers on the topic[24]), but an agency problem between the banker and the supervisors, who represent the interests of the DIF: insufficiently capitalized banks shirk, i.e., they stop monitoring their assets. To avoid this problem, we assume now that when the value of the bank's assets hits some threshold A_R chosen by the regulator, the bank is liquidated and the shareholders are expropriated.[25] This regulatory threshold A_R is designed in such a way that bankers are never tempted to shirk.

Proposition 9.2.

(i) *Under the assumption of proposition 9.1 (that is, $y/D < (a+1)/(\lambda a) - 1$), bank shirking can be eliminated if bank regulators impose liquidation whenever the bank's assets fall below the following threshold:*

$$A_R^O = \frac{a(D+y) + ry/\Delta\mu}{a+1}. \tag{9.8}$$

(ii) *When y/D is larger than $\Delta\mu/(r + a\Delta\mu)$, this liquidation threshold can be implemented by imposing a minimum capital ratio:*

$$\frac{A-D}{A} \geqslant \rho_R \equiv \frac{y(r + a\Delta\mu) - D\Delta\mu}{y(r + a\Delta\mu) + aD\Delta\mu}. \tag{9.9}$$

The condition $y/D > \Delta\mu/(r + a\Delta\mu)$ ensures that the minimum capital ratio ρ_R is positive. When it is not satisfied, banks can be allowed to continue for negative equity values. We focus here on the more interesting case of proposition 9.2, where $\rho_R > 0$.

Notice that when liquidation costs are large enough, the first-best liquidation threshold

$$A_{FB} = \frac{a}{a+1} \frac{y}{1-y}$$

is smaller than the regulatory threshold A_R^O defined in (9.8). This means that bank supervisors are confronted with time consistency problems: even if *ex ante* agency considerations imply that a bank should be closed whenever $A \leqslant A_R^O$, *ex post* it is optimal to let it continue (and provide liquidity assistance). These forbearance problems are examined in section 9.6.

---

[24]See Santos (2000) for a review.

[25]This is similar to protected debt covenants, whereby bondholders (or banks) retain the option of restructuring a firm before it is technically bankrupt. See Black and Cox (1976) for a formal analysis.

We now examine the policy implications of our first results. We interpret bank solvency regulations as a closure rule intended to avoid shirking by insufficiently capitalized banks: every time the asset value of the bank falls below A_R^O, the bank should be closed. However, we argue that bank assets are opaque and cannot be marked to market in continuous time. The traditional view of the role of supervisors was to evaluate these assets periodically through on-site examinations. In particular, most academic papers[26] assume that A_t is observable only through costly auditing that has to be performed more or less with uniform frequency across banks. We argue in favor of a more modern modeling strategy whereby bank supervisors can rely on market information and adapt the intensity or frequency of their examinations to the market assessment of the bank's situation. This can be done by conditioning risk weights on market ratings of assets (pillar 1) or using yield spreads of bank liabilities and private ratings to reassess the solvency of the bank (pillars 2 and 3). In our model, it would mean inferring A_t, the (unobservable) value of the bank's assets, from the market price of equity (if the bank is publicly listed), i.e., inverting the function $A \rightarrow E(A)$. This is how our model captures the notion of "indirect market discipline": using as much publicly available information as possible to allocate scarce regulatory resources in priority to the banks in distress. In our model, it leads to a simple policy recommendation of organizing a regulatory framework with two regimes:

- A light regime for "healthy" banks (those for which asset value A is way above the closure threshold A_R^O, where A is inferred from accounting data and market information), only imposing accurate reporting and transparency.

- A heavy regime for "problem" banks (those for which A gets close to A_R^O), imposing restrictions on what the bank can do and closely examining its books.

This two-regime regulatory framework (a simplified version of the prompt corrective action provisions of the Federal Deposit Insurance Corporation Improvement Act, or FDICIA[27]) is examined formally in section 9.6. For the moment, we discuss direct market discipline and, more specifically, how the subdebt proposal can, under certain conditions, reduce capital requirements.

---

[26]The seminal paper on this topic is Merton (1978). More recent references are Fries et al. (1997) and Bhattacharya et al. (2002).

[27]The consequences of FDICIA are assessed in Jones and King (1995) and Mishkin (1996).

9.5 Market Discipline and Subordinated Debt

We now consider that the bank is mandated to issue a certain volume B of bonds, each paying a continuous coupon c per unit of time.[28] These bonds are subordinated to deposits: if the bank is liquidated (when asset value hits threshold A_L), the DIF receives λA_L but bondholders receive nothing. Anticipating this possibility, bondholders require a coupon rate c above the riskless rate r. To maintain the convenience of the stationarity of the bank's financial structure, we assume that bonds have an infinite maturity (unless of course the bank is liquidated) but are randomly renewed according to a Poisson process of intensity m.[29] In more intuitive terms, a fraction $m\,dt$ of outstanding bonds is repaid at each instant at its face value B and the same volume $m\,dt$ is reissued,[30] but at its market value $B(A)$. This is where market discipline comes in:[31] if the bank's asset value A deteriorates (for example, if bankers stop monitoring their assets), the finance cost of the bank increases immediately, since at each instant a fraction m of the bonds has to be repaid at face value B and reissued at market value $B(A) < B$ (notice also that $B' > 0$). In the appendix, we show that the value of equity becomes

$$E(A, B) = A - y - D - B\frac{c + m}{r + m} + (D + y - A_L)\left(\frac{A}{A_L}\right)^{-a}, \qquad (9.10)$$

where $a(m)$ is the positive root of the quadratic equation

$$\tfrac{1}{2}\rho^2 x(x + 1) - \mu x = r + m.$$

The new regulatory threshold A_R^{SD} is the smallest value of A_L that guarantees that bankers will not shirk. It is defined implicitly by

$$A_R^{SD}\frac{\partial E}{\partial A}(A_R^{SD}, B) = \frac{yr}{\Delta\mu},$$

where A_L is taken to equal A_R^{SD}. After easy computations, we obtain

$$A_R^{SD} = A_R^O + \frac{a(m)}{a + m}\left(\frac{c + m}{r + m}\right)B. \qquad (9.11)$$

---

[28] The mandatory subdebt proposal has been extensively discussed (see, for example, Calomiris 1998; Estrella 2000; Evanoff and Wall 2000, 2001). The only formal analysis I am aware of is Levonian (2001). However, Levonian uses a Black-Scholes type of model in which the bank's returns on assets are exogenous. For empirical assessments of the feasibility of the subdebt proposal, see Hancock and Kwast (2001) and Sironi (2001).

[29] This approach is borrowed from Leland and Toft (1996) and Ericsson (2000).

[30] The average maturity of bonds is thus $\int_0^{+\infty} mte^{-mt}\,dt = 1/m$.

[31] The disciplining role of periodical repricing of debt has been shown by Levonian (2001). It is close in spirit to the disciplining role of demandable deposits (Calomiris and Kahn 1991; Carletti 1999).

Not surprisingly, this threshold is higher than A_R^Q (all else being fixed), since the bank is now more indebted. However, the capital ratio becomes

$$\rho_R^{SD} = 1 - \frac{D + B}{A_R^{SD}}. \tag{9.12}$$

It is smaller than $\rho_R = 1 - D/A_R^Q$, whenever $A_R^{SD}/(D + B) < A_R^Q/D$, which is equivalent to

$$a(m)\frac{c + m}{r + m} < a + \frac{y}{D}\left(a + \frac{r}{\Delta\mu}\right). \tag{9.13}$$

Since $a(m)$ increases with m (which $a(0) = a$ and $a(+\infty) = +\infty$), we see that this condition can be satisfied, but m (the frequency of renewal of bonds, which is inversely proportional in our model to their average maturity) and $(c - r)/r$ (the relative spread on subordinated debt) have to be small enough. Thus, we obtain the following proposition.

Proposition 9.3. *If banks are mandated to issue subordinated bonds on a regular basis, regulators can reduce capital requirements (tier 1) if two conditions are satisfied: the average maturity must not be too small*[32] *(m small) and the coupon paid on the bonds must not be too large (c/r close to 1). However, the total requirement, capital + subdebt (tier 1 + tier 2), is always increased.*

Proposition 9.3 shows the limits of the mandatory subdebt proposal. Only when properly designed (that is, with a maturity that is not too small or a frequency of renewal that is not too large) and when markets are sufficiently liquid and bank assets not too risky (so that the relative spread $(c-r)/r$ is not too large) can mandatory subdebt allow regulators to decrease capital requirements.

9.6   Market Discipline and Supervisory Action

We now come to what we consider to be the most convincing rationale for market discipline: preventing regulatory forbearance by forcing regulators to intervene before it is too late. As is well documented in the literature on banking crises, banking authorities are very often subject to political pressure for bailing out the creditors of banks in distress. To capture this in our model, we consider what would happen if subdebt holders were de facto insured in the case where the bank is liquidated (that is, whenever the value of its assets hits the regulatory threshold).

---

[32]Recall that in our model, bonds theoretically have an infinite maturity but are randomly repaid with frequency m. The average (effective) maturity is $1/m$.

This bailout obviously does not affect the social value of the bank but only leads to a redistribution of wealth between the DIF and bondholders. Bonds become riskless[33] and perfect substitutes for deposits in the view of equityholders. The frequency of renewal of bonds ceases to play any disciplining role.

Proposition 9.4. *If subdebt holders are insured by the DIF, subdebt ceases to play any disciplining role: direct market discipline can work only in the absence of regulatory forbearance.*

Proposition 9.4 shows the existence of some form of complementarity between market discipline and supervisory action: direct market discipline can work only if supervisors can credibly commit not to bail out bondholders.

We now examine a second form of complementarity between market discipline and supervisory action: if financial markets are suitably efficient and liquid, and if banks issue publicly traded securities (equity or bonds), the market prices (or yields) of these securities will provide objective signals about the situation of these banks. We do not address the difficult statistical question of which security (equity or subordinated bonds) gives the most useful information to bank supervisors.[34] Our model has only one state variable, A, and both the equity price $E(A)$ and the subdebt price $B(A)$ are monotonic functions of A and thus sufficient statistics for A. In our simple model, by observing market prices of either equity or bonds, regulatory authorities can perfectly infer the true value of A.

Our model is obviously not appropriate for analyzing such statistical considerations. It is, however, well adapted to study another, equally important question: namely, how market discipline can limit forbearance. Market information is then viewed as providing objective signals that oblige supervisors to intervene. Indirect market discipline is thus useful in two ways: it allows supervisors to save on audit costs for the banks that are well capitalized, and simultaneously it forces supervisors to intervene early enough when a bank is in trouble. This is captured in our model in the following way.

We consider that bank supervisors are required to inspect banks whenever the value of their assets hits an inspection threshold A_I (with $A_I > A_R$). Inspection allows them to detect shirking and close the banks that do shirk. The value of equity is still given by equation (9.6) (for simplicity, we return to the case with no subordinated debt):

$$E(A) = A - y - D + (D + y - A_R)\left(\frac{A}{A_R}\right)^{-a}.$$

---

[33] Arbitrage considerations then imply that the coupon rate c must equal r.

[34] On this topic, see, for example, Bliss (2001), Evanoff and Wall (2002), Gropp et al. (2002), and the references therein.

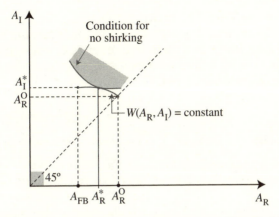

Figure 9.3. The optimal combination of inspections (threshold A_I^*) and closures (threshold A_R^*). Note: W is proportional to the social value of the bank, net of auditing costs.

But now the condition for no shirking becomes

$$\forall A \geqslant A_I, \quad AE'(A) \geqslant \frac{yr}{\Delta\mu}, \tag{9.14}$$

which is equivalent to

$$A_I - a(D + y - A_R)\left(\frac{A_I}{A_R}\right)^{-a} \geqslant \frac{yr}{\Delta\mu}. \tag{9.15}$$

This formula shows that for any closure threshold A_R, there is a minimum inspection threshold A_I that prevents shirking: it is given by equality in equation (9.15). The corresponding curve in the (A_R, A_I)-plane is represented in figure 9.3. Notice that the previous case (no inspection, closure at A_R^O) corresponds to the intersection of this curve with the first diagonal ($A_R = A_I = A_R^O$).

In figure 9.3, we represent the optimal combination of inspection and closure thresholds by (A_R^*, A_I^*). It is obtained by maximizing the social value of the bank:

$$V(A, A_R) = A - y + [y - (1 - \lambda)A_R]\left(\frac{A}{A_R}\right)^{-a},$$

net of the expected present value of auditing costs:

$$C(A, A_R, A_I) = E\left(\int_0^{T_R} \xi \mathbf{1}_{A_t \leqslant A_I} e^{-rt}\, dt\right), \tag{9.16}$$

where the auditing cost ξ is incurred only when the asset value of the bank lies in the interval $[A_R, A_I]$, $\mathbf{1}_{A_t \leqslant A_I}$ is the indicator function that takes a value of 1 when $A_t \leqslant A_I$ (and 0 otherwise). Here, τ_R denotes the first time that $A_t = A_R$ (closure time). It can be shown that the expected present value of auditing costs C is proportional to A^{-a}:

$$C(A, A_R, A_I) = A^{-a} \phi(A_R, A_I). \tag{9.17}$$

Thus, after simplification by A^{-a}, we obtain the following proposition.

Proposition 9.5. *The optimal value of the closure threshold A_R^* and the inspection threshold A_I^* can be obtained by maximizing*

$$W(A_R, A_I) = (\gamma - (1 - \lambda)A_R)A_R^a - \phi(A_R, A_I) \tag{9.18}$$

under the incentive-compatibility constraint (equation (9.15)).

We have that $A_R^* < A_R^O$, which indicates that prompt corrective action allows the reduction of capital requirements. When auditing costs are small, A_R^* becomes close to the first-best closure threshold A_{FB}, which means that prompt corrective action also reduces the severity of the time consistency problem of bank supervisors.

Proposition 9.5 illustrates the substitutability between pillar 2 (supervisory action) and pillar 1 (capital requirements). This was already a feature of Merton's (1978) model, in which the frequency of bank examinations could be substituted for more stringent capital requirements. However, here the introduction of pillar 3 (market discipline) changes the picture: the intensity of regulation can be modulated according to market information (in the spirit of the prompt corrective action provisions of FDICIA), and symmetrically, supervisors can be forced to intervene when market signals reveal the distress of a bank (so that forbearance becomes more costly to supervisors or politicians). Notice also that market discipline decreases the (*ex post*) benefits of forbearance by reducing the bank closure threshold (capital requirements), another illustration of the complex interactions between the three pillars of Basel II.

9.7 Conclusion

This paper develops a formal model of banking regulation that permits analysis of the interactions between the three pillars of Basel II. It differs from previous models in several important ways:

- it is a dynamic model, in which solvency regulations are interpreted as closure thresholds rather than as complex tools intended to correct the mispricing of deposit insurance;

- the justification for regulation is not (primarily) to prevent asset substitution by banks (deposits are not subsidized in our model), but rather to prevent shirking by the managers of undercapitalized banks;

- bank supervisors can use market information as a complement to the information provided by bank examinations; thus, they can save on scarce supervisory resources and allocate them in priority to the banks in distress; and

- the returns on banks' assets are endogenous, since they depend on the monitoring decisions of bankers.

Although very simple, this model allows a formal analysis of the interactions between the three pillars of Basel II. In particular, we show in proposition 9.3 that mandatory subdebt (direct market discipline) may, under some restrictions, allow regulators to decrease capital requirements. More importantly, we show that market discipline and supervisory action are complementary rather than substitutes (propositions 9.4 and 9.5): one cannot work well without the other.

In terms of policy implications, our theory points to a serious rebalancing of the three pillars of Basel II. The initial motivation of Basel I was to guarantee a level playing field for international banking, given that the large banks of some countries could take enormous risks without having much capital, benefiting from implicit guarantees by their governments. So the fundamental idea behind the Cooke ratio was harmonization, i.e., to set a uniform standard for internationally active banks. It turns out that the Cooke ratio (or more generally, the risk-based capital methodology), although imperfect, was revealed to be extremely useful as an instrument for measuring bank risk. That is probably why it was applied rapidly (with minor changes) by the regulatory authorities of many countries within their jurisdictions (although it was initially designed for large, internationally active banks).

Probably in response to the harsh critiques of the crudeness of the Cooke ratio, the Basel Committee began a process of complexification, alternating new proposals and consultation periods with the banking industry (Basel Committee 1999, 2001, 2003). The outcome of this long process is an extremely complex instrument (the McDonough ratio) that results from intense bargaining with large banks, and will probably never be implemented without further changes.

In this analysis, we argue that banking authorities should instead keep arm's-length relationships with bankers and that scarce supervisory resources should be used, according to priority, to control the behavior of banks in distress, rather than to implement an extremely complex regulation that will ultimately be bypassed in some way or other by the largest or most sophisticated banks. By contrast, there is an urgent need (once again) to guarantee a level playing field in international banking. The development of large and complex banking organizations with multinational activities implies that supervisory authorities of different countries urgently need to harmonize their institutional practices. Market discipline can provide a very useful tool for defining a harmonized and clear mandate for banking authorities across the world, in an attempt to eliminate political pressure and regulatory forbearance. This should be the top priority of the Basel Committee.

9.8 Mathematical Appendix

Here we derive the mathematical formulas used in our analysis.

9.8.1 First-Best Value of the Bank

The value of the bank (when assets are monitored) equals the expected present value of future cash flows βA_t, net of the monitoring cost ry, until the stopping time τ_L (the first time t that A_t hits the liquidation threshold A_L) when the bank is liquidated. The formula is

$$V = E\left[\int_0^{\tau_L} e^{-rt}(\beta A_t - ry)\, dt + \lambda A_L e^{-r\tau_L}\right]. \tag{9.19}$$

Using classical formulas (see, for example, Dixit 1993; Karlin and Taylor 1981), we obtain

$$V = A - y + \{y - (1 - \lambda)A_L\}\left(\frac{A}{A_L}\right)^{-a}, \tag{9.20}$$

where A is the current value of A_t and a is the positive root of the quadratic equation

$$\tfrac{1}{2}\sigma^2 x(x + 1) - \mu x = r. \tag{9.21}$$

9.8.2 Value of the Bank's Equity

In the absence of regulation, equityholders choose the liquidation threshold that maximizes the value of their equity. Using the same classical formulas as we use to establish equation (9.20), we obtain

$$E(A) = (A - y - D) + (D + y - A_L)\left(\frac{A}{A_L}\right)^{-a}, \tag{9.22}$$

As for the total value of the bank (equation (9.20)), the second term is an option value that is maximized when

$$A_L = A_E \equiv \frac{a}{a+1}(D+y).$$ (9.23)

At this threshold, the value of the bank's equity has a horizontal tangent (as represented in figure 9.2):

$$E'(A_E) = 0.$$ (9.24)

If equityholders decide to stop monitoring, the dynamics of asset value become

$$\frac{dA}{A} = (\mu - \Delta\mu)\,dt + \sigma\,dW,$$

but they save the monitoring cost ry. Shirking becomes optimal for equityholders whenever the instantaneous loss of equity value $E'(A)A\Delta\mu$ is less than this monitoring cost. Because $E'(A_E) = 0$ (see equation (9.23)), this condition is always satisfied in the neighborhood of the liquidation point. However, we have to check that this incentive constraint binds after the bank becomes insolvent. This is true whenever

$$\lambda A_E \leqslant D \quad \text{or} \quad \lambda a(D+y) \leqslant (a+1)D,$$

which is equivalent to the condition of proposition 9.1, namely

$$\frac{y}{D} \leqslant \frac{a+1}{\lambda a} - 1.$$

This ends the proof of proposition 9.1.

9.8.3 Minimum Capital Ratio

Suppose that bank regulators impose a closure threshold $A_R \leqslant D/y$: if the bank's asset value hits A_R, the bank is liquidated and shareholders receive nothing. By an immediate adaptation of equation (9.22), shareholders' value becomes

$$E(A) = A - y - D + (D + y - A_R)\left(\frac{A}{A_R}\right)^{-a}.$$ (9.25)

The condition for eliminating shirking is

$$\forall A \geqslant A_R, \quad E'(A)A\Delta\mu \geqslant yr.$$ (9.26)

Using equation (9.25), we see that this is equivalent to

$$\forall A \geqslant A_R, \quad A - a(D + y - A_R)\left(\frac{A}{A_R}\right)^{-a} \geqslant \frac{yr}{\Delta\mu}. \tag{9.27}$$

Provided that $A_R \leqslant y + D$ (this will be checked *ex post*), the left-hand side of equation (9.27) is increasing in A, therefore equation (9.27) is equivalent to

$$A_R(a + 1) - a(D + y) \geqslant \frac{yr}{\Delta\mu}$$

or

$$A_R \geqslant A_R^O \equiv \frac{a(D + y) + yr/\Delta\mu}{a + 1}. \tag{9.28}$$

A_R^O represents the minimum asset value that preserves the incentives of the banker. The associated capital ratio is

$$\rho^R = \frac{A_R^O - D}{A_R^O} = \frac{y(a + r/\Delta\mu) - D}{a(D + y) + yr/\Delta\mu}.$$

9.8.4 Subordinated Debt

Consider now that the bank issues a volume B of subordinated bonds, paying a coupon cB per unit of time, and randomly renewed with frequency m. The market value of these bonds $B(A)$, as a function of the bank's asset value, satisfies the differential equation

$$rB(A) = cB + m(B - B(A)) + \mu AB'(A) + \tfrac{1}{2}\sigma^2 A^2 B''(A), \tag{9.29}$$

with the boundary conditions

$$B(A_L) = 0 \quad \text{and} \quad B(+\infty) = cB/r.$$

The solution of this equation is

$$B(A) = B\frac{c + m}{r + m}\left[1 - \left(\frac{A}{A_L}\right)^{-a(m)}\right], \tag{9.30}$$

where $a(m)$ is the positive root of the quadratic equation

$$\tfrac{1}{2}\sigma^2 x(x + 1) - \mu x = r + m. \tag{9.31}$$

In a comparison with equation (9.21), we see immediately that $a(0) = a$. Moreover, equation (9.31) shows that $a(m)$ increases with m.
  The value of equity becomes

$$E(A, B) = A - y - D - \frac{c + m}{r + m}B$$

$$+ (D + y - A_L)\left(\frac{A}{A_L}\right)^{-a} + \frac{c + m}{r + m}B\left(\frac{A}{A_L}\right)^{-a(m)}. \tag{9.32}$$

9.8.5 Auditing Costs

By definition, the expected present value of auditing costs is defined by

$$C(A, A_R, A_I) = E\left[\int_0^{\tau_R} \xi \mathbf{1}_{A_t \leqslant A_I} e^{-rt} \, dt \,\Big|\, A\right],$$

where τ_R is the first time that A_t hits the closure threshold A_R. By the usual arguments (see Dixit 1993), one can establish that C satisfies the following differential equation:

$$rC = \mu A C'(A) + \tfrac{1}{2}\sigma^2 A^2 C''(A), \quad A \geqslant A_t,$$

with the limit condition
$$C(+\infty) = 0.$$

Therefore, $C(A) = k A^{-a}$, where a is (as before) the positive solution of the equation
$$r = -\mu x + \tfrac{1}{2}\sigma^2 x(x+1),$$

and k is a constant that depends on A_R and A_I:

$$k = \varphi(A_R, A_I).$$

References

Basel Committee. 1988. International convergence of capital measurement and capital standards. Basel Committee on Banking Supervision 4 (July). Basel, Switzerland: Bank for International Settlements.

———. 1999. A new capital adequacy framework. Consultative Paper, Basel Committee on Banking Supervision. Basel, Switzerland: Bank for International Settlements.

———. 2001. The new Basel Capital Accord. Second Consultative Paper, Basel Committee on Banking Supervision. Basel, Switzerland: Bank for International Settlements.

———. 2003. The new Basel Capital Accord. Third Consultative Paper, Basel Committee on Banking Supervision. Basel, Switzerland: Bank for International Settlements.

Berger, A. N., and G. F. Udell. 1994. Did risk-based capital allocate bank credit and cause a "credit crunch" in the United States? *Journal of Money, Credit and Banking* 26:585–628.

Bernanke, B., and C. Lown. 1991. The credit crunch. *Brookings Papers on Economic Activity* 2:205–47.

Bhattacharya, S., M. Plank, G. Strobl, and J. Zechner. 2002. Bank capital regulation with random audits. *Journal of Economic Dynamics and Control* 26:1301–21.

Black, F., and J. C. Cox. 1976. Valuing corporate securities: some effects of bond indenture provisions. *Journal of Finance* 31:351–67.

Bliss, R. R. 2001. Market discipline and subordinated debt: a review of some salient issues. Federal Reserve Bank of Chicago *Economic Perspectives* 25(1): 24–45.

Blum, J. 1999. Do capital adequacy requirements reduce risks in banking? *Journal of Banking and Finance* 23:755–71.

Buchinsky, M., and O. Yosha. 1997. Endogenous probability of failure for a financial intermediary: a dynamic model. Unpublished paper, Brown University.

Calem, P. S., and R. Rob. 1996. The impact of capital-based regulation on bank risk-taking: a dynamic model. Board of Governors of the Federal Reserve System, Finance and Economics Discussion Series, no. 96-12.

Calomiris, C. W. 1998. Blueprints for a new global financial architecture. U.S. House of Representatives, Joint Economic Committee, October 7.

Calomiris, C. W., and C. Kahn. 1991. The role of demandable debt in structuring optimal banking arrangements. *American Economic Review* 81:497–513.

Carletti, E. 1999. Bank moral hazard and market discipline. Mimeo, FMG, London School of Economics.

Dixit, A. K. 1993. *The Art of Smooth Pasting*. Chur, Switzerland: Harwood.

Dixit, A. K., and R. S. Pindyck. 1994. *Investment under Uncertainty*. Princeton University Press.

Ericsson, J. 2000. Asset substitution, debt pricing, optimal leverage and maturity. *Finance* 21(2):39–70.

Estrella, A. 2000. Costs and benefits of mandatory subordinated debt regulation for banks. Unpublished paper, Federal Reserve Bank of New York.

Evanoff, D. D., and L. D. Wall. 2000. Subordinated debt and bank capital reform. Federal Reserve Bank of Chicago Working Paper 2000-07.

———. 2001. Sub-debt yield spreads as bank risk measures. *Journal of Financial Services Research* 20:121–45.

———. 2002. Measures of the riskiness of banking organizations: subordinated debt yields, risk-based capital, and examination ratings. *Journal of Banking and Finance* 26:989–1009.

Fries, S., P. Mella-Barral, and W. Perraudin. 1997. Optimal bank reorganization and the fair pricing of deposit guarantees. *Journal of Banking and Finance* 21:441–68.

Froot, K., and J. Stein. 1998. Risk management, capital budgeting, and capital structure policy for financial institutions: an integrated approach. *Journal of Financial Economics* 47(1):55–82.

Furfine, C. 2001. Bank portfolio allocation: the impact of capital requirements, regulatory monitoring, and economic conditions. *Journal of Financial Services Research* 20:33–56.

Furlong, F., and N. Keeley. 1990. A reexamination of mean–variance analysis of bank capital regulation. *Journal of Banking and Finance* 14(1):69–84.

Gennotte, G., and D. Pyle. 1991. Capital controls and bank risk. *Journal of Banking and Finance* 15:805–24.

Gropp, R., J. Vesala, and G. Vulpes. 2002. Equity and bond market signals as leading indicators of bank fragility. European Central Bank Working Paper 150.

Hancock, D., and M. L. Kwast. 2001. Using subordinated debt to monitor bank holding companies: is it feasible? *Journal of Financial Services Research* 20:147-87.

Hancock, D., A. J. Laing, and J. A. Wilcox. 1995. Bank capital shocks: dynamic effects on securities, loans, and capital. *Journal of Banking and Finance* 19:661-77.

Hellwig, M. 1998. Banks, markets, and the allocation of risks in an economy. *Journal of Institutional and Theoretical Economics* 154:328-45.

Holmström, B. 1979. Moral hazard and observability. *Bell Journal of Economics* 10(1):74-91.

Jackson, P., C. Furfine, H. Groeneveld, D. Hancock, D. Jones, W. Perraudin, L. Radecki, and N. Yoneyama. 1999. Capital requirements and bank behaviour: the impact of the Basel Accord. Basel Committee on Banking Supervision Working Paper 1.

Jones, D. J. 2000. Emerging problems with the Basel Accord: regulatory capital arbitrage and related issues. *Journal of Banking and Finance* 24(1-2):35-58.

Jones, D. J., and K. K. King. 1995. The implementation of prompt corrective action: an assessment. *Journal of Banking and Finance* 19:491-510.

Karlin, S., and H. Taylor. 1981. *A Second Course in Stochastic Processes*. New York: Academic Press.

Kim, D., and A. M. Santomero. 1988. Risk in banking and capital regulation. *Journal of Finance* 43:1219-33.

Koehn, M., and A. Santomero. 1980. Regulation of bank capital and portfolio risk. *Journal of Finance* 35:1235-44.

Leland, H. 1994. Corporate debt value, bond covenants, and optimal capital structure. *Journal of Finance* 49:1213-52.

Leland, H., and K. B. Toft. 1996. Optimal capital structure, endogenous bankruptcy, and the term structure of credit spreads. *Journal of Finance* 51:987-1019.

Levonian, M. 2001. Subordinated debt and the quality of market discipline in banking. Unpublished paper, Federal Reserve Bank of San Francisco.

Merton, R. C. 1974. On the pricing of corporate debt: the risk structure of interest rates. *Journal of Finance* 29:449-69.

——. 1977. An analytic derivation of the cost of deposit insurance and loan guarantees: an application of modern option pricing theory. *Journal of Banking and Finance* 1:3-11.

——. 1978. On the cost of deposit insurance when there are surveillance costs. *Journal of Business* 51:439-52.

Milne, A., and A. E. Whalley. 2001. Bank capital regulation and incentives for risk-taking. University Business School Discussion Paper, London.

Mishkin, F. S. 1996. Evaluating FDICIA. In *Research in Financial Services: Private and Public Policy* (ed. G. Kaufman), volume 9, pp. 17-33.

Morgan, D. 2002. Rating banks: risk and uncertainty in an opaque industry. *American Economic Review* 92:874-88.

Peek, J., and E. Rosengren. 1995. Bank regulation and the credit crunch. *Journal of Banking and Finance* 19:679–92.

Saidenberg, M., and T. Schuermann. 2003. The new Basel Capital Accord and questions for research. Unpublished paper, University of Pennsylvania Wharton School, Financial Institutions Center.

Santos, J. A. C. 1996. Glass-Steagall and the regulatory dialectic. Federal Reserve Bank of Cleveland *Economic Commentary*, February.

———. 2000. Bank capital regulation in contemporary banking theory: a review of the literature. Working Paper 90. Basel, Switzerland: Bank for International Settlements.

Sironi, A. 2001. An analysis of European banks' SND issues and its implications for the design of a mandatory subordinated debt policy. *Journal of Financial Services Research* 20:233–66.

Thakor, A. V. 1996. Capital requirements, monetary policy, and aggregate bank lending: theory and empirical evidence. *Journal of Finance* 51:279–324.

Chapter Ten

The Three Pillars of Basel II: Optimizing the Mix

Jean-Paul Décamps, Jean-Charles Rochet, and Benoît Roger

10.1 Introduction

The ongoing reform of the Basel Accord[1] relies on three "pillars": capital adequacy requirements, supervisory review, and market discipline. Yet the articulation of how these three instruments are to be used in concert is far from clear. On the one hand, the recourse to market discipline is rightly justified by common-sense arguments about the increasing complexity of banking activities, and the impossibility for banking supervisors to monitor these activities in detail. It is therefore legitimate to encourage monitoring of banks by professional investors and financial analysts as a complement to banking supervision. Similarly, a notion of gradualism in regulatory intervention is introduced (in the spirit of the reform of U.S. banking regulation, following the FDIC Improvement Act of 1991).[2] It is suggested that commercial banks should, under "normal circumstances," maintain economic capital way above the regulatory minimum and that supervisors could intervene if this is not the case. Yet, and somewhat contradictorily, while the proposed reform states very precisely the complex refinements of the risk weights to be used in the computation of this regulatory minimum, it remains silent on the other intervention thresholds.

---

[1]The Basel Accord, elaborated in July 1988 by the Basel Committee on Banking Supervision (BCBS), required internationally active banks from the G10 countries to hold a minimum total capital equal to 8% of risk-adjusted assets. It was later amended to cover market risks. It is currently being revised by the BCBS, which has released for comment a proposal of amendment, commonly referred to as Basel II (Basel Committee 1999, 2001).

[2]The FDIC Improvement Act of 1991 requires that each U.S. bank be placed in one of five categories based on its regulatory capital position and other criteria (CAMELS ratings). Undercapitalized banks are subject to increasing regulatory intervention as their capital ratios deteriorate. This prompt corrective action (PCA) doctrine is designed to limit supervisory forbearance. Jones and King (1995) provide a critical assessment of PCA. They suggest that the risk weights used in the computation of capital requirements are inadequate.

It is true that the initial accord (Basel Committee 1988) has been severely criticized for being too crude,[3] and for introducing a wedge between the market assessment of asset risks and its regulatory counterpart.[4] However, it seems strange to insist so much on the need to "enable early supervisory intervention if capital does not provide a sufficient buffer against risk" and to remain silent on the threshold and form of intervention, while putting so much effort on the design of risk weights. Similarly, nothing very precise is said (apart from the need for "increased transparency"!) about the way to implement pillar 3 (market discipline) in practice.[5] The important question this raises is: what should be the form of regulatory intervention when banks do not abide by capital requirements?

In this paper, we address this question by adopting the view, consistent with the approach of Dewatripont and Tirole (1994), that capital requirements should be viewed as intervention thresholds for banking supervisors (acting as representatives of depositors' interest) rather than complex schemes designed to curb banks' asset allocation. This means that we will not discuss the issue of how to compute risk weights (it has already received a lot of attention in the recent literature), but focus instead on what to do when banks do not comply with capital requirements, a topic that seems to have been largely neglected.

Our analysis allows us to address the imbalance in the literature between pillar 1 and the other two pillars. Perhaps one reason for this imbalance is that most of the formal analyses of banks' capital regulation rely on static models, where capital requirements are used to curb banks' incentives for excessive risk-taking and where the choice of risk weights is fundamental (see, for example, the Bhattacharya and Thakor (1993) review). However, as suggested by Hellwig (1998), a static framework fails to capture important intertemporal effects. For example, in a static model, a capital requirement can only impact banks' behavior if it is binding. In practice, however, capital requirements are binding for a very small minority of banks and yet seem to influence the behavior of other banks. Moreover, as suggested by Blum (1999), the impact of more stringent capital requirements may sometimes be counterintuitive, once intertemporal effects are taken into account. The modeling cost is obviously additional complexity, due in particular to transitory effects. In

---

[3] Jones (2000) also criticizes the Basel Accord by showing how banks can use financial innovation to increase their reported capital ratios without truly enhancing their soundness.

[4] See our discussion of the literature in section 9.2.

[5] In particular, in spite of the existence of very precise proposals by U.S. economists (Evanoff and Wall (2000), Calomiris (1998), and see also the discussion in Bliss (2001)) for mandatory subordinated debt, these proposals are not discussed in the Basel II project.

order to minimize this complexity, we will assume here a stationary liability structure, and rule out those transitory effects. Also, for simplicity, we will only consider one type of asset, allowing us to derive a Markov model of banks' behavior with only one state variable: the cash flows generated by the bank's assets (or, up to a monotonic transformation, the bank's capital ratio).

We build on a series of recent articles that have adapted continuous time models used in the corporate finance literature to analyze the impact of the liability structure of firms on their choices of investment and on their overall performance. We extend this literature by incorporating features that we believe essential to capture the specificities of commercial banks.

We model banks as "delegated monitors" à la Diamond (1984) by considering that banks have the unique ability to select and monitor investments with a positive net present value and finance them in large part by deposits. Liquidation of banks is costly because of the imperfect transferability of banks' assets. Also, profitability of these investments requires costly monitoring by the bank. Absent the incentives for the banker to monitor, the net present value of his investments becomes negative. We show that these incentives are absent precisely when the bank is insufficiently capitalized. Thus, incentive-compatibility conditions create the need for the regulator, acting on behalf of depositors, to limit banks' leverage and to impose closure well before the net present value of the bank's assets becomes negative. This is the justification for capital requirements in our model.

Notice that there are two reasons why the Modigliani and Miller (1958) theorem is not valid in our model. The value of the bank is indeed affected both by closure decisions and by moral hazard on investment monitoring by bankers. Closure rules (i.e., capital requirements) optimally trade off between these two imperfections. However, these capital requirements give rise to a commitment problem for supervisors: from a social welfare perspective, it is almost always optimal to let a commercial bank continue to operate, even if this bank is severely undercapitalized. Of course, this time inconsistency problem generates bad incentives for the owners of the bank from an *ex ante* point of view, unless the bank's supervisors find a commitment device, preventing renegotiation.

The rest of the paper is organized as follows. After a brief review of the literature in section 10.2, we describe our model in section 10.3. In section 10.4 we provide the justification for solvency regulations: a minimum capital requirement is needed to prevent insufficiently capitalized banks from shirking. In section 10.5 we introduce market discipline through compulsory subordinated debt. We show that, under certain circumstances, it may reduce the minimum capital requirement.

Section 10.6 analyses supervisory action. We show that direct market discipline is only effective when the threat of bank closures by supervisors is credible. In this case, indirect market discipline can also be useful in allowing supervisors to implement gradual interventions.

10.2 Related Literature

We will not discuss in detail the enormous literature on the Basel Accord and its relation with the "credit crunch" (good discussions can be found in Thakor (1996), Jackson et al. (1999), and Santos (2000)). Let us briefly mention that most of the theoretical literature (e.g., Furlong and Keeley 1990; Kim and Santomero 1988; Koehn and Santomero 1980; Rochet 1992; Thakor 1996) has focused on the distortion of banks' asset allocation that could be generated by the wedge between market assessment of asset risks and its regulatory counterpart in Basel I. The empirical literature (e.g., Bernanke and Lown (1991); see also Thakor (1996), Jackson et al. (1999), and the references therein) has tried to relate these theoretical arguments to the spectacular (yet apparently transitory) substitution of commercial and industrial loans by investment in government securities in U.S. banks in the early 1990s, shortly after the implementation of the Basel Accord and FDICIA.[6] Even if one accepts that these papers have established a positive correlation between bank capital and commercial lending, causality can only be examined in a dynamic framework. Blum (1999) is one of the first theoretical papers to analyze the consequences of more stringent capital requirements in a dynamic framework. He shows that more stringent capital requirements may paradoxically induce an increase in risk taking by the banks that anticipate having difficulty meeting these capital requirements in the future.

Hancock et al. (1995) study the dynamic response to shocks in the capital of U.S. banks using a vector autoregressive framework. They show that U.S. banks seem to adjust their capital ratios much faster than they adjust their loans portfolios. Furfine (2001) extends this line of research by building a structural dynamic model of banks' behavior, which is calibrated on data from a panel of large U.S. banks in the period 1990–97. He suggests that the credit crunch cannot be explained by demand effects but rather by the increase in capital requirements and/or the increase in regulatory monitoring. He also uses his calibrated model to simulate the effects of Basel II and suggests that its implementation would not

---

[6]Peek and Rosengren (1995) find that the increase in supervisory monitoring had also a significant impact on bank lending decisions, even after controlling for bank capital ratios. Blum and Hellwig (1995) analyze the macroeconomic implications of bank capital regulation.

provoke a second credit crunch, given that average risk weights on good-quality commercial loans will decrease if Basel II is implemented.

Our objective here is to design a tractable dynamic model of bank behavior where the interaction between the three pillars of Basel II can be analyzed. Our model builds on two strands of the literature:

- Corporate finance models like those of Leland and Toft (1996) and Ericsson (2000) that analyze the impact of debt maturity on asset substitution and firm value.

- Banking models like those of Merton (1977), Fries et al. (1997), Bhattacharya et al. (2002), and Milne and Whalley (1998) that analyze the impact of solvency regulations and supervision intensity on the behavior of commercial banks.

Let us briefly summarize the main findings of these articles.

Leland and Toft (1996) investigate the optimal capital structure which balances the tax benefits coming with debt and bankruptcy costs. They extend Leland (1994) by considering a coupon bond with finite maturity T. They maintain the convenient assumption of a stationary debt structure by assuming a constant renewal of this debt at rate $m = 1/T$. Leland and Toft (1996) are able to obtain closed-form (but complex) formulas for the value of debt and equity. In addition, using numerical simulations, they show that risk shifting disappears when $T \rightarrow 0$, in conformity with the intuition that short-term debt facilitates the disciplining of bank managers.[7]

Ericsson (2000) and Leland (1998) also touch on optimal capital structure but are mainly concerned with the asset substitution problem arising when the managers of a firm can modify the volatility of its assets' value. They show how the liability structure influences the choice of assets' volatility by the firm's managers. Both consider perpetual debt but Ericsson (2000) introduces a constant renewal rate which serves as a disciplining instrument.

Mella-Barral and Perraudin (1997) characterize the consequences of the capital structure on an abandonment decision. They obtain an under-investment (i.e., premature abandonment) result. This comes from the fact that equityholders have to inject new cash in the firm to keep it as an ongoing concern. Similarly, Mauer and Ott (2000) consider the investment policy of a leveraged company and also obtain an under-investment result for exactly the same reason. These papers thus offer a continuous-time version of the debt-overhang problem first examined

---

[7] Building on Calomiris and Kahn (1991), Carletti (1999) studies the disciplining role of demandable deposits for commercial banks.

in Myers (1977): the injection of new cash by equityholders creates a positive externality for debtholders and the continuation (or expansion) decisions are suboptimal because equityholders do not internalize this effect. Anderson and Sundaresan (1996) and Mella-Barral (1999) elaborate on this aspect by studying the impact of possible renegotiation between equityholders and debtholders. They also allow for the possibility of strategic default.

In the other strand of the literature, Merton (1977, 1978) is the first to use a diffusion model for studying the behavior of commercial banks. He computes the fair pricing of deposit insurance in a context where supervisors can perform costly audits. Fries et al. (1997) extend Merton's framework by introducing deposit withdrawal risk. They study the impact of the regulatory policy of bank closures on the fair pricing of deposit insurance. The optimal closure rule has to trade off between monitoring costs and costs of bankruptcy. Under certain circumstances, the regulator may want to let the bank continue even when equityholders have decided to close it (the underinvestment result).

Following Leland (1994), Bhattacharya et al. (2002) derive closure rules that can be contingent on the level of risk chosen by the bank. Then they examine the complementarity between two policy instruments of bank regulators: the level of capital requirements and the intensity of supervision. In the same spirit, Dangl and Lehar (2001) mix random audits as in Bhattacharya et al. (2002) with risk-shifting possibilities as in Leland (1998) so as to compare the efficiency of Basel Accords (1988, I and II) and VaR regulation. They show that VaR regulation is better, since it reduces the frequency of audits needed to prevent risk shifting by banks.

Calem and Rob (1996) design a dynamic (discrete time) model of portfolio choice, and analyze the impact of capital-based premiums when regulatory audits are perfect. They show that regulation may be counterproductive: a tightening in capital requirement may lead to an increase in the risk of the portfolios chosen by banks, and similarly, capital-based premiums may sometimes induce excessive risk taking by banks. However, this never happens when capital requirements are stringent enough.

Froot and Stein (1998) model the buffer role of bank capital in absorbing liquidity risks. They determine the capital structure that maximizes the bank's value when there are no audits nor deposit insurance. Milne and Whalley (1998) develop a model where banks can issue subsidized deposits without limit in order to finance their liquidity needs. The social cost of these subsidies is limited by the threat of regulatory closure. Milne and Whalley study the interaction between two regulatory instruments: the intensity of costly auditing and the level of capital requirements. They also allow for the possibility of banks' recapitalization. They show that banks' optimal strategy is to hold an additional amount of capital (above the regulatory minimum) used as a buffer against future solvency shocks. This buffer reduces the impact of solvency requirements.

Finally, Pagès and Santos (2001) analyze optimal banking regulations and supervisory policies according to whether or not banking authorities are also in charge of the deposit insurance fund. If this is the case, Pagès and Santos show that supervisory authorities should inflict higher penalties on the banks that do not comply with solvency regulations, but should also reduce the frequency of regulatory audits.

We now move on to the description of our model.

10.3   The Model

Following Merton (1974), Black and Cox (1976), and Leland (1994), we model the cash flows x generated by the bank's assets by a diffusion process:

$$\frac{dx}{x} = \mu_G \, dt + \sigma_G \, dW, \tag{10.1}$$

where dW is the increment of a Wiener process with instantaneous drift μ_G and instantaneous variance σ_G^2. We also assume that all agents are risk neutral with an instantaneous discount rate $r > \mu_G$.

Equation (10.1) is only satisfied if the bank monitors its assets. Monitoring has a fixed (nonmonetary) cost per unit of time, equivalent to a continuous monetary outflow rb.[8] b can thus be interpreted as the present value of the cost of monitoring the bank's assets forever. In the absence of monitoring, the cash-flow dynamics satisfies instead[9]

$$\frac{dx}{x} = \mu_B \, dt + \sigma_B \, dW, \tag{10.2}$$

where "B" stands for the "bad" technology (and "G" for the "good" technology) and $\mu_B \equiv \mu_G - \Delta\mu \leqslant \mu_G$ and $\sigma_B^2 \equiv \sigma_G^2 + \Delta\sigma^2 \geqslant \sigma_G^2$. For technical reasons, we also assume that $\sigma_G^2 < \frac{1}{2}(\mu_G + \mu_B)$.

---

[8]If monitoring cost also has a variable component, it can be subtracted from μ_G. This monitoring cost captures the efforts that bankers have to exert in order to extract adequate repayments from borrowers, or alternatively the forgone private benefits that could have been obtained by related lending. Being nonmonetary, this cost does not appear in accounting values but it does affect the (market) value of equity for bankers.

[9]For simplicity, we assume that the bad technology choice is irreversible: once the bank has started "shirking," the dynamics of x is forever given by equation (10.2). Reversible choices would lead to similar results, with slightly more complicated formulas. Reversibility would also complicate our analysis of regulatory forbearance in section 10.6.

Notice that, when $\Delta\sigma^2 = 0$, we have the classical first-order stochastic dominance (pure effort) problem. When $\Delta\sigma^2 > 0$, there is also a risk-shifting component.

If the bank is closed, the bank's assets are liquidated for a value λx (i.e., that is proportional to the current value of cash flows[10]). λ is given exogenously and satisfies

$$\frac{1}{r - \mu_B} < \lambda < \frac{1}{r - \mu_G}. \tag{10.3}$$

The first inequality means that closure is always preferable to the "bad" technology:

$$E_{x_0}\left[\int_0^{+\infty} e^{-rt} x_t\,dt \,\bigg|\, \text{bad technology}\right] = \frac{x_0}{r - \mu_B} < \lambda x_0.$$

The second inequality captures the assumption that outsiders are only able to capture some fraction $\lambda(r - \mu_G) < 1$ of the future cash flows delivered by the bank's assets. However, due to the fixed monitoring cost rb, liquidation is optimal when x_0 is small. Indeed, the net present value of a bank which continuously monitors its assets is

$$E_{x_0}\left[\int_0^{+\infty} e^{-rt}(x_t - rb)\,dt \,\bigg|\, \text{good technology}\right] = \frac{x_0}{r - \mu_G} - b,$$

so the "good" technology dominates closure whenever x_0 is not too small:[11]

$$\frac{x_0}{r - \mu_G} - b > \lambda x_0 \quad \Longleftrightarrow \quad x_0 > \frac{b}{v_G - \lambda},$$

where

$$v_G = \frac{1}{r - \mu_G} > \lambda,$$

while we denote by analogy

$$v_B = \frac{1}{r - \mu_B} < \lambda.$$

In the absence of a closure threshold (i.e., assuming that banks continue forever), the surpluses generated by the good (G) and the bad (B) technologies would be represented in figure 10.1.

---

[10]Mella-Barral and Perraudin (1997) assume instead a constant liquidation value.

[11]Gennotte and Pyle (1991) were the first to analyze capital regulations in a framework where banks have an explicit monitoring role and make positive NPV loans. In some sense, our paper can be viewed as a dynamic version of Gennotte and Pyle (1991). This implies that banks' assets are not traded and thus markets are not complete. In a complete-markets framework, the moral hazard problem can be solved by risk-based deposit insurance premiums and capital regulation becomes redundant.

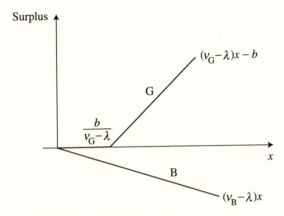

Figure 10.1. Economic surpluses generated by the good (G) and the bad (B) technologies.

The economic surplus generated by the good technology is therefore positive when x is larger than the NPV threshold $b/(v_G - \lambda)$, while the surplus generated by the bad technology is always negative. We now introduce a closure decision, determined by a liquidation threshold x_L.

Assuming for the moment that the bank always monitors its assets ("good technology"), the value of these assets $V_G(x)$ is thus determined by the liquidation threshold x_L, below which the bank is closed:

$$V_G(x) = E_x \left[\int_0^{\tau_L} e^{-rt}(x_t - rb)\, dt + e^{-r\tau_L} \lambda x_L \right], \qquad (10.4)$$

where τ_L is a random variable (stopping time), defined as the first instant where x_t (defined by (10.1)) equals x_L, given $x_0 = x$.

Using standard formulas,[12] we obtain

$$V_G(x) = v_G x - b + \{b - (v_G - \lambda)x_L\}\left(\frac{x}{x_L}\right)^{1-a_G}, \qquad (10.5)$$

where

$$a_G = \frac{1}{2} + \frac{\mu_G}{\sigma_G^2} + \sqrt{\left(\frac{\mu_G}{\sigma_G^2} - \frac{1}{2}\right)^2 + \frac{2r}{\sigma_G^2}} > 1. \qquad (10.6)$$

The continuation value of the bank is thus equal to the net present value of perpetual continuation $(v_G x - b)$ plus the option value associated with the irreversible closure decision at threshold x_L. Interestingly,

---

[12] See, for instance, Karlin and Taylor (1981).

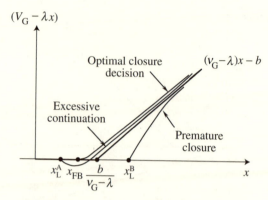

Figure 10.2. The continuation value of the bank for different closure thresholds.

this option value is proportional to x^{1-a_G}, thus it is maximum for a value of x_L that does not depend on x, namely

$$x_{FB} = \frac{b}{v_G - \lambda} \frac{a_G - 1}{a_G}. \tag{10.7}$$

Proposition 10.1. *The first-best closure threshold of the bank is the value of the cash flow x_L that maximizes the option value associated with the irreversible closure decision. This value is equal to*

$$x_{FB} = \frac{b}{v_G - \lambda} \frac{a_G - 1}{a_G},$$

where a_G is defined by formula (10.6). The first-best closure threshold x_{FB} is smaller than the NPV threshold $b/(v_G - \lambda)$.

The continuation value of the bank as a function of x (i.e., $V_G(x) - \lambda x$) is represented below for different values of x_L:

- x_L^A corresponds to excessive continuation ($V_G'(x_L^A) < \lambda$);

- x_L^B corresponds to premature closure ($V_G'(x_L^B) > \lambda$);

- x_{FB} corresponds to the optimal threshold ($V_G'(x_{FB}) = \lambda$);

- $b/(v_G - \lambda)$ corresponds to the positive NPV threshold.

We now introduce the second characteristic feature of commercial banking, namely deposit finance: a large fraction of the bank's liabilities consists of insured deposits,[13] with a volume normalized to 1. For the moment, we assume that these deposits are the only source of outside funds for the bank (we later introduce subordinated debt) and that issuing equity is prohibitively costly.[14] In the absence of public intervention,[15] liquidation of the bank occurs when the cash flows x received from its assets are insufficient to repay the interest r on deposits. In this case, the liquidation threshold is thus

$$x_L = r. \tag{10.8}$$

We also assume that when this liquidation takes place, the book value of the bank equity (which, in our model, is equal to the book value of assets $v_G x$ minus the nominal value of deposits) is still positive:

$$v_G r > 1, \tag{10.9}$$

but liquidation does not permit repayment of all deposits:

$$\lambda r < 1. \tag{10.10}$$

Condition (10.9) captures the fact that, in the absence of liquidity assistance by the central bank (introduced in section 10.6), solvent banks may be illiquid.[16] Condition (10.10) ensures that deposits are risky.

The PV of deposits is computed easily:

$$D_G(x) = 1 - (1 - \lambda x_L)\left(\frac{x}{x_L}\right)^{1-a_G}, \tag{10.11}$$

leading to the market value of equity

$$E_G(x) = V_G(x) - D_G(x)$$

---

[13]For simplicity, we assume that these are long-term deposits. It would be easy to introduce a constant frequency of withdrawals, as in our treatment of subordinated debt in section 10.5.

[14]Bhattacharya et al. (2002) instead make the assumption that the bank can costlessly issue new equity. In that case, the closure threshold is chosen by stockholders so as to maximize equity value. Milne and Whalley (1998) make the intermediate assumption that new equity issues entail an exogenous fixed cost.

[15]Public intervention can consist either of liquidity assistance by the central bank, or on the contrary closure by the banking supervision authorities. This is analyzed in the next sections.

[16]This assumption is in line with Bagehot's doctrine for a lender of last resort (see, for example, chapter 2 for a recent account of this doctrine). In our model, it guarantees that optimal capital requirements are positive. However, it is not crucial: even if it is not satisfied, optimal capital requirements are positive if b is large enough (see below).

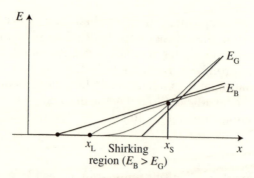

Figure 10.3. Comparing equity values under
good and bad technology choices.

or

$$E_G(x) = v_G x - b - 1 + (b + 1 - v_G x_L)\left(\frac{x}{x_L}\right)^{1-a_G}. \tag{10.12}$$

Notice that, since $\lambda x_L < 1$, deposits are risky. As a result, the PV of deposits $D(x)$ is less than their nominal value 1, the difference corresponding to the liability of the deposit insurance fund.[17] If instead the bank ceases to monitor its assets, the value of equity becomes, by a simple adaptation of the above formula (replacing v_G by v_B and b by zero),

$$E_B(x) = v_B x - 1 + (1 - v_B x_L)\left(\frac{x}{x_L}\right)^{1-a_B}, \tag{10.13}$$

where

$$a_B = \frac{1}{2} + \frac{\mu_B}{\sigma_B^2} + \sqrt{\left(\frac{\mu_B}{\sigma_B^2} - \frac{1}{2}\right)^2 + \frac{2r}{\sigma_B^2}}. \tag{10.14}$$

By comparing the value of equity in the two formulas, it is easy to see that in general $E_B(x) > E_G(x)$ for x in some interval $]x_L, x_S[$, as suggested by figure 10.3.

10.4   The Justification of Solvency Requirements

Figure 10.3 illustrates the basic reason for imposing a capital requirement in our model: as long as $E'_G(x_L) < E'_B(x_L)$, there is a region $[x_L, x_S]$ where, in the absence of outside intervention, the bank "shirks" (i.e., chooses the bad technology) which reduces social welfare, and ultimately provokes failure, the cost being borne by the Deposit Insurance Fund

---

[17]This liability is covered by an insurance premium $1 - D(x_0)$ paid initially by the bank. We could also introduce a flow premium, paid in continuous time, as in Fries et al. (1997).

(DIF). As shown by proposition 10.2, this happens when the monitoring cost b is not too small. In order to avoid shirking, banking authorities (which could be the central bank, a Financial Services Authority, or the DIF itself) set a regulatory closure threshold x_R below which the bank is closed. In practice, this closure threshold can be implemented by a minimal capital requirement. Indeed, the book value of equity is equal to the book value of assets $v_G x$, minus the nominal value of deposits, which we have normalized to 1. The solvency ratio of the bank is thus

$$\rho = \frac{v_G x - 1}{v_G x}.$$

This is an increasing function of x. A continuation rule $x \geqslant x_R$ is thus equivalent to a minimum capital ratio

$$\rho \geqslant \frac{v_G x_R - 1}{v_G x_R} \overset{\text{def}}{=} \rho_R.$$

Proposition 10.2. *When the monitoring cost b is not too small, a solvency regulation is needed to prevent insufficiently capitalized banks from shirking. The second-best closure threshold (associated with the optimal capital ratio) is the smallest value x_R of the liquidation threshold such that shirking disappears. It is given by*

$$x_R = \frac{(a_G - 1)b + a_G - a_B}{a_G v_G - a_B v_B}. \tag{10.15}$$

Regulation is needed whenever $x_R > r$, which is equivalent to

$$b > \hat{b} = \frac{r[a_G v_G - a_B v_B] - (a_G - a_B)}{a_G - 1}. \tag{10.16}$$

Proof. See the appendix (section 10.8). □

Notice that, when regulation is needed ($x_R > x_L = r$), the implied solvency ratio ρ_R is always positive:

$$\rho_R = \frac{v_G x_R - 1}{v_G x_R} > 0.$$

This is because we have assumed that $v_G r > 1$, which means that, in the absence of public intervention, banks become illiquid before they become insolvent.[18]

---

[18] Even without this assumption, ρ_R is positive whenever b is large enough. This is in line with most corporate finance models with moral hazard (e.g., Holmström and Tirole 1997): when the cost of effort (or the level of private benefits) is large enough, capital is needed to prevent moral hazard.

Notice also that when b is very large, the liquidation value of the bank λx_R becomes greater than the nominal value of deposits (normalized to 1) and deposits become riskless. In this case the incentives of banks' stockholders are not distorted by the limited liability option: they optimally decide to close the bank when x hits the first-best threshold x_{FB} and the moral hazard constraint does not bind. We focus on the more interesting set of parameter values for which undercapitalized banks do indeed have incentives to shirk.

10.5 Market Discipline

There are several reasons why market discipline can be useful. First it can produce additional information that the regulator can exploit (this is usually referred to as "indirect" market discipline). Consider, for example, a setup à la Merton (1978) or Bhattacharya et al. (2002) where x_t is only observed through costly and imperfect auditing. As a result, there is a positive probability that the bank may continue to operate in the region $[x_L, x_R]$ (because undetected by banking supervisors). If shirking is to be deterred, a more stringent capital requirement (i.e., a higher x_R) has to be imposed, to account for imperfect auditing (see Bhattacharya et al. (2002) for details). In such a context, requiring the bank to issue a security (say subordinated debt) whose payoff is conditional on x_t, and that is traded on financial markets, would indirectly reveal the value of x_t and dispense the regulator from costly auditing.[19] This idea is explored further in section 10.6.

When x_t is publicly observed, as in our model, the supervisors can have recourse to a second form of market discipline (sometimes called "direct" market discipline), which works by modifying the liability structure of banks. This is the idea behind the "subordinated debt proposal" (Calomiris 1998; Evanoff and Wall 2000), which our model allows us to analyze formally.

Following this proposal, we assume that banks are required to issue a certain volume s of subordinated debt, renewed with a certain frequency m. Both s and m are policy variables of the regulator. To facilitate comparison with the previous section, we keep constant the total volume of outside finance.[20] Thus, the volume of insured deposits becomes $d = 1 - s$. To simplify the analysis, and obtain simpler formulas than Leland

---

[19]Of course, if the bank's equity is already traded, then this advantage disappears and the question becomes more technical: which security prices reveal more information about banks' asset value?

[20]It would be more natural to endogenize the level of outside finance but this would introduce a second state variable and prevent closed-form solutions. We are currently working on an extension of this paper in this direction.

and Toft (1996), we assume (as in Ericsson 2000) that subordinated debt has an infinite maturity, but is renewed according to a Poisson process of intensity m. The average time to maturity of subordinated debt is thus

$$\int_0^{+\infty} mte^{-mt}\, dt = \frac{1}{m}.$$

In this section, we consider a situation in which the regulator can commit to a closure threshold x_R. We focus on the case where $\lambda x_R < d$, so that deposits are risky, while subdebt holders (and stockholders) are expropriated in case of closure. We use the same notation as before (for any technology choice $k = B, G$):

$$V_k = \text{value of the bank's assets,}$$
$$D_k = \text{PV of insured deposits,}$$
$$E_k = \text{value of equity,}$$

while S_k denotes the market value of subordinated debt.

Starting with the case where the bank monitors its assets ($k = G$), the values of V_G and D_G are given by simple adaptations of our previous formulas:

$$V_G(x) = v_G x - b + [b - (v_G - \lambda)x_R]\left(\frac{x}{x_R}\right)^{1-a_G},$$

$$D_G(x) = d - (d - \lambda x_R)\left(\frac{x}{x_R}\right)^{1-a_G}.$$

S_G is more difficult to determine. It is the solution of the following partial differential equation, which takes into account the fact that, with instantaneous probability m, subordinated debt is repaid at face value s but has to be refinanced at price $S_G(x)$:

$$rS_G(x) = sr + m(s - S_G(x)) + \mu_G x S_G'(x) + \tfrac{1}{2}\sigma_G^2 x^2 S_G''(x),$$
$$S_G(x_R) = 0,$$

leading to

$$S_G(x) = s\left[1 - \left(\frac{x}{x_R}\right)^{1-a_G(m)}\right], \tag{10.17}$$

where

$$a_G(m) = \frac{1}{2} + \frac{\mu_G}{\sigma_G^2} + \sqrt{\left(\frac{\mu_G}{\sigma_G^2} - \frac{1}{2}\right)^2 + 2\frac{r+m}{\sigma_G^2}}. \tag{10.18}$$

We immediately notice a first effect of direct market discipline: the exponent $1 - a_G(m)$ decreases when m increases. Thus, the value of S_G increases in m. The value of equity becomes

$$E_G(x) = V_G(x) - D_G(x) - S_G(x)$$

$$= v_G x - 1 - b + [d + b - v_G x_R]\left(\frac{x}{x_R}\right)^{1-a_G} + s\left(\frac{x}{x_R}\right)^{1-a_G(m)}.$$
$$(10.19)$$

When $m = 0$, we obtain the same formula as in the previous section (no market discipline): this is due to our convention to keep constant the total volume of outside finance[21] $(s + d = 1)$. Notice also that the value of equity is reduced when s is increased (while keeping $s + d = 1$): this is because $a_G(m) \geqslant a_G$. Thus the bank will only issue subordinated debt if it is imposed by the regulator (or if it reduces the capital requirement).

A simple adaptation of formula (10.19) gives E_B, the value of equity when the bank shirks:

$$E_B(x) = v_B x - 1 + [d - v_B x_R]\left(\frac{x}{x_R}\right)^{1-a_B} + s\left(\frac{x}{x_R}\right)^{1-a_B(m)},\qquad(10.20)$$

where

$$a_B(m) = \frac{1}{2} + \frac{\mu_B}{\sigma_B^2} + \sqrt{\left(\frac{\mu_B}{\sigma_B^2} - \frac{1}{2}\right)^2 + 2\frac{r+m}{\sigma_B^2}}.\qquad(10.21)$$

Thus, a necessary condition for shirking to be eliminated is $\Delta \geqslant 0$, where

$$\Delta = x_R[E_G'(x_R) - E_B'(x_R)].$$

A simple computation gives

$$x_R E_G'(x_R) = a_G v_G x_R - (a_G - 1)(d + b) - s[a_G(m) - 1],$$
$$x_R E_B'(x_R) = a_B v_B x_R - (a_B - 1)d - s[a_B(m) - 1].$$

Thus

$$\Delta = [a_G v_G - a_B v_B]x_R - [(a_G - a_B)d + (a_G - 1)b + s\{a_G(m) - a_B(m)\}].$$
$$(10.22)$$

Now, let $x_R(m)$ define the minimum value x_R that satisfies the inequality $\Delta(x_R) \geqslant 0$. Remark that $x_R(m)$ is implicitly defined by the equation $\Delta(x_R(m)) = 0$. We show in the appendix (section 10.10) that $(E_G - E_B)(x) \geqslant 0$ for all $x \geqslant x_R(m)$. We deduce the following proposition.

---

[21]Of course, even when $m = 0$, the liability of the DIF is reduced when a fraction s of insured deposits is replaced by subordinated debt. But this is exactly offset by the default premium demanded by subordinated debtholders.

Proposition 10.3. *With compulsory subordinated debt, the minimum solvency ratio that prevents bank shirking becomes*

$$x_R(m) = \frac{(a_G - 1)b + (a_G - a_B)d + (a_G(m) - a_B(m))s}{a_G v_G - a_B v_B}$$

or equivalently

$$x_R(m) = x_R(0) + s\frac{(a_G(m) - a_B(m)) - (a_G - a_B)}{a_G v_G - a_B v_B}. \qquad (10.23)$$

- *If the difference between the variances of the bad and good technologies, $\Delta\sigma^2$, satisfies $\Delta\sigma^2 > 0$, then the minimum solvency ratio x_R is a U-shaped function of m, with a minimum in m^*, where $1/m$ is the average time to maturity of subordinated debt.*

- *If $\Delta\sigma^2 = 0$ (pure effort problem), then $m^* = +\infty$, which means that $x_R(m)$ is decreasing for all m.*

- *Market discipline reduces the need for regulatory bank closures when m and $\Delta\sigma^2$ are small.*

In order to understand the intuition behind this result, let us recall that $x_R(m)$ is defined implicitly by the tangency point between the values of equity under the good and the bad technologies:

$$\frac{\partial(E_G - E_B)}{\partial x}(x_R(m), m) = 0.$$

Given that the value of the bank's assets and the value of deposits are fixed (once x_R has been fixed), the changes in the value of equity come from changes in the value of subordinated debt. The question is therefore: under what conditions does an increase in the frequency of renewal of subordinated debt increase the derivative of S_G less than the derivative of S_B (so that shirking becomes more costly for bankers)? Proposition 10.3 shows that this is true essentially when $\Delta\sigma^2$ and m are small.

Figure 10.4 illustrates a case where the gap between E_G and E_B has been widened by an increase in m (see dashed line), giving the shareholders more incentives to choose the "good" technology. This last property is expressed by the following condition:

$$\frac{\partial^2(E_G - E_B)}{\partial x \partial m}(x_R(m), m) > 0.$$

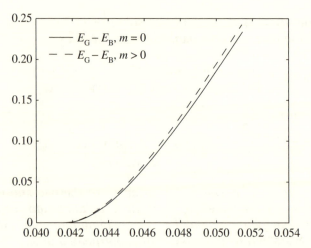

Figure 10.4. The impact of an increase in m on the gains of equityholders when adopting the good technology. The continuous line represents the difference between E_G and E_B as functions of x. The dashed line represents the same function after m has been increased and x_R modified accordingly.

Proposition 10.3 clarifies the conditions under which market discipline is a useful complement to solvency regulations: $\Delta\sigma^2$ and m have to be small. Indeed, when $\Delta\sigma^2$ is large, m^* is negative and $x_R(m) > x_R(0)$ for all relevant values of m (i.e., positive). In this case the introduction of subordinated debt is counterproductive, since it forces the regulator to increase the minimum capital requirement. The intuition is that the incentives for gambling for resurrection are, in this case, increased by the presence of subordinated debt. By contrast, when $\Delta\sigma^2$ is small, m^* is positive and, for m smaller than m^*, the opposite inequality is true: $x_R(m) < x_R(0)$. Thus when the risk-shifting problem is not too big ($\Delta\sigma^2$ small), then for m small, market discipline reduces the level of regulatory capital.[22] We now study how the efficiency of market discipline is affected by the attitude of supervisory authorities.

10.6 Supervisory Action

The "second pillar" of Basel II is supervisory review.[23] The Basel Committee states several principles for a sound supervisory review, including: "Supervisors should review and evaluate banks' internal capital adequacy assessments...[and] take appropriate supervisory action if they

---

[22]More precisely, the regulatory requirement on equity (tier 1) is reduced.

[23]"The Committee views supervisory review as a critical complement to minimum capital requirements and market discipline" (Basel Committee 2001, p. 30).

are not satisfied with the results of this process" (Basel Committee 2001, p. 31). However, this is easier said than done. Indeed, banking authorities are very often subject to political pressure for supporting banks in distress. In our model, this means providing public funds to the banks who hit the threshold x_R. Given our irreversibility assumption, it is indeed always suboptimal (even *ex post*) to let banks go below this threshold. On the other hand, closure can be (*ex post*) dominated by continuation, when net fiscal costs are not too high. Therefore, whenever a bank hits the boundary $x = x_R$, the government considers the possibility of recapitalizing the bank up to $x_R + \Delta x$ with public funds.

We denote by $y > 0$ the net welfare cost of these public funds, due to the distortions created by the imperfections of the fiscal system. Whenever the government intervenes, the level of recapitalization Δx and the new asset's value[24] of the bank[25] $V_{k,BO}$ (for a technology $k \in \{G, B\}$) are determined by

$$V_{k,BO}(x_R) = \max_{\Delta x \geqslant 0} \{V_{k,BO}(x_R + \Delta x) - y\Delta x\}. \qquad (10.24)$$

The function $V_{k,BO}$ is determined together with (10.24), by the usual differential equation that expresses absence of arbitrage opportunities and the "no-bubble" condition: $V_{k,BO}(x) \sim v_k x$ for $x \to +\infty$. Therefore, $V_{k,BO}(x)$ is necessarily of the type

$$V_{k,BO}(x) = v_k x - b_k + \theta_k x^{1-a_k},$$

where the constant θ_k is determined by (10.24) and $b_k = 0$ when $k = B$ and b when $k = G$. In the appendix (section 10.9), we show that the optimal Δx is actually 0^+. This means that the government injects the minimum amount needed to stay above the critical shirking level x_R. This can be interpreted as liquidity assistance.

Technically, x_R becomes a reflecting barrier (see, for example, Dixit 1993) and the boundary condition for $V_{k,BO}$ becomes

$$V'_{k,BO}(x_R) = y.$$

The new formula for V_G is

$$V_{G,BO}(x) = v_G x - b - \left(\frac{y - v_G}{a_G - 1}\right) x^{1-a_G} x_R^{a_G}.$$

---

[24]This new asset's value reflects that future government intervention is anticipated, every time the bank again hits the threshold $x = x_R$.

[25]The letters "BO" refer to the bailout operation.

Notice that this liquidity assistance implies that $V_{G,BO}(x_R)$ is now different from zero,[26] given that banks are allowed to continue after they hit x_R. Interestingly, the impact on the value of bank equity, and thus on the incentives for shirking, essentially depends on the behavior of the government toward subdebt holders when the bank hits $x = x_R$. Let us examine successively the case of full expropriation and the case of complete forbearance.

If subdebtholders (and of course equityholders) are wiped out, the decision to rescue the bank only affects the deposit insurance fund, which becomes the residual claimant of the assets' value of the bank. However, the differential equation and boundary conditions that characterize the value of subdebt are the same as before and thus S_k is unchanged. Therefore, the differential equations that characterize E_k ($k = G, B$) are also unchanged and so are the functions E_k themselves. Market discipline is thus compatible with public liquidity assistance, provided that subordinated debtholders lose their stake if the bank is rescued.

The situation is different in the case of complete forbearance, i.e., if subdebtholders are fully insured when the bank hits the critical threshold x_R: $S_k(x_R) = s$. In this case it is easy to see that subdebt becomes riskless and thus its value is identically equal to s. But then the subdebt term vanishes from the differential equation that characterizes E_k. This means that market discipline becomes completely ineffective.

These results are summarized in the next proposition.

Proposition 10.4. *Public liquidity assistance to the banks that hit the critical threshold x_R is compatible with market discipline, provided there is no regulatory forbearance, i.e., if subordinated debtholders are fully expropriated when the bank is rescued. If, however, subdebtholders are fully insured, market discipline becomes completely ineffective.*

Proposition 10.4 thus shows that *direct* market discipline is effective when the credibility of supervisors to close insufficiently capitalized banks is established. We now go further and show how *indirect* market discipline (i.e., information revealed by the market prices of the securities issued by the banks) can be used to implement a more elaborate regulatory policy, but again when regulatory forbearance is excluded. This illustrates that market discipline is indeed a useful complement to the two other pillars of Basel II: supervision and capital requirements.

As already discussed in section 10.5, a branch of the academic literature has studied the optimal mix between capital requirements and

---

[26]When $y > V'_G(x_R)$, the cost of public funds is so high that the government prefers to close the bank. Whenever $y < V'_G(x_R)$, $V_{G,BO}(x_R) > 0$, which guarantees that bailout is socially preferable (*ex post*) to closure.

regulatory audits. In this literature, the value of the bank's assets (or cash flows x as in our model) is privately known to the banker. It can only be observed by the regulator if a costly audit is performed, which is modeled by a Poisson process, the intensity of which is chosen by the regulator. Since the regulator wants to avoid excessive continuation, he has to set a higher closure threshold than if x was publicly observable.[27] However, this threshold can be reduced by an increase in the intensity of auditing, thus suggesting substitutability between supervision and capital requirements.

Our model allows us to extend this literature by integrating the third pillar of Basel II, namely market discipline, into this picture. Suppose indeed that the bank has issued at least one security (equity, certificate of deposits, or subordinated debt) that is publicly traded on a secondary market. In our model, the price of such a security is a one-to-one function of the state variable x. By inverting this function, the regulator can infer the value of the bank's cash flows to condition its intervention policy.[28] In such a context, the role of bank supervisors has to be reexamined: instead of a constant intensity of audit across all banks, bank supervisors can adopt a gradual intervention policy (in the spirit of the U.S. regulatory reform following the FDIC Improvement Act). For example, the regulator can set two thresholds x_R and x_I (with $x_R < x_I$), where x_R is as before a closure threshold, but x_I is only an inspection threshold: whenever $x < x_I$, the bank is inspected,[29] the technology chosen by the bank is revealed, and it is closed if and only if the bank has chosen the bad technology ($k = B$).

With this regulatory policy, the value of equity when the technology is "good" is the same as in section 10.3 (with x_R replacing x_L):

$$E_G(x) = v_G x - b - 1 + k_G x^{1-a_G},$$

with

$$k_G = [b + 1 - v_G x_R] x_R^{a_G - 1}.$$

---

[27] Here also, the regulator faces a credibility problem.

[28] An important empirical literature discusses the predictive power of subordinated debt prices or spreads on banks' probabilities of failure (see, for example, Evanoff and Wall 2001; Hancock and Kwast 2001; Sironi 2001). Covitz et al. (2002) argue that endogeneity of liquidity premiums can significantly decrease this predictive power. They argue that mandating a regular issuance of subdebt can reduce this endogeneity, thus improving information content of spreads and ultimately increasing market discipline. Evanoff and Wall (2003) show how subdebt spreads can be used as a complement to capital requirements as a way to reduce regulatory forbearance.

[29] We assume that the regulatory audit policy is deterministic. It would be easy to consider the more general case of stochastic audits.

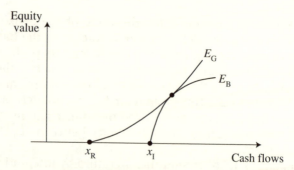

Figure 10.5. Optimal capital requirement x_R for a given inspection threshold x_I. It can be proved that this minimum level of x_R decreases with x_I, which establishes that the substitutability between capital requirements and supervision is maintained when market discipline is introduced.

However, the value of equity when the bank shirks is now a function of x_I:

$$E_B(x) = \begin{cases} v_B x - 1 + k_B x^{1-a_B} & \text{for } x \geqslant x_I, \\ 0 & \text{otherwise,} \end{cases}$$

with

$$k_B = [1 - v_B x_I] x_I^{a_B - 1}.$$

For a given value of x_I (and thus for a given function E_B), there is a minimum value of x_R such that E_G remains above E_B. It is obtained when the two curves are tangent, as suggested by figure 10.5.

Figure 10.5 illustrates well how the three pillars of Basel II can be optimally mixed: indirect market discipline (i.e., information given to supervisors by market prices of securities issued by banks) could allow a very "light" supervisory policy: only banks with $x \in \,]x_R, x_I[$ are audited, and the capital requirement is reduced to x_R (which is less than the one obtained in proposition 9.2, in the absence of audit).

10.7 Concluding Remarks

Our objective in this article has been to design a simple dynamic model of commercial bank behavior, where the articulation between the three pillars of Basel II can be analyzed. We interpret the first pillar (capital adequacy requirement) as a closure threshold rather than an indirect means of influencing banks' asset allocation. We show that market discipline (the third pillar) can be used to reduce this closure threshold, especially if there is a risk of regulatory forbearance. We also reexamine the traditional view of the supervisory role (the second pillar).

We suggest that supervisors can modulate the intensity of their interventions (from a simple audit to the closure of the bank) according to reliable signals given by market prices of the securities issued by banks (indirect market discipline). However, two caveats are in order: direct market discipline can only be effective if banking supervisors are protected from political interference, and indirect market discipline cannot be used under all circumstances, since market prices become erratic during periods of crisis. This shows that Basel II proposals seem to be dangerously insufficient: important reforms of the supervisory system have to be implemented as well, in order to guarantee independence of banking supervisors from political powers and also proper behavior during future crises.

10.8   Appendix: Proof of Proposition 9.2

Since by construction $E_G(x_R) = E_B(x_R) = 0$, a necessary condition for elimination of shirking is $E_G'(x_R) \geqslant E_B'(x_R)$. The minimum value of x_R that satisfies this inequality is defined implicitly by $\Delta(x_R) = 0$, where

$$\Delta(x_R) = x_R[E_G'(x_R) - E_B'(x_R)].$$

But formulas (10.12) and (10.13) (with x_R replacing x_L) imply

$$x_R E_G'(x_R) = v_G x_R + (a_G - 1)[v_G x_R - 1 - b],$$
$$x_R E_B'(x_R) = v_B x_R + (a_B - 1)[v_B x_R - 1].$$

Therefore,

$$\Delta = [a_G v_G - a_B v_B]x_R - [(a_G - 1)b + a_G - a_B],$$

which establishes formula (10.15). Conversely, we have to prove that $(E_G - E_B)(x) \geqslant 0$ for $x \geqslant x_R$ when x_R is given by formula (10.15). The proof is a particular case of the one developed in section 10.10 with $m = 0$, $d = 1$, and $s = 0$. Thus we have established that regulation is needed when $x_R > x_L$, which is equivalent to condition (10.16).

10.9   Appendix: Optimal Recapitalization by Public Funds Is Infinitesimal (Liquidity Assistance)

Consider a bank that hits the regulatory threshold x_R. When government injects funds Δx, the new continuation value of the bank at x_R becomes

$$V_{k,BO}(x_R) = \max_{\Delta x \geqslant 0} \{V_{k,BO}(x_R + \Delta x) - y\Delta x\}. \tag{10.25}$$

Recall the expression for $V_{k,BO}$:

$$V_{k,BO}(x) = v_k x - b_k + \theta_k x^{1-a_k}. \tag{10.26}$$

We want to establish that a finite $\Delta x > 0$ is never optimal. Let us assume by contradiction that such a Δx is optimal. The first-order condition leads to

$$V'_{k,BO}(x_R + \Delta x) = y.$$

Now, because of equation (10.25),

$$V_{k,BO}(x_R + \Delta x) = -y\Delta x + V_{k,BO}(x_R)$$
$$= V_{k,BO}(x_R) - V'_{k,BO}(x_R + \Delta x)\Delta x. \tag{10.27}$$

Given that, for $\theta_k \neq 0$, $V_{k,BO}$ is either convex or concave, the above equality is only possible when $\theta_k = 0$, $V_{k,BO}$ is affine, and the optimal Δx is either 0 or infinity. Since by assumption $y > v_G$, the optimal Δx is always zero.

10.10   Appendix: Proof of Proposition 9.3

We have to prove that

$$(E_G - E_B)(x) \geqslant 0 \quad \text{for all } x \geqslant x_R(m).$$

This result is a straightforward consequence of the following lemma.

Lemma 10.1.

$$E'_G(x) > E'_B(x) \quad \text{for all } x > x_R(m). \tag{10.28}$$

Proof of lemma 10.1. For all $x > x_R(m)$,

$$xE'_G(x) - xE'_B(x)$$
$$= (v_G - v_B)x + (1 - a_G)\{d + b - v_G x_R(m)\}\left(\frac{x}{x_R(m)}\right)^{1-a_G}$$
$$- (1 - a_B)(d - v_B x_R(m))\left(\frac{x}{x_R(m)}\right)^{1-a_B}$$
$$+ s(1 - a_G(m))\left(\frac{x}{x_R(m)}\right)^{1-a_G(m)}$$
$$- s(1 - a_B(m))\left(\frac{x}{x_R(m)}\right)^{1-a_B(m)}. \tag{10.29}$$

Introducing into this equality the inequalities $x > x_R(m)$, $1 - a_G < 1 - a_B < 0$, and $(d + b - v_G x_R(m)) > 0$, we obtain

$$xE_G'(x) - xE_B'(x) > ((v_G - v_B)x_R(m) + (1 - a_G)\{d + b - v_G x_R(m)\}$$
$$- (1 - a_B)\{d - v_B x_R(m)\})\left(\frac{x}{x_R(m)}\right)^{1-a_G}$$
$$+ s(1 - a_G(m))\left(\frac{x}{x_R(m)}\right)^{1-a_G(m)}$$
$$- s(1 - a_B(m))\left(\frac{x}{x_R(m)}\right)^{1-a_B(m)}$$
$$= (a_G(m) - a_B(m))s\left(\frac{x}{x_R(m)}\right)^{1-a_G}$$
$$+ s(1 - a_G(m))\left(\frac{x}{x_R(m)}\right)^{1-a_G(m)}$$
$$- s(1 - a_B(m))\left(\frac{x}{x_R(m)}\right)^{1-a_B(m)}.$$

Since $a_B(m) < a_G(m)$, this is greater than

$$(a_G(m) - a_B(m))s\left(\frac{x}{x_R(m)}\right)^{1-a_G}$$
$$+ s(1 - a_G(m))\left(\frac{x}{x_R(m)}\right)^{1-a_G(m)} - s(1 - a_B(m))\left(\frac{x}{x_R(m)}\right)^{1-a_G(m)}$$
$$= (a_G(m) - a_B(m))s\left(\left(\frac{x}{x_R(m)}\right)^{1-a_G} - \left(\frac{x}{x_R(m)}\right)^{1-a_G(m)}\right)$$
$$> 0$$

since $1 - a_G(m) < 1 - a_G < 0$ and $x > x_R(m)$. Thus our result. □

References

Anderson, R., and S. Sundaresan. 1996. Design and valuation of debt contracts. *Review of Financial Studies* 9:37–68.

Basel Committee. 1988. International convergence of capital measurement and capital standards. Basel Committee on Banking Supervision 4 (July). Basel, Switzerland: Bank for International Settlements.

———. 1999. A new capital adequacy framework. Consultative Paper, Basel Committee on Banking Supervision. Basel, Switzerland: Bank for International Settlements.

———. 2001. The new Basel Capital Accord. Second Consultative Paper, Basel Committee on Banking Supervision. Basel, Switzerland: Bank for International Settlements.

Bernanke, B., and C. Lown. 1991. The credit crunch. *Brookings Papers on Economic Activity* 2:205–47.

Bhattacharya, S., M. Plank, G. Strobl, and J. Zechner. 2002. Bank capital regulation with random audits. *Journal of Economic Dynamics and Control* 26:1301–21.

Bhattacharya, S., and A. V. Thakor. 1993. Contemporary banking theory. *Journal of Financial Intermediation* 3:2–50.

Black, F., and J. C. Cox. 1976. Valuing corporate securities: some effects of bond indenture provisions. *Journal of Finance* 31:351–67.

Bliss, R. 2001. Market discipline and subordinated debt: a review of salient issues. *Economic Perspectives, FRB of Chicago* 1:24–45.

Blum, J. 1999. Do capital adequacy requirements reduce risk in banking? *Journal of Banking and Finance* 23:755–71.

Blum, J., and M. Hellwig. 1995. The macroeconomic implications of capital adequacy requirements for banks. *European Economic Review* 39:739–49.

Calem, P. S., and R. Rob. 1996. The impact of capital-based regulation on bank risk-taking: a dynamic model. Board of Governors of the Federal Reserve System, Finance and Economics Discussion Series, no. 96-12.

Calomiris, C. W. 1998. Blueprints for a new global financial architecture. (Available at www.house.gov/jec/imf/blueprnt.htm.)

Calomiris, C. W., and C. Kahn. 1991. The role of demandable debt in structuring optimal banking arrangements. *American Economic Review* 81:497–513.

Carletti, E. 1999. Bank moral hazard and market discipline. Mimeo, FMG, London School of Economics.

Covitz, D. M., D. Hancock, and M. L. Kwast. 2003. Market discipline in banking reconsidered: the role of deposit insurance reform and funding manager decisions and bond market liquidity. Paper presented at the NYFed–Chazen Institute Conference, October 2003, New York.

Dangl, T., and A. Lehar. 2001. Basel Accord vs value-at-risk regulation in banking. Discussion Paper, Department of Business Studies, University of Vienna, Austria.

Dewatripont, M., and J. Tirole. 1994. *The Prudential Regulation of Banks.* Cambridge, MA: MIT Press.

Diamond, D. 1984. Financial intermediation and delegated monitoring. *Review of Economic Studies* 51:393–414.

Dixit, A. K. 1993. *The Art of Smooth Pasting.* Chur, Switzerland: Harwood.

Ericsson, J. 2000. Asset substitution, debt pricing, optimal leverage and maturity. *Finance* 21(2):39–70.

Evanoff, D. D., and L. D. Wall. 2000. Subordinated debt and bank capital reform. Federal Reserve Bank of Chicago, Working Paper 2000-07.

——. 2001. SND yield spreads as bank risk measures. *Journal of Financial Services Research* 20:121–46.

——. 2003. Subordinated debt and prompt corrective regulatory action. Federal Reserve Bank of Chicago, Working Paper 2003-03.

Fries, S., P. Mella-Barral, and W. Perraudin. 1997. Optimal bank reorganization and the fair pricing of deposit guarantees. *Journal of Banking and Finance* 21:441–68.

Froot, K., and J. Stein. 1998. Risk management, capital budgeting, and capital structure policy for financial institutions: an integrated approach. *Journal of Financial Economics* 47(1):55–82.

Furfine, C. 2001. Bank portfolio allocation: the impact of capital requirements, regulatory monitoring, and economic conditions. *Journal of Financial Services Research* 20:33–56.

Furlong, F., and N. Keeley. 1990. A reexamination of mean–variance analysis of bank capital regulation. *Journal of Banking and Finance* 14(1):69–84.

Gennotte, G., and D. Pyle. 1991. Capital controls and bank risk. *Journal of Banking and Finance* 15:805–24.

Hancock, D., and M. L. Kwast. 2001. Using subordinated debt to monitor bank holding companies: is it feasible? *Journal of Financial Services Research* 20:147–87.

Hancock, D., A. J. Laing, and J. A. Wilcox. 1995. Bank capital shocks: dynamic effects on securities, loans, and capital. *Journal of Banking and Finance* 19:661–77.

Hellwig, M. 1998. Banks, markets, and the allocation of risks in an economy. *Journal of Institutional and Theoretical Economics* 154:328–45.

Holmström, B., and J. Tirole. 1997. Financial intermediation, loanable funds, and the real sector. *Quarterly Journal of Economics* 112:663–92.

Jackson, P., C. Furfine, H. Groeneveld, D. Hancock, D. Jones, W. Perraudin, L. Radecki, and N. Yoneyama. 1999. Capital requirements and bank behaviour: the impact of the Basel Accord. Basel Committee on Banking Supervision Working Paper 1.

Jones, D. J. 2000. Emerging problems with the Basel Accord: regulatory capital arbitrage and related issues. *Journal of Banking and Finance* 24:35–58.

Jones, D. J., and K. K. King. 1995. The implementation of prompt corrective action: an assessment. *Journal of Banking and Finance* 19:491–510.

Karlin, S., and H. Taylor. 1981. *A Second Course in Stochastic Processes*. New York: Academic Press.

Kim, D., and A. M. Santomero. 1988. Risk in banking and capital regulation. *Journal of Finance* 43:1219–33.

Koehn, M., and A. Santomero. 1980. Regulation of bank capital and portfolio risk. *Journal of Finance* 35:1235–44.

Leland, H. 1994. Corporate debt value, bond covenants, and optimal capital structure. *Journal of Finance* 49:1213–52.

——. 1998. Agency costs, risk management, and capital structure. *Journal of Finance* 53:1213–43.

Leland, H., and K. B. Toft. 1996. Optimal capital structure, endogenous bankruptcy, and the term structure of credit spreads. *Journal of Finance* 51:987–1019.

Mauer, D. C., and S. H. Ott. 2000. Agency costs, underinvestment, and optimal capital structure: the effect of growth options to expand. In *Innovation, Infrastructure and Strategic Options* (ed. M. J. Brennan and L. Trigeorgis). Oxford University Press.

Mella-Barral, P. 1999. The dynamics of default and debt reorganization. *Review of Financial Studies* 12:535–79.

Mella-Barral, P., and W. Perraudin. 1997. Strategic debt service. *Journal of Finance* 2:531–56.

Merton, R. C. 1974. On the pricing of corporate debt: the risk structure of interest rates. *Journal of Finance* 29:449–69.

——. 1977. An analytic derivation of the cost of deposit insurance and loan guarantees: an application of modern option pricing theory. *Journal of Banking and Finance* 1:3–11.

——. 1978. On the cost of deposit insurance when there are surveillance costs. *Journal of Business* 51:439–52.

Milne, A., and E. Whalley. 1998. Bank capital regulation and incentives for risk taking. Discussion Paper, City University Business School, London, U.K.

Modigliani, F., and M. Miller. 1958. The cost of capital, corporate finance and the theory of investment. *American Economic Review* 48:261–97.

Myers, S. 1977. Determinants of corporate borrowing. *Journal of Financial Economics* 5:147–75.

Pagès, H., and J. Santos. 2001. Optimal supervisory policies and depositor-preference laws. Discussion Paper. Basel, Switzerland: Bank for International Settlements.

Peek, J., and E. Rosengren. 1995. Bank regulation and the credit crunch. *Journal of Banking and Finance* 19:679–92.

Rochet, J.-C. 1992. Capital requirements and the behaviour of commercial banks. *European Economic Review* 43:981–90.

Santos, J. A. C. 2000. Bank capital regulation in contemporary banking theory: a review of the literature. Working Paper 90. Basel, Switzerland: Bank for International Settlements.

Sironi, A. 2001. An analysis of European banks' SND issues and its implications for the design of a mandatory subordinated debt policy. *Journal of Financial Services Research* 20:233–66.

Thakor, A. V. 1996. Capital requirements, monetary policy, and aggregate bank lending. *Journal of Finance* 51:279–324.